THE
HERO'S
FIGHT

THE HERO'S FIGHT

PATRICIA
FERNÁNDEZ-
KELLY

AFRICAN
AMERICANS
IN
WEST
BALTIMORE
AND
THE
SHADOW
OF
THE
STATE

PRINCETON UNIVERSITY PRESS
PRINCETON AND OXFORD

Copyright © 2015 by Princeton University Press
Published by Princeton University Press, 41 William Street, Princeton, New Jersey 08540
In the United Kingdom: Princeton University Press, 6 Oxford Street, Woodstock,
Oxfordshire OX20 1TR

Cover illustration by Ben Wiseman. Jacket design by Isometric Studio.

press.princeton.edu

Second printing, and first paperback printing with a new preface by the author, 2016

Library of Congress Control Number: 2014951729

Cloth ISBN 978-0-691-16284-3

Paper ISBN 978-0-691-17305-4

British Library Cataloging-in-Publication Data is available

This book has been composed in Minion Pro, Rockwell Std, and OSP-Din

Printed on acid-free paper. ∞

Printed in the United States of America

10 9 8 7 6 5 4 3 2

We've only to follow the thread of the
hero path and where we had thought
to find an abomination, we shall find a
god; and where we had thought to slay
another, we shall slay ourselves; where
we had thought to travel outward, we
shall come to the standard of our own
existence, and where we had thought to
be alone, we shall be with all the world.

—JOSEPH CAMPBELL
The Hero with a Thousand Faces

To Melanie who made all things possible

And to the children who taught me:
Tawanda, Belinda, Sherise, Earl, Joy,
Malik, and Curtis

CONTENTS

Preface to the Paperback Edition   xi

Acknowledgments   xvii

Introduction   1

1   D. B. Wilson   20

2   Baltimore: From Factory Town to City in Decline   38

3   Big Floyd   54

4   Intersections of Poverty, Race, and Gender in the American Ghetto   72

5   Shaping the Inner City: Urban Development and the American State   95

6   Distorted Engagement and Liminal Institutions: Ruling against the Poor   113

7   Little Floyd   132

8   Down the Rabbit Hole: Childhood Agency and the Problem of Liminality   151

9   Clarise   172

10   Paradoxes of Social Capital: Constructing Meaning, Recasting Culture   192

11   Towanda   213

12   Cultural Capital and the Transition to Adulthood in the Urban Ghetto   232

13 Lydia   253

14 Faith and Circumstance in West Baltimore   275

15 Manny Man   296

16 Divided Entrepreneurship and Neighborhood Effects   315

        Conclusion: Distorted Engagement and the Great
        Ideological Divide   342

        Appendix   357

        Notes   361

        Bibliography   375

        Index   405

PREFACE TO THE PAPERBACK EDITION

ONE YEAR AGO, ONLY TWO MONTHS AFTER THIS BOOK WAS FIRST published, the nation was riveted by new developments in West Baltimore. The needless, still incomprehensible death of Freddie Gray, a twenty-five-year-old resident of Sandtown-Winchester, offered yet another illustration of the extent to which impoverished people in America's inner cities endure harsh surveillance, containment, and punishment. That event was the latest in a string of deaths involving unarmed black men. Together they form a pattern in demand of analysis and political response. The Black Lives Matter movement may be seen as the outraged effect of those concerns.

Like many young men in destitute neighborhoods, Freddie Gray lived and died in line with a familiar story—the son of a drug-addicted mother, he was affected by lead poisoning in childhood and subsequently diagnosed with learning deficiencies in schools where teachers and counselors are overworked and underpaid. As a teenager, in the absence of meaningful employment opportunities, he gravitated towards drug commerce, the main source of revenue for kids like him. He was a small dealer without a violent record in an unforgiving setting where people like him can be detained simply for *looking* suspicious. After being arrested, he was handcuffed and thrown, without safety restraints, into the back of a vehicle. By the time he arrived in the police station, his spine had been nearly severed, allegedly, as a result of a bumpy ride. He died seven days later, one more casualty in the American State's long assault on the urban poor.

In the wake of Gray's death, reactions divided along known ideological demarcations. Conservatives lamented the ensuing civil disturbances, portraying them as "riots" caused by the disorderly desires of "looters," a good way to perpetuate stereotypes about African Americans living in poverty. More liberal channels focused on "police brutality," a term that encodes anxieties about the misuse of power on the part of public servants mandated to protect local communities. Lost in the ideological cacophony was the *institutional context* that makes the death of impoverished black men like Freddie Gray possible and nearly inevitable; a context formed by a multitude of liminal government institutions in a relationship of distorted engagement vis-à-vis the urban poor. Mainstream government agencies relate with *most* people as citizens and consumers. By contrast, these liminal government institutions—welfare offices, correctional facilities, public schools, and other such entities—interact with indigent clients as burdens on the society, perennial outsiders, and sources of pollution. An exclusive focus on police brutality makes it appear as if the main problem confronted by inner-city residents were abusive cops. In this book, I contend that more is at play—institutional guidelines and practices that limit the choices of vulnerable residents but also those of government employees.

Most police officers grow up in working-class environments; they choose their profession aiming to serve the public. Surely, they must be held accountable for their personal choices—including the perpetration of arbitrary violence—but those choices are not made in a vacuum. For more than three decades, police have been asked to behave like combatants in an occupied territory; they are seen by many local residents as intruders. Their training seldom includes specifications on how to engage with individuals and families as neighbors, not criminals. The model of community policing that once served as the stock of vintage American art and literature has virtually disappeared. In its stead is a profusion of militarized agencies, which often treat residents as enemies and potential sources of revenue—Baltimore, Maryland, and Ferguson, Missouri, are but two cases revealing the much larger and ominous landscape of government omnipresence.

What remains absent in narratives about police brutality is a deeper understanding of the forces that shape American destitution. A main purpose of this book is to redress that omission. In addition to the criminal justice system, a panoply of liberally inspired government agencies aimed at helping the poor have become forces that contribute to the perpetuation of poverty. Public schools, dispensers of public assistance, and rehabilitative programs of various kinds operate under contradictory conditions; on the one hand, their expressed mission is to provide a safety net for vulnerable individuals and families. In that respect, they are in correspondence with traditions of public responsibility towards people labeled as "underserved," "less fortunate," or "underprivileged." On the other hand, the internal policies and practices of those agencies are shaped by suspicion and conditionality. Underfunded and thinly staffed, offices charged with services for the poor—public assistance, child protection, juvenile corrections and counseling, even rehabilitation—often require special forms of certification (urine specimens, for example), which ordinary Americans would find it onerous and even insulting to be asked to provide. This is but one indicator of the differential treatment bestowed on impoverished people. Contempt, suspicion, and actual and symbolic violence are grafted on liminal institutions charged with their management.

The Hero's Fight offers an in-depth look at the effects of such agencies and such practices in the lives of inner-city residents. Poverty in American cities consists of more than material deprivation; it also entails the unintended consequences of pervasive government intrusion in the lives of the poor, a large number of whom live in racially segregated neighborhoods. In light of my findings, the treatment and demise of unarmed black men at the hands of the police cannot be explained as the sole effect of individual cruelty and carelessness; it is also the result of enduring institutional distortions that have been given little attention until now. People like Freddie Gray confront lethal conditions of *hypervisibility* in urban settings marked by acute disinvestment.

For the better part of a century, "big government" has been the butt of disdain on the part of conservatives and libertarians. Nevertheless, this book shows that, contrary to what President Ronald Reagan vehemently affirmed in his 1981 inaugural address, government as a whole is not the problem. The historical record shows that the American state has a long history of forward-looking legislation that, in partnership with the private sector, forged conditions of economic prosperity, personal freedom, and democratic participation. Government initiatives like the 1862 Homestead Act, the 1935 Social Security Act, and the

Servicemen's Readjustment Act of 1944—the GI Bill—enabled immigrants from Europe and their descendants to find avenues for progress. The children of despised Irish, Poles, and Italians went on to become legitimate Americans because of their hard work and compliance with mainstream norms but also thanks to the proactive stance of the American State as a promoter of public well-being and its creation of channels for the acquisition of property, educational betterment, and political participation. It is in the margins of such a noble landscape that liminal institutions operate as mechanisms for the containment and subjugation of poor Americans.

For that reason, this book aims to invigorate dialogue and debate about the liberal American State and its relationship to a divided society in which race and class continue to subvert the expressed objectives of agencies charged with the mitigation of poverty. My hope is that greater attention to the role played by liminal institutions will lead to a nuanced rethinking of their programs and practices. New approaches to assuage the punitive slant with which service agencies operate is required. Reform of the criminal justice system has begun but it is not enough. Urgent change is needed in child protective services, whose cumbersome and punitive practices fracture the authority of impoverished parents without effectively addressing cases of egregious abuse. The same may be said about programs that cast destitute individuals and families as broken vessels in search of help from the government. Since the valiant deployment of the war against poverty more than fifty years ago, top-down measures have yielded meager benefits. The voices of local residents must be heard. The unique character of poverty in America will endure unless our approach towards poverty undergoes a meaningful transformation. This book is offered in the spirit of confidence that research such as I conducted in West Baltimore can be used to freshly address the blotch of dispossession in the world's wealthiest nation.

This book is also an attempt to re-symbolize the way in which African Americans living in poverty are cast both in specialized writings and by the media. Such populations tend to be portrayed either as the target of social policy or as distant "others" whose behavior both fascinates and terrifies observers. The gaze of mainstream America focuses on how different the poor are from the norm. That is consistent with a long history of nation building partly achieved through the virtual and actual ousting of black people never fully integrated into the broader society. The forfeiting of policies deliberately intended to provide economic opportunity to emancipated slaves and their descendants set into motion a process that continues to this day. Forty Acres and a Mule was once envisioned as a way to set things straight by providing property and means of production to people recently relieved from bondage. At present, Forty Acres and a Mule represents the nation's inability and unwillingness to fulfill that promise. Even the great advances brought about by the Civil Rights Movement have not countered the disadvantages resulting from centuries of economic marginalization.

Against that backdrop, *The Hero's Fight* offers analytical chapters that address subjects such as globalization and industrial restructuring, economic sociology, cultural sociology, religion and poverty, and entrepreneurship and neighborhood effects, all of current interest and vital to the development of social policy. Nevertheless, the book's ambition goes further by pursuing a theoretically informed ethnography. Although mixed methods have long been part of sociology, ethnographic research has sometimes been seen as supplemental, not vital to the scientific endeavor. Here I argue otherwise by suggesting a model combining rigorous analysis and high standards in qualitative research.

The book includes biographical and analytical chapters. The biographies follow real people, whom I knew for nearly a decade of formal research. Some of them are still part of my life. Their stories take us back to the early years of the twentieth century when slavery was not a distant memory and migration from the rural South offered the promise of renewal and progress. The absence of biographical accounts focusing on poor individuals is but a symptom of the way in which we view them—not as persons able to articulate the reasons for their behavior or as forgers of plausible descriptions of their existential conditions, but as mere illustrations of public problems to be addressed by social engineers. I hope the chapters ahead correct that misapprehension.

It is true that residents in West Baltimore face many problems, but most of them are not of their own making. Under difficult circumstances, they fight back. As this book shows, abandoned children, welfare mothers, and young delinquents strive mightily to become agents in the construction of their own lives. Under appalling conditions of disinvestment, neglect, intense supervision, and violent treatment they retain, on the whole, a sense of purpose and a hope that they will be recognized as full members of American society.

The same hope lies at the core of this book.

Patricia Fernández-Kelly

March 21, 2016

ACKNOWLEDGMENTS

MELANIE Z. STRUB HAS BEEN A SISTER AND FRIEND FOR NEARLY four decades. Without her unconditional love this book would not exist. To her it is dedicated.

Unending gratitude goes to Miguel A. Centeno, Mitchell Duneier, Barbara Ehrenreich, Susan Fiske, Alice Goffman, Natasha Iskander, Jennifer Lee, Douglas Massey, Cecilia Menjívar, Harvey Molotch, Alexandra Murphy, Alejandro Portes, Saskia Sassen, Harel Shapira, Andreas Wimmer, and Viviana Zelizer, all admirable scholars whose work inspires me.

I am forever thankful to the remarkable group at Princeton University Press: Peter Dougherty, Eric Schwartz, Fred Appel, Ryan Mulligan, Ellen Foos, Casey LaVela and her associates, Molan Goldstein, and Jan Williams. Their dedication sustained me throughout the publication process.

Alexander Barnard, Denisse Calle, Ernesto Castañeda, René Flores, Linda Pittari, Lenore Sylvan, and Connie Tate, read this manuscript and offered suggestions that enhanced it.

Andy Chen, Princeton '09, designed the cover. He reflects my indebtedness to undergraduate and graduate students across time.

INTRODUCTION

AT THE BEGINNING OF 2016, NEARLY FIFTY MILLION PEOPLE—15 percent of the American population—still face high levels of actual or near destitution. In a country with a $17.9 trillion economy and durable traditions of opportunity and democracy, countless individuals live in conditions marked by the paucity of resources and insufficient means to attain social and economic advancement. Why does entrenched deprivation persist in the United States? Why do so many people continue to face economic and social marginalization fifty years after President Lyndon B. Johnson famously declared a "War on Poverty"?

This book, the result of long-term observations in Baltimore's western neighborhoods, offers answers to that question by concentrating on the specific relationship between the American State and the urban poor. On the basis of historical and ethnographic research, I argue that poverty, of the kind found in American inner cities, encompasses more than material scarcity; it also entails exceptional and systematic interactions between government officials and vulnerable people, a disproportionate number of whom are racial minorities.

Under normal circumstances, exchanges between the American State and ordinary persons have been shaped by the government's corporate coherence and its capacity to act on behalf of groups with varying interests—what the sociologist Peter Evans (1997) calls *embedded autonomy*. In that setup, public servants enjoy a salutary measure of distance from *and* connection to social segments endowed with divergent power and influence. Agents of the state typically view individuals as consumers and citizens regulated by market competition and large-scale narratives of individual achievement through hard work.

As a result, most Americans have a limited relationship with the government, and that relationship, when it arises, customarily involves the interchange of information and monetary assets. As long as they observe established laws and regulations, people expect to be left alone by the government. It is the state's relative independence as well as its civic involvement that have largely accounted for America's developmental success.

In the case of the urban poor, the delicate balance between detachment and connection has been suspended; the poor are perceived and treated differently by the state. Whether explicitly or not, government agencies mandated to address the needs of impoverished individuals and families define them as potential felons and social burdens. Populations so viewed face overwhelming and atypical intrusions on the part of agencies whose procedures are based on ambivalent benevolence and a penchant for retribution. Regular contact between the American State and impoverished Americans may thus be described as a form of *distorted engagement* marked by suspicion, surveillance, containment, and penalization. Against the backdrop of *quantitative* disparities in wealth, such treatment produces *qualitative* differences in the experiences of ordinary and destitute Americans. A major purpose of this book is to account for such differences as they are lived through by actual people.

Hovering relentlessly over the inner city are the police and a multitude of social workers, administrators of correctional facilities, teachers and counselors in public schools, the penal system, halfway houses, group homes, dispensers of food vouchers, shelters, personnel in training programs and community-based organizations, therapeutic centers, and those ubiquitous publicly funded researchers conducting yet another costly study about the causes and consequences of poverty. The totalizing presence of the state in those environments illustrates the unique relationship between government agents and vulnerable social sectors, one that deviates from standard norms of social interaction and deportment.

Central to this argument are the ways in which the unique relationship between the state and the urban poor affects life at the local level. Children growing up in deprived, racially segregated neighborhoods have a diminished sense of what it is like to move up and muster material resources through education—they have seldom met anyone who has succeeded by staying in school, but they are prompt to tap public agencies as a means to gain a measure of control and self-sufficiency. A youngster's call to 911 can render a mother powerless even when she believes her attempts at discipline are legitimate. Departments of child protection, installed in the name of impeccable liberal principles, can thus contribute to the subversion and erosion of the already weakened authority of low-income parents. The overrepresentation of the poor among alleged child abusers is, in many cases, an effect of the zeal with which public officials suspect impoverished parents of ill behavior.

Something similar may be said about programs that place security guards and "school resource officers" in educational facilities to monitor the activities of students, a matter that has led to the criminalization of minor offenses, formerly managed by teachers and principals but now grounds for expulsion and jail time even among the very young. Representing another example are attempts at monitoring crime that rely on intensified police surveillance and interdiction rather than collaboration with local residents. Finally, the comparatively large number of young, single mothers in poor neighborhoods is not only the effect of personal ignorance or bad judgment but also the result of economic stagnation in tandem with government omnipresence, a combination that leads poor girls to see motherhood as the only path to signify adult status.

A common feature connects the examples above: in the absence of alternative resources for economic progress and self-expression, government agencies become critical sites of encounter between the urban poor and the outside world. Bureaucratic interference is to life in poverty what marketing bombardment is to the society at large.

Investigating the exceptional relationship between the American State and the urban poor paradoxically sheds light on government actions that have increased the capacity of ordinary Americans to achieve prosperity. In the United States, policies aimed at increasing education and wealth largely explain the emergence of a successful middle class, that is, a thriving contingent of working people endowed with property rights, personal mobility, and access to a variety of material and educational assets. Where incentives to the accumulation of human and material capital have been absent, the result has been marginalization, unnecessary suffering, and the persistence of entrenched poverty. Palliation, as embodied in multiple and costly programs for low-income populations, has been a sad parody of capitalist provisos that, despite flaws, have always worked in the American context. In other words, the solution to poverty in the United States cannot continue to depend on attempts to mitigate the effects of dispossession or modify personal behaviors; it should rely instead on the deployment of significant resources to produce genuine gains in formal education and property accumulation.

That recommendation exposes the limits of prevalent ideological trends. For more than a century, conservative writers have bloviated against government programs, contending that they bolster dependence, lassitude, and deviance. Such rants, however, have been indifferent to the effects of racial discrimination and class bias and have not recognized the state's powerful and constructive role in forging the American Dream. Liberals and progressives, on the other hand, have viewed the government as part of the solution to problems confronted by impoverished people, but they have been reluctant to investigate the ways in which public service agencies perpetuate anomalous conditions in poor neighborhoods. As a result, they have turned a blind eye to the deleterious effects of ineffective, politically compromised, and woefully underfunded programs. Conservative accounts have been amply denounced but the unintended consequences of liberal presumptions about the poor have been left virtually untouched (O'Connor 2001). While conservative interpretations *demonize* disadvantaged populations, liberal positions *infantilize* them. The content of this book suggests that we should cast a less approving, graver glance at the liberal premises underlying government approaches to poverty (see also Menjívar and Kil 2002).

By doing that, I hope to reopen a long overdue project—a progressive critique of the American State. For too long, assailing the role and size of government has been the mission of conservatives and libertarians, a way for them to assert their ideological authenticity. By contrast, liberals and progressives have taken a defensive position that has often led to compromise and capitulation. Even the abandonment and circumvention of the term *liberal* during the Bush years illustrates that sort of cowardice (Massey 2005). The stories told in this book call for a more aggressive defense of liberal principles *and* a more trenchant review of existing government programs. It should be a top responsibility of the state to own up to and review premises that may be hampering the ability of public servants to address with integrity the needs of vulnerable groups, many of whose constituents are children.

REDISCOVERING THE URBAN POOR

I first made incursions into the neighborhoods of Upton, Sandtown-Winchester, and Liberty Heights in 1989, seeking to interview men affected by deindustrialization. Two years earlier, William J. Wilson had published the now classic book *The Truly Disadvantaged: The Inner City, the Underclass, and Public Policy* (1987), one of the main themes of which was the devastating effect of industrial decline on the employment prospects of African Americans. Last to be hired and last to join labor unions, Black workers had been first to be dismissed when jobs in the manufacturing sector were relocated to other parts of the world as globalization accelerated in the 1970s.

Ejection from well-paying employment, Wilson argued, had contributed to the formation of an underclass consisting primarily of men detached from the labor force and families whose main income was in the form of public assistance. The importance of his findings was demonstrated by an avalanche of studies that followed the publication of *The Truly Disadvantaged* (e.g., Gans 1995; Jencks 1993; Massey and Denton 1993; Sharkey 2013; Sampson 2013). Wilson developed his argument in two subsequent volumes, *When Work Disappears: The World of the New Urban Poor* (1997) and *More than Just Race: Being Black and Poor in the Inner City* (2010).

Baltimore was an ideal location to further investigate the effects of industrial recomposition on urban dwellers. Situated at the point of encounter between northern and southern states, along the Mason-Dixon Line, that city had been a vibrant industrial mecca whose prosperity, for a good portion of the twentieth century, was anchored in the activities of the Bethlehem Steel Company. At its peak, in the 1970s, the firm employed more than 180,000 people throughout the Northeast. Thirty thousand worked at its Sparrows Point, Baltimore, plant alone. By 1986, when I first arrived in that city, fewer than 15,000 people worked for Bethlehem Steel, and by 2009 the number had plummeted to 2,500.

Such a precipitous reduction of industrial jobs called for a systematic inquiry into the effects of economic change upon inner-city residents.

Armed with a battery of questions, I conducted in-depth interviews with a convenience sample of thirty African American men who had held jobs in manufacturing and manufacturing-related sectors—welders, pipe fitters, assemblers, packers, couriers, and office clerks. Through them I met others, including fifteen women who had worked in industry at some point in their lives. Altogether, I interviewed fifty-three persons for that early project. Their stories offered a glimpse into events that had led from aspiring youth and seemingly secure employment to displacement.

My exploratory study confirmed what Wilson had documented in Chicago: men and women who had held humble but decent positions in factories and other workplaces providing input and services to manufacturing now languished without stable employment. Some, like Donald B. Wilson, whose story I relate in chapter 1, had been able to save and purchase a home, thus gaining a footing in the upper echelons of the working class. Most of them, however, now held itinerant jobs or dabbled perilously at the margins of the law. For their children, the outlook was even worse.

Industrial decline, I discovered, was only part of a larger, more disturbing picture marked by the impact of residential segregation, long-term poverty, and government intrusion on a new generation born even as narrow channels for upward mobility were closing down. My initial interest had been industrial recomposition, but as I carried out my research, I found myself surrounded by youngsters of all ages, children filled with vitality, beauty, and ambition; children who wanted to be athletes, doctors, teachers, and police officers; children who, at the same time, knew by the age of four or five that the texture of their hair and the color of their skin were flaws in need of apology and correction. They were sons and daughters who, long before adolescence, had faced dislocation and assumed responsibilities that even adults would have met with great trouble; children older than their chronological age, sometimes wise, often difficult, and always captivating. It was mostly from those children that I obtained the lessons contained in this book.

I knew those children well and for enough time to watch them change from vessels of promise to shattered casualties in a war they had not initiated. By the age of twelve or thirteen, many of those I had met only five years earlier as giggling boys and girls seeking approval, their eyes fiercely engaging other eyes, were now withdrawn and distant, their gaze averted, hiding in a place within that no one could easily reach. Teenagers whose hands I had held when they were youngsters, during visits to the zoo and the aquarium, were now single mothers living on public assistance or drug kingpins standing on corners waiting for the next client to arrive. Some were in prison. At least two were dead.

It was the story of children growing up in West Baltimore that riveted my attention. I witnessed their efforts to make sense of conditions that were barely comprehensible. I heard them explain the logic behind their actions, while their mothers, and sometimes fathers, despaired of their behavior. For nearly ten years, many of those children and their families were an integral part of my life.

As I progressed in my investigation, harrowing questions arose: How to portray the behind-the-scenes struggles of people who are permanently viewed as misfits? How to account for lives diminished by scarcity, drug addiction, and violence, not solely as a result of individual choices gone awry but also as the outcome of collective indifference and misguided policies? How to recover the biographical dimensions of those represented by the popular media mostly as a pretext to review disturbing statistical facts? Those questions constituted the challenge. Years later, the answers are laid out in this book.

The stories told in these pages are American stories. Roughly between 1990 and 1997, I cultivated relationships with members of fifty families living in West Baltimore. For six of those years I sponsored four of the children in those families to attend a parochial school in Baltimore's Waverly district. I saw myself as backup, another pair of hands and another mind in the service of youngsters who had very few resources. Beyond all that is known about racial discord and the gulfs created by class inequality, it was hard to accept that the richest country in the world—a nation with a comparatively benign colonial past, a history of consistent development, and a bountiful spirit—had turned away from the descendants of slaves who had contributed to its prosperity. It is one thing is to learn about race and inequality from books; it is an altogether different matter to learn about those subjects through the direct observation of young lives being destroyed before reaching full bloom. I was moved not by charity but by solidarity. As an immigrant in awe of the values that sustain America, I could not passively accept the extreme conditions of abandonment that I witnessed in West Baltimore.

My involvement ran against prevailing trends and attitudes. Families like those I knew in Baltimore do not elicit compassion; investing in them has not been part of the national impulse. Data about charitable contributions, indicators of the country's generosity, support that claim. In 2012, Americans spent $316.23 billion in philanthropic giving—about 2 percent of GDP, and an increase of 3.5 percent from 2011. About 32 percent of those contributions went to religious organizations that often channel funds to help the poor (Giving USA 2013). Yet only a fraction of those resources reached impoverished urban families, whose members numbered nearly twenty million (U.S. Department of Health and Human Services 2012).

Government programs do not fare better. Temporary Assistance for Needy Families (TANF), since 1996 the successor to Aid for Families with Dependent Children (AFDC), allocates about $8.00 per day to minors living in poverty (McGuire and Merriman 2005). From the mid-1970s until its rescission, AFDC served one in twenty Americans, but its spending did not surpass 1 percent of the federal budget. When added to the Supplemental Income for the Disabled and the Supplemental Nutrition Assistance (food stamp) Programs, it did not reach beyond 5 percent of federal outlays (Page and Larner 1997). In 2013, total federal spending on TANF benefits was $16.5 billion (Falk 2013). For a single point of comparison, that year Americans spent nearly $343 billion in entertainment and more than $217 billion in apparel and services (U.S. Bureau of Labor Statistics 2013a).

Americans who see it as a moral imperative to support the poor in less advanced countries plagued by corruption, economic distress, or natural disaster do not feel the same toward their fellow citizens living in distressed neighborhoods. Mostly we blame the domestic poor for their afflictions. We find it difficult to grow a sense of connection toward unemployed men, women on welfare, girls toting babies on inner-city streets, or boys in handcuffs passing like shadows before our eyes as we watch the evening news. Yet such people—the central concern of this book—are as American as the descendants of immigrants from Europe and other parts of the world whose judgmental gaze often defines the public image of impoverished Blacks.

Throughout the period of my involvement in West Baltimore, a wide chasm separated my experience from that of my colleagues at the Johns Hopkins Institute for Policy Studies (IPS) where I worked as a research scientist. There, the poor constituted a social category in need of modification through social engineering. My colleagues had impressive credentials. Among them were scholars and researchers, as well as former public servants and politicians. They administered projects aimed at understanding or mitigating indigence and its discontents, including crime, imprisonment, drug addiction, unemployment, school abandonment, domestic violence, child maltreatment, and premature motherhood. No social pathology was left untouched at the IPS.

Despite their complexity and high cost, projects addressing such dysfunctions circled mostly around one objective: compelling the poor to adhere to middle-class standards of conduct—incentives to promote marriage as a solution to poverty are an enduring example; the federal government still allocates $150 million to the pursuit of that goal. Undergirding such efforts is a simple idea: if only the poor would behave like affluent people, their problems might disappear (O'Connor 2001). The emphasis in policy circles was, and continues to be, on changing individuals, not on modifying the circumstances that have caused deviant behaviors in the first place—high levels of residential segregation, large inequalities in the distribution of social and financial resources, and punitive government programs that stifle constructive action.

One summer morning in the mid-1990s, a former housing commissioner for the city of Baltimore, and a senior fellow at the IPS, stopped me on my way to my office to ask about Clarise, the young girl whom I had mentored for nearly five years and whose life is recounted in chapter 9 of this book. Clarise, who was thirteen at the time, was receiving high grades at her parochial school, swam proficiently, and had just completed an acting course at the Bryn Mawr School, a well-regarded educational institution in Baltimore. That stint had culminated in a performance at the Peabody Center for the Performing Arts attended by members of her family. She had glowed and taken a bow on that day, when promise about her future was fresh and untainted. Yes, I had much to report about Clarise but, as I began to answer my colleague's question, she interrupted me; what she *truly* wanted to understand were the reasons behind my attentiveness to the girl for such an extended period of time. I shifted my reply, but she cut me short again with her own, memorable response: "It's because you don't want her to get pregnant, right? She's an experiment. Good luck with that!" Our conversation had ended before it began.

The ring of skepticism in the woman's last syllable made a lasting impression on me, but more disturbing was the intimation that Clarise's story was important only as the expression of a social problem, not as the unfolding of a real life. Rare only in their honesty, my colleague's remarks mirror common perceptions about the urban poor and must be compared with the conversations we regularly entertain about our own sons and daughters. We would deem it insulting to characterize the care we bestow upon our own children solely as an attempt to prevent them from becoming social burdens. In our minds, we bracket that possibility and celebrate their achievements as evidence of our parental skill or manifestations of their intellectual and moral acumen. It is different for the poor—they have no biography. Impoverished people in general and African Americans in particular have been reduced to flattened representations of social problems. Individuals have been rendered insignificant, the rationale behind their actions buried beneath harsh judgment and simplification.

It is mostly for this reason that I interweave seven biographical accounts with analytical chapters in this book. They serve as anchors for my narrative and ground my theoretical formulations. My hope is to shine a light on events that are hidden behind statistical accounts and bureaucratic and academic jargon. The neighborhoods I studied are not exceptions; they represent typical outcomes in the evolution of American cities. Each biographical sketch reflects the normative experience of larger populations in dejected urban districts throughout the United States. Although I use synonyms, the biographies are of real people, not composites.

By taking this approach, I endeavor to highlight the significance of including personal stories as part of the ethnographic mission, not as a way to tell colorful anecdotes but as a means to affirm a fundamental tenet of the social sciences: when seen and compared as part of a larger universe of observations, biographical narratives reveal patterns that can only be explained through attention to social context. Whether it is the higher likelihood of imprisonment, out-of-wedlock motherhood, or dependence on public assistance, events characteristic of a specific population may be interpreted as the by-products of individual choices but also as the statistically probable effects of invisible yet real forces in the society. In this book, biography is meant to complement structural analysis (Ragin 2008; Ragin and Amoroso 2010).[1]

CONTEXT AND SIGNIFICANCE

Questions about poverty in the United States are not new. Numerous writings over the last five decades highlight the paradox of destitution in the planet's wealthiest country. Some draw attention to cultural traditions inherited from nineteenth-century England that hold the poor responsible for their own afflictions and require that they lift themselves and each other through diligence and virtuous living. Classic works like Michael Katz's *The Undeserving Poor: America's Enduring Confrontation with Poverty*—first published in 1990 and reissued in 2013—provide brilliant historical accounts of public views that cast impoverished people as defective outsiders. Other authors, Herbert Gans (1995), for example, note the extent to which powerless groups are often used as scapegoats to shift attention away from corporate abuses and political failures or to codify social ills, like gross income inequalities and racial discrimination. In that voluminous literature, however, there are few attempts to investigate the relationship between agents of the state and people living in poverty. The part played by bureaucratic intrusion in shaping identity among the urban poor has been assumed rather than investigated. It exists in academic narratives as a backdrop, not as an active force shaping existential realities.[2]

That is surprising because studies of the state have been central to sociological research. From Max Weber (1919) and Emile Durkheim (1893/1997) to Charles Tilly (1975, 2006) and Theda Skocpol (1979, 1995), authors have investigated the origin and function of governing apparatuses. There is also a large literature on public service agencies, but its goals are narrow and pragmatic, focusing on directives to improve personnel performance and procedural quality (Berman et al. 2012). Notable writings, like *Regulating the Poor* by Frances Fox Piven and Richard Cloward (1971/1993) or Jill Quadagno's *The Color of Welfare* (1996), explore aspects of the relationship between the state and the urban subproletariat—the first by providing an explanation of welfare policies as safety valves for the economic system, the second by investigating the role of race in the configuration of social policies. Despite their lasting importance, such analyses do not seek to clarify in any detail the effect of sustained contact between individuals and families and state agencies.

Especially relevant to the content of this book are works by David Garland (1990, 2010), David Harvey (2007), and Loïc Wacquant (2008, 2009), who offer absorbing analyses of changes undergone by the state in the latter part of the twentieth century. Garland's influential tract *Punishment and Society: A Study in Social Theory* (1990) articulates an innovative approach to the study of imprisonment, shedding light on the interactions between the state and inner-city residents. Similarly, David Harvey's *A Brief History of Neoliberalism* (2007) provides an inspired account of the way market deregulation has resulted in the rearrangement of state functions, some of them now explicitly directed at the containment of populations made superfluous by industrial recomposition. Like Garland, Harvey focuses on systemic changes occurring during the latter part of the twentieth century. Neither author, however, investigates those structural transformations from the perspective of social agents directly affected by them.

In contrast, Loïc Wacquant (2008, 2009) lucidly describes the relationship between the postindustrial state and marginal groups. His objective is to understand the effect of neoliberalism and globalization upon the working and nonworking classes, the urban poor, in particular. He contends that the masculine hand of the state, offering punishment and confinement, has supplanted the feminine hand of the nanny state that paralleled Keynesian economic reform during the 1960s. He also notes that a consequence of hardening policies over time has been a steep increase in the number of people living behind bars. Although they represent less than 13 percent of the American population, impoverished Blacks constitute 40 percent of those who are incarcerated. According to Wacquant, that astonishing fact is not a coincidence; in the age of economic globalization, imprisonment has become a means to contain and control a surplus population of discarded workers (see also Pager 2009; Western 2007; Alexander 2010). As with Garland and Harvey, Wacquant's intent is not, for the most part, to clarify the responses of individuals and families to measures implemented by segments of the state. This book complements analyses by such authors.

Rethinking Ethnography

Central to my effort is the ethnographic tradition and ways in which it can be pushed further in the twenty-first century. Ethnography still holds the promise of depth and moral suasion at a time when dazzling inventions are reshaping the way we transmit and receive information, often to the detriment of serious understanding. A short electronic text can prompt action; postings in social media can multiply our capacity to interact with others, but stories of consequence necessary to accrue deep knowledge can only be obtained through painstaking research and one-to-one interaction. This book is partly an attempt at testing the limits of ethnographic narratives while honoring theoretical analysis.

Ethnographic research came of age during the first decades of the twentieth century as a means to memorialize cultures at risk of being absorbed or eliminated by Western expansion and the advent of modernity. Early anthropologists believed that steep divides existed between the world of the ethnographer and the world populated by informants, whether located in New Guinea (Malinowski 1922), Samoa (Mead 1928), Polynesia (Firth 1925), the Andaman Islands (Radcliffe-Brown 1922), Southern Sudan (Evans-Pritchard 1940), or Ghana (Fortes and Evans-Pritchard 1940).

Later in the twentieth century, the availability of rapid transportation and the improvement of communications technology made it possible to undertake ethnographic research in urban settings. Exemplary of this trend were scholars from the Chicago school of sociology who developed ethnography as a centerpiece of their studies. The boundaries between observers and people once regarded as different or foreign began to dissolve. Ethnography became a tool to understand not only those living in exotic locations but also those in modern societies.

New questions then emerged about the use of the interview method as a means to advance scientific goals. Authors shifted attention to the evolving relationship between the observer and the observed as they interact with one another trying to clarify meanings and significance, establish cognitive boundaries, and develop internally plausible narratives about specific areas of experience. Fading memories, the imprecision of language, and the play of emotions diminish the self-evident character of spoken accounts. For that reason, the goal of in-depth interviews is not to take the statements of informants at face value, as if they revealed *truth,* but to identify *experiential patterns* in the testimonies of individuals sharing common characteristics (Fernández-Kelly 2012).

When seen in counterpoint to other interviews displaying common characteristics, personal accounts can become part of a virtual totality reflecting the structural factors that explain collective behavior (Burawoy et al. 1992; 2000). Theoretical propositions can then be *rubbed* against empirical findings to later re-construct and refine theory (see also Knorr Zetina 1982). As Arthur Conan Doyle once remarked, "It is a capital mistake to theorize before one has data. Insensibly one begins to twist facts to suit theories, instead of theories to suit facts" (Conan Doyle 1891/2012: 93). Ethnography without theory is mere anecdote but theory without ethnographic research often leads to vacuous speculation.[3]

Although ethnography has been yielding valuable insights for more than one hundred years—longer if early attempts starting in the sixteenth century are included—it has also been criticized for various reasons. Some scholars argue that because ethnographers depend on small numbers, their methodology yields idiosyncratic, not scientific, knowledge. Others assert that the interview method contradicts objectivity because of its dependence on the spoken word, known to be ambiguous and susceptible to contradictory interpretations. Yet others maintain that ethnography *samples on the dependent variable* and, therefore, betrays principles of scientific integrity.

Such criticisms tend to impose the language and logic of *quantitative* methodologies upon procedures whose justification lies elsewhere (Ragin and Amoroso 2010). Unlike that of quantitative methods, the logic behind ethnographic research, including interviews and participant observation, is not mainly to generalize findings to large universes but to obtain a deep understanding of the factors accounting for social action. It is, in fact, the purpose of ethnographic projects to sample on the dependent variable as a way to gain further knowledge of social processes. There is nothing anecdotal about narratives based on systematic research resulting from sustained observation over extended periods of time.

In other words, ethnographic research aims to create internally plausible explanations about specific areas of experience, explore meanings and the sui generis logic behind events, and raise questions that can be subsequently pursued through a plurality of methods. Triangulation—the iteration between theoretical propositions and quantitative and qualitative analyses—constitutes the mainstay of science both as a process and as a result. [4]

A Word about Methodology

My intent in this book is to flesh out C. Wright Mills's memorable dictum that sociology should be anchored at the intersection of biography and history (Mills 1959/2000: 3). Toward that purpose I mesh ethnographic research, theory, and analysis. Each of the seven biographical sketches that anchor my account represents a prism through which broader structural forces may be appreciated. I selected each portrait as a reflection of normative experiences in the lives of children, adolescents, and adults living in West Baltimore. Each one offers insight into the progression of events that leads to typical outcomes in distressed neighborhoods. I aim not at embellishment but at explanation from the point of view of the observer, as well as from the perspective of social actors responsible for behaviors that may seem incomprehensible or even reproachable to outsiders. Every biographical narrative in this book re-presents the life of a real individual.

I followed an exploratory study about deindustrialization in Baltimore, described at the beginning of this introduction, with a two-tiered methodology. A first level consisted of open-ended interviews and sustained interaction with more than two hundred and sixty individuals distributed in approximately sixty families over the course of nearly ten years.

Several of the families in the sample were related and resided in close proximity to one another. Their boundaries were indeterminate and fluid. Fictive kinship often affected how individuals saw their membership in larger units—godparents and foster parents are common in West Baltimore. Interviews and casual exchanges were sometimes short, while others extended over weeks. Some were interrupted, only to be resumed months later. In a few cases, original conversations were followed by efforts at clarification years later.

I supplemented interviews with participant observation and community mapping. Participant observation involved sustained contact with scores of individuals over the period of my research. Community mapping, an underrated technique in ethnographic research, consisted of exploring urban spaces in the company of people at the center of my investigation.[5] The purpose of those explorations was to obtain information about key elements in physical spaces from the point of view of the social actors whose behavior and perceptions I was attempting to understand.

Community mapping is an invaluable vehicle to obtain factual information and, more importantly, knowledge about how a neighborhood is felt and perceived by those who live within its boundaries. Without community mapping, elements shaping the life of residents—from playgrounds as a turf for negotiation and economic interaction to imaginary borders separating gang territories—would be invisible to an outsider.

Results from those methodologies are used in this book as a backdrop against which I view the character of patterned behaviors and lived denouements. They provide context and allow me to distinguish between unique events unfolding in the lives of individuals and normative developments affecting the collectivity, in this case, low-income African American families in West Baltimore.

The second tier in my approach encompassed biographical testimonies collected from the members of ten families most prominently featured in this book. Here, the challenge was to accurately represent their experience. Because I was more than a distant observer, many of the events described in these pages happened to West Baltimore dwellers as much as they happened to me. The lessons I derived from my interactions were not the result of dispassionate study—as much as that can ever happen in ethnographic research—but the consequence of deliberate and deep involvement. My goal was not to attain a false sense of objectivity or clinical expertise but to make empathy work as a springboard for understanding (Ortner 2006).[6]

I use life narratives as texts that express people's interpretation of their own circumstances. Case histories and personal narratives require that we view the statements of informants as constructions emerging from singular social, economic, and political conditions. Such constructions give voice to subjects in their own terms, allowing them to reflect upon personal and collective culture. Accounting for the meanings that individuals and collectivities impose upon their own actions is critical to the development of theory and the crafting of policy. In consonance with John Van Maanen's (2011) retelling of Clifford Geertz's classic proposition, I contend that it is not enough to observe how social actors behave but also necessary to understand what *they* think they are doing.

ORGANIZATION OF THE BOOK

The book comprises eight sections, each formed by two chapters; seven chapters include ethnographic accounts and are complemented by analytical chapters. Chapter dyads stand independently and can be read as self-contained efforts to address specific dimensions of poverty in American cities.

I begin with the story of Donald B. Wilson whose life reflects Baltimore's transition from vital industrial hub to urban setting in permanent decline. That chapter is paired with an account of Baltimore's evolution, with a focus on Upton, Sandtown-Winchester, and Lower Park Heights, the neighborhoods where I conducted most of my research.

The second section begins with the biography of Big Floyd (chapter 3), a man of lesser gifts than D. B. Wilson but who cultivated similar ambitions while confronting a dearth of employment opportunities and an abundance of bureaucratic interference, two features of life in the postindustrial city. I close with a discussion of the effects of economic dispossession and state intrusiveness on gender relations in inner-city neighborhoods (chapter 4).

In section three, I present a historical account (chapter 5) and theoretical framework (chapter 6) based on ideas put forth by Peter Evans (1995). I argue that America represents a mature developmental state whose policies account for much of the country's prosperity. Nevertheless, government's approach to impoverished and racially distinct populations substantially deviates from a developmental stance. I discuss *distorted engagement* as a way to gain a better grasp of the distinctive relationship between the American State and the urban poor.

Subsequently I investigate specific features of distorted engagement, first by reviewing the life of Little Floyd (chapter 7) and then (chapter 8) through an exploration of child protection agencies as an example of the mechanics integral to institutions addressing the needs of impoverished populations. The ambiguous character of public assistance ushers in unexpected consequences: on the one hand, having limited capacity to protect children from extreme abuse and neglect; on the other hand, fracturing the authority of parents and dividing families.

The fifth section begins with the story of Clarise Twigg (chapter 9) supplemented by a discussion of social capital under conditions of isolation and reduced access to resources (chapter 10). Social capital has been portrayed as a palliative for poverty and downward mobility, but the ethnographic evidence presented here suggests that a strong base of material and human resources is a precondition for social capital to result in qualitative improvements.

I then explore other dimensions of social and cultural capital, leading with the story of Towanda Forrest (chapter 11) to illustrate typical developments in the trajectory of girls growing up in inner-city neighborhoods. In chapter 12, I develop a complementary argument, claiming that early motherhood is partly the result of compressed time protocols and the absence of material and social assets to mark the transition to adulthood. In lieu of other means to affirm maturity, youngsters turn to their bodies to establish their adult status.

In chapter 13, I review the life of Lydia Forrest, a woman who struggled for the better part of two decades to live in dignity while receiving public assistance and who imposed a higher meaning on her actions through religious conversion. Her story is one of agency in the face of factors undermining the capacity for individual advancement. I follow with a study of the relationship between poverty and religion in chapter 14.

In the last section of the book I present the story of Emmanuel Travis Williams—Manny Man, as he was known in the streets (chapter 15). I use that story to show the workings of neighborhood effects and two kinds of entrepreneurship, one that often fails in poor residential areas—because of the paucity of investment, purchasing power, adequate training, and institutional connections—and one that tragically succeeds through reliance on the drug trade (chapter 16). In urban environments like West Baltimore, drug peddling has acquired normative status as a means to make a living. Countless young men have yielded to its lure. Many have ended up behind bars serving sentences disproportionate to their transgressions. Others, like Manny Man have lived intense lives punctuated by turmoil and violence. They represent squandered energy and talent.

The conclusion revisits the book's argument in relation to the liberal-conservative divide.

I now turn to the story of Donald B. Wilson, a man of honor in the Baltimore that once was.

1   D. B. WILSON

DONALD BRADLEY WILSON WAS ONLY NINETEEN WHEN HE ARRIVED in the promising city of Baltimore, Maryland, in the summer of 1959. The winds of history were blowing strong in the aftermath of school desegregation and the first inklings of the civil rights movement, but the young man from Mayesville, South Carolina, had other things on his mind, like endurance and high hope. Not that he was unaware of the troubles caused by racial friction or that he didn't welcome progress, but in his view, discrimination was just part of human nature. Either you learned to live with it or it hammered you down. Years later he told me, "If you can't change it, don't let it bother you. Peoples blame discrimination for everything; they make excuses, but really it's their own fault if they can't make it." In this, Mr. Wilson held a truly American outlook.

I cannot remember exactly when we met, so gradually did our paths converge. It must have been in 1987, at the beginning of my decade in Baltimore. By then he was driving a Yellow Cab that I often boarded on my way to the airport, rushing south along Martin Luther King Jr. Boulevard, past the odious skyscrapers that formed the now defunct George Murphy Homes. Never at a loss for words, Mr. Wilson treated me to detailed critiques of the welfare state. The government, he thought, pampered the idle at the expense of the taxpayer. Harboring opposing views, we argued in earnest, eventually finding nicknames for each other. He called me Doc; I called him D. B.

Our early encounters invariably concluded with one of his business cards clasped between my fingers as he reminded me that I could call him directly, bypassing the Yellow Cab dispatcher. Donald Wilson carried a portable telephone long before such a practice became popular among the members of the executive class, and his motives were far from showy—he wanted to keep downtime to a minimum, the same principle he had observed throughout his working life. Not for Mr. Wilson the long waits in line at the Pennsylvania train station, hoping for the infrequent but lucrative ride to Pikesville or DC. Not for him the complaints about low fares in a city that could hardly afford them. He had a bevy of "regulars" to fill most of his day. They relied on him because, to tell the truth, you could set your watch by Mr. Wilson's movements. He seldom missed a call, and he was never late. If he was not available, the rasp of his voice, poured out in rhyme, greeted his patrons in a recorded message:

> You know my name, you are getting closer and closer, but you haven't found me yet. If you want to reach me, I'll give you a clue: leave your telephone number; that's all you have to do. Thank you and have a nice day.

In addition to integrity, Mr. Wilson had humor.

When he was a boy growing up with seven brothers and sisters in rural South Carolina, D. B. always knew where authority and comfort resided. His father was a strict man who showed no hesitation in using the occasional lashing. Such measures were seldom necessary because, according to D. B., "a single look of him was enough to freeze you on the spot." His approach to discipline was premodern: it was not enough, or even necessary, that his children love him; more important was that they stand in awe before their father, as the Good Book says. There was, in his mind, a key distinction between adults and youngsters: the former should tower over the latter. And the older Mr. Wilson had no doubt that a disregard for the differences between children and grown-ups would signify the collapse of civilization.

Decades later, as we traversed the streets of West Baltimore with their rows of abandoned houses and their climate of defeat, Donald Wilson would reflect on the enigmatic outcomes of resettlement. The people who had first arrived in those neighborhoods were not all that different from him or, for that matter, his own father. As part of the Great Black Migration, they had arrived seeking opportunity, willing to work hard and sacrifice for their children.[1] Legal segregation was still in effect during the 1940s and early 1950s, and maybe just for that reason, families shared a feeling of unity, a need to stand together against leveling pressures. That was especially true with respect to the young. D. B. remembered that

> Families looked out for other peoples' childrens, and if you was a child, you knew that. You could go to the house next door or across the street like it was your own. But if you got into trouble, look out! You mama would find out before you got home. You saw her standing at the door with the strap in her hand, and you didn't have to ask no questions—you knew what was comin'.

Now the young people wandered about without surveillance or fear of their elders, and the neighborhoods looked like war zones. Apparently, the older Mr. Wilson had been right all along.

And it wasn't only the way parents related to children that had changed. West Baltimore had once been inhabited by distinguished personalities, like Thurgood Marshall who litigated before the U.S. Supreme Court and prevailed against all odds, bringing about the legislative agenda that demolished segregation and ushered in the civil rights movement. Donald Wilson could recall the names of celebrities and businessmen, some of them very wealthy, who had lived in close proximity to ordinary folks, the sons and daughters of sharecroppers like him.

Long before Pennsylvania Avenue had become an open market of illicit pleasures, it had been a fashionable strip lined with nightclubs, dance halls, and theaters, including the famous Royal, and the Senator. All the great entertainers of the era had performed in those gilded places; from Lena Horne to Louis Armstrong and James Brown. They were remembered as part of a period marked by greater confidence and civility. In the 1970s, things had started to shift: "It was the drugs and the welfare that finished the city," Mr. Wilson told me. "Peoples just got lazy."

Throughout the 1960s, Blacks living in West Baltimore held modest jobs, and they struggled to make ends meet. But on Sundays, when they went to church, partly to pray and partly to see and be seen by others, they donned the symbols of self-affirmation and optimism. Families walked down the streets on their way to Old Bethel AME or First Baptist clothed as beautifully as their means would allow. The men in double-breasted suits, vivid neckties, and their indispensable Stetsons embellished with a discreet feather on the hatband. Girls in tight, shiny braids overlaid with multicolored baubles, the cuffs of their socks peeking above immaculate patent leather shoes. Boys in trousers and white shirts, hair pressed hard against their heads. But in that radiant display of human pride, no other group shone more brightly than the women in their plumed or bejeweled hats, dressed in silk or lace, gloves covering their hands, their throats encircled in pearl strings. The garments and trinkets were cheap but the effect was stylish.

Collective symbols and deportment were different in the 1990s. The new generations had no way of knowing what the past had been like and how bright the days ahead had seemed. They gazed upon the "old heads" and their quaint ways with contempt.[2] Church was not among their frequent destinations. Instead of formal wear, they favored clothes that were casual, costly, and subversive: jeans with a leg rolled up below the knee or trousers baggy enough to show their underpants; T-shirts sporting loud, insolent slogans; climbing boots, running shoes, and sneakers, all with the laces undone.

The young people bought the footgear at high prices from firms like Nike, K-Swiss, New Balance, and Timberland. The shirts and pants bore labels from Tommy Hilfiger, Apollo, and Nautica. Especially among older adolescents, but even in the prepubescent set, off-brand dressing was a mark of inadequacy that could attract heaps of abuse from friends and foes alike. Youngsters would rather stay home than go to school in the wrong threads. Their grandmothers and grandfathers had been satisfied to scrimp for garments that said, "I am respectable." The children went hungry and sometimes stole or killed for clothes that screamed "I don't give a fuck!"

Some of the old migrants from the South were still living in West Baltimore in the last decade of the twentieth century. They stayed, driven by a sense of continuity and also because they couldn't afford to move elsewhere. They had watched their neighborhoods change in ways they never did. Age had bent their backs and weakened their knees, but they still looked elegant heading for church. I loved to watch them on Sundays, moving deliberately or standing gravely at their places of worship, the gentlemen still wearing those fine hats with the diminutive feathers, the ladies still in their fancy dresses and bonnets. Out of step with the times, their numbers had dwindled together with those of the holy buildings where they found refuge.

Once the center of community life and cultural dignity, many churches were now shells, mere pieces of real estate with little appeal or monetary value. Some had been altered to serve secular purposes. Others had been boarded up and thrust into permanent disrepair. Desperate addicts searching for easy dollars had eventually stolen their copper pipes and wrought-iron frames to sell for a pittance at the junkyards. At least one church had been turned into a shooting gallery. Then again, as D. B. liked to say, "When the churches go, Doc, the whole community goes."

The ravages of urban decline had been far in the distant future when Donald B. Wilson was still growing up on the farm in South Carolina. He had been born into a modest but upright family. His father, Henry, and his granddaddy, Johnny Wilson, had been sharecroppers. Although there wasn't much to go around, D. B. had fond memories of his childhood. It was a first-rate experience to be a youngster in the rural South when kin surrounded you. He told me:

> I can go back to when I was six, seven years old. Every morning we went about five miles to school 'cause it was all country and there was no transportation. It was cousins and other relatives, about thirty of them, and we used to walk, run really, to school. But first we had to do our chores. Sometime we had to go in the field and haul cotton; sometime we picked the cotton or plow the land. We did a lot of things people does in the farm. After school, we come back home and study a little, and later we worked till the sun goes down and you can't see. Those were the good old days.

School began at 9:00 a.m. at the Mayesville Institute, a large barn-like structure with a cement floor and small desks lined up in the front. The teacher, Miss Bella Ward, had down-to-earth goals: to ensure that her pupils knew the basics and that they became good citizens. Every afternoon, during the winter months, the students, Donald included, went out to play and collect wood. They had to make sure it was warm inside the building the next day. "The federal government," said D. B., "provided food, like apples, so the childrens could have good nutrition, and they also gave us stamps to buy flour and gasoline." Families did wonders with the little they had, and the young people, for the most part, didn't realize they were poor. When you know those around you and they know you, it's hard to engage in invidious comparisons or yearn for things you don't know exist.

Henry Wilson, Donald's father, was in his early twenties when he married fifteen-year-old Geneva Radisson. Their union lasted almost forty-six years and was only interrupted by Geneva's death in 1988. Through thick and thin, the couple went on, in due course buying fourteen acres of arable land that is still owned by the family. D. B. attributes his success and that of his siblings to his elders' strong principles. All they wanted was for their children to have an education and do well in life. Their loyalty to family and community were unwavering:

> My parents wasn't nothing like the parents today that let the children do whatever they want. When my mother went and cook, you either ate or, when she cleaned up, if you hadn't touched the food, it went right back into the kitchen. That was it! My father too was firm about that.

In addition, the elder Mr. Wilson was a stickler about punctuality:

> It was ten o'clock, say, on a Saturday morning and he tell you, "See, boy, see the sun behind the tree? If you go to town, you gotta get back by the time the sun is *on* the tree top." And he meant what he said; if you wasn't back when you was supposed to, you had somethin' coming.

Although he was a dependable provider and a devoted husband, Henry Wilson was not a saint; temptation could derail his good intentions. Said D. B. many years later:

> My daddy, he was a religious man but he had his ups and downs like everyone else: he cussed, he said wild things, and he liked to gamble a lot. So when you're out there rolling dice and playing cards, anything can happen, like womens; he loved the womens, yes, he did! But come Sunday morning: holy man! He din't do no wrong!

Henry and Geneva Wilson had eight children—six boys and two girls, all of whom fared well as adults. First came Henry Jr., who volunteered for the Marine Corps when he was seventeen but who, in D. B.'s droll account, "cried to get out." Although he wasn't a marine for long, he learned a trade: how to lay bricks. Later he worked as a mason. With his wife, Alice, he had four children. D. B.'s eldest sister, Sandra, became a schoolteacher. Like Henry Jr., she never left the South, and even today, she looks after the family farm. When she was younger, she worked on it with her husband; after he died, she leased out the land. By the 1990s, neither cotton nor corn was cultivated on that farm—soybeans had become the crop of choice.

After Sandra came Buford, who grew up to be a crew officer in the army and held his post until retirement. He put two of his children through the Marine Corps. Dorothy, the Wilson's second daughter, left Mayesville for New York in 1960, when she was twenty-five, in search of a better life leaving behind her first husband and children. When she remarried and could afford to, she sent for her three children and had two more with her new husband.

Robert, the next born, was the first to head for Baltimore, and Albert and Donald followed. Robert worked in construction and ultimately was hired by the Koppers Company, one of Baltimore's large industrial firms. Albert found a job at the local A&P supermarket in Dundalk, which later became part of the Super Fresh franchise. He retired in 1993 after many years of faithful service. Donald's younger brother, Leroy eventually married and went to live in New York.

Although tossed asunder by migration and resettlement, the Wilson siblings maintained strong, lasting ties. They found jobs for one another, depended on shared assets, met regularly to play and gossip, and periodically converged in Mayesville for a family reunion. They cultivated a sense of shared history because, as D. B. explained, "You need to know where you coming from if you're gonna make something of youself."

As a youngster on the farm, and from time to time, Donald visited Mary, his father's sister, who had lived in Baltimore since the 1940s. When he grew older and became concerned about his future, he went looking for a job in that city and stayed with Mary. First he worked setting and waiting tables at the Chartreuse, a restaurant situated at the corner of Eagle and Charles. After a year, he moved on to the Tower Engineering Company, where he was a construction worker. Even later, he became a mechanic at Jerrysville Chevrolet. He also began supplementing his income by driving a taxi. Baltimore was expanding, and it wasn't hard to make a living in those days.

When he was twenty-one, D. B. went back to Mayesville to marry his childhood sweetheart. He was "crazy in love with her," but after he and his young wife returned to Baltimore, things didn't work out as planned. He wasn't ready to slow down. Smoking, drinking, and carousing were part of his routine:

> I had a little street in my life, staying out, partying; my wife never knew when I was coming home. We had a daughter but the marriage didn't last. After that I had to search my soul because I was the one who caused the trouble.

Magnified by the contrast with his parents' unbreakable union, Donald's failure was all the more painful; he was forced to take a hard look at his priorities.

In 1963 his cousin Jill, who was also living in Baltimore, introduced him to Beverly Elaine Jeter, who would become his second wife. Bev, as she was known by her family, was still striking in her fifties. Like Donald, she had been married before. When they first met, she was working as a seamstress in a factory to support her two children, seven-year-old Robert and five-year-old Teresa. According to D. B., it was love at first sight: "You know how it is when you see someone in the street and something just clicks? That's the way it was with me." The couple married in 1967.

This time it was a charm. Together they had another child, Donald Jr. In the summer of 2010, the Wilsons celebrated their forty-third wedding anniversary. D. B. speaks lovingly about his two stepchildren, whom he regards as his own.

As a young man, recently married for the second time, and determined to make progress, D. B. left no stone unturned in search of better employment. Personable and resourceful, he often tapped at opportunity's door. But even by piecing together two or sometimes three jobs, his ambition remained larger than his income. Then came a defining moment: when he was twenty-six, D. B. went to work for the Koppers Company. It was his association with that firm that gave a permanent boost to his future. Here is how he explained that transition:

> In those days I was driving a cab, and I read in the paper that Koppers was looking for a mail clerk. I went down and filled an application and I jus' kept going about my business until one day, Earl

Bundy, the director of personnel, call me and he wants me to show up the next morning at nine o'clock. It was a hard decision, but I took the job in the mailroom at Scott Street. I sorted mail and I delivered mail for about six years.

Along with Bethlehem Steel, Baltimore Gas and Electric, and the McCormick Spice Company, Koppers was one of the brightest jewels in Baltimore's industrial crown. At its peak, in the 1960s, it hired nearly 30,000 people, mostly in the assembly of parts for heavy machinery, aircraft, and ships. Not lacking in perspicacity or initiative, D. B. took a chance on Koppers, suspecting that the firm's evolution was closely tied to Baltimore's prosperity. He was right.

The kernel from which the Koppers Company had grown in the nineteenth century was the Bartlett and Hayward plant at 200 Scott Street, D. B.'s original site of employment. Two cast-iron dogs, "Sailor" and "Canton," flanked the building's entry. They had been crafted in the 1850s to celebrate the Newfoundland ancestors of the Chesapeake Bay ducking dog, symbols of the interest that the original Bartlett and Hayward partners had in hunting—a talisman of the firm's success.[3]

Stored in the Baltimore Museum of Industry is a collection of photographs tracing the evolution of the Bartlett and Hayward plant from late nineteenth century foundry to mid-twentieth-century industrial behemoth. Originally, the plant specialized in the assembly of stoves and stove parts, but it soon branched out to include artistic wrought iron for construction purposes. Architectural ornamentation in cast and wrought iron was all the rage in the Victorian era. Homes and businesses boasted their wealth and prominence through the lavish use of Bartlett and Hayward's facades.[4] Most of the exquisite fronts and balconies in the Mount Vernon residential area, one of Baltimore's tonier neighborhoods, were designed and assembled at Bartlett and Hayward, as were the signature staircase and railings in the Peabody Library and the fence around the Washington Monument on Mount Vernon Place.

As it became better known, the firm's influence reached far beyond Baltimore. The ceiling in the Hall of Columns at the nation's Capitol was produced at Bartlett and Hayward. In New Orleans, two churches, the city's customhouse, and some of the balconies that made the French Quarter famous had casting built by the same company. It was said in humor at the time that New Orleans had received two mixed blessings from Baltimore: slaves and wrought iron.

In the late 1930s, Bartlett and Hayward was acquired by the Koppers Company and thus became part of a manufacturing emporium dedicated to the production of piston rings, airplane propellers, and Lentz-type steam engines for cargo ships. Koppers was a main government supplier during World War II. Its workforce expanded as rapidly as its national reputation. The Maryland State Archives gives testimony of the firm's ascending star, including a transcription of a speech delivered by Governor Herbert Romulus O'Conor on April 30, 1941, "at a ceremony meant to celebrate the delivery to the Ordinance Department of the United States Army of the first Anti-Aircraft Gun Carriers manufactured by the Koppers Company, Bartlett and Hayward Division."[5] O'Conor also stated, "The occasion is inspiring [be]cause it is . . . evidence of the completeness with which the people of Maryland have addressed themselves to the stupendous task of adequate national preparedness."[6] He assured an attentive audience, "I bring to the officers and workers of the Koppers Company, Bartlett Hayward Division, the confidence of the people of Maryland."[7]

Koppers was also a main contractor for the U.S. Maritime Commission. With Bethlehem Steel at Sparrows Point, it produced scores of Liberty ships. Admiral Emory Scott Land, the Navy's top commander, recognized the contributions of industry to the war effort by remarking, "Nuts and bolts and sub-assemblies, and a thousand other parts and supplies are furnished for the Victory Fleet by plants both large and small."[8] Koppers was one of those plants. In 1944 it won an "M" Award from the Maritime Commission and was listed as one of only two firms in Maryland manufacturing precision equipment for naval use.[9] By the mid-twentieth century, the Koppers Company managed seven plants, including the Bartlett Hayward Metal Products Division, sprawled over several city blocks. When Donald Wilson first arrived on its premises, Koppers was among Baltimore's main sources of livelihood for working-class families.

In the 1970s, steadily employed at Koppers, D. B. saw his brood expand. After she became pregnant, his wife, Beverly, gave up her factory job. With three children under the age of five, she didn't have a free moment. She stayed home until her babies were old enough to go to school and then became a student herself, hoping to get her high school diploma. Through her husband's mediation, she then found a job at Koppers. Robert, D. B.'s older brother, had been the first to be hired. "Good things happens when you got connections in the right places," D. B. declared with a grin. "It's never lonely at the top." Beverly worked at Koppers until 2003 as a quality control inspector, the last one to look over the finished products as they were prepared for delivery.

When he was in his early thirties, and after six years of service as a mail clerk, Donald Wilson was ready for a change. He began contemplating a job as a bus driver with the Greyhound Company. Not that he had grown tired of Koppers, quite the opposite, but long-distance travel, he thought, would bring about higher revenues. Never mind the long days and the necessary absences from home, the pay would be worth the pain. Koppers, however, wouldn't accept his resignation. Says D. B.:

> It was Easter Sunday, 1967. That's when I was going to take the job at Greyhound, but my supervisor calls me aside an says, "I hear you're leaving us. . . . First, I think you owe Mr. Fried [his boss] an explanation."

Throughout the preceding years, Mr. Fried had been generous:

> So I told him [Fried] and, right on the spot, he offered me a $2,500 raise to be the head chauffeur. That was a lot of money back then. It was an honor to get that opportunity, me a young man out of the South. . . . All I do is drive the executives from point A to point B, wherever they had to go.

D. B. cherished his new position: "It was like going back to school, everything was about learning. Either you got the point or you didn't," and D. B. did. So he stayed. As head chauffeur, he had access to a company car and his own expense account. He wore a suit. Toward the end of his years at Koppers, his annual earnings had risen to nearly $50,000 a year, to say nothing about benefits. Combined with Beverly's wages, Wilson's income put the family squarely at the prosperous top of the working class.

Equally important was the knowledge that now sustained him: he was valued for his good work and deportment, an irreplaceable member of the Koppers family. From his father, he had first acquired a regard for punctuality and order. His new position reinforced those values because "at Koppers everything was by the clock, you had to be on time or things fell apart." Other, equally important insights, had followed. "Your company," he said, "makes a big difference on how you act and how you perform."

It gives you backbone, and expectations about how to dress and how to behave. You do things to keep the respect of the other people who work with you. You don't want to lose face and so you do your job as well as you can. For me, the job—it changed my whole attitude and way of thinking about my life.

By 1986, after nineteen years of employment at Koppers, D. B. had many accomplishments to boast about. For starters, he had put his three children through college. Robert became an accountant solidly employed by the federal government. Donald, the second boy, is a software specialist employed at United Airlines in Roxville. Teresa too is a government employee. All are married and have children of their own.

Access to property, the mark of a middle-class life, had also been within reach. At the time of D. B.'s promotion, he and his wife were renters. They lived on the 600 block of Newton Street, the area known as Poplar Grove, part of Old West Baltimore. Working at the Koppers Company allowed them to move up by moving out. In 1973, shortly after he became a head chauffeur, D. B. and Beverly bought a home in Glen Oaks, a county subdivision adjoining their old neighborhood. As with other good things, business associates were involved in that process:

It was like this: my wife and me, we was saving to buy a home all along but it was Mr. Fried, my boss, who gave me the push to do it sooner. "Donald," he said, "you're making all this money; I want you to take it and put it to use. Buy a house." It was his idea that really led my wife and me to go in that direction.

A stable job and encouragement from his boss bolstered D. B.'s ambition and strengthened his relationship with Beverly. She, prudent and smart, got most of the credit for the couple's advancement. Explained D. B.:

All the while I was saving, but I have to thank my wife [for buying the house] because she's a good provider. From the beginning, she said, "If you bring it home, I'll put it to good use," and that's what she did. I give her all I earn. Every month I took an allowance, maybe twenty or thirty dollars; a lot of money for that time, but she kept the rest.

Glen Oaks, the residential area where the Wilsons went to live, came into being in 1948, when city authorities contracted the Elba Construction Company to build a few houses around Chinquapin Park. Triangular in shape and bordered in the south by the Belvedere Shopping Center, the neighborhood was first inhabited by upwardly mobile Jews, the children of immigrants who, as a mark of their own success, began leaving for the suburbs in the 1960s. Baltimore's Jewish saga, filled with strife and vitality, has been told before but seldom with as much feeling as in Barry Levinson's movie *Avalon* (1990). It shows how exodus from the city entailed both triumph and defeat; it buttressed achievement but fractured community. There are few Black faces in *Avalon*, but the connection between the Jewish and African American journeys is inescapable. When earlier residents left Glen Oaks, seeking to relocate farther away from the inner city, Black families quickly replaced them. By the time D. B. went looking for a new home, he had no difficulty finding it: "The real estate man," he explained, "had a deposit from someone else, but we made an offer and took the house 'as is.' We got it for $37,000 in 1973, but [by 2003] it was worth more than $70,000. All the improvements, we done ourselves. It's all paid off now."

A charming residential district, Glen Oaks stands as a living testimony to the accomplishments of working people like Donald B. Wilson. Its streets are well aligned; its houses tidy and dignified. Most of the residents are homeowners. Large trees border the sidewalks. Throughout Lent, tulips infuse the ground with color. Along Belle Avenue, where the Wilsons live, the foliage forms a canopy during the summer months. The interplay of shade and light gives the houses a picturesque appearance.

The Wilsons' house is a two-story structure and features a red brick facade. Iron bars protect the front windows, a legacy from the time when he was traveling as part of his duties at Koppers and wanted his family to be safe from potential prowlers. The entrance is topped by a forest-green awning. Flowerpots brighten the exterior. The effect is warm and cheerful.

By 2006, most of D. B.'s neighbors were retired. They too worked hard in all the respectable trades. He estimates that more than half owed their jobs to the federal government. Miss Pierce, who lived two houses down from the Wilsons, used to be a schoolteacher. Mr. Jones, almost a block away, was with the post office most of his life. Winnie Carp, across the street, held a job at the Department of Labor. According to D. B., she was "strictly old religion." The refrain pasted on her front window for all passersby to see bore witness to her faith; in bright cutout letters it read "Jesus Saves." Crime, even the occasional petty offense, was almost unknown in the neighborhood, but Winnie Carp still watched over her block like a hawk. Alert to interlopers, potholes, or broken pipes, she represented feelings of solidarity lost in other parts of West Baltimore.[10] When a family had to travel, it could count on Winnie to look after its property and water the plants.

Parked in front of the Wilsons' house, you could see the backyard, where D. B. stored his cars. In the late 1990s, he sold a yellow Mustang that he had intended to repair as a hobby. The underside was rusting and D. B., who worked long hours, had no time to fix it. On the other hand, the Mercedes-Benz he bought while he worked at the Koppers Company was still there in 2000, a thrilling machine with a shiny gray exterior. In contrast to the cab that he drove during weekdays, it was D. B.'s private car, the high mark of his accomplishments, the means of transportation he used when visiting friends, returning to Mayesville to see relatives, or accompanying Beverly to the New Rehoboth Baptist Church on Sundays.

Not that D. B. went to church all that often. He was a religious man in a quiet, big-hearted way, but the service was simply too long:

> It's supposed to start at eleven o'clock, but the sermon takes off around twelve or twelve thirty, and that's just halfway throughout the whole thing! Can't take it, Doc, can't take it. But my wife, she's a good soldier; she teaches Sunday school and does all kinds of work for the church.

Protestations notwithstanding, I can remember a few Sundays when, yielding to my requests, D. B. drove me to the Baltimore airport in his Mercedes, fresh out of church, dressed to the nines, a gold armlet bounding his wrist. By every possible standard, he had a good life. Yet not even his desire or integrity could forestall the economic onslaught that altered Baltimore's incipient fortunes and D. B.'s own. He was only forty-six and not ready for retirement when the Koppers Company fired him in 1986, after nearly two decades of faithful service. Defenseless against the pressures of foreign competition, Koppers had been sold off and "streamlined" a few years earlier. Many of its manufacturing operations had gone overseas, in search of lower production costs. Its Baltimore workforce had shrunk rapidly.

For a while, before his discharge, D. B. had been aware of plans to curtail production. Rumors abounded, but he had heard the story firsthand from Mr. Fried—the same man who had been his mentor and promoter. Advance warning, however, was weak comfort for the shock that followed D. B.'s dismissal. Despite his optimism and resilience, he was deeply wounded. Our conversations would invariably gravitate to memories of his years at Koppers. Many times he had driven the big shots back and forth to the airport, impeccably dressed, always on time, using a personal account to sign for miscellaneous expenses, doing his job well, conscious of his importance in the larger edifice of industry. I could imagine him engaged in lively exchanges with salesmen and managers as he traversed the Baltimore streets. Something of a philosopher, he must have shared with them, as he had with me, his views of the world and, especially, American society. All that had been abruptly taken from him.

The blow was hard, but D. B. was not a man to stay down for long. As in every other American city, government programs were being implemented in Baltimore to ease the trauma of dislocation caused by the decline of industry. D. B. was open to new possibilities. Bureaucratic design, however, can't give you back the texture of a life constructed over long periods of time, redolent with cherished, familiar details. When D. B. joined a government-funded retraining program, he found it deeply wanting. He said:

> After Koppers sold out, . . . I went to Catonsville Community College for a year to learn how to operate machinery. I was learning to work the milling machine, you know, to ground down steel and design

different parts, but I didn't care for the work at all. So I started looking for something else.

Retraining didn't just mean an exploration of novel alternatives; it
also meant less money and lower status. His former job had endowed
him with autonomy, resources, and the pleasure of conversation. He
could not fathom working in a factory, tied to a machine, bored by routine, hidden away in nameless corners, unknown and unremarkable.
It was unlikely that he would even be able to apply his newly acquired
skills. Manufacturing jobs were not expanding. The situation called for
drastic action, and D. B. moved swiftly:

> When I was out in Catonsville, learning to work the milling machine,
> I met an old friend of mine. He says to me, "Why don't you buy your-
> self a cab permit?" I said, "No one will sell me one." He said, "If I find
> someone, . . . do you have the money to pay for it?"

Soon enough, D. B. was in conversation with Mark Joseph, proprietor
of the Baltimore Yellow Cab Company:

> He told me he had a permit going for $13,500. Then you had to buy
> a car, and consider all the pros and cons going with the cab business,
> insurance, other things. So I end up putting up $23,000 just to start
> off. That's how I became part of the Yellow Cab fleet.

Although driving a taxi was never the same as being the head chauffeur at the Koppers Company, it offered some of the elements that D.
B. relished: self-reliance, variety of experience, and contact with a wide
spectrum of people. It was also while he was driving the taxi that Baltimore's reigning misery came into full view. With mock disdain, D. B.
would point to the young girls standing in line by the money machines
on the first day of the month. He knew they were on welfare. "See that?"
he would ask me rhetorically, "Those are our tax dollars, Doc, flying
away, never to be seen again!"

Together we often traversed Lower Park Heights, melancholy and
beautiful with its large, decaying homes and its old synagogues turned
into soup kitchens or community centers. Driving east from Belvedere
to Reisterstown Road, he sometimes stopped at the 7-Eleven where he
bought ice cream for children he regularly drove to school at the behest

of their parents or sponsors. He would point to the Chinese eateries and the Lake Trout market, "where people can get the best fish in town," one of the small pleasures savored by people who live in constant danger and uncertainty.

D. B. would also notice the boarded-up houses speckling every block, and the multitude of small businesses fueled by the drug trade, the pawnshops, the liquor stores and especially, the bail and bond companies. One boasted a large sign with the slogan: *"In and Out Bail and Bond—We have the Key to set you Free!"* Businesses can afford to make fun of disaster when, for many residents, a visit to the Western District police station is a routine occurrence. Tellingly, funeral parlors also dot the streets of West Baltimore.

If you travel south from Lower Park Heights, you will eventually come to the area known as Pigtown, so called because hogs were once hauled down its main avenue on their way to the slaughterhouses. Travel east and you will encounter the vestiges of an old industrial zone. It is there that the remains of the old Koppers Company can still be found. Most of it is now rubble. The two iron dogs that used to welcome the visitor to 200 Scott Street—Wilson's place of work for several years—are gone, dislodged when the building was demolished in the 1980s. The entrance to a condominium building now stands in their place. Only the plant where Beverly Wilson worked for nearly thirty years is still standing.

In the summer of 1998, twelve years after his departure from the Koppers Company, D. B. Wilson and his wife attended the twenty-fifth Jeter and Peake annual family reunion in Spartanburg, South Carolina. This was partly to honor the memory of Beverly's ancestors and partly to enjoy the gifts of sheer sociability. Traveling down from points in the Midwest, Northeast, and Atlantic Seaboard, more than one hundred people attended the event, which was far from casual.

Held at the Quality Hotel and Conference Center in Hearon Circle, the ceremony began with a banquet and dance on the evening of the Fourth of July. The next day, a buffet breakfast and testimonial service was followed by another dinner. There was ample opportunity for small talk, but religious exuberance permeated the ceremony. Moments for prayer and reflection alternated with lively conversation and laughter. Beverly Wilson offered welcoming remarks. Donald, her husband, participated in the lighting of candles. Evangelist Clara Jeter, Bev's sister-in-law, blessed the food.

In addition to the distinctive Southern fare of fried chicken, spare ribs, and collard greens, other symbols of cultural unity were distributed—they had been lovingly assembled by some of the Jeter and Peake women. Among the tokens were paper napkins and bookmarks imprinted with the date of and reason for the gathering, and pamphlets containing pictures and stories of departed kin. Every family in attendance received a copy.

On the cover of the booklets was the outline of a sturdy oak, each one of its limbs branching out to represent a descendant of Jimmie and Mattie Jeter, the oldest members of the lineage. "Back to the roots: South Carolina," read the caption below the genealogical tree. Upon opening the little book you found, among other things, the pictures of Milton Jeter, from Washington, DC, and the late Eugene Peake, from Aliquippa, Pennsylvania, founders of the annual reunion. Further along, the family's evolution was narrated in some detail. Two pages were dedicated to the Jeter coat of arms and its location in world history. The name dates back to the Middle Ages, and its origin is French. Without irony, complaint, or qualification, the booklet made a claim on both European and African ancestries. The final section listed the names of every member of the extended family, including that of Beverly Elaine Wilson, Donald B. Wilson, and their children and grandchildren.

"It was a grand party," D. B. told me upon his return from Spartanburg to Baltimore. "With that sort of faith, you can't have no fear."

And so it goes. America's inner city may be in permanent decay, filled with despair and marked by neglect; corporations may turn their backs on loyal employees; unforgiving markets will demolish human undertakings. But among people like Donald B. Wilson and his family, traditions endure, a source of strength in a topsy-turvy world.

2   BALTIMORE: FROM FACTORY TOWN TO CITY IN DECLINE

ONE CITY, ONE MAN

Donald B. Wilson's biography, summarized in the previous chapter, reflects changes experienced by the city of Baltimore during the second half of the twentieth century and the first decade of the new millennium. It shows the extent to which one single fragile life can be affected by structural forces that also impinge upon the constitution of physical spaces and the character of urban living.

Wilson grew up on a South Carolina farm, arrived in Baltimore as a young man in 1959, held a string of low-paying jobs, and then, in his mid-twenties, found employment at a major industrial firm. Nineteen years later, he was abruptly dismissed when the company yielded to the pressures of globalization, but not before he had acquired some of the elements of comfort and prosperity. Would Wilson have fared as well as he did without a vibrant manufacturing sector to bolster his aspirations and sense of self? Those who believe that admirable values can overcome all obstacles will point to the man's personal virtues—his stamina, resilience, optimism, and work ethic—to conclude that he would have succeeded, no matter what.

An alert reading of his life trajectory suggests otherwise. Wilson's youth was filled with opportunities for failure. He faltered and lived dangerously before finding a job that gave him safe harbor and the incentives to refashion goals. It was employment by an industrial firm—the Koppers Company—that enabled Wilson to realize his ambition, providing him with the material and human resources to sustain his marriage, purchase a home, raise his children to become professionals, and secure the elements of a middle-class life. Without a stable job and the benefits associated with it, those outcomes would not have ensued. One thing is certain: opportunities that were available when Wilson was young are no longer within the reach of most unskilled and semiskilled workers. International economic trends and industrial recomposition at the domestic level have played a role in that development.

GLOBALIZING BALTIMORE

Baltimore's transition from burgeoning industrial center to struggling service entrepôt and tourist destination was largely the result of global integration starting in the mid-twentieth century (Centeno and Cohen 2010; Fernández-Kelly 1984; Harvey 2011; Arrighi 1994, 2010; Portes and Walton 1981; Sassen 1999, 2001, 2008; Sennett 2000, 2007). By the 1960s, computer technology and cheap but rapid transportation freed employers from spatial constraints and diminished their dependence on local workforces. Companies began to relocate assembly operations to parts of the world, like Asia and Latin America, where wages were low and workers lacked means for negotiation. Able to roam across borders in search of optimal conditions, employers had few incentives to increase real wages for American workers.[1]

During the 1970s and 1980s, an epidemic of plant closings caused massive layoffs in places like New York, Pittsburgh, Detroit, and Baltimore. Baltimore alone lost 90,000 manufacturing jobs between 1970 and 1998 (Chapelle 2000: 232). The sputtering smokestacks that had dotted the old industrial landscape gradually went still.

Estimates of the time give an idea of the depth of industrial restructuring at the national level. After conducting the first influential study on that subject, economists Barry Bluestone and Bennett Harrison (1984: 9) concluded that "somewhere between 32 and 38 million jobs [throughout the nation] were lost during the 1970s as the direct result of private disinvestment in American business." Large firms eliminated nearly 100,000 jobs per year simply by closing down domestic branch plants. Economist David M. Gordon (1996) calculated a total loss of three to four million jobs between 1978 and 1982—one out of every four positions in large manufacturing facilities (Bluestone and Harrison 1990; Harrison 1997).

Observers noticed with alarm the tendency of companies to renege on past commitments to employees under the guise of increasing efficiency and flexibility (Gordon 1996; Harrison 1997). Writings by Michael Piore and Charles Sabel (1986) took a more optimistic view, emphasizing the opportunities that the new economy was creating for entrepreneurs. Despite varying positions, there was consensus about the irrevocable character of economic change in the United States.

Figure 1 shows the dramatic rearrangement of the U.S. economy since the mid-twentieth century. In 1960, one-third of all U.S. jobs were in manufacturing, and services represented a small fraction of employment (13.7 percent). By 1999, those proportions were reversed—only 16.4 percent of jobs were in manufacturing and more than 70 percent were in services. That trend continued in later years.

Deregulation and privatization paralleled neoliberal discourses consistent with the globalizing shift (Arrighi 2010; Harvey 2007). Signal pieces of legislation were blunted or repealed to allow markets to perform lithely. The consequences of such decisions were felt as far along as the first decade of the twenty-first century. For example, some key provisions in the Glass-Steagall Act of 1933, which had established the Federal Deposit Insurance Corporation and set in place measures under Franklin D. Roosevelt to discourage speculation, were repealed in 1980; other stipulations in the same law were dismantled in 1999. Such steps would facilitate the near collapse of the banking industry in 2008. Chipping away at the regulatory apparatus became a counterpart to industrial restructuring.

Milton Friedman, the Nobel Prize–winning economist and a major advocate of neoliberalism under the Reagan administration, saw the relocation of manufacturing from places like Baltimore to points like Hong Kong, Singapore, South Korea, and the U.S.-Mexico border as an effective mechanism to invigorate the economy and democracy in developing regions. Globalization, he believed, would restore economic balance by creating opportunities for the expansion of high-end economic sectors—like electronics, finance, and insurance—in advanced nations while allowing greater economic competitiveness in emerging countries (Friedman 1962/2002). In the views

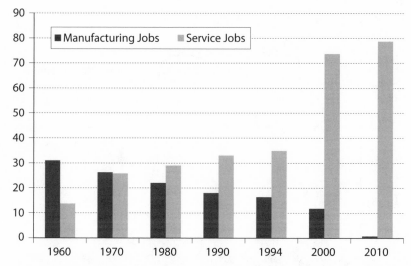

FIGURE 1. Employment in Manufacturing and Services, 1960–2010. Source: Bureau of Labor Statistics, U.S. Department of Labor

of economists like Friedman, global integration would also benefit workers by enabling companies to market cheaply made goods at lower prices, thus enhancing the purchasing power of ordinary consumers.

But there was more to economic change than cost-benefit calculations. Globalization was also a political trend whose effect was to realign the balance of power between investors and workers to the advantage of the former (Fernández-Kelly 1984). Such programmatic ends encompassed an assault upon labor unions launched by conservative politicians and like-minded intellectuals. As part of a current that had begun in the early twentieth century, unions were increasingly portrayed as enemies of free enterprise and tools to achieve socialist, even communist, ends.

Along with unions, the government came under attack and was increasingly portrayed as an impediment to freedom and market competition. In his 1981 inaugural address, President Ronald Reagan famously stated, "government is not the solution to our problem; government *is* the problem." In that spirit, and soon after he took office, he approved the decertification of the Professional Air Traffic Controllers Organization (PATCO), dealing a nearly fatal blow to workers who,

FIGURE 2. Percent of Employed Workers with Union Membership, 1930–2003. Source: Mayer, Gerald (2004) "Union membership trends in the United States." Congressional Research Service. Library of Congress. Washington.

ironically, had voted overwhelmingly to install him as president. What many people saw as a historical betrayal ushered in an era of steady union decline.

Figure 2 synthesizes data about trends in union membership between 1930 and 1999. In the mid-1950s, nearly 30 percent of workers in the United States belonged to unions, although union membership was lower there than in most comparable countries. By 1970, less than 25 percent of American workers were unionized. That proportion further declined to 18 percent in 1980 and to an abysmal 13 percent at the end of the twentieth century. In 2010, the union membership rate was 11.9 percent, down from 12.3 percent a year earlier, and the number of wage and salary workers belonging to unions declined by 612,000 to 14.7 million. Today, only 6.9 percent of workers in private business belong to labor unions, in contrast to 36.2 percent of workers employed by government (U.S. Bureau of Labor Statistics 2011).

The weakening of labor organizations and a reduction of their bargaining power vis-à-vis employers was compounded by minimal or negative increases in hourly wages. Figure 3 shows that real hourly

FIGURE 3. Year-to-year percentage growth in median weekly earnings, U.S., 1979–2013.
Source: Bureau of Labor Statistics, U.S. Department of Labor

wages dropped, especially during the 1980s, as much as 6 percent in the United States. It was only after 1995 that they rebounded, partly as a result of vigorous activity in the financial and speculative sectors.

Diminishing opportunities for native-born workers in blue-collar employment matched increases in automation and greater reliance on domestic and international subcontracting as a means to disperse the economic and political risks of production. On Mexico's northern border, in cities like Tijuana and Ciudad Juárez, thousands of assembly plants, or *maquiladoras*, gave testimony to the new competitive strategies. Older sectors, like clothing, but also emerging industries, like electronics, increased their reliance on subcontracting chains connecting large companies with small firms and even individuals doing piecework at home in locations within and outside the United States (Fernández-Kelly 1984; Fernández-Kelly and Sassen 1991; Fernández-Kelly and Shefner 2007; Shefner and Fernández-Kelly 2011).[2]

Poverty and inequality increased during the period of industrial recomposition. Between 1980 and 1998, the number of people living below the poverty line in the United States increased from 29 million to nearly 32 million. Statistically, that change was small, showing that the percentage of the total population living in poverty remained nearly static—from 12.95 to 13 percent. In absolute numbers, however, poverty expanded appreciably by nearly 3 million.

At the national level, destitution among people under the age of eighteen increased from 11 million in 1980 (18.3 percent of the child population) to more than 12 million at the end of the decade (19.5 percent of all minors). In Baltimore alone, the number of individuals living below the poverty line expanded by 25,000 during the same period. With ebbs and flows, trends in poverty continued in the new millennium. In 2012, four years after a nearly catastrophic recession, African Americans experienced almost unprecedented unemployment levels. Almost a third of the Black population in Baltimore now lives below the poverty level (U.S. Census Bureau 2012b).

As Figure 4 shows, low-income groups have been especially affected by social spending reductions partly fueled by neoliberal policies. At the national level, the share of total income going to the 5 percent highest-income households grew from 16.5 percent in 1980 to 18.3 percent in 1988, and the share of the highest fifth increased from 44.1 percent to 46.3 percent during the same years. By contrast, the portion of total income accruing to the lowest fifth fell from 4.2 percent at the beginning of the 1980s to 3.8 percent in 1988. The share of the second-poorest fifth went from 10.2 percent to 9.6 percent (Center for Budget and Policy Priorities 2010). Economic inequalities in the United States now approach those of some countries in the less developed world.

Globalization and industrial recomposition dramatically recast the options of working-class people, both in the United States and abroad. They also led to record levels of capital accumulation among the members of a new corporate class operating across international borders (Sassen 2014).

As the twenty-first century advances, the effects of international economic integration seem positive among those endowed with professional standing and education, regardless of national origin. Educated people everywhere have at their disposal channels for economic mobility that did not exist before and, despite national differences, have more in common with one another than with poor and poorly educated people in their own countries. That partly explains how and why poverty remains invisible to so many Americans, including some affluent Blacks.

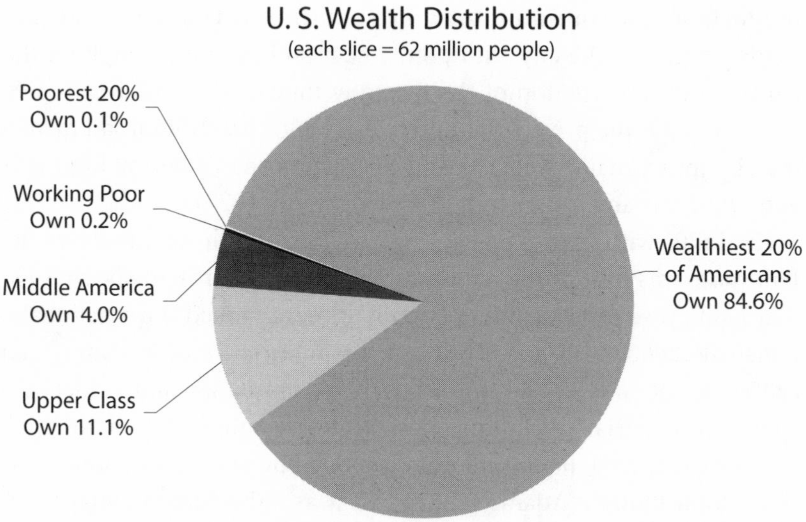

U. S. Wealth Distribution

(each slice = 62 million people)

Poorest 20%
Own 0.1%

Working Poor
Own 0.2%

Middle America
Own 4.0%

Wealthiest 20%
of Americans
Own 84.6%

Upper Class
Own 11.1%

FIGURE 4. U.S. income/wealth distribution (source TK)

In the next section, I summarize in more detail Baltimore's development and examine the evolution of the city's western neighborhoods. That analysis sets the stage for the presentation of another life, that of Big Floyd Twigg, whose experience parallels that of Donald B. Wilson, but at a more recent time and under less auspicious circumstances.

BALTIMORE BEGINNINGS

Founded in 1729, Baltimore was named after Cecilius Calvert, Second Lord of Baltimore, a nobleman in the Irish House of Lords and the first proprietor of the Maryland Colony (Chapelle 2000: 2).[3] Since then, and throughout the eighteenth century, the city grew rapidly as a repository for sugar-producing colonies in the Caribbean, and it played a key role in events leading to and including the American Revolution.[4]

Given its strategic position and transportation connections to the American Midwest and the Pacific Ocean, Baltimore continued to expand in the nineteenth century, partly as a result of a new demand for industrial workers. Many immigrants were employed in factories, which multiplied with the introduction of steam power. Textile production and flour mills grew in number. Roads, canals, and railroads connected the city with points near and distant throughout the nation. The construction of the federally funded National Road (U.S. Route 40) and the private Baltimore and Ohio (B&O) Railroad turned the city into a major shipping and manufacturing center by linking it with domestic and overseas markets (Skidmore 1977).

In 1870, with approximately $33 million worth of foreign trade, Baltimore was fifth in the nation as a commercial crossroads; by 1900 that figure rose to $130 million, and Baltimore ranked third nationally (Chapelle 2000: 146). In addition to its importance as a commercial center, the city was also a vigorous trading conurbation and a chief outlet for raw materials, including grain products, cotton, and leaf tobacco.

As it prospered, Baltimore was celebrated by writers and politicians alike. John Quincy Adams referred to it as "The Monumental City" because of its imposing architecture and assortment of plazas, fountains, and graceful sculptures in public spaces. With the growth of an affluent class, art and literature flourished. Edgar Allan Poe lived and died in Baltimore, and it was there that he wrote "The Raven."

The city was full of contrasts. Wealthy merchants built fortunes and donated funds to civic and cultural institutions, their riches matching those of others urban dwellers in great American cities. Industrial expansion, however, paralleled increases in the number of immigrants living and toiling in squalor. Germans and then Irish dominated the ethnic landscape. The descendants of Jews, Bohemians, Poles, Italians, Lithuanians, and Greeks who had arrived in the nineteenth century lived side by side with African Americans born within and outside the United States. Baltimore's immigration history mirrors the broader nation's experience, but the city is somewhat unique for its combination of sizable immigrant groups coexisting with a large antebellum Black population.

Over the last three decades of the nineteenth century, the number of industries in Baltimore trebled, and capital investment increased sixfold (Chapelle 2000: 148). Slaughtering and meatpacking increased. Clothing, foundries, machine shops, and copper and steel mills proliferated, as did the steel rails made at Sparrows Point by the Maryland Steel company. That outfit was purchased in 1916 by Bethlehem Steel, a firm founded in Pennsylvania in 1852 that subsequently became a key force in Baltimore's industrial development.

Bethlehem Steel grew to become the second-largest producer of its kind in America, operating its Sparrows Point plant in Baltimore for the better part of the twentieth century. Between 1916 and 1945, the company manufactured the steel for many of the country's most prominent landmarks, including New York City's George Washington Bridge and Madison Square Garden and San Francisco's Golden Gate Bridge and Municipal Railway.[5]

Commercial and manufacturing activity promoted affluence and economic development, but large numbers of workers continued to live in overcrowded, disease-ridden slums while working long hours for paltry wages. The adoption of machinery since the early 1900s led to the replacement of skilled and unskilled workers in manufacturing, adding dislocation to the afflictions of the urban poor and provoking new forms of political mobilization.

Labor unions proliferated. By 1900, approximately twenty thousand individuals belonged to nearly seventy different workers' organizations (Chapelle 2000: 150). Strikes were frequent and often violent. The period following World War I witnessed growing union recognition, gains in wages, and improved working conditions. All in all, hardship but also opportunity marked the trajectory of immigrant workers and their descendants. Blacks, by contrast, faced special circumstances imprinted with the legacy of slavery, emancipation, and imperfect incorporation.

THE AFRICAN AMERICAN JOURNEY

Baltimore features significantly in African American history because of the early efforts of Quakers and other religious groups in the abolitionist struggle. Many denounced slavery as a practice grossly inconsistent with the ideals of equality and freedom proclaimed in the Declaration of Independence (Chapelle 2000). The combined activities of abolitionist societies and legislation easing the manumission process gradually led to a significant growth of Baltimore's free Black population. By the early nineteenth century, free Blacks outnumbered slaves. Frederick Douglass, a leading abolitionist, worked as a ship's carpenter in Baltimore. Although born a slave, he rose to become an internationally recognized orator and fighter for human rights.

Before the Civil War, African Americans in Baltimore created community institutions similar to those built by immigrants. After the war, however, they did not attain as full a level of integration as their immigrant counterparts. While incentives were put into place by local and federal authorities to assimilate immigrants, people of African descent faced steep deprivation and prejudice. By 1870, almost forty thousand Blacks lived in Baltimore, representing 15 percent of the population, but most of them languished in poverty. By contrast, residents of European ancestry became the tenants of Baltimore's lively ethnic neighborhoods, like Little Italy, Greek Town, and Locust Point, the latter known also as Little Warsaw (Janvier 1933; Wright 1921/1971).[6]

The twentieth century, as well, witnessed large demographic changes as a result of the Great Black Migration, which transferred large numbers of African Americans seeking improved opportunities from the rural South to northeastern and midwestern cities. Baltimore's Black population grew from 23.8 percent in 1950 to 46.4 percent in 1970 (Chapelle 2000:194; Wright 1921/1971). By 2000, 58 percent of those residing in Baltimore were African American. Hard hit by deindustrialization, the city moved from a manufacturing-based economy to one focused on services and tourism. A series of developmental strategies implemented in the 1970s and '80s under the legendary Mayor Donald Schaeffer led to the "Baltimore Renaissance," one of the signal accomplishments of which was the revitalization of Baltimore's Inner Harbor (Smith 1999).

The loss of industry and the ascent of tourist attractions like the Inner Harbor have benefited skilled workers, visitors, and tourists but not impoverished Blacks. Although African Americans represent more than half of Baltimore's residents, and a large proportion of them are poor, they remain almost invisible to the casual observer. High levels of residential segregation are partly to blame, as well as developments like the Inner Harbor that attract populations with large disposable incomes but produce scant employment for local residents.[7]

For impoverished people living in segregated neighborhoods, globalization was the latest of multiple historical setbacks hardening their living conditions. Emblematic of that trend are the western neighborhoods of Upton, Sandtown-Winchester, and Lower Park Heights where I conducted most of the research for this book.

WEST BALTIMORE AS LANDSCAPE

On a map, West Baltimore resembles a reclining hourglass comprising approximately fifteen square miles. To the southeast are Upton and Sandtown-Winchester, to the northwest is Lower Park Heights, and farther north is the sprawling area known as Liberty Heights. The three sections join at Druid Hill Park, a large expanse of green where the Baltimore Conservatory and Zoo are located.

Upton, the neighborhood where most of the families described in this book lived, is one of the poorest in the city of Baltimore. Ninety-eight percent of its residents are African American. The majority are renters, not property owners. Mortgages and other loans are virtually unavailable. In 1990, the average price of a home in Upton was $7,442, a bad investment by any measure. Arson and abandonment were frequent, as evidenced by the abundance of charred and boarded-up buildings that often became safe houses for drug dealers. Owners found it more profitable to burn down their properties than to repair them. Partly as a result, vacancy rates were high, as was the level of unemployment and underemployment. Business activity was puny, with the exception of a myriad of grocery stores and liquor shops inherited by Korean immigrants from an earlier cohort of Jewish entrepreneurs.

Outsiders see West Baltimore as an enigmatic zone constituting one of three ghettos encroaching upon the city. Lower Park Heights and Upton bear foul reputations. It is there that the projects smoldered and "the element"—a euphemism used by real estate brokers to designate poor residents—clusters. In the 1970s, the now defunct George Murphy Homes, a publicly subsidized housing complex, was known as "the Valley of Death." Images of crime, deprivation, and racial resentment engulfed West Baltimore in the 1990s, and they still do. Upton, in particular, appeared as a hodgepodge of small streets and alleyways strewn haphazardly on the wrong side of the Pennsylvania-Ohio railroad tracks. A smaller demarcation, Sandtown-Winchester, was targeted for urban revitalization under Kurt Schmoke's mayoralty in the 1990s, and other mayors have continued those efforts more recently. The results, so far, have been lackluster.

West Baltimore's development has been uneven. Well into the 1960s, Lower Park Heights was a solid middle-class tract populated by the

children and grandchildren of Eastern European Jews. Several imposing synagogues still stand in the area as legacies of its shining past.
Its stature in the collective imagination has been celebrated by Barry
Levinson, a Baltimore native, in popular films like *Tin Men* (1987),
Avalon (1990), and *Liberty Heights* (1999). Over the course of a century,
economic and demographic changes transformed Lower Park Heights
from an urban space of hope and advancement into a segregated tract
marked by social isolation and destitution.

Upton and Sandtown-Winchester, on the other hand, illustrate
enduring poverty; their present is eerily reminiscent of their past. The
two neighborhoods emerged in the late eighteenth century as areas
populated by European immigrants employed in the expanding commercial districts of Baltimore. Irish, German, Polish, and Bohemian
waves first, followed by Eastern European Jews, coexisted in Upton.
Many residents were unskilled manual workers and domestic servants employed by the wealthy families of Old Baltimore Town and
Bolton Hill. Others were manumitted slaves vying with immigrants for
unskilled jobs. Fierce competition for wage employment marked the
relationship between Blacks and Whites living in those areas.

The first decades of the nineteenth century witnessed increased
immigration and population mobility prompted by the war of 1812.
Generalized turmoil was followed in Upton and Sandtown-Winchester
by increases in the rates of homicide and pauperism. Historical
accounts of the time are filled with descriptions of disease, filth, and
crowded living conditions. Epidemics of smallpox, diphtheria, and
measles were common.

As far back as 1894, the U.S. Department of Labor conducted and
published a study of slums in urban areas that focused on Chicago, Philadelphia, New York, and Baltimore. Upton was prominently displayed
as part of that report. In 1821, a noted physician characterized a section
in Sandtown-Winchester as "A nest of houses tenanted by Negroes and
divided by an alley [where] disease and death have year after year luxu-
riously rioted among the miserable and abandoned victims who have
there nestled together" (Commissioner of Labor 1894: 127).

Conditions did not improve during the second half of the nineteenth century. By the 1860s, local government sought to make provision for the protection and maintenance of "unfortunate helpless

maniacs" who were appearing on the streets of West Baltimore. There was a great increase in the number of idle and wandering poor, chiefly women with children and without husbands, and old men who were destitute, helpless, and without work. References mention multitudes of arrivals, especially Irish who flocked to the area, "worn-out Negroes, and infant beggars" (Commissioner of Labor 1894: 153).

European immigrants in Upton and Sandtown-Winchester followed a well-known trajectory: they lived poorly and worked tirelessly; they saved money, hoping to move to better places. They viewed the slum and its squalid tenements as temporary calamities to be endured in the search of a good life. For the majority, economic advancement meant relocating to other, more prosperous, neighborhoods. That option was out of reach for African Americans who were shunned as a result of strict racial demarcations (Massey and Denton 1993).

When European immigration slowed down during the first part of the twentieth century, it was followed by new arrivals from the rural South as part of the Great Black Migration. The forebears of families described in this book came mainly from the Carolinas, Virginia, and West Virginia. Rural-urban migration further polarized class distinctions in the already crowded neighborhoods. As immigrants moved to more attractive locations, permanent enclosure, on the basis of color and race, became West Baltimore's trademark, illustrating a common phenomenon in American cities: the transformation of immigrant slums into Black ghettos (Massey and Denton 1993; Philpott 1991).

Yet, impoverished people were not the only occupants of Upton and Sandtown-Winchester. The rigidity of color boundaries, during the period that preceded desegregation in the 1960s, meant that even middle-class Blacks, many of whose forebears had never been slaves, and some of whom were immigrants from the Caribbean, could not settle in White areas. Some were professionals; others were involved in crafts and small businesses. Despite their relative affluence, their mobility was restricted. The confinement of poor and affluent Blacks to the same urban space gave Upton and Sandtown-Winchester a singular profile marked by class differentiation amidst racial homogeneity.

Unable to move, affluent Blacks sought to carve out spaces within the ghetto. Among such enclaves of relative prosperity were Edmonson Village, Lafayette Square, and Druid Hill Avenue—labeled by W.E.B.

DuBois as one of the best colored boulevards in the world. Marble Hill, an area within the larger Upton, was known for its dignified row houses featuring ornamented front steps of white stone and wrought-iron banisters. It was there that Black intellectuals, political leaders, and musicians lived. Donald Wilson (chapter 1) remembered many of them from his youth. Thurgood Marshall, Billie Holiday, and the Mitchell family once resided in Upton.

Baltimore's segregated society also led to the growth of a widely celebrated Black entertainment district. Pennsylvania Avenue emerged as a prime center of culture in the 1920s and took second place only to Harlem, whose artistic vitality has been widely celebrated (Chapelle 2000: 192). The ornate Douglass Theater, later known as the Royal, featured big-name musicians like Eubie Blake, Count Basie, Cab Calloway, and Duke Ellington. After World War II, Ella Fitzgerald, Nat King Cole, Dizzy Gillespie, and Billie Holiday all performed at the Royal, as did later the Supremes, the Platters, and James Brown. Bars, nightclubs, and theaters were owned by and catered to Blacks, who were barred from White neighborhoods.

On a broader scale, as more White families fled to the suburbs, prompted by the accelerated arrival of Blacks during the first half of the twentieth century, property values plummeted and banks turned their backs on neighborhoods that rapidly became predominantly African American. Discontent led to intermittent unrest, dealing yet another blow to private enterprise and business activity. Countless commercial establishments closed down in the wake of civil disturbances ignited by the assassination of the Reverend Martin Luther King Jr. in 1968. Together with the ravages of industry, those events thrust West Baltimore into a state of permanent decline.[8]

Finally, reforms resulting from the civil rights movement enabled middle-class Blacks to move away from the inner city for the first time. With them left the last vestiges of class diversity in Baltimore's western neighborhoods. This further undermined the social and economic base (Wilson 1987). Churches that had stood as bastions of order and mainsprings of leadership were boarded up or sold. Their shells stand as silent witnesses of an older, less desperate past. Small businesses once owned by African Americans lost their clientele to a growing assortment of shopping malls that sprang up like mushrooms in the wider metropolitan area.

According to census figures, Upton and Sandtown-Winchester contain roughly 43,000 residents, 41 percent of whom have incomes below the poverty level. Mean household earnings amount to $10,723, and 71 percent of the households have earnings below $12,499. Only 20 percent of Upton occupants are homeowners. Open unemployment reaches 12 percent, and 42 percent of all adults in the area do not participate in the labor force. Almost 60 percent of mothers are eligible for public assistance.

It is in that environment that Big Floyd struggled to become a man. I present his story in the next chapter.

3   BIG FLOYD

THE WINTER OF 1994 WAS BITTER BY BALTIMORE STANDARDS. A sky as drab as cinder hung over the city almost without break between January and March. Dampness and cold were punctuated by an ice storm shortly after New Year's Day. Suddenly, the barren trees changed into luminous statues, their branches heavy with stalactites. At the entrance of the Johns Hopkins University, a decorative row of winter cabbages glistened like crystalline rock under the brief morning sun. Seven miles away, close to the George Murphy Homes, blue plastic bags taken from local stores dangled from the electrical lines along Franklin Avenue. They were either blown into place by the wind or hung there by children at play. Now, they seemed like birds waiting to soar, fluttering with the mild breeze, almost cheerful in the surrounding squalor.

The season was harsh, but things were looking up for Floyd Mitchell Twigg Sr.—Big Floyd. For one thing, he was making plans to marry Iliad, the woman who had given birth to his daughter Shatirya, the previous year. For another, it seemed like he was finally going to get a real job after a long spell of hustling and failure. He was full of hope, but that wasn't rare; Big Floyd had a hopeful disposition.

So many times had he stated his longings that he was beginning to sound like a man obsessed. "You just wait an' see," he would tell me, repeating the sentences like a mantra. "As soon as I get back on my feet, I'm gonna marry Iliad and get them babies, all of them, under the same roof. We're gonna be a real family." That had been his goal since childhood: to be a family man. He thought about his other children—Melinda, then twelve; Clarise, almost eleven; and Little Floyd, then eight. On and off for the past five years, they had been living with relatives or in foster homes after being declared "children in need of assistance" by the Department of Child Protective Services.

Despite the time elapsed since his separation from his children, Floyd still thought he was facing a temporary reversal. Things would get better. He would yet fulfill his desire to reunite with his kids; he would do the right thing, as his father had told him to do when he was just a boy.

Big Floyd was born in New York City twenty-nine years earlier, but his people had originally come from Virginia. As a child he had lived in a small row house in Harlem with his father, stepmother, two younger half-brothers, one half-sister, and a mentally disabled uncle whose name was Ben. His biological mother had died when he was only three, leaving him and his older sister, Rita, behind. Rita, whom they called Boo, had lived most of her life in Baltimore.

At first, Floyd had liked Harlem. That was when his father, Ernie, was working at the Compton Iron Works, just across the Hudson River, a job he held for more than a decade, mostly in the 1970s. Floyd could remember his father's daily departures to work. Long before dawn, his footsteps would wake him hours before he had to rise in reluctant preparation for school. Ernie, who was tall and light-skinned, and spoke with the slow beat of the south, would gather his lunch box in the dark, button up his worn-out jacket and wave at Floyd who slept on the living room sofa.

Then came his forewarning: "Jus' pay mind to the Bible, son: Depart from evil, and do good so you shall abide in the House of the Lord forever." Ernie's favorite words came from the Book of Psalms, but it would take Floyd many years to understand their meaning: "Guess he just wanted to remind the two of us that we was good people trying to do better." Memories such as those kept him going years later when things got rough.

Before he became a welder, Ernie had held a string of menial jobs at Compton. He worked for nine years at low pay and with few benefits, grateful to have steady employment. He never was late or missed a shift and, although he longed to ditch the small rented quarters where he lived with his family, he was proud of his record. Not everyone could boast about keeping a family together through hard work as he could. All along, Alma, his wife, cleaned houses to supplement Ernie's income.

They were getting by all right. And then, in 1978, Ernie became a union man. Not just any union man but a member of the United Steel Workers of America, Local 2188. John Schmidt, the shop steward, impressed by Ernie's spirit and diligence, had recommended him for the welding job. Now Ernie could look ahead, start saving money, move into a bigger house, and prosper.

With his mind set on buying a home, Ernie renewed his effort at work. He bought a used Ford car. Floyd could remember his father driving the family around on weekends to see neighborhoods where they might want to live. It was like "dreaming about the future," said Floyd years later.

Ernie's ambition, however, would soon be tested. In 1980, when Floyd was almost fifteen, the Compton factory, one of the most productive in the region, closed down unable to withstand foreign competition. New economic trends were afoot. A recession seemed imminent. Companies were shifting manufacturing operations to less developed countries. Good jobs were hard to come by, especially among those in the lower strata of the working class. Last to be hired during the preceding boom and first to be fired in the subsequent downturn, Blacks were hit the hardest.

For a while Ernie went about from odd job to odd job, unable to secure a permanent position. He was not alone in his troubles; many of his friends and neighbors had been laid off too or couldn't find work. Now, his union card lay still on the nightstand without use or purpose, eventually to be discarded as trash. Still very young, Floyd saw the neighborhood go from bad to worse as his family began to splinter. "We was like lost in a storm," he recalled. "Things weren't right and I didn't care for New York no more."

Alma, Floyd's stepmother, was the first to let go of the common purpose. Cleaning houses didn't pay enough to cover the rent and also put food in her children's bellies. Uncle Ben's disability benefits were too small to be shared in times of need. He and young Floyd took up too much space in the small home, anyway. Never overly generous toward her stepson, Alma now became miserly. She saw no option but to go on welfare. Yet she couldn't apply for assistance with her husband still there—social service regulations were strict; they did not allow men to live with women on government aid. Ernie, Uncle Ben, and Floyd, would have to move out, at least, temporarily. Maybe later, when things changed, they could get back together again. They never did.

She was all about wishful thinking, said Floyd. As far as Ernie was concerned, that was pretty much the end of the road. His sense of manhood wounded, he took a long time to recover. I first met him in 1993, at the house of his daughter Boo. Still genial, he had long ago given up on regular work.

Just shy of his fifteenth birthday, Floyd was sent to live in West Baltimore with his favorite aunt, Lucy, Ernie's younger sister. He was beaming with renewed anticipation as he arrived in Baltimore's Penn Station. The city wasn't big like New York; it seemed tamer, more welcoming with its long rows of brick houses and shaded streets.

Lucy and her two sons, Trevor and Carlos, who were sixteen and thirteen at the time, lived on the 1100 block of Biddle Street. They occupied the upper level of an attached single-family home. Their quarters were crowded, but they had three bedrooms, a kitchen, and a bathroom, in addition to a small porch and sitting area adjacent to the front door. In the summer, they could use the grill in the backyard for an occasional barbecue. Lucy had worked as a clerk at the post office for almost twenty years. She had a modest but stable income, enough to support her children and welcome Floyd into her home.

In the fall of 1979, Floyd began attending Frederick Douglass High School. Like other educational facilities in poor neighborhoods, this one was named after a leading figure in the struggle for racial justice. Douglass had been born a slave and became renowned for his verve and brilliance. His memory was now bestowed on a decrepit structure more suitable for a warehouse than for the instruction of youngsters.

The irony was not lost on Floyd, who remembered DHS as "an old building where somethin' was always falling apart and there wasn't enough books for the kids. [It] would have made Frederick Douglass cry." Clamorous and distracting, the school contradicted expectations: "The students, man! They was always making noise and you couldn't think straight. It was hard getting the studyin' done."

Despite the limitations of the environment, Floyd maintained average grades throughout his high school years and demonstrated a special interest in English literature. One of his teachers, Mrs. Hoover, was caring and "really smart." He used to read the books she assigned and pretend he was a fictional character, "living far away, away from Balti-more and New York." Other than that, there was little that captured his youthful imagination.

Before and after school hours Floyd had to face the perilous journey from and back to his home. Street corners were busy commercial points where youngsters earned quick money by peddling crack and weed—tickets to oblivion. Floyd didn't care for drugs and therefore bypassed the lure of the local market without difficulty. The problem was with the sporadic violence that erupted wherever drugs were present. Drive-by shootings were not uncommon, though they happened mostly at night. What worried Floyd were the unexpected flare-ups and the accidental deaths. He had lived less than three months in Baltimore with his aunt Lucy when a little girl a block away fell instantly dead on the front steps of the house where she was staying. Two boys, scarcely eleven, had been toying with a handgun.

Floyd had lived in Baltimore less than a year when he met Benita Wallace, a neighborhood girl nearly a year older than him. The two shared a common childhood experience: she too had lost her mother as a toddler. Unlike Floyd, however, Benita had been in foster care and, from the age of twelve, had lived with her grandmother Missie. By the early 1990s, when I first met her, Benita had fallen into crack and alco-hol abuse—she died of cirrhosis in 2002, at the age of thirty-seven—but in her teens she had been willful and bright.

Floyd remembered Benita Wallace as "always having to get her own way." Years later, I often saw her sitting in her aunt Lydia's living room, grinning vapidly, arms folded, waiting for a bit of food and the occasional twenty-dollar bill. Bloated and listless, she gave little evidence of youth, although she was still in her twenties. Her flame had burned out long ago, and her three children, Melinda, Clarise, and Little Floyd, were but a vague, intermittent presence. That's not what she had expected when, as a girl, she pursued Floyd's company. He had been good-looking and strong; her desire drew her to him.

Shortly after they started going together, Benita knew she was preg-nant. Already a high school dropout, she regarded her condition as a sign of impending maturity—she should now start acting "responsible," like a grown woman. Avid for independence, she was tired of living where she didn't belong and wasn't wanted; she yearned for a home of her own, and she knew where to get it. Few in her circle escaped public assistance. "The welfare" was such a common experience that it never dawned on her there might be an alternative.

With her grandmother, Benita first went to the local clinic to confirm her pregnancy. Having seen many youngsters become mothers too early in life, Missie was in a huff, but not surprised: "Dem girls nowadays," she said, "they just do what they want to do without paying no mind to the consequences." Benita didn't take her grandma's disapproval too seriously. She knew she could rely on her.

Missie and the gravid Benita had spent tiresome hours waiting for a doctor and then more hours at the welfare office to see a social worker. The girl had been there several times before with an older cousin and didn't have fond memories of the place. "It was hateful, nasty, 'cause they [the social workers] treat you like you nothing, like they so much better and you a piece of shit."

At this time, however, she didn't let other people's attitude bother her. More important things were on her mind. She needed the social worker, disdainful as she may have been, to help with the application. Waiting lists for public housing were long. It would take time to find a spot. Only the social worker could give her a hand.

When her first daughter, Melinda, was born, in May 1980, Benita was still living with Missie, her grandmother. Almost another year elapsed in boredom and occasional despair before there was any change in her housing situation. Then, two years later, Benita received authorization to occupy a small unit on the tenth floor of one of the towering structures at the George Murphy Homes. She was elated as she took over the new apartment, and although he wasn't supposed to, Floyd virtually moved in with her right away.[1] For the next four years, the couple struggled to build a family.

Shortly after Benita moved into the Murphy Homes, Floyd turned eighteen. He had grown into a muscular frame and a withdrawn manner, a combination that presented new liabilities. Gone was his confident, accepting smile. His reserve was easily mistaken for surliness, his reticence for antagonism. He thought that a man should "better stay to hisself and not show weakness 'cause [otherwise] people take advantage."

Floyd's notion of manliness interfered with sociability. And despite his interest in English literature, he had limited use of the language.

Unable to communicate fluidly and hampered by toughness, he retreated into the armor that often cloaks impoverished men. To conceal his frailty, he cultivated a hermetic style that guaranteed survival within the contours of the ghetto but was of little use elsewhere, especially when seeking jobs.

Despite all that, and eager to support his children, Floyd began looking for paid employment even before getting his high school diploma. He worked in all the usual places: as an attendant at a fast-food restaurant, as a helper at a construction site; even as a janitor in one of the local grade schools. Shortly after graduation, he was hired at minimum wage by the Atlas Storage Company, on Carlton Street, and he kept that job for more than two years, not an easy feat in the kind of position that shows perpetual turnover.

The pay was low and the treatment was rough. Loading and unloading trucks filled most of Floyd's time, but he didn't mind—he thought he was making progress. Added to Benita's monthly check and food stamps, his wage allowed for a few creature comforts: a fancy refrigerator, nice furnishings, and best of all, two telephones with call-waiting and call-forwarding service—one of the trademarks of a middle-class life in the latter part of the twentieth century. Things, he was sure, would improve. They did not.

Even before Melinda's birth, Benita had begun to dabble in drugs, first marijuana and, later, crack cocaine; it was her way to escape the drudgery of daily life.[2] Her second daughter, Clarise, was born in February 1982 and her son, Little Floyd, in March of the following year. She had shed the yoke of her grandmother's tutelage only to strive alone, caring for three young children with whom she had little in common but a biological connection.

For a while she tried to be a good mother, to dust and mop and feed her babies on time, but increasingly she started looking for company in the neighborhood, going to parties, running the streets, having a blast. She hungered for friends, popularity, and constant excitement—the good times she had left behind when she first became pregnant. Floyd's association was no longer enough and, besides, he didn't turn out to be the kind of companion she had hoped for. He didn't know "how to party." He didn't drink or smoke. He couldn't even make money like other men. She thought he was lazy.

Benita wasn't alone in her misgivings. Other women in her family shared the same notions. Her aunt Lydia, for instance, thought that Floyd was "a regular bum, just hangin' on to the girl so he don't have to do real work." Then again, Lydia held similar opinions about most men. Her own husband, James Culver, was an itinerant mechanic who could not be trusted to make a steady living.

Things were different with Lydia. Although she was on welfare, she cleaned five houses for cash every week. She took pride in being industrious, trustworthy, and resourceful. In her case, "The welfare" was only a supplement, not a primary source of livelihood. "But the mens," she bemoaned, "they don't want a real job, [they don't want] nothin' to tie dem down." It was mostly the dealers who got rich. A devout Jehovah's Witness, Lydia would grow disgusted at the thought of drugs. She had seen her neighborhood destroyed by the trade. All the same, she felt the dealers were at least "trying to support themselves and their families." Men like Floyd were inept even at crime. She could understand why Benita was getting fed up with him.

Floyd deeply resented Lydia's charges. Under assault, chastened by his failed efforts at finding a better position, he began to lash out, awkwardly trying to maintain control over Benita. Sadly, he had little ammunition to prevail in the war of the sexes. Conflict escalated. The couple argued bitterly over his inability to support the family, over her frequent absences and suspected infidelities, over the filth that had accumulated in the small apartment, over the children's unmet needs.

A few times Floyd had resorted to physical force—slapping Benita, not with enough strength to bruise her but hard enough to dread his own power. "I couldn't believe I done it," he confided, "she was my girl; we gone through a lot together and now I was hittin' her like she was a dog." On one of those occasions, Benita had called the police and Floyd had spent a long night cooling off behind bars.

With growing frequency, the two were unable to harmonize obligations. Floyd wanted desperately to keep his position at Atlas, but he began to miss days waiting for Benita to show up after her binges. His foreman at the warehouse grew impatient. Floyd tried to improve his attendance record. While he was at work, he worried and wondered about the three children who were often left alone. Clarise, his middle child, would remember searching for food in the garbage dumpsters of the projects during her parents' absence.

Sometime in the winter of 1987, Benita's cousin and Lydia's oldest daughter, Felicia Forrest, found Melinda, Clarise, and Little Floyd crouching in a corner of the apartment they inhabited with their parents. They were alone, scantily dressed, hungry and shivering under dirty blankets. Felicia took them to her mother, Lydia, who promptly called Child Protective Services. It was within days that the youngsters were rent asunder. Melinda went to her Aunt Margaret, who lived in Prince Georges County, Clarise remained in Lydia's custody, and Little Floyd was eventually assigned to foster care. He had not yet celebrated his fourth birthday. Furious, Benita blamed Floyd for everything and threw his belongings out the window.

Now, it looked to Floyd as if having his family split up was life's recurrent theme. How well he could remember the day, long ago, when his stepmother, Alma, had asked him and his father to leave. That unhappy recollection fueled his resolve to set things straight. He would yet find a way to get his children back. But he couldn't do it without a job, and Floyd had just lost the one he had held at the Atlas Storage Company. His supervisor had finally concluded that Floyd had too much on his mind to be a good worker. Unemployed and cast aside, the man had no other option but to find shelter at the home of his sister Boo, whose real name was Rita. They had always been close, especially since Floyd's arrival in Baltimore.

He bounced around like his father had done in older times, but at a younger age, unable to find decent employment. As early as four o'clock in the morning, he could be seen standing with other men at the intersection of Franklin Street and Fulton Avenue, waiting to catch a ride to perform day labor in the county, not knowing where he was bound or whether he would get paid. His time was often wasted—there wasn't enough work to go around.

He would then begin the slow retreat, stopping at McDonald's to buy a Happy Meal before arriving, idle and without honor in Boo's house. The weeks turned into months. Gradually, he settled into a predictable pattern of blundering attempts at independence. Time became flat; interrupted once in a while by the visit of his children. It was that tenuous connection that kept Floyd going. He kept the faith. Things were going to get better; he knew they would.

It was on a clear summer morning in 1990 that he met Iliad Hardwick, who was twenty-two and, by the standards of the time, not doing poorly. She had been born into a family of some regard. Her mother was a nurse who had married the White owner of a small car repair shop after her first husband's death. She had named her daughter after the famous Greek epic in testimony of her highbrow aspirations.

Iliad had a high school diploma and was taking courses at the local community college. Her goal was to become an accountant and drop her job as a cashier at the Giant Supermarket. She was dark, trim, and poised, and almost as tall as Floyd. He was impressed by her speech and gentle manner. Here was a well-spoken woman who longed for a good life as much as he did. Their romance was intense, and soon they were living together in the upper level of a converted single-family home on Rosedale Road in Lower Park Heights. In the spring of 1992, Iliad learned that she was pregnant with her first baby. Unable and unwilling to keep her job, she applied for public assistance and received some help to pay the rent from her mother and stepfather. Floyd was still chasing rides to the county.

They squeezed opportunity out of circumstance. It occurred to Floyd that this was a proper moment to regain custody of his son who had languished in foster care for too long. He had been unable to act sooner, mostly because of Boo who had refused to let Little Floyd live in her house. She was already supporting four children—three of her own and one belonging to her best friend, who was temporarily homeless, and spent most of her nights in shelters. But now, Floyd reasoned, Boo's name and address could appear in the boy's records while, in fact, he could live with his father and Iliad.

And so it was that a sympathetic social worker believed the ruse and the boy moved into the flat on Rosedale Road. Big Floyd thought he was starting to deliver on his promise. It was just a matter of time before he would reclaim his two daughters. After all, he was planning to get married.

On October 25, 1992, Shatirya Twigg-Hardwick was born, weighing in at seven pounds and ten ounces. It was a happy day for her parents, Big Floyd Twigg and Iliad Hardwick, but even more pleasing for Little Floyd who had recently rejoined the family. During his first visit to the maternity ward, he offered Iliad a colorful balloon and a box of chocolates. With greater expression than he normally allowed himself, Big Floyd applauded his son's gesture. There were laughter, and hugs, and a sense of renewed optimism.

Autumn ended, and winter set in with its usual heaviness. Life began to unravel again. All along, Iliad had backed Floyd's attempts to recover custody of his son. She wanted to be selfless, with a heart big enough to embrace another woman's child. But she had been deluding herself all along. What she really wanted was to give her full attention to the newborn Shatirya. She had lovingly constructed the name in honor of her two best friends, Shanna Robbins and Tirya Bonson, who had seen her through thick and thin. She was mesmerized by the baby's perfect little fingers and shapely head. She didn't want anything to come between them, but Little Floyd seemed to be around all the time, seeking prominence and attention, impossible to ignore in the small flat.

And another thing: although Boo was receiving public assistance on behalf of the boy, Iliad found it increasingly difficult to extract money from her to cover his needs. She begrudged having to share her own check. As if that were not enough, she too was growing impatient with Big Floyd's inability to secure a real job. Her meager income was becoming the sole support of the family.

For months, Iliad kept those concerns to herself. She knew how to handle Big Floyd; he always yielded to her wishes. With quiet determination she found ways to get rid of Little Floyd, at least part of the time. Her excuses multiplied. Some days he was sent away because Iliad felt ill, others because she had to go out shopping, or take Shatirya to the pediatrician, or visit her family, or help a friend. There was irony to this unfolding of events because more and more, after school and on weekends, Little Floyd ended up at the house of Aunt Boo—the same Aunt Boo who had so strenuously declined to give him shelter in the first place.

Constantly moving without rhyme or reason, the child had no home to call his own, despite his father's well-meaning efforts. The situation worsened when Iliad's parents, tired of the permanent crisis, withdrew their support. It took only three months for the family to face eviction. In the subsequent year they moved three times, always to dismal and dangerous places. By then, Little Floyd was part of the picture only once in a while.

Early in their relationship, Iliad and Floyd had talked about the way they wanted their common life to shape up. To create a safe haven for the children had been a major priority from the outset of their love affair. For that they needed a home. Iliad had applied for public housing when she first knew she was pregnant. She had been told that it would take close to a decade before anything became available but, at the end of 1993, a small miracle happened: she received permission to move into the twelfth floor of Flag House, a notorious housing development not far from Baltimore's Little Italy.

Flag House exists now only in memory. It was imploded in 1999 as part of one of those surreal events that characterize American public policy but, when it was still standing, I knew it well. At the gate, a guard in uniform sat protected behind a bulletproof window. Tenants often wobbled out, dazed under the effect of drugs. Panhandlers and drug dealers gathered nearby, a few feet away from the lobby. The elevators smelled of urine and vomit, and the walls were scrawled with obscenities. This was not the home Iliad had envisioned, but it was better than periodic eviction. It was there that the small family settled in, and it was there that Little Floyd was finally invited back.

Matters of national import were about to affect Floyd and his family in even more dramatic ways. The case for welfare reform had been gaining momentum throughout the Reagan and first Bush administrations. Charles Murray's influential book, *Losing Ground: American Social Policy, 1950–1980*, had been published in 1984, setting the stage for new thinking about the poor. It would later be regarded as "the book that ended welfare as we know it." Partly as a result, by the early 1990s, under the Clinton Administration, public attention was fixated on Washington's attempts to "move people from welfare rolls to payrolls."

Popular radio programs aired the voices of ordinary Americans calling in support of government plans to revive the work ethic among the poor. Daytime television presented the plight of single mothers, extolling those who had been able to overcome great obstacles in the pursuit of genuine employment and full responsibility. On shows like *Oprah*, *Montel Williams*, and *Sally Jessy Raphael*, audiences heaped derision on guests—advocates as well as welfare recipients—who dared raise their voices in defense of jobless mothers. Gradually, the range of contempt broadened to encompass the men who had fathered their children;

"deadbeat dads" became the lightning rod of popular anger and political expediency.

As a result, several bills were passed, at the federal and state levels, to ensure that delinquent fathers were brought into the harness of the law.[3] Those mandates trickled down into the directives of social workers. To continue receiving public assistance, women were now required to name the fathers of their dependent minors and file legal claims for child support. Men had to appear regularly before district judges to explain why they were unable to provide financial sustenance for their sons and daughters. From the point of view of policy makers, this was a first step in the right direction: to end the abuses that for two generations had saddled taxpayers with an unfair burden. At the grassroots level, the new measures had unintended consequences.

In June 1993, Big Floyd received his first summons to appear at Prince Georges District Court on behalf of his eleven-year-old daughter, Melinda, who had been living with her aunt, Margaret, for over three years in Prince Georges County. He was puzzled by the official document. He couldn't understand the legal wording or its cryptic, impersonal tone. Eventually, he understood that he should appear before a judge at the appointed date. There were stiff penalties for not showing up, but that was beside the point. Floyd was eager to see the judge; he wanted to voice his desire to become a real father, to explain why he hadn't reclaimed his daughter sooner, to bare his soul and receive absolution. He wanted everyone to know that he was not a deadbeat dad.

So he borrowed money that he knew he couldn't repay to make the long trek from West Baltimore to Prince Georges County. It took him almost ninety minutes to get to the courthouse, first by train, then by bus, then walking a few blocks. Another hour elapsed as he waited for his turn in a crowded antechamber at the official building. When, at last, he came face to face with the district judge, his interview lasted less than two minutes.

The magistrate was uninterested in the particulars of Floyd's case. He just wanted the man to know that, until he began making child-support payments, he would have to appear in court twice a year to offer an explanation. Floyd walked away crestfallen. Six months later and still without a stable job, he received another summons. Again, he found his way to the courthouse. Most shaming about the experience was its damning innuendo. "That judge," he told me, "he looks at me like I don't want to support my family, but it ain't true. I rather be blind than a deadbeat."

During the days between residing on Rosedale Road and the move to Flag House, Floyd, Iliad, and their baby were being regularly evicted from apartments they couldn't afford. The courts were mailing child-support summonses with the proviso not to be forwarded by the post office. In transit to Flag House, Floyd never saw his third court order.

Perhaps, in the imagination of policy makers, a man like Floyd Twigg should have remembered that the time had arrived for his biannual visit to the district court. In the real world, however, the document was never missed. Moving repeatedly over short periods of time fills one's life with tumult and anticipation. Every departure erases a bit of the past and opens up new possibilities. The long trips to the hall of justice had been expensive and humiliating. They left impressions best left unrecalled.

Then, in January, 1994, Floyd got a real break from an unlikely source. Minister Louis Farrakhan, the controversial reformer, had been making a mark in Baltimore's Black neighborhoods for several years. Known for his philosophy of discipline and self-reliance, he had captured the attention of prominent members of the city council. By 1993, the People of Islam Security Company (PISCO)—one of Farrakhan's creations—had obtained a contract to provide services in a few housing projects.[4]

PISCO was almost alone in creating jobs for ghetto dwellers in the 1990s. And so it was that Floyd Mitchell Twigg Sr. became a PISCO employee and a security guard at Bethany Gardens, a publicly subsidized residential complex. There was a probationary period attached to his new position, but knowing he was qualified for the job gave him confidence. He was in high spirits. Iliad acquired new respect for him. He wore an impeccable uniform with the self-importance of a newly appointed officer. Little Floyd beamed with pride, a wide grin dancing on his beautiful golden face. "Way to go, Floyd" he chanted, "Way to go!"

One bitter cold day in March 1994, with a heavy snowfall in the weather forecast, Big Floyd entered one of the police stations in the city of Baltimore to request the clearance card that would end his probationary period and turn his temporary hire into a permanent job. After years of defeat, he was secure in his expectations. He didn't smoke or drink, and he didn't do drugs. He had never been in trouble with the law except for the time when Benita had called the cops on him after the slapping incident. That had been a long time ago, and besides, the charges had been dropped. As he entered the police station, Floyd thought of his clean record. This was his big chance. It was only a matter of time before he would be able to gather all of his children under the same roof.

He approached the reception desk at the police station. Sitting behind a computer, the officer in turn took his documents with some interest. His job was to verify that applicants to security-related jobs were unencumbered by pending matters of legal import. For a few seconds, he looked intently at the computer screen, pressing the scroll key several times. His face did not betray emotion. Then he asked Floyd to wait and stepped away from his post in the same professional manner he had displayed from the outset. As he watched the officer retreat into a back office, Floyd put back his Social Security card in his wallet, and took a seat.

Moments later, Floyd saw three police officers approaching him. The search had shown that a warrant had been issued for his arrest. For all the officers knew, Floyd could have been guilty of murder. Now, one of the cops was reciting his Miranda rights, another one was pressing his wrists into handcuffs, and the third stood nearby in a defensive stance. Big Floyd was in a daze. This couldn't be happening to him. "I done nothing wrong. I was just tryin' to get a job. I never broke the law," he protested with little conviction. The officers had probably heard the same statements hundreds of times before.

That evening, under a charcoal sky and snow blowing hard, Big Floyd Twigg was transported without ceremony to the Prince Georges jailhouse. It was in Prince Georges County that the warrant for his arrest was issued after he had failed to appear in court for the third time to explain why he was not making child-support payments. Inadvertently, he had become a felon at the very moment that he was attempting to secure the job that would allow him to provide for the daughter on whose behalf he had been summoned to appear before a judge. It is unlikely that the arm of justice would have reached him so speedily, had he not entered the police station voluntarily as part of the process to secure a paid position.

That bitter irony was wasted on Lydia Forrest, Benita's aunt, who, upon hearing the news, exclaimed, "It serves him right! That bum is no good; he had it comin.'" Such an absence of empathy was consistent with her perception that Floyd, having first disgraced her niece, had gone on to leech sustenance from Iliad and her family. Now, at last, he was receiving a proper punishment. As a good Jehovah's Witness, she believed that God chastises the wicked.

Incarcerated for the first time in his life, Floyd called Iliad. His bail was set at $25,000. Ten percent of that amount had to be posted as bond to get him out of jail before the date of his hearing; otherwise he was likely to languish in captivity for at least three months until his day in court was scheduled. Numb with fright, he couldn't feel the fingers of his hands. Random thoughts flashed through his mind. "I dunno why, but I started thinkin' about Durell Muncie, jus' like that. He was with me in high school. We was like brothers. Then he got into trouble. Stole somethin' I think. Went to jail and didn't make bail. When he came out, he had no home to go to, his girl didn't want him. His mother didn't want him. He ended up in a street corner, beggin'. It was sad."

Iliad took a resigned outlook toward the new troubles and mobilized rapidly in search of the money to free Floyd. Despite the old grudges and rancor, she thought first of Lydia Forrest and Benita Wallace only because they were Floyd's kin. But Lydia would hear nothing of it. She was prepared to see Floyd rot in jail, and besides, she had no money. Benita didn't have money either.

Iliad had known that all along, but she had wanted to make a point: "They always passing judgment, but when the time comes to be there like family, they worse than anyone else." As for her parents, it would have been useless to put the case before them, for the same reason. There were few other options. Floyd, however, was not entirely without resources. A family acquaintance appreciated the disproportion between the man's trespass and the punishment he was being dealt and put up the bond on his behalf. Three days later, Big Floyd walked out of jail, much to Lydia's dismay.

It was difficult for Floyd to express any feeling; he choked up every time he had to speak from the heart. Yet he was grateful for the narrow escape. His eyes filled with tears at the thought of what could have happened. Now, there was hope again. The experience had been demeaning, but he was out, able to walk the streets and rejoin his girl and his baby. His supervisor at PISCO did not hold the incident against him. He still had a job, despite the missed days. Still under probation, he would get his clearance card after explaining in court the circumstances that had landed him in jail.

Tempered by the latest calamity, Floyd set out with resolve to be a security guard. He was on rotating shifts and that meant that he worked nights every other week. In 1995, he earned six dollars an hour, only slightly above the minimum wage, and the job carried no benefits, but Floyd didn't mind. At last, he had work that he could be proud of. The following summer, he took a second job as a janitor in the maintenance department of the Johns Hopkins University. Although this was a temporary position, Floyd and his family saw it as another step in the right direction. With one foot inside the door, it would be easier for him to become a permanent hire. That would have been a dream come true because Hopkins had, since the 1980s, replaced Bethlehem Steel as the largest employer in the city of Baltimore. To have a job at that university meant employment security and benefits.

Often in those days, I would spot Floyd, during his lunch break, outside the Dairy Maid at the corner of Saint Paul and Thirty-Third Streets. He would rush to hug me and recount the latest news. Iliad was about to have another baby. She was happy. They were moving into a new house. This time it was a true home—still publicly subsidized under Section 8 but not in the projects, thank God! He had finally regained custody of Melinda, who would soon come to live with them. Clarise was still under Lydia's care, but they saw her all the time. Things were very good, very good indeed.

On September 2, 1995, Big Floyd Twigg and Iliad Hardwick were married at Saint John's Church in Lafayette Square. Only relatives and a small group of friends attended, but that still made for more than fifty people. The simple ceremony was followed by a picnic in Druid Hill Park, to which everyone contributed something. There were paper streamers hanging from the trees, the smell of hot dogs in the air, and much laughter and conversation. Grownups chatted while children played.

It was still early in the afternoon when Big Floyd and his family, bathed in warm summer light, returned to their new home. For a moment, the man stood waving good-bye in front of the pretty house with the iron gate, which he and his flock inhabited under Section 8 of the Housing Act. Iliad, now more than seven months pregnant, leaned by Floyd's side, cradling a sleepy Shatirya in her arms. Melinda, Clarise, and Little Floyd lingered on the front steps, waiting for the door to open.

From a distance, the scene was fitting of a Norman Rockwell painting. At last, Big Floyd had delivered on his promise.

4 INTERSECTIONS OF POVERTY, RACE, AND GENDER IN THE AMERICAN GHETTO

A TALE OF TWO MEN

One way to understand the life of Big Floyd Twigg is by comparison with that of Donald B. Wilson, sketched in chapter 1. Both men had similar hopes and dreams. Family values were as important to D. B. as they were to Big Floyd. Both men understood, to varying degrees, the elements of discipline necessary to retain a job. On the other hand, the two were unique in terms of personality, temperament, and resourcefulness—Wilson was a lively conversationalist, always eager to connect with others; Big Floyd was timid, even surly, unwilling to express emotions out of caution and perhaps shame. His actions were often tentative and fruitless. Varying personal endowments surely had an impact upon the outcomes of the two men's lives.

The two men were also set apart by wide generational divides. Born on a South Carolina farm, Wilson grew up poor, but his parents supported each other; he was surrounded by a multitude of brothers and sisters and aunts, uncles, and cousins. The opposite was true of Big Floyd who was born in an urban setting, lost his mother at an early age, and saw his family splinter when he was a teenager. Donald Wilson's steady progress contrasts with Floyd's history of false starts and deflated hopes. Factors related to the timing of migration and household composition may account for some of the differences in the men's experiences.

Beyond those features, two other elements explaining the men's divergent fates crisply emerge from an examination of their biographies. The first one consists of differences in the economic context that enabled Donald Wilson to thrive and made it less likely for Floyd Twigg to succeed. While D. B. benefited from the expansion of industry in the city of Baltimore and from his long-term employment with a manufacturing firm, Big Floyd arrived to young adulthood at a time when industrial decline had been taking place for nearly two decades. Without an economic foundation to buttress their aspirations, young men like Floyd Twigg faced fewer and less palatable options than had been available only a generation earlier to men like Wilson. That shift augured poorly for family stability and financial progress.

The other force at play entailed dissimilar levels of government interference in the lives of the two men. Wilson's steady job and modicum of prosperity sheltered him from bureaucratic intrusion. Twigg's economic and social fragility turned him into an easy target for imputations of idleness and irresponsibility which culminated in his arrest for dereliction of child-support payments. State invasiveness is a major reality shaping the lives of poor people in America.

A comparison of the two cases illustrates a broader point concerning the intersection of state action, race, and class, which in turn affects almost every dimension of social existence, including romantic and sexual relationships. Definitions of what it means to be a man or a woman are given form by economic determinants but also by policies put into place by government agencies (Gordon 1994, 2002; Skocpol 1995). The experiences of Donald Wilson and Big Floyd Twigg reflect the changing meaning of masculinity among working and non-working-class men in urban settings. Gender emerges in that context as a central vector in the constitution of inequality.

Below, I discuss gender and gender relations as they unfold among impoverished African Americans living in West Baltimore. I follow, in chapter 5, by presenting a historical account that begins to clarify the role of government policies in promoting both economic progress and the exceptional character of American poverty.

GENDER, EMPLOYMENT, AND INDUSTRIAL DECOMPOSITION

A major consequence of rapid economic change since the 1970s was the transformation of gender definitions in advanced industrial countries, including the United States. Even before globalization eroded

FIGURE 5. Women in the U.S. Workforce, percentage. Source: Bureau of Labor Statistics, U.S. Department of Labor

the capacity of working-class men to support families, ideological shifts strengthened the push for women's equality before the law, in the labor market, and in education. The sexual revolution, begun in the preceding decade, lifted the stigma of premarital sex and divorce. Reproductive rights, especially the right to abortion, were part of an evolving cultural landscape that gave women greater freedom and expanded their participation in the public arena. An effect of those transformations was the steady growth in the number of two-earner households among both professional *and* working-class people (Fernández-Kelly 2008).

Figure 5 shows the trajectory of women's formal employment in the United States between 1900 and 2010. In the 1970s, as the capacity of men to earn a family wage declined, working-class women entered the labor force in droves, primarily to lift family earnings but also in a climate of support fueled by the feminist movement.

Female labor force participation in the United States increased from nearly 20 percent in 1900 to 45 percent in 1988, with much of the growth among mothers in families with annual earnings below $20,000. By 1988, 67 percent of mothers who were single parents, 65 percent of mothers in dual-parent families, and 53 percent of mothers with children under the age of three were in the labor force (Hayghe 1997). Those proportions grew during the 1990s—in contrast to men's

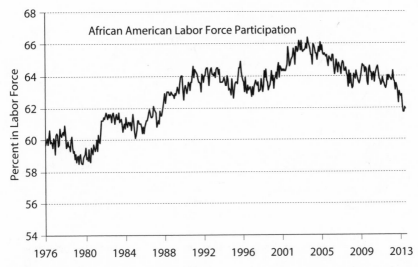

FIGURE 6. African-American Labor Force Participation, 1976–2013. Source: Economic Data, Federal Reserve Bank of St. Louis

labor force participation, which dropped from nearly 88 percent in 1950 to 76 percent in 1990.

The overall trend is striking: between 1970 and 2007, women's formal employment went from 37 percent to 48 percent, while men's labor force participation declined from 80 percent to 73 percent (Lee and Mather 2008). By 2011, 60 percent of adult women were working outside the home with that figure representing an unprecedented 46.8 percent of the total labor force (U.S. Bureau of Labor Statistics 2012).[1]

Among African Americans, gender differences in the labor market have been more pronounced than among Whites. Black women exhibited high rates of employment in services, many as maids and nannies, well into the 1950s, but aspirations rose in the wake of the civil rights movement, making menial work a less than popular option. In the 1970s, Black women made progress in education and professional employment. By contrast, African American men experienced continual decline.

Figure 6 shows that between 1976 and 2013, the labor force participation of African American males went from 60 percent to 62 percent. That trend was punctuated by ebbs and flows. Black men's employment rate went from 64 percent in 1990 to 65 percent in 1996, roughly

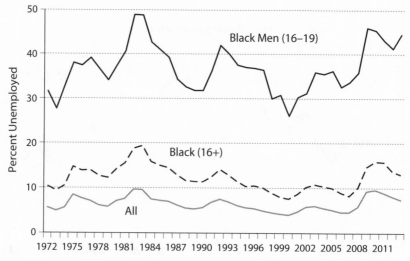

FIGURE 7. Unemployment rate by race and age, 1972–2013. Source: Bureau of Labor Statistics, U.S. Department of Labor

the period when Big Floyd Twigg—whose story is told in the previous chapter—was undertaking hapless efforts to find a job. Tangible improvements were felt toward the end of that decade, thanks largely to the financial bonanza that took place under the Clinton Administration. Yet labor force participation among African American men dropped to an unprecedented 66 percent in 2005 (Lee and Mather 2008).

In the two years that followed the Great Recession of 2008, joblessness among Black men grew to even higher levels: while unemployment in the general population reached 9.1 percent; it was 16.2 percent among African Americans as a whole and higher still—17.5 percent overall—for African American males. Stunningly, nearly 41 percent of Black adolescents had no jobs as recently as 2010, a percentage higher than the nation's total unemployment rate during the Great Depression of the 1930s (Levine 2013).

As shown in figure 7, recent unemployment figures are but the last episode in a dismal evolution affecting young African American men. Black males aged sixteen to twenty-four with a high school education or less saw their employment slide from 1.03 million in 1979 to 898,000 in 2001. In 1992, among those in the same age group, the national unemployment rate was 30 percent; by 2004 it had dropped only slightly to 26 percent. In 2004 as well, the idleness index in that group was 18 percent in contrast to 6 percent among comparable White men and 12 percent among Hispanics (Falco and Schmeiser 2006).

Joblessness, in tandem with a long history of discrimination, has had devastating social effects. High rates of unemployment and under-employment paralleled a rapid growth in the number of African American men who were incarcerated or on parole or probation. As Becky Pettit and Bruce Western (2002) persuasively note, if Black men living behind bars were included in nationwide unemployment calculations, the labor force participation of African American males would appear even bleaker.

As of 2014, approximately 2,300,000 persons were incarcerated in U.S. state and federal prisons and jails, that is, about 1 percent of all adults in the nation (Wagner 2012; U.S. Bureau of Labor Statistics 2011). Most were men, and 40 percent were African American. One in ten Black men is locked up on any particular day throughout the United States. In addition, about 7,225,800 adults were on probation or parole in 2014 (U.S. Bureau of Justice Statistics 2014).[2]

In 1995, the year of Big Floyd Twigg's arrest, fully 32 percent of Black men in Washington D.C. between the ages of eighteen and thirty-four, were admitted to jails or prisons. The equivalent figure in Baltimore was 36 percent. Nearly one decade later, in 2005, 52 percent of men living in Baltimore were incarcerated or on parole or proba-tion (Justice Policy Institute 2010); Schiraldi and Ziedenberg 2003). By 2012, more than 60 percent of young African American men in Baltimore had spent at least one day in jail over the course of their lives (*Baltimore Sun* 2013).

The continuous drop in the labor force participation of Black males over the last thirty years is partly explained by the absence of employ-ment opportunities for poorly educated men, under conditions of industrial recomposition and rising demands for workers endowed with what Robert Reich (1992, 2011), the secretary of labor during the Clinton administration, called *symbolic skills*. For men without such endowments, the choice has often been involvement in the informal and criminal economies or in legitimate but low-paying employ-ment. As part of any specific demographic group, African American men represent one of the largest contingents of working poor in the

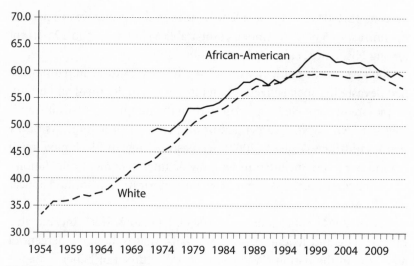

FIGURE 8. African American Women's Labor Force Participation. (source TK)

United States (Duneier 1994; Newman 2000). That means that even for employed Black men with low skill levels, survival is difficult.

By comparison, African American women have fared much better. Figure 8 shows trends in their employment. In the 1950s, their participation rate was anywhere between 12 to 15 percent higher than among White women (Aziz 2009; McConnell, Brue, and Macpherson 2010). That gap began to close in the 1980s, but it increased in the next decade, and since then, the propensity of Black women to work outside the home has remained slightly higher than among White women (Fullerton and Toosi 2001; Toosi 2002). Altogether, between 1970 and 2005, the labor force participation of Black women went from 48 percent to 62 percent, up by three points since 1995.

Many Black women have been able to move up in the social and economic ladders as a result of unique cultural and economic factors. Seen as less threatening than men, they have faced less discrimination in education and employment. There are more Black men in American prisons than in American colleges, but the proportion of Black women in institutions of higher learning has increased rapidly. By 2004, Black women constituted 59.3 percent of all first-time, full-time Black students attending four-year institutions in the United States, compared

with 54.5 percent in 1971 (2004). Between 1990 and 2005, the graduation rates for Black women rose from 34 percent to 46 percent, and by
2012, that figure was 48 percent. Sixty-three percent of college-educated
Blacks are women; only 37 percent are men.

On the other hand, among African American women living in poverty, the main survival alternatives have been taking low-paying jobs
within the formal and informal economies or dependence on public
assistance. In 2012, 39.8 percent of those receiving Temporary Assistance for Needy Families were African American, and most of them
were women (U.S. Census Bureau 2012a).[3]

WOMANHOOD AND MANHOOD RECAST

The previous section serves as a backdrop to examine the effects of
economic standing upon notions of masculinity and femininity among
impoverished African Americans. Like men in that group, Black
women have run against high levels of prejudice, but the triple burden
of subordination in terms of sex, class, and race,has given them a paradoxical advantage as providers of cheap labor. Not compelled to live out
the dangerous prescriptions of dominant masculinity, they have faced a
lower probability of incarceration. African American men, on the other
hand, have been portrayed as potentially devastating to the integrity
of a nation founded upon White masculine domination (Hill Collins
2008; Quadagno 1996). Resistance has been high against Black men's
integration, even in positions of lesser authority and power.

Cultural and generational divides have further impeded the incorporation of Black men into the economy. Roughly between 1907 and
1972, the Great Black Migration ushered in renewed expectations in
people from the rural South streaming into midwestern and northeastern cities in search of opportunity (Best 2007; Lemann 1992; Philpott
1991). New arrivals saw even humble employment in urban settings as
progress as compared with what they had left behind.[4]

By contrast, the children and grandchildren of internal migrants—like
many second- and third-generation immigrants—often shunned menial
employment, partly because they were skeptical that it would bring
about social and economic advancement. Having seen their fathers and

grandfathers fall behind despite their hard work and compliance, they had no reason to believe that poorly paid jobs would lead to upward mobility (Anderson 2000; Bourgois 1996). History and social structure shaped their context, but lived experience molded their choices. Material and ideational factors combined to produce unique conditions marked by high levels of disconnection from the labor force (Wilson 1987, 1997, 2010).

Elevated rates of unemployment and underemployment among African American men worked against their long-term relationships with women. Evidence of that is the growth of Black female-headed households over time. The very concept of what it means to be a man, a husband, and a father has been affected by diminishing opportunities in the labor market.

That process is aptly illustrated by the experience of young men in West Baltimore. In 1996, at the age of seventeen, Jared Wilkins had become a high-school dropout. He had lived all his life on the same decrepit block and saw himself as a hustler able to flip found objects and gifts for income. Once in a while he sold drugs, but he didn't have a permanent supplier; he therefore found other ways to survive. Inventiveness, he thought, was a necessary condition to become a real man. In earnest he told me:

> You got to hold your own, you know, look out for youself; if not, you dead. So I do what I can to get ahead and not by stealing or nothing like that but by trading, flipping stuff that I find and stuff that people give me. . . . I'd like a good job but I don't see good jobs around, and school—school is just a waste of time in the 'hood. So, maybe I get my GED and I go to trade school. I don't know 'bout other options.

Jared's parents, Frank and Lucinda Wilkins, had been married for more than twenty years, but their relationship was tumultuous. Lucinda's greatest grudge against her husband was his incapacity to keep a job. Frank had held a string of low-paying positions—janitor, busboy, clerk, and common laborer in construction. Lucinda, on the other hand, clung fiercely to her job at the post office. She was the main provider of her family, and although Jared, her firstborn, had been a disappointment, she had three younger children, between the ages of eight and fifteen, to look after. She thought of herself as a Christian woman and, for that reason, remained married to Frank despite his affair with Tamika Lawson, a twenty-two-year-old neighbor with whom he had fathered five-year old Alonso. Frank believed it had been the struggle to stay afloat that had led him to cheat on his wife:

> I know it was a mistake, but I couldn't see that then. Tamika, she was good to me and didn't judge me; she's a sweet girl. Lucinda [his wife], she's all so high and mighty, always thinking I'm lazy. So I try to do right, you know, to have a decent job, but when it don't work, Lucinda ain't there for me. Tamika, she had no complaint, so she made me feel like a man. But I know it was a mistake because I believe in family first.

Such experiences have a long history. Working-class and impoverished men have always faced dire straits in a society where masculinity is associated with economic power, sexual prowess, and social prominence. In *The Hidden Injuries of Class* (1993), Richard Sennett and Jonathan Cobb memorably describe the feelings of inadequacy shared by White men working in factories who saw themselves as losers because of their inability to meet definitions of manly success measured by wealth and status. Even during a period of economic prosperity, and while holding comparatively secure jobs, such men felt the sting of shame and failure.

More recently, Lillian Rubin's book, *Families on the Fault Line* (1994), shows how men, whether Latino, White, or African American, bemoaned the loss of patriarchal prerogatives in the aftermath of deindustrialization and the decline of labor unions. White men, in particular, underwent great losses as well-paying jobs in the industrial sector were surrendered to outsourcing. For nearly a century, starting in the late 1800s, such men had been the target of exploitation but also found opportunity in a thriving manufacturing economy. By the 1970s, they saw their star wane even as White women made signal advances that challenged masculine standing.

Black men experienced an even sharper kind of reconfigured manhood. Last to be hired in industry, even as the American economy was undergoing reductions in industrial employment, they were first to be laid off or fired. As the stories in this book show, residential segregation and racial exclusion limited Black men's options to a larger extent than in any other segment of the population (Massey and Denton 1993;

Sampson 2013). Economic globalization and industrial restructuring also broadened the gulf between those able to benefit from new opportunities and those left behind (DiMaggio and Cohen 2003; Sennett 2007).[5]

William Julius Wilson (1997) first called attention to the singular effects of what he called *the disappearance of work*. One of those effects was the virtual collapse of notions of masculinity dependent on paid employment. Laws, like those that brought about the family wage in the early 1900s, tied manhood with a capacity to support women and children (Coontz 1993; Gordon 1994; Skocpol 1995). In the case of African American men, that ability was always limited, but it was utterly crushed in the latter part of the twentieth century as a result of deindustrialization.

Instead of accepting demeaning jobs, which their forebears held without obtaining sizable benefits, young Black men sought significance and empowerment through extralegal means. Unable to provide for families or to hold rank vis-à-vis women, they redefined success by rejecting marriage in favor of sexual appeal and personal independence (Anderson 2000). My interviews with members of sixty families living in West Baltimore show the consistency of that pattern across generations.

As described in the previous chapter, Ernie Twigg, Big Floyd's father, had yearned for the American Dream as vigorously as did Donald Wilson, the protagonist of chapter 1. Ernie's memories of his youth in Harlem included hard work and marriage. After the death of his first wife, he wed for the second time, partly to re-create a normal family for his children. His son, Floyd, could remember Ernie contemplating the purchase of a home in a good neighborhood. The man's job at the Compton Iron Works made that goal plausible but the closing of the firm, where he had worked for five years, put an end to his hopes. His displacement was the first tumble in a downward spiral. Alma, Ernie's wife, skeptical about his employment prospects, soon enacted new living arrangements and fell back on public assistance; something she thought would require separation from her husband. Bureaucratic requirements made it impossible for women in stable unions to receive aid.

As a result, the family was broken into pieces. Young Floyd was sent away to an alien environment in West Baltimore, where he confronted violence, uncertainty, and a dearth of educational opportunities. Restless and eager to become a grown man, he entered a relationship with a girl whose past resembled his own. That misadventure had dire consequences, as it nearly always does under similar circumstances. But contrary to popular views, Floyd's decision was not motivated by moral laxness or a rejection of normative values; instead, he was led by a conventional yearning for adulthood and home building. His story illustrates a familiar phenomenon: young men and women hoping to construct lives in accordance with mainstream expectations but whose aims are truncated by poverty and marginalization.

PARENTING BY ANY OTHER NAME

Appendix 1 shows a breakdown of sixty households included in this study The names of irregular or itinerant members appear in parentheses. The ages of constituents are also noted in parentheses after each name. Table 1 summarizes main characteristics.

Roughly 265 individuals are included in table 1. Of those, less than 20 percent (fifty) were men between the ages of sixteen and fifty-five. Twenty were permanently employed and only nine held jobs paying more than the minimum wages. Most households were formed by women and children and do not include men as permanent members. Men appear as shadowy figures that enter and exit households intermittently.

Many of those men, however, try to preserve connections with their children. Statistical accounts give the impression that female-headed

TABLE 1

Characteristics of Household Sample in West Baltimore (1997)

	Male	Female	Total
Heads of household	4	56	60
Mean age heads of household	33	32	32
No. of household members (excluding heads)	107	96	203
Mean age household members (excluding heads)	20	12	16
Permanently employed men 16–55 years of age[a]	31	—	—
Mean household size	2	2.5	4.5
Total sample	111	152	263

[a] Percentage of all men in the sample who are 16–55 years of age and who are permanently employed.

households exist wholly without the participation of fathers (Gabe 2011). That is seldom the case among impoverished African Americans. Richardson (2010), for example, notes the important role men serving as real or fictive uncles play in the well-being of male adolescents. In addition, despite personal limitations and economic vulnerability, a large number of fathers cultivate a regular or sporadic communication with their sons and daughters. Two examples will suffice to illustrate those dynamics:

Always in trouble with the law for multiple violations since he was a teenager, Anton Freeman, a twenty-eight-year-old Baltimore man, was determined to stay in touch with his seven-year-old daughter, Camilla. Although he wasn't married to the child's mother, Anton saw fatherhood as a noble goal and thought that if things went right, he would be a good provider:

[My] plan is to clean up my act and get a real job so that I can give my daughter a home. . . . She has a good mother, but kids—they need a father too.

. . . So I don't want to disappear from her life; I buy her things when I can and I take her places when I can, and my mother babysits for her. We're not together, but still, we are a family.

Similarly, in 1997, Damon Artis, a thirty-five-year-old laborer with a temporary job in a Baltimore market told me:

Not everybody has the money to buy a family. . . . You think family is jus' about love? It ain't, it takes an income to keep people together. Well, I don't have money, but what I have I share with my boy—he's just three but he got my name. . . . I want him to know me and my life.

Feelings, like those expressed by Damon Artis, are behind the common tradition among African Americans—especially those living in poverty—to name male children after their fathers while adding the qualifier "Little" to affirm the child's bond to his progenitor. Language reflects the desire of parents to acknowledge ties and responsibility. Big Damon did not have much to give Little Damon, other than his name and his story.

Similarly, the tendency of women to assemble names for their children, both male and female, out of snippets taken from the names of girlfriends, relatives, and mates expresses a desire to honor social bonds and strengthen children's relationships with adults. Shatyria Twigg, Floyd Twigg's baby by Iliad Hardwick, bore a combined name that paid tribute to two of her mother's best friends. In environments woefully characterized by the absence of material assets and what Mark Granovetter (1973) calls "weak ties," language becomes a crucial resource used to validate potentially useful connections for children (see also Willis 1981).

THE POVERTY OF MASCULINITY

Among impoverished men and women, children are seen as valuable resources, and the capacity to bear children is often viewed as a sign of maturity. Elements other than parenting are also present in the search for masculine status. Defending kin and turf through participation in gangs is part of that quest.[6]

Most men in poor neighborhoods do not join gangs but images of gangs pervade the thoughts of male adolescents in American inner cities. Demetrius Brown, who turned eighteen in 1997, thought of gangs as the byproduct of mutually protective friendship. An ally and sidekick of Emmanuel (Manny Man) Travis—whose story I develop in chapter 15—Demetrius believed that

> [y]o' homies are the people you trust; they there when you need help; when others don't care. If someone wants to hurt you or steal from you, you homeboys will represent you. . . . Manny, he's a stand-up guy; that's why people respect him. He take care of his own.

Accounts of gangs often characterize them as substitutes for broken families. An equally persuasive conceptualization is that of gangs as *complements*, not replacements, for kinship networks (Sánchez-Jankowski 1991; Vigil 2002; Ward 2012). Poorly educated young men without promising employment depend on reciprocal exchanges resulting from gang membership to secure scarce assets, which later they redistribute among kin and friends. In Demetrius Brown's terms:

> You crew is like you team. What you get together you own together and tha's how you get stuff, say for your mother, you girl, you kid.

You don't need to do nothing wrong; it just happens that you friends take care of you and you take care of your own.

Similarly, Darnell Watson, a sixteen-year-old boy living with his mother and two younger siblings, explained his gang-related activities as part of a plan to assume manly responsibilities:

My crew is like blood. . . . We've sworn to die for each other; I love my bros like I love my mother. We not bad people; sometimes we steal but it's for a good cause, 'cause my little brother and my sister, they need things my ma can't afford. If I don't look out for them, who gonna?

Such pursuits of masculine status are dangerous. A lone individual is less prone to violence than one forced to save face vis-à-vis his home-boys. Time and time again, some of the worst crimes are committed by young men in packs. That is because, when gathered together, social actors rapidly fall into position within hierarchies of authority; each individual is thus pressured to engage in performances appropriate to his rank. Young men in groups tend to play to each other, aiming to gain control or at least acceptance from cronies (Goffman 2009, 2014).

When guns are readily available, the stage is set for disaster. Nineteen-year-old Tyrell Cameron represents a typical trajectory. In 1994, bright and gregarious, he took part in a burglary gone wrong with two friends, one of whom, twenty-year-old Marquis Young, carried a concealed .22-caliber handgun. When the clerk at the convenience store they were robbing confronted Marquis, the boy saw no alternative but to shoot him. He couldn't bear to risk his reputation as a tough guy vis-à-vis his crime associates. Tyrell was at the scene without knowing his friend's full intentions but that didn't matter: he was charged with first-degree murder and is still serving a thirty-five-year-to-life prison sentence. In poor neighborhoods, the reenactment of masculinity is a matter of life and death.

MAN-CHILDREN IN THE LAND OF SCARCITY

It is not easy to reach adulthood when you are young, Black, and poor. The paucity of resources, including a proper education and remunerative employment, retards the acquisition of a grown-up status. The body ages, but the condition of poverty perpetuates dependence and limited ability—the main traits of childhood and adolescence. As a result, depictions of impoverished males as not fully mature are rooted in popular judgments and government policies. The notion that unemployed men are lazy and undependable is as widespread among impoverished people as among pundits and politicians. Programmatic designs and bureaucratic procedures catering to the needy invariably assume the same. Poverty is explicitly or implicitly viewed as the effect of personal deficiencies, not structural constraints.

In the transition to maturity, young men and women of all kinds are asked to assume greater responsibility for their choices and behavior. Progress in school and the expectation of futures circumscribed by affluence and respectability give the children of the middle and upper classes a vested interest in complying with mainstream norms. Among such youngsters, dominant values are brought into correspondence with personal actions (Levey Friedman 2013; Zelizer 1994). That imagined progression is consistent with Robert K. Merton's (1938) analysis of the relationship between culturally defined goals and the institutional means necessary to achieve them.[7]

Institutional channels for the realization of dominant values, however, remain insufficient or nonexistent among impoverished youngsters. As a result, the poor grow up chronologically but not in a social sense. Big Floyd Twigg, for example, saw himself as a man struggling to build a family but that view was diametrically opposed to the opinions of those around him. His kin and acquaintances saw him perennially as a boy, unable to support himself or his children, prone to impulse, morose, and deceitful. Lydia Forrest, whose niece, Benita, had given birth to three of Floyd's children, best expressed feelings held at the local level: "Floyd ain't alone, no ma'am. Most [men] don't want to work. They want their mama to feed them forever, even when they big and fat!"

Those remarks echo common beliefs among impoverished women but they are also embedded in media portrayals. The image of the slothful Black man has a long history in American culture, dating back to the times of slavery and beyond. Even popular programs of the 1970s that purported to affirm Black progress—*Good Times*, *Sanford and Son*, and *The Jeffersons*, for example—tended to reproduce stereotypes, casting Black men as immature, indolent, and dim-witted. It was the presumption of Black men's limited capacity that buttressed the humor in those representations.

Among poor Black women, dissatisfaction about African American men sharply contrasts with yearnings for normative manhood. Lydia Forrest's neighbor, Amelia Thomas, a thirty-two-year-old mother of four who lived on public assistance, voiced a common perception: "A real man," she told me,

> [is one] who can take care of his family, support his wife, bring home some cash, protect his children. I think there was men like that a long time ago, but not now. My grandpa was like that. Things are different now; it's the women who have to fend on their own, while the men get into trouble and cheat on you. They the ones who behave like children. I should know; tha's how I ended up on welfare!

Kiyah Mason, in her mid-twenties, another dweller of the Murphy Homes, declared:

> Sure, I want to get married, have a nice home, give my children a good father and a good life, but where that man? He ain't nowhere. I jus' see gangbangers, dealers, and bums. There ain't no one to marry.

An illustration of the mystifications surrounding gender relations among the poor was Lydia Forrest's response to Big Floyd's release after a period of brief incarceration. She was furious; harsh punishment is what she thought the man deserved. That Big Floyd had been arrested while searching for a job to support his children and that he longed to assume masculine duties were points lost to her. She remained skeptical. Lydia's outrage was more than a symptom of social anomie or lack of collective cohesion; it also mirrored frustration resulting from the breakdown of standard gender definitions and the inability of men to gain economic standing.

The tendency to infantilize impoverished man for their lack of ability to function as breadwinners parallels women's search to redefine their own circumstances. That, in turn, affects men's views of women's intentions. While women tend to cast men as financially impotent and morally suspect, men think of women as castrating and materialistic. Women's yearnings for security and intimacy are perceived as entrapments. In her early twenties, Davinia Fitzpatrick, a mother of three, typically stated:

> You got to be careful with men. They can cling to you like the flu, but they don't have a lot to offer. So, it's better for a girl to be independent, carry her own weight, don't depend on a man for yo' life.

In vivid contrast, thirty-two-year-old Alfonso Williams, who worked for the Baltimore sanitation department, contended:

> Women want just one thing: money. If you got bling, they like you, and some will do almost anything for you; but if you broke or hit a spell of hard luck, they out of yo' life like a bat out of hell. And you learn you lesson—better to be alone than to have you life wrecked by some greedy ho. I know; I been married twice and twice divorced, and the reason [for the breakups] was always money.

The two previous statements give new meaning to the expression "*at cross purposes.*" Lacking information about the way economic, political, and social processes affect individual lives, men and women blame one another for, in one case, irresponsibility and, in the other, greed.

Stylized representations of manhood and femininity have dispersed throughout the cultural landscape, including music and dancing. Hip-hop, especially rap music, often gives voice to gender resentment. The representation of women as hos and bitches is but a veiled expression of men's loss of masculine status. To think of such musical statements as evidence of misogyny—as some commentators have argued—misreads a complex reality marked by men's diminished power (Rose 2008). As with other forms of artistic expression, rap music amplifies and discloses strains and anxieties surrounding human interactions—in this case, those pertaining to gender. The violence of ghetto music makes sexual politics visible through symbolic means.

Hip-hop was central to the worldview of Emmanuel Travis Williams, who had become a successful drug dealer by the age of eighteen.[8] Endowed with a keen business sense and fearlessness, he harbored transparent thoughts about women. He saw young female flesh as a pennant, a mark of his budding masculinity and dominance. He took that position as a protective shield while aiming for something better in the future:

I'm just hedging my bets, see? Cause I'm still young and I can be a playa. I'm a man, see? And when you's a man with bling, women want it all. They can crush you if they hot and smart, so I jus' play it cool; nothing to gain, no need for pain. . . . But ten years from now, say, when I got enough cash, I'm gonna find someone real good and nice, like my Ma, to get married, have children, the big house, the dog, you name it. . . . Like that.

Given the reduced ability of impoverished African American men to uphold mainstream expectations, women too have had to rethink the meaning of femininity by emphasizing personal autonomy and rejecting romantic illusions of marriage and family. Such yearnings remain alive among members of the Black middle classes but even there, women find their implementation difficult, given the scarcity of eligible men of like status and reduced levels of intermarriage with members of other groups. Under such circumstances, marriage levels among African American women remain low.

Singular for its level of fragmentation, the experience of urban Blacks underscores the role of gender as a pivotal force shaping inequality between and within social groups. Adding to the resulting distress, public policies often harden the conditions faced by poor men and women.

GENDER, POVERTY, AND GOVERNMENT POLICY

In the United States, a long-held trust in individual agency as the path to prosperity, in tandem with racial and class discord, has led to the conceptualization of the poor as deviant. Such views have been pronounced among libertarians and conservatives whose way of thinking is as alive in present-day America as it was in nineteenth-century England (Katz 1990). Liberals, on the other hand, give greater salience to social structure and context, but they too see individual will and behavior as main causes of both poverty and economic progress. As a result, most government programs for the needy focus on personal conduct and transformation, not on the redistribution of economic, political, and human resources (O'Connor 2001).

State policies vis-à-vis vulnerable groups are thus imprinted with indeterminacy—what may be called *the ambivalence of collective benevolence*, that is, a tendency to treat claimants with a mixture of compassion and hostility. I examine that paradox more fully in chapter 6. Here, I merely summarize the effects of public policies upon gender relations among impoverished groups.

Government programs for the poor bear the legacy of patriarchal imperatives that deem women and children to be under the charge of men. That premise was consciously incorporated into family wage and protective legislation at the beginning of the twentieth century (Coontz 1993). Masculinity was equated with the capacity of men to support women and children through participation in the labor market; femininity was tied to women's role as mothers and wives specializing in reproductive labor (Fernández-Kelly 2008).

Such notions had differential effects in terms of socioeconomic status. During the first half of the twentieth century, middle-class and affluent women relied mostly on the incomes of men for their own support and that of their children. Educated single women depended on a small number of professions, including teaching, or self-employment to attain a modicum of financial independence.

For women without masculine support or education, the options were few and grim. That was a main reason for the implementation, in 1935, of Aid for Dependent Children (ADC), an initiative minted as part of Franklin D. Roosevelt's New Deal. The program's objective was to support minors in low-income families (Gordon 1996; Stier and Tienda 2001; Tienda and Stier 1991), mainly the children of White women whose husbands had died in war. ADC thus evinced an understanding of the state as a proxy for male support. Through actions aimed at protecting women and children, the government became a stand-in for manly responsibility. The families of patriots killed in the nation's defense were seen as worthy of public assistance.

Although ADC faced vigorous criticisms in the fear that it would discourage marriage, it endured as an expression of public commitment to the deserving poor. That legitimizing narrative changed dramatically in the 1960s as more African American women became dependent on the program, now renamed Aid for Families with Dependent Children. AFDC became the single most significant policy instrument providing assistance to impoverished mothers in the latter part of the twentieth century. It also became the permanent target of those who saw it as a bounty of rewards for the undeserving poor.

Strict regulations and meager payments characterized AFDC throughout its history. In the early 1990s, as the program experienced biting attacks and imminent reform, the average monthly payment under AFDC was three hundred dollars for a mother with two children. Such miserly allotments contrasted with the extravagant salaries earned by corporate CEOs and by financial speculators benefiting from the high-tech bubble. It was the recipients of welfare payments, however, who bore the brunt of public condemnation; media outlets increasingly portrayed them as corrosive to the nation's character.

Most consequential, however, were the explicit and implicit assumptions behind government programs for the poor. Although the expressed purpose of policies like AFDC was to protect children, their procedures evinced antagonism and deprecation toward single mothers. Among other duties, overworked social workers had to exercise surveillance over their clients to ensure that women on welfare did not receive support from men. That entailed reaching into the deep crevices of personal life, driving women away from potential partners and erasing the latter from public records, even when they played a part in family sustenance.

Ethnographic research, including my own, shows that poor African American men perform a more significant role in the lives of families than is apparent from a review of relevant statistics (Edin and Nelson 2013). That role is often invisible as a result of bureaucratic rules and regulations. Such was the case for Mary Washington, a thirty-year-old Baltimore woman who received public assistance on behalf of her four children, aged three to fifteen. Mary remembered:

> Alfred Morris was his name, the father of my four children, and he was not a bad man but I had to kick him out 'cause he couldn't support us and I couldn't get welfare if the social worker knew he was living with us. For a while, he stuck around. Nowadays he don't see the children much, but he sends gifts, you know, like clothing and toys . . . sometimes.

Like many others, Mary supplemented her income by cleaning houses and taking care of an older woman in a suburban home. She kept her boyfriend, Steven, at bay because she didn't want her children to get the wrong idea or for the man to get too close.

Until 1996—when AFDC was replaced by TANF (Temporary Assistance for Needy Families) as part of a move to end "welfare as we know it"—a woman applying for public assistance had to lie if she received contributions from her children's father, even when those contributions were tiny and irregular. That led to the erasure of men from the public record. Lydia Forrest, whose turbulent relationship with her husband, James Culver, lasted for more than two decades, spoke of him as "the man who don't exist." Although James struggled with excessive drinking, he never relented in his attempts at providing for his family. His contributions, however, were small. To defray expenses, Lydia combined them with public assistance and the cash she received for her work as a maid. In regular interaction with social workers, she concealed both her informal job and her marriage to James. Blotting out her husband was a permanent feature of life.

In other words, infantilization, erasure, and various forms of actual and symbolic violence circumscribe the experience of impoverished Black men. In the 1990s, feminist fervor was tapped to further castigate low-income fathers. Daytime television was filled with programs focusing on the plight of welfare mothers, now portrayed as the victims of wayward men unwilling to support them and their children. "Deadbeat dads"—a phrase perversely combining harsh judgment with a term of endearment—captured the public's imagination, giving rise to stringent legislation forcing men to meet their parental duties. The deadbeat dad joined the welfare queen in the mythical pantheon of condemnation against the poor.

Forced to denounce their children's fathers as a precondition to receiving public assistance, women had to adopt an even more adversarial stance vis-à-vis former husbands and lovers. Such laws accentuated gender fragmentation while criminalizing men. The consequences were deep and dire even among those, like Big Floyd, whose hope had been to hold a stable job and make child-support payments. The new rules included procedural details so disconnected from the realities faced by impoverished men as to make compliance not only difficult but, in many cases, impossible. When unable to follow the new rules, men like Floyd ended up in jail. This further eroded their ability to fulfill parental duties.[9]

In other words, the fractious exchanges between men and women in poor neighborhoods are partly related to the implementation of programs ostensibly designed to meet human needs but whose operations have had unexpected and ruinous consequences. Such programs reflect a specific relationship between the American State and impoverished people that is characterized by a focus on suspicion, surveillance, and punishment. As I contend in the next chapter, that tendency is not accidental but the result of long-standing historical processes that single out impoverished people for special treatment. In their operations, institutions serving vulnerable populations differ markedly from those addressing the needs of mainstream groups.

5 SHAPING THE INNER CITY: URBAN DEVELOPMENT AND THE AMERICAN STATE

TO GAIN FURTHER UNDERSTANDING OF THE TORTUOUS RELATION-ship between the state and the urban poor in America, it is necessary to examine historical and structural processes underpinning today's policies. Toward that objective, I present a theoretical framework based on ideas put forth by Peter Evans (1995), one of whose objectives has been to explain different levels of efficacy in government structures. I argue that America represents an advanced developmental state whose actions have been instrumental in the preservation of democratic institutions and capitalist markets. A review of pertinent facts reveals the willingness and ability of the American State to promote the advancement of individuals and groups through education and wealth accumulation, the two channels by which most Americans have prospered.

I then contrast such policies to those enacted on behalf of poor and racially distinct populations, Blacks in particular. With respect to them, the American State has taken approaches that differ noticeably from those it adopted to buttress economic progress and social assimilation among European immigrants and their descendants. A trajectory of systematic exclusion backed by the force of law gives the African American experience its exceptional profile.

My analysis serves as an introduction to chapter 6 where I examine the notion of *distorted engagement*, a concept intended to shed light on the unique ways in which state agencies relate to the urban poor.

THE STATE IN A THEORETICAL FRAMEWORK

In 1995, Peter Evans, a leading figure in the study of Latin American development, introduced the concept of *embedded autonomy* to explain the varying degree to which national states are able to implement policies on behalf of differentiated social sectors. On the basis of research in Brazil, India, and Korea, he noted the pervasive influence of the state, as an institution and social actor, despite predictions about its fading importance in the age of globalization (Evans 1995: 11; see also Appadurai 2001; Sassen 2008). His focus was on industrial development—information technology, in particular—but his work has wider ramifications insofar as it clarifies the conditions under which states can advance not only the interests of the powerful and wealthy but also those of the popular classes. To explain why some states are more effective than others, Evans offered a comparative institutional analysis.

Following Max Weber, he defined states as "compulsory associations claiming control over territories and the people within them" (Evans, Rueschemeyer, and Skocpol 1985: 7), adding that there has been comparatively little effort to describe governing apparatuses with dissimilar structures and capacities to impose civic-minded programs. This is important because not all government structures behave the same under similar conditions. To address that matter, Evans distinguished between predatory and developmental states.

Predatory states, according to Evans, lack the capacity to stop incumbents from pursuing their own goals at the expense of populations outside their proximate sphere; personal ties become the only source of cohesion and that, in turn, perpetuates nepotism and patron-client relationships. Predatory states illustrate the absence of bureaucratic discipline in the sense defined by Max Weber; they tend to be a legacy of historical processes, like colonialism, that led to widespread subordination and disempowerment at the national and international levels.

Developmental states, by contrast, are characterized by selective, meritocratic recruitment to government positions, a condition that brings about long-term career rewards, personal engagement, and corporate coherence. That, argues Evans, creates distance between public officials and the interests of specific groups, thus increasing the propensity of the state to impose impartial policies in the service of civic-minded goals.

Neutral selection criteria to fill government jobs, explicit rules and procedures, and legitimating narratives focusing on service, nation, and professionalism further enable state agents to maintain independence vis-à-vis the larger society. This is consistent with Weber's formulations, which emphasize autonomy as the mark of the modern state (Weber 1919).

Evans, however, deviates from Weber's conceptualization by observing that developmental states, although featuring a measure of distance from civil society, are also wedged in networks whose ties bind them to collective interests, and provide institutionalized channels for the negotiation of goals and policies. In other words, the distinguishing features of developmental states are both corporate coherence *and* connectedness, a combination that Evans encapsulates in the concept of *embedded autonomy*. He uses that term to designate conditions under which public officials are not so far removed from civil society as to care only about their vested interests, but not so rooted in specific segments of civil society as to represent solely the objectives of those social segments.

Although the balance between social detachment and connectedness remains difficult to specify empirically, such ideas have heuristic value. They allow us to think of *embedded autonomy* as a feature permitting states to implement programs that may have limited or even deleterious effects on specific individuals and groups but which are beneficial to the larger society. Developmental states maintain civic distance while promoting forward-looking transformations (see also Chalmers 1999; Cummings 1999).

The theoretical scheme put forth by Peter Evans has been most influential among students of emerging states in Asia, Latin America, and Africa, but it is equally valuable in any attempt to understand advanced industrial countries. From that perspective, America represents a mature developmental state. Since its inception, as an independent country, the United States has been remarkable for the solidity of its institutions. The framers of the Constitution imagined a nation in which government would be limited in scope but would act to promote personal freedom and prosperity. More than a rhetorical catchphrase, "Liberty and the Pursuit of Happiness" became a summation of the values that define the body politic: respect for the rule of law, democracy, fair play, and an aptitude for self-correction. Just as Evans would have anticipated, the American State has been dually endowed with corporate coherence and social connectedness.

Whether national states are able to implement developmental measures or devolve into instruments of predation largely depends on accumulated history. The genesis and progression of the American experiment has attracted uninterrupted attention at least since the publication of Tocqueville's pioneering book, *Democracy in America* (1835/2003). A plethora of authors—historians, sociologists, political scientists, philosophers, economists, and even poets and novelists—have described the events that culminated in the creation of an enduring democracy and high levels of affluence in the United States.

Below, I summarize that evolution with two objectives in mind: first, to illustrate the consistent developmental character of the American State and, second, to note its deviations from that stance with respect to poor and racially distinct populations.

MODERNIZING THE AMERICAN STATE

Starting in the nineteenth century, the collective dreams of social mobility and economic advancement in America were forged through the cooperation of three social sectors: (a) capitalist investors, (b) a labor force comprising large numbers of immigrants, and (c) a striving national state. Foundational outlooks and actions defining government in the United States are related to the country's immigrant past. Even in its early stages, the arrival of immigrants, mostly from Europe, forced earlier settlers to make accommodations despite fear and racial prejudice. Benjamin Franklin, one of the country's founders, and a signatory of the Declaration of Independence, was known to loathe German newcomers, whom he saw as a danger to the integrity of the new nation (Lack 1919; Seavey 1999).

Years later, German Americans—their children and grandchildren by then firmly established in the new country—were equally prone to look down upon even more recent arrivals. That trend has continued to the present, creating sustained momentum for the perpetuation of racial and ethnic inequalities but also opening spaces for opportunity and advancement. Successive waves of immigration have encountered a measure of tolerance and, in most cases, assimilation.

Rapid industrialization during the second half of the nineteenth century heightened the demand for labor in the United States. Vast in its domains but sparsely populated, the nascent industrial power continued its expansion through the recruitment of immigrants, mostly Irish, Italians, Poles, Germans, and East European Jews (Portes and Rumbaut 2015). It has become a tenet of American culture to celebrate the nation's immigrant past, but most of us give less attention to the dual character of nineteenth-century immigrants—on the one hand, humble people avid for improvement and, on the other, workers responding to exploitation through protest and sometimes fierce mobilization.

Contrary to romantic versions that glorify unity and consensus, the advent of modernity in the United States was redolent with strife. We remember the story behind the Statue of Liberty but forget the Haymarket Affair in Chicago, a violent episode that accelerated the formation of labor unions and is recognized throughout the world, on May 1, as a day to honor workers. Both the unveiling of the Statue of Liberty and the bloody Haymarket Affair occurred in the same year, 1886, giving testimony to America's split identity.

The tumultuous character of class struggle in nineteenth-century America paralleled the development of a manufacturing economy buttressed by immigrant labor and entrepreneurship. Some of the most prominent industrial moguls of the time were foreign born or the children of immigrants—Andrew Carnegie, Charles M. Schwab, Claus Spreckels, and Henry Ford are examples—and so were the throngs of laborers arriving on the country's shores. In the absence of protective legislation, and with boundless opportunities for exploitation, many of those workers rebelled against capitalist abuses (Morris 2006). The era of robber barons and tycoons was also the age of raw class conflict in the United States. It was not a coincidence that Karl Marx anticipated the advent of socialism in England but also in America, where clashes between captains of industry and workers repeatedly took place. A prolific writer and revolutionary, Marx made regular contributions to the *New York Tribune*, a newspaper that voiced the grievances of the American working class (Ledbetter 2008).

Out of that turbulence, a social compact emerged by the early twentieth century in which the American State acted as an arbiter and mediator, upholding the interests of both investors and laborers, while putting forth legislative actions to anchor a modern market economy. The ousting of radical elements—including organizations like the Industrial Workers of the World (Wobblies)—led to the formation of labor unions whose members exchanged compliance for better wages, increased benefits, and safer working conditions (Hannan and Freeman 1987). Investors gained advantages through access to a dependable, mostly male, workforce. Government intervened with a variety of programs supporting profits for capitalists and purchasing power for ordinary Americans. Subsidized housing, the expansion of railroads and freeway systems, the proliferation of services, and the creation of new suburbs for upwardly mobile people were among the accomplishments that buttressed modernity in the United States (Duany, Plater-Zyberk, and Speck 2001).

Partly to accommodate plural and combating interests between investors and workers, government also implemented a wide legislative agenda to give immigrants and their children a stake in the society. Such laws—which included homestead and land grant acts—stimulated productivity and afforded property rights to ordinary Americans (Hymann 2008). Industry benefited from protectionist measures aimed at bolstering domestic demand by reducing competition with foreign imports. At the turn of the twentieth century, momentous initiatives, including the family wage and protective legislation, limited women's and children's participation in paid employment while at the same time providing economic gains to working-class families. Incentives for education were followed by the consolidation of a public school system financed through taxes assessed on the basis of real estate values. Access to property and education became the path for most Americans to succeed (Hochschild and Scovronick 2004)

Despite its devastating effects, the Great Depression of the 1930s did not cancel the state's proactive vision; it was during that period that Franklin D. Roosevelt's New Deal took shape. The passage of the 1935 Social Security Act is but one example of the extent to which government agents were willing to act on behalf of vulnerable groups. That piece of legislation, still molding the lives of Americans, was instrumental in the near eradication of poverty among the elderly. It also provided benefits to those unemployed as a result of downturns in the economic cycle and offered basic earnings to the blind and disabled. Such improvements were secured amidst raucous objections by conservatives and libertarians, who saw government intervention in social matters as detrimental to the nation's integrity.

As the effects of the economic downturn waned in the late 1930s, the federal government continued a series of legislative initiatives that eventually led to the modernization of cities and the expansion of suburbs. Stimuli to the auto-manufacturing industry and renewed investments in rail transportation conjoined a nation where a series of loosely connected political units had previously existed. In the short period that encompassed the two world wars, the United States went from a middling agricultural economy to a fully urbanized industrial power.

The period following the Second World War witnessed ever-increasing prosperity, partly as a result of government incentives to boost industry and the implementation of Keynesian measures that expanded the purchasing power of ordinary Americans. Immigrants, now mainly from Mexico, filled labor demand, primarily in agriculture. In 1944, the passage of the Servicemen's Readjustment Act—the first GI Bill—enabled men who had served in the armed forces to obtain, among other benefits, monetary supports to advance their education and federally subsidized housing loans to purchase a home (Bennett 1996; Humes 2006). Such policies were decisive to the creation of a working class endowed with extensive property rights and secondary education, thus equipped to achieve economic betterment and greater political participation.

In the 1960s, civil rights legislation—unpopular in many circles—asserted the will and power of the federal government to address the political aspirations of marginalized groups, African Americans and Hispanics in particular. School desegregation beginning in the mid-1950s, the Civil Rights Act of 1965, and a push to back affirmative action through legislative action followed. Similarly, the 1965 Immigration and Nationality Act enabled family reunification by allowing legal residents and citizens to bring close relatives from abroad to the United States; it also made it possible for large numbers of people from

Asia and Latin America to lawfully enter the country, thus ushering in processes of demographic change that continue to this day.

Throughout the 1980s and 1990s, the introduction of other pieces of legislation, even when their sponsors failed to implement them—various attempts at health care reform are examples—provided further evidence of the American State's inclination to act on behalf of constituencies with varying degrees of might and influence. Even more recently, the Affordable Care Act, signed into law by Barack Obama in 2010, underscores the transformative role of government. Although that program confronted virulent attacks from conservatives on the right and progressives on the left, it stood as evidence of the capacity of public officials to enact legislation that transcends segmented political and ideological interests.[1]

A review of historical facts thus shows that on the whole, the American State has been an active participant in social and economic reform as well as an implementer of measures aimed at facilitating the operation of markets, stimulating the formation of a disciplined workforce, and crafting legislation whose end result has been, if not a fully equitable society, then at least a highly functioning republic. In the face of anomalies, failures, and delays, the tendency in the United States has been for the state to assume what Peter Evans identifies as a vigorous developmental stance and to display in its policies a good measure of embedded autonomy.

UNEVEN DEVELOPMENT

Within the general framework outlined above, the role of the American State has varied depending on multiple factors, including the often contested relationship between federal, state, and local levels of governance. Certain populations and geographical areas have been refractory to trends in development. Appalachia, for example, appears in the nation's landscape as a redoubt of concentrated poverty mostly affecting the descendants of Scottish and Welsh immigrants who first settled the area in the mid-nineteenth century. Such populations endure high levels of dependence on welfare programs and food stamps, low rates of formal employment and education, and a disproportionate number of

pregnancies and births to young, single mothers. Family disorganization, domestic violence, alcoholism, and drug addiction are widespread
in the region (Billings and Blee 2000). Such tribulations are strikingly
similar to the ones found in inner-city neighborhoods. The commonal-
ity of experience between impoverished Appalachians—a White rural
population—and the urban poor, who tend to be African American,
suggests that social dysfunctions are more the result of material scarcity, social isolation, and the absence of constructive government policies than the effect of culture or even race.[2]

In the Appalachian case, poverty has partially resulted from practices that eerily resemble the operations of rapacious states in less
developed countries. The untrammeled extraction of natural resources
by agricultural and mining firms; the absence of investment in modern
economic sectors; the dearth of effective regional governments; and a
lack of political power on the part of common workers has led to what
Andre Gunder Frank (1967) first called the "development of underdevelopment." With respect to Appalachia, the American State has been
detached as well as disconnected, leaving the matter of development, or
its absence, in the hands of local elites.[3]

Similar, and central to the lives of impoverished African Americans
described in this book, was the role that the American State played in
the evolution of inner cities, first populated by European immigrants
and then by Black internal migrants. Throughout the second half of the
nineteenth century and beyond, international immigrants that filled
the ranks of an expanding industry gradually *moved up* in the society
by *moving out* of decrepit slums to suburban developments made possible by the concurrence of vigorous private investment and government
subsidies. Despite repeated egresses, cities remained strong, thanks
to the resilience of neighborhoods replenished by the new arrival of
foreign-born workers, mostly from Europe.

Key elements at that stage were the demand for unskilled and semiskilled labor and the capacity of immigrants, frequently seen as members
of inferior races, to gain status as *Whites*. Crossing the color line became
the mark of assimilation for modest but determined people aiming to
gain admission into the broader society (Roediger 2006, 2007).

A different kind of population movement began in the early twentieth century, accelerating between 1950 and 1970. In a few decades,

American cities were revolutionized by the Great Black Migration—
one of the largest demographic changes ever witnessed in the United
States (Wilkerson 2011). In 1905, two-thirds of American Blacks were
concentrated in southern states. By 1972, nearly 80 percent of all African Americans had moved to northeastern and midwestern cities. They
were propelled by aspirations akin to those that had mobilized international immigrants. So great were the similarities between the two
groups that in the 1930s, members of the Chicago school of sociology
believed that Blacks would rapidly assimilate, following the trajectory
of their European predecessors. Robert E. Park—whose contributions
to the sociology of urbanization are as relevant today as they were when
he was alive—believed that African Americans would undergo even
more rapid social incorporation, given that they held an advantage over
foreign-born immigrants: a knowledge of English (Park 1928). Park's
prediction did not materialize.

An expedient way to understand the causes of that development
is by reference to the differential accumulation of wealth holdings
among Blacks and Whites, as first described by sociologists Melvin
Oliver and Thomas Shapiro (1995/2006). On the basis of historical
research, Oliver and Shapiro note that since the early stages of the
nation's evolution and especially during the second half of the nineteenth century, the U.S. government devised and implemented a large
number of initiatives, including investment stimuli and fiscal policies,
meant to give ordinary Americans an ability to accumulate financial
assets and pass them on to younger generations through mechanisms
such as inheritance.

That was the original purpose of laws that enabled tens of thousands of humble workers of immigrant background to take possession
of lands as trustees of the state and later to retain the fruits of their
labor, passing those gains on to their children. The Homestead Act
of 1862, for example, allowed impecunious individuals—mostly men
but also some women and manumitted slaves—access to up to sixty-
five hectares of land, with the proviso that they cultivate it and build a
home within its limits. When successful, such tenants received title to
the property after a period of five years (Portfield 2005). A multitude
of humble workers braved cruel winters in midwestern, northern, and
western states in search of prosperity. By the early twentieth century,

when homesteading became rare, more than one-tenth of the American territory had been ceded to striving individuals and families.

Although the Homestead Act devastated indigenous populations, and was marred by abuses on the part of rich and powerful speculators, it also benefited ordinary Americans. That piece of legislation stands as an illustration of successful developmental efforts on the part of the American State. In tandem with the expansion of industry and the hard work of individuals, government incentives such as the Homestead Act fueled the growth of a thriving working class.[4]

Something similar may be said about the Morrill Land-Grant Acts which, starting in the 1860s, allowed for the creation of colleges whose purpose was "to promote the liberal and practical education of the industrial classes in the several pursuits and professions in life" (Morrill Act of 1862, chap. 130, sec. 4). Although their focus was on "the mechanic arts" and "agriculture," those laws proscribed the exclusion of "other scientific and classical studies." They made possible for each eligible state to receive up to 30,000 acres of public land, either within or contiguous to its boundaries, to foster higher education. Adjustments were implemented after the Civil War to extend the scope of the Land Grant Acts. Numerous institutions of enduring consequence were thus born, including Cornell University, the Massachusetts Institute of Technology, and the University of Maryland at College Park. The significance of these and other legislative measures in the forging of the American Dream cannot be overstated.

It is instructive to contrast items of legislation—such as the 1787 Northwest Ordinance, the Morrill Acts of 1862 and 1890, the Homestead Act of 1862, and the Servicemen's Readjustment Act of 1944 (GI Bill)—with the movement to afford emancipated slaves forty acres and a mule in the aftermath of the Civil War as compensation for more than two hundred years of bondage. That proposed measure did not match the scope and vast resources deployed by the Land Grant Acts, or subsequent laws to uplift the standing of veterans of the armed forces, but it adhered to similar principles by giving people the means to thrive and anticipating that they would use such means in the pursuit of self-reliance, wealth, and civic engagement.

The "Forty Acres and a Mule" program was never implemented; it came to represent the failure of policies aimed at restoring to African

Americans the fruits of their labor. For countless Blacks living in the American South, the alternatives to landownership were share-cropping and personal services, both paths leading to cumulative indebtedness across generations, not to the growth of wealth holdings through investment and inheritance (Earle 2004; Foner 1988/2002; Mitchell 2000).

When reviewing such processes, even using the word *poverty* to designate their effects seems a misnomer—the historical facts point to *dispossession*, a term that more accurately describes the loss of economic footing over time (see also Harvey 1998/2009, 2012; Wacquant 2008, 2009).

Later, the Great Black Migration that began in the early 1900s resulted in the massive redistribution of African Americans from the rural South to midwestern and northeastern cities but not in an improvement of the conditions under which Blacks could muster assets. Developmental policies to foment social and economic progress in the case of European immigrants and their progeny and their absence in the case of African Americans and their successors partially explain the divided fates of Blacks and Whites in America.

The aftershocks of historical neglect and dispossession over extended periods of time are still being felt. In 1995, when Oliver and Shapiro published their illuminating book, the wealth ratio between African Americans and the descendants of European immigrants in the United States was one dollar to twelve—a worrisome differential to start with. By 2011, as a result of the severe economic downturn that began three years earlier, Blacks had further lost 53 percent of their reserves. The gap between Black and White wealth holdings is now one to twenty.

Such large inequities have become part of a durable and ongoing national argument. Throughout the country, people bemoan Black poverty and its ailments by highlighting the capacity of immigrants from Europe, Asia, and Latin America to overcome racial prejudice and exploitation. If Irish, Poles, Jews, Cubans, and Italians were able to move up the social and economic ladders—so the argument goes—why didn't more Blacks succeed as well? Analysts like Thomas Sowell (1981) and Charles Murray (2013) revert to cultural factors in their attempts to explain different rates of success among Whites and Blacks. Even comedians like Bill Cosby exalt and demand personal responsibility as a solution to ghetto dysfunctions. Legions of politicians and pundits follow their lead.

Such opinions overlook the exceptional character of the Black journey; there is no basis to claim that immigrants had an experience akin to that of African Americans except in the most superficial sense. Although both populations endured geographical relocation, the conditions under which they migrated and, more importantly, the character of their reception in areas of destination were radically different.[5]

European immigrants and their successors faced exploitation but also opportunity. With the passage of time, and as a result of their own struggles, they benefited from reforms implemented by the American State and from the growing prosperity induced by functioning markets. By comparison, Blacks from the rural South confronted unparalleled hatred in urban settings, a dearth of programs to promote their social integration, and high levels of bureaucratic intrusion (Massey and Denton 1993).

In other words, those who think of the immigrant and Black experiences as equivalent phenomena fail to notice the timing and mode of economic insertion of Black migrants in areas of settlement, the scale of racial animus that greeted their arrival in American cities, and the deleterious effects of government policies that compounded their strife. The sons and daughters of European immigrants got the Homestead Act and the GI Bill; the descendants of African slaves got the forfeiture of Forty Acres and a Mule and, eventually, underfunded and politically compromised welfare programs (Kilty and Segal 2006). What is surprising, therefore, is not that a disproportionate number of Blacks have fallen prey to poverty and its disorders but that so many of them have made it despite monumental obstacles not faced by any other group.

RACIAL PREJUDICE AND MARKET FAILURE

In addition to the absence of developmental action on the part of the American State, two other factors have delayed social assimilation and economic advance among African Americans. First was the timing of the Great Black Migration which, at its apex in the 1970s, coincided with the shrinkage of the U.S. manufacturing base and its transition to an information- and service-based economy (Cowie, Heathcott, and Bluestone 2003). Blacks with low levels of education were increasingly unable to find employment of the kind that had buoyed upward mobility among European immigrants. Last to arrive in cities that were shedding mills and assembly lines, they were also less likely to secure jobs in what remained of industry.[6] Big Floyd's story, recounted in chapter 3, is but an example of that trend.

Even more significant were the obstacles faced by African Americans when attempting to step over the color line. A growing literature on *Whiteness* as an ideational category shows that the racialization of European immigrants was based on their lowly position in the edifice of social class and thus faded as they obtained wealth and education (Roediger 2006). African Americans, on the other hand, faced unprecedented levels of hostility contingent not solely on their weak economic status but also on their physical appearance (Wimmer 2013). As a result, they found it ever more difficult than Europeans to become socially *White*. Even among those able to acquire financial means and formal education, prejudice remained a major hindrance limiting their occupational and residential choices (see also Fiske 2000, 2013).

Largely for those reasons, the arrival of Blacks in American cities provoked the massive departure of White residents, with devastating effects upon the resource base of neighborhoods. Practices like *blockbusting* brought about the collapse of property values (Philpott 1991; Hutchison and Heynes 2011). That, in turn, had a ruinous impact on public school funding and on the willingness of banks and other financial institutions to operate according to conventional market standards (Massey and Denton 1994). An example is the practice known as *redlining*, that is, the systematic denial of mortgages and insurance to residents in poor, racially segregated neighborhoods. The paucity of financial assets to purchase or refurbish properties has been a major obstacle confronted by low-income Blacks. The departure of productive investment in poor urban areas rapidly brought about a classic instance of urban underdevelopment consistent with the theories of scholars like André Gunder Frank (1967).

In other words, Black ghettos are defined by the reduced operation of markets; they constitute spaces on the fringes of capitalism, and because investment is to the city as oxygen is to living organisms, poor urban neighborhoods endure a permanent state of suffocation (Harvey 1998/2009). Already buffeted by a changing economy, African Americans arriving in cities during the first half of the twentieth century were reduced to something less than the source of cheap labor that their European predecessors once had been. To them was left the ordeal of superfluity in inner cities deserted by capital for reasons external to the laws of supply and demand. With respect to such processes, the American State has remained inert, in part because of the lack of political voice among African Americans in general and low-income Blacks in particular.

Critics stand in judgment of the anomalous and sometimes frightening sights in inner cities: abandoned houses, graffiti-laden surfaces, young men peddling drugs in broad daylight, girl prostitutes, elevators in publicly subsidized housing that smell of vomit and urine, drive-by shootings. Yet more significant, and causally related to those symptoms, is what remains invisible to the eye: the absence of productive investment and nurturing government policies of the kind that forged success among mainstream populations.

CAPITAL RETROGRESSION, PREDATORY CAPITAL, AND STATE OMNIPRESENCE

The exodus of financial and human resources from inner cities—what many label *White flight* and I call *capital retrogression*—paralleled quick residential segregation and high levels of social isolation. The spaces left empty by the dearth of productive investments were then occupied by two social actors: government bureaucracies and the drug trade. Capital retrogression, predatory commerce, and bureaucratic interference became the unholy trinity circumscribing the experience of impoverished inner-city residents.

In other words, capital disinvestment prompted by the arrival of African American migrants in American cities made it possible for illegal forms of commerce to infiltrate urban spaces. Beginning in the 1970s and accelerating in the 1980s, Black neighborhoods became appealing markets for the traffic of illicit substances of the most dangerous kind, including heroin and crack cocaine (Jonnes 1996). Bereft of power and representation, local residents were ideal targets for the transactions of shady entrepreneurs aiming to reduce their exposure and liability. Drug lords flooded the inner city, knowing that it would provide a haven unequalled by other settings where inhabitants had more wealth and influence. The scandalous peddling of crack cocaine, in South Central Los Angeles, to finance the Contra insurgency in Nicaragua in the 1980s is a case in point (Webb 1999). This was no conspiracy, merely a logical response to cost-benefit calculations and political expediency.

Capital retrogression and the subsequent flooding of poor residential areas with dangerous drugs may be best explained from the vantage point of economic sociology, whose main contention is that for free markets to operate efficiently, actors must yield to social norms that place limits on their behavior. The emphasis is on the *social underpinnings of economic action* because without boundaries created by accountability and trust, markets cannot properly function (Portes 2010). When left alone, *Homo economicus* drifts toward chaos and the degradation of the economic process itself (Schumpeter 1942/1975: 82–85).

Social norms affecting market operations often appear in the guise of informal agreements that promote interdependence, reciprocity, and the avoidance of shame. Merchants, for example, may refrain from profitable transactions for moral reasons or reduce gains by donating to charitable causes, partly motivated by a desire to protect the standing and trust they will need for future dealings. Short-term profits are thus subordinated to long-term advantages. Conventions imposed by social networks play a critical role in the maintenance of productive economic exchanges, and so does government action when geared toward the maintenance of orderly exchanges and the fulfillment of common interests.

America's inner cities illustrate what markets look like when liberated from mainstream norms and expectations. Similar processes took effect in less developed countries, like Bolivia and Colombia during the 1980s, when enfeebled governments and atomized societies made it possible for executives of the drug trade to attain control tantamount to that of true states. Unhampered in their drive for profits, they amassed extravagant fortunes amidst a population almost untouched by their economic bonanza. The absence of limits imposed upon them by cohesive social networks and organized government action eliminated the need for accountability, trust, and solidarity (Cross and Peña 2006).

Similarly, in American inner cities, the absence of productive invest-ments created new opportunities for a thriving commerce unencum-bered by the need to preserve loyalties or avoid shame. During the 1980s and 1990s, vast amounts of drugs were deployed in West Baltimore—and every other poor neighborhood in the nation—making their con-sumption as much a matter of demand as one of supply. In places where other resources were scarce, drugs were everywhere: in "balloon rooms" dotting the decrepit streets, in the pockets of seven-year-old lookouts, in crack houses and shooting galleries, and in stores whose ostensible mission was to sell canned food. Where constructive opportunities for economic advancement were absent, drug peddling offered aspiring youngsters a means to generate income (Sullivan 1989).

Drugs exacerbated the already dire conditions in poor areas, turn-ing them into war zones. Significantly, however, there is no inevitable line of causation between drug consumption and urban decay. Most consumers of controlled substances in the United States do not live in Black ghettos; demand permeates every corner of the society, with affluent Whites representing the richest market. Americans of all kinds have felt the devastating consequences of addiction; and still, the use of drugs for recreational purposes has grown in highly functional settings, including business districts and wealthy homes in America's suburbs (Jonnes 1996: 308–325). The majority of places where drugs are routinely used have not experienced the atrocious effects visible in America's racially segregated neighborhoods; most people who use drugs do not become addicts, and most places where drugs are used do not become infernos.

The calamities resulting from drug use and commerce in America's inner cities are linked more closely to economic breakdown and social isolation than to personal dysfunction. In districts that have financial resources, political influence, and protective social connections, the consumption of drugs is at best a matter of leisure and at worst a pre-dicament faced by isolated individuals and families. It is different in areas of concentrated indigence where the lack of resources accentuates the vulnerability of residents. In such environments, drug consumption acts as an epidemic touching almost every aspect of life. No amount of therapeutic intervention or retributive action can make up for the absence of political and economic power.

Still, in lieu of productive investment or effective measures to reduce residential segregation, the American State has responded with a multiplicity of programs aimed at palliation but also repression. Combined with capital retrogression and the operations of predatory merchants, state agencies mandated to alleviate the consequences of historical neglect complicate the unique character of urban dispossession. The government's approach to drug consumption in poor neighborhoods, for example, has included a wide range of punitive measures and pointed surveillance beneath a thin layer of magnanimity. In such settings, most approaches to drug addiction focus on individual behaviors rather than structural changes; they combine narratives of personal empowerment with harsh consequences when individuals relapse. This is emblematic of the way in which the American State has dramatically deviated from its developmental stance. With respect to poor and racially distinct populations, laws and policies have been geared toward control and restraint rather than social incorporation.

In the next chapter, I continue my examination of the factors surrounding state action in poor neighborhoods by introducing the notion of *distorted engagement.*

6

DISTORTED ENGAGEMENT AND LIMINAL INSTITUTIONS: RULING AGAINST THE POOR

THE SIGNS OF ECONOMIC DEVASTATION AND RACIAL IMPLOSION are everywhere in West Baltimore: lines of decaying row houses on whose steps young men gather to chat and peddle drugs for lack of anything better to do; homes left over from the Victorian era, still bearing the marks of a genteel past, their doors and windows now boarded up, their walls covered with graffiti; streets oddly punctuated by people's belongings—broken furniture and scattered clothing—tossed aside in the course of evictions. Parks and playgrounds sit forlorn during the day but are brought to life at night by the purveyors of illicit pleasures; women in garments that reveal and cling to the body, their vacant eyes searching, anxious to keep the party going. These are the physical markers of enduring decay. Another one is the overwhelming presence of government offices in the same precincts.

In 1993, there was only one bank open for business in the fringes of Upton and Sandtown-Winchester, two of the West Baltimore tracts where I conducted my research. There were no large chain supermarkets or fresh produce stores. By contrast, there were fifteen public agencies, including five community centers, seven halfway houses, two courthouses, and one office charged with the protection of children. By 2013, those numbers had been surpassed. West Baltimore now boasts no fewer than twenty public and private organizations addressing social ills connected to poverty, including parole and probation, emergency food provision, care for victims of domestic violence, juvenile corrections, community psychiatry, and the ever-present Child Protective

Services. The sole enumeration of entities intended to address poverty and its afflictions in an area less than fifteen miles in radius calls for further scrutiny.

A plausible reason for the large number of public service agencies in poor neighborhoods is the nation's desire to lend a helping hand to those in need. Police departments and prisons play a critical role in the preservation of public safety; welfare offices enable countless families to survive during periods of crisis. Without child protection agencies, some of the most fragile members of our society would be at further risk of abuse or neglect. And no one would argue that shelters, psychiatric care, and rehabilitative centers are superfluous in urban spaces where a disproportionate number of residents struggle with drug addiction and mental illness. All in all, the concentration of public agents in inner-city neighborhoods could be seen as evidence of the public's commitment to vulnerable populations.

Overt intentions, however, can conceal latent institutional functions. Although agencies serving inner-city dwellers are designed to fulfill compassionate goals, a close look at their operations reveals multiple contradictions. Such agencies allocate most of their budgets to infrastructure, subcontracted initiatives, and various forms of compensation—including wages, salaries, and benefits—with smaller proportions dedicated to actual services. In their inner spaces, stretched-thin employees—administrators, social workers, counselors, case managers, family advocates, parole officers, and teachers—labor under ambiguous expectations that demand both sympathy and permanent suspicion toward those whom Michael Lipsky (1980) calls "non-voluntary clients."

In his influential book, *Street-Level Bureaucracy: Dilemmas of the Individual in Public Service* (1980), Lipsky draws attention to personnel in government agencies whom he identifies as part of the policy-making community. While consultants and high-level officials design programs and craft regulations, it is employees at the grassroots level who must adapt their abstract formulations through daily exchanges that involve confrontation and negotiation. Their contact with residents in poor neighborhoods is often filled with tension as clients contest or seek to subvert strict rules. Public service agencies are the terrain where laws crafted in the rarified halls of government clash with local realities.

Although government agencies serving the poor often lack the resources to fulfill their stated goals, their concentration in segregated urban spaces has a significant effect upon the character of community life. It fosters adversarial relations between representatives of the state and residents lacking both political power and economic resources. Their procedures stimulate a series of unique dispositions that markedly differ from those made possible by the relationship between ordinary people and mainstream institutions.

While agencies designed to address the needs of poor people focus on surveillance, control, and retribution, those that deal with mainstream populations act in accordance to market dictates, treating individuals as consumers and citizens rather than victims or drains on the national treasure. In fact, the mark of middle-class living is a reduced contact with the public sector. Most Americans have few direct and regular dealings with government bureaucracies. By contrast, impoverished populations have multiple and recurrent exchanges with agents of the state.

Compared with less developed countries where governments are often weak and therefore unable to infiltrate the daily life of the poor, in the United States the public sector has amassed the material and human resources needed to routinely encroach into the very core of community life. State omnipresence has thus become a key factor eroding the capacity of inner-city residents to mobilize resources and create alternative means of subsistence or defense. In tandem with capital retrogression and the workings of predatory drug merchants, state programs for the poor exacerbate social fracture and economic stagnation.

In other words, a distinctive aspect of life in the urban ghetto, one whose ramifications are not properly understood, is the extent to which the state penetrates the daily existence of individuals and families. In environments where poverty levels reach above one-third of the population, and nearly half of men in prime working age are unemployed, local bureaucracies exert a pervasive influence on the character of social intercourse.

THE THEORETICAL CLAIM

I use *distorted engagement* to describe conditions in which government agencies designed to address the problems of poverty supplant and transform normative exchanges in the economic, social, and symbolic realms. As an analytical tool, the concept is inspired by the word *anamorphosis,* used in the field of optics to denote the misshapen projection of intelligible objects through reflecting surfaces, a phenomenon equivalent to that of state agents whose exchanges with marginal populations appear as a disfigured version of conventional interactions. The concept gives contrast to *embedded autonomy,* the phrase employed by Peter Evans to designate a true developmental relationship between government and civil society (see chapter 5).

Distorted engagement materializes through *liminal institutions* like prisons, welfare offices, public schools, rehabilitative centers, providers of subsidized housing, the court system, and child protection agencies, which become locations for the enactment of what Pierre Bourdieu (1991: 87) called *symbolic violence* (see also Bourdieu and Wacquant 1992/2002: 167). Although the term *liminal* has been used by sociologists and anthropologists in various ways (Menjívar 2010; Turner 1974), I use it here in reference to public agencies, departments, or offices that operate on the implicit or explicit assumption that their claimants are likely deceitful and undeserving; therefore, they must be subjected to special treatment.

To be poor is to be marred by a discrediting blotch. For that reason, the attendant procedures of liminal institutions often violate normative rules of communication and deportment along lines best described by Goffman (1963/1986) in his discussion of stigma. Liminal institutions have expressed goals, such as eradicating crime and safeguarding the public (police departments, courts of law, and prisons), providing income and services to poor families (welfare departments, Medicaid, and food stamps), and protecting minors (child protection agencies), but woven into their fabric run the common threads of misgiving and contempt. Interactions with such agencies often entail humiliating procedures, including special forms of certification or the provision of bodily fluids for inspection.

By comparison, mainstream institutions interact with citizens who are assumed to command assets, rights, and responsibilities that reinforce their feelings of agency. The presumption is that, when presented with a balance of rewards and penalties, individuals will behave in accordance with dominant values because that is the least costly and most beneficial course of action. In that case, the person is constituted as a self-reliant agent in competition with others similarly endowed. Mainstream institutions organize behavior and exercise power but afford social actors a measure of real and imaginary leeway to make choices—the *illusio touted* by Pierre Bourdieu (1991) that prompts all members of the society to participate in social games and interfaces. Such ideas are in agreement with Michel Foucault's insight in *The Archaeology of Knowledge* (1969/1982: 35) that "Man is an invention of recent date," that is, a construction whose attributes, actions, and demeanor are sustained by standard and generalized rationality.

Liminal institutions, on the other hand, express ambivalent benevolence, that is, society's uncertainty over the adequate treatment of marginal groups whose members are simultaneously viewed as hapless victims and conniving scoundrels. Such institutions build on the premise that the people they serve are suspect and are positioned on the fringes of society because of their vulnerable status and presumed deficiencies, moral as well as intellectual.

When clustered in physical spaces—as they often are in impoverished neighborhoods—liminal institutions contribute to the cultivation of a specific way of life. Frequent interaction with the agents of surveillance and regulation imprints the bodies of low-income people with a distinctive *habitus,* that is, a set of cultural manifestations anchored in the physical being and in the routine, unself-conscious practices of individuals (Bourdieu 1979/1984).

In that respect, and like the very rich evoked by F. Scott Fitzgerald, the urban poor are different—the wealthy may have more money but the urban poor have more state agents inspecting their lives and molding their actions. In both cases, practices and outlooks flow from concrete experiences. Social insularity, residential segregation, a paucity of educational and employment opportunities, and repeated contact with personnel in liminal institutions produce types of embodied knowledge not found in or transferrable to other settings. This too has an effect upon the capacity of impoverished people to function, relate, or secure jobs in mainstream environments.

In other words, persons for whom government agencies and state bureaucracies are a main and continuing point of reference develop behaviors and manners of being that diverge from those found among members of populations whose principal relationship, real as well as symbolic, is with markets and with mainstream government institutions.[1] In the first instance, individuals learn to see themselves from early childhood as subjects of regulations and discourses so constrictive and detrimental as to incite mostly manipulation, resistance, and circumvention. Antagonism suffuses the relationship between marginal populations and agents of the state.

In the second case, when persons are primarily construed as consumers and citizens endowed with a measure of autonomy, the opposition between individuals and the state is muted; buffered by polite terms and euphemisms. Power is still involved in that setup but it is power diluted by persuasion and co-optation not intensified by oppression and brutality. The difference between liminal and mainstream institutions is, therefore, one of quality as well as quantity. Liminal institutions take to a higher level of performance a critical function of the state: the legitimized deployment of violence in figurative and actual senses.

Distorted engagement thus entails temporal and spatial dimensions; it designates a process as well as an effect. As a process, it consists of the increasing capacity of state agencies to penetrate community life through regulation and supervision, superseding the operation of markets and conventional social interchanges. From that point of view, distorted engagement represents an extension of the total institution—the generalized *panopticism* rooted in disciplinarian state policies examined by Michele Foucault (1995).

As an effect, distorted engagement points to the overpowering presence of state delegates within physical circumscriptions. Government agents act as intermediaries between marginal populations and bodies of legislation whose object is suppression and control rather than social integration. In their daily lives, a multitude of public servants struggle to overcome bureaucratic restrictions and ambiguities in the service of poor people. Their efforts often meet limited results because distorted engagement is not a direct effect of policy making that can be tweaked to improvement but the legacy of long-standing historical trends involving race and social class, which resist change.

UNPACKING DISTORTED ENGAGEMENT

Distorted engagement may be unfolded into three distinct components: (a) *palliation*, that is, the substitution of ameliorative social policies for productive investment; (b) *acute regulation* in the form of measures aimed at restricting individual agency; and (c) *violence*, deployed through material and symbolic resources. I review these features next.

Palliation versus Investment

In lieu of productive investment to address the consequences of intergenerational dispossession, the American State has deployed substantial resources into relief programs to alleviate the consequences of poverty. Those expenditures appear large only when seen out of context. They pale by comparison to the outlays that buttressed developmental tools that enabled the descendants of European immigrants to prosper. Two examples will suffice to support that contention.

Throughout the post–World War II era, the Veterans Administration—the entity charged with the management of the GI Bill—alternated between the second- and third-highest-spending federal agency, a position far ahead of comparable government branches providing social services to citizens, including the poor (Congressional Quarterly 1975). In 1950, the peak postwar moment of federal expenditures on veterans, the federal government devoted almost $8 billion directly to that function, that is, almost a quarter of all disbursements for that year (Congressional Quarterly 1975: 1335). The total spent on the GI Bill's education title alone surpassed the cost of the Marshall Plan in Europe.

Between 1940 and 1973, as much as one-third of the population—including veterans and their dependents—may have directly benefited from the elaborate and generous welfare system created through the expansion of such benefits. In 2009, the U.S. Department of Veterans Affairs was still the second-largest federal agency after the Department of Defense; it managed a budget of $87.6 billion and employed nearly 280,000 people at hundreds of medical facilities, clinics, and benefits offices. By contrast, Temporary Assistance for Needy Families, the program that replaced Aid for Families with Dependent Children in the mid-nineties, absorbed approximately $38 billion—that is, 1.5 percent—of a $2.7 trillion federal budget the same year (Knight and Worden 1995: 34).[2]

Two conclusions emerge from that comparison. First, programs for the poor deploy very small fractions of the federal and state budgets. Belying conservative critiques, such programs have been severely underfunded, especially in comparison with initiatives that aim to bolster middle-class and affluent ways of life. Second, and more significant, programs for the poor constitute a kind of vicarious investment—a mimicking of the relationship between market forces and competing individuals. In contrast, items of legislation like the GI Bill supported the capacity of social actors to compete in the labor market through the pursuit of education and the acquisition of property.

In the first case, the effect was not only the erosion of personal agency, as conservatives have accurately observed, but also a new set of calculations and relationships between individuals and state agencies, based on the obliteration of market forces buttressing social interactions in the larger society. Laws like the GI Bill stand as evidence of efficacy on the part of the American State. Conservative critics get it wrong when focusing exclusively on the deleterious impact of government policies on the poor while neglecting the part that government has played in improving the life chances of mainstream populations. On the other hand, liberal authors have mostly focused on cuts in government expenditures for the poor without examining the foundational deficiencies of those programs.

Similar in character to Aid for Families with Dependent Children—and its successor since 1996, Temporary Assistance for Needy Families—has been a constellation of ameliorative programs implemented by federal and state governments for more than fifty years to address the needs of the urban poor. From Medicaid to training and literacy initiatives, housing and urban development, mental health and counseling services, remedial and "enriching" programs for failing students, and grants awarded to community-based organizations, such endeavors constitute attempts to *make up for the absence of direct investment and the normal operation of markets*. For the most part, those initiatives have not reduced poverty by much. Even successful initiatives such as Head Start, a publicly funded effort to provide intensive educational services to very young children in poor families, have seen their effects thwarted for lack of continuity and proper support (Puma et al. 2012).

Ironically, although government programs for the poor have not eradicated poverty, they have been successful in other ways by sustaining a dynamic sector consisting of program designers and administrators but also researchers, many of whom have mustered fortunes through the implementation of demonstration projects and other grant-financed endeavors supported by philanthropic foundations and public agencies. They complement a thriving contingent formed by not-for-profit organizations, policy makers, academics, consultants, and media personalities, all of whom make a living by analyzing or purporting to change the conditions created by historical dispossession (O'Connor 2001).

Examples of this are found in studies of mental health among deprived populations, which display a tendency to conceal the true causes of psychological distress. Their conclusions often benefit big pharmaceutical firms seeking to deploy their products. That represents the *medicalization* of reasonable responses to the anomalous circumstances created by social isolation and poverty. It is likely that a disturbing number of impoverished children diagnosed with attention deficit disorder are not exhibiting behavioral dysfunction but reacting to the intolerable conditions of their lives (see Horowitz 2003). In other words, the economic stagnation and social disconnection of American inner cities have stimulated a bounty of ideas to address the very problems they create.

This is evident in initiatives aimed at urban revitalization. Especially since the 1970s, writings on how to restore investment in depressed neighborhoods have multiplied. Michael Porter, a leading figure in business economics, refueled dialogue on that subject after the publication of his paper "The Competitive Advantage of the Inner City" (1995). Following the logic behind his influential book *The Competitive Advantage of Nations* (1998), Porter pointed to an apparent paradox consisting of obdurate deprivation combined with high purchasing power at the aggregate level in declining neighborhoods. Many ghettoes are in optimal locations that could attract capital outlays. Yet "the establishment of sustainable economic foundations with wealth creation, employment opportunities, and improved infrastructure still is out of reach" (Porter 1995: 54). Porter's statement remains valid today.

He argued that past efforts at urban revitalization did not succeed because they were guided by models designed to meet the immediate needs of individuals rather than to create the necessary infrastructure to mobilize financial resources. They have depended on subsidies, preferential designs, or expensive plans to stimulate tangential fields like housing, real estate, and neighborhood development—mostly benefiting government subcontractors, not necessarily the poor.

Lacking an overall strategy, such endeavors have treated the inner city as an island separate from the surrounding economy, a feature that, in Porter's opinion, has undermined the creation of viable companies along the way. As a remedy, he recommends measures to reinforce local demand, a proper evaluation of existing human resources, and integration with regional clusters, that is, "those unique-to-a region collections of related companies that are competitive nationally and even globally" (Porter 1995: 60).

The late economist Bennett Harrison and his colleague, Amy K. Glasmeier (1997), promptly responded with a friendly rebuttal to Porter. In their opinion, business alone cannot redevelop the inner city; government and community organizations must also be included. Harrison and Glasmeier emphasized the role of grassroots organizations as potential instruments to invigorate distressed urban areas.

Neither Porter nor Harrison and Glasmeier were entirely right or wrong about inner-city development. Porter paid no attention to the role played by racial discrimination and past history in the formation of urban ghettoes, and he did not credit the government for actions that have constructively supported the operation of markets in the larger society. Harrison and Glasmeier saw the potential of community-based organizations to promote economic vitality but failed to notice that, as they currently exist, many of those organizations are part of the thick institutional web that contributes to maintaining irregular conditions in poor neighborhoods. Underfunded and limited in scope, those organizations are ill equipped to make up for market failure.

In fact, affluent residential areas are notable for the absence of community organizations (Brooks-Gunn et al. 1993; Brooks-Gunn, Duncan, and Aber 2000); they are not needed in prosperous urban spaces, given the level of connectedness between residents and functioning markets and mainstream institutions. Both Porter and Harrison and Glasmeier underestimated the extent to which the government's occupation of spaces left vacant by the departure of productive investment has contributed to the creation of conditions outside the scope of capitalist enterprise.

More recently, Howard Husock (2003) described how low-income housing programs, like other antipoverty initiatives, have complicated the conditions faced by low-income people in urban settings. Housing vouchers, community development corporations, urban enterprise zones, and even the Community Reinvestment Act have worked to diminish the autonomy of residents. Yet other authors (Peters 2009; Sealander (2003); Streensland (2007); Wagner and Barton Gilman 2012; Winston 2006) have addressed similar problems in other sectors of palliative government policy, from homelessness to subsidized housing, drug rehabilitation, and primary and secondary instruction. The overall conclusion is inescapable: amelioration has not been an effective substitute for productive investment.

In other words, programs guided by liberal principles of relief and aid have not reproduced the vital effects of markets in depressed urban areas. Although individuals and families often depend on them for support, the programs have mostly benefited those who implement them. Capital retrogression and state omnipresence constitute main impediments to the social and economic integration of impoverished, racially distinct people in urban areas.

Acute Regulation

A major function of the state since antiquity has been to impose compliance among those living under its jurisdiction through aggression, coercion, co-optation, and persuasion. Fending off external threats, occupying territories through conquest, and redistributing goods and services have also been among the state's prerogatives, as has been the legitimized use of violence to discipline those who deviate from normative standards of behavior (Tilly 2006). Americans are beholden to a multiplicity of laws, but even in a context characterized by a persistent legislative impulse, regulations affecting the poor are unique.

A major cause underlying the differential treatment of needy people in the United States relates to the country's legacy from England. In his celebrated book, *The Protestant Ethic and the Spirit of Capitalism* (1912/2002), Max Weber describes the affinity between principles of diligence and the accumulation of material goods. His analysis underscores personal responsibility and rectitude as conditions for the mustering of wealth, which, in turn, becomes a sign of virtue and merit.

For that reason, poverty has been interpreted as a manifestation of moral lassitude and lack of self-control. In the work that first brought him to public attention, Herbert Spencer (1851/2012) wrote at length against England's Poor Laws. Such regulations were so harsh as to lead many, including Charles Dickens, Spencer's contemporary, to denounce them in novels like *A Christmas Carol* (1843) and *A Tale of Two Cities* (1859/2012). Yet Spencer saw even minimal attempts at relief as misguided efforts that perpetuated laziness among the indigent.

Such ideas, nascent in nineteenth-century England are still alive in the United States. They operate around a key differentiation between the deserving and undeserving poor (Katz 1990/2013). While the victims of unforeseen disaster may provoke sympathy, those who are able-bodied and yet impoverished elicit antipathy; they are thought to threaten the moral fiber of the society. Unemployed Black men are especially susceptible to judgment, as are single mothers in need of support.

The 1935 Social Security Act was originally envisioned by visionaries like Frances Perkins as a tool to afford basic rights such as income, medical services, housing, and child care to individuals by virtue of their status *as citizens*, not their moral worth. The vociferous debate that surrounded the law's passage evinced deep rancor toward impoverished people deemed as undeserving. The resulting compromise, still embodied in present-day laws, was a fragmented system of protection with a top tier benefiting creditable populations—older people, some unemployed, the White widows of soldiers, and the physically disabled—and a lower tier charged with supplying public assistance to the unworthy—unmarried mothers, mentally impaired individuals, and the victims of addiction (Jencks 1993). Because the distinction between deserving and undeserving poor is so deeply rooted in the American psyche, the tendency has been for public officials to temper their attempts at legislative reform with guarantees that unworthy individuals won't benefit from government largesse.

Thus, regulations affecting low-income people are exceptional by the extent to which they violate normative standards of privacy and decorum. The invasive guidelines regulating AFDC payments have been noted before (chapter 4). Similar policies tend to exhibit a secular preoccupation over the sexual habits of vulnerable people. The late Stephen Jay Gould (1985) tells the story of Carrie Buck, an eighteen-year old Virginia resident who was sterilized, in the 1920s, without her consent after she gave birth to a daughter out of wedlock. Both Carrie and her mother had been deemed to be "mentally feeble," a phrase used at the time to designate people with a variety of brain-related deficiencies. The objective of sterilization was to impede additional births to poor people who were seen as incapable of controlling their sexual appetites and thus representing a potential contaminant to society.[3]

Nearly seventy years later, in the 1990s, court hearings were held throughout the nation to push for the compulsory implantation of Norplant, a birth control patch, in the arms of adolescent mothers receiving public assistance. Restrictions were also put in place to ban access to income on the part of women who became pregnant while receiving welfare payments (Wingert and Kantrowitz 1993). As an African American politician in Baltimore stated at a public hearing regarding such matters, "it is only proper for the public to ask young ladies [single mothers on welfare] to act with a better sense of responsibility if they want to receive public funds."[4]

The effect of legislative heavy-handedness has not been solely the diminution of personal autonomy among impoverished people but also the development of styles pivoting around confrontation, subversion, and reluctant accommodation. Multiple authors investigating living conditions in inner cities, from Elliott Liebow (1967) to Carol Stack (1971/1997), Katherine Newman (2008), Elijah Anderson (1999), Mitchell Duneier (2000), and Löic Wacquant (2008), provide evidence of the extent to which recurrent contact with agents of the state shapes personal and collective modes of interaction that include riffing, bantering, and loud argumentation as part of day-to-day exchanges. Such elements are the result of repeated contact with ruling bureaucracies. Mannerisms and gestures distinctive of ghetto residents partly originate through contact with personnel in surveillance and regulatory agencies.

High levels of residential segregation in inner-city neighborhoods have also contributed to the cultivation of behavioral repertories that, ironically, are favored by youngsters in more prosperous settings, as shown by the crossover appeal of hip-hop and the fashions surrounding it. The popularity of such styles and bearing depends on the whiff of resistance and rebellion they emit. Because middle-class youngsters tend to lead lives fraught with restrictions, they resonate with the emotional and aesthetic power of ghetto deportment and imagery.

Other forms of subliminal political resistance and confrontation occur in the very places where services are rendered. Lynne Haney (1996) describes the way in which young women under court supervision use the ideas and counsel tendered by a caring social worker to sabotage her recommendations. The social worker advises girls in trouble to shed boyfriends whom she sees as the source of their difficulties, but the young women parade their paramours as indicators of their own power and sexual allure. Other social workers advise young mothers "to take the bull by the horns" as a way to become self-reliant. The women use the same catchphrase to undermine order in the residential facility where they live, demonstrating a sarcastic capacity for independent thinking.

Even more recently, Haney (2010) compares therapeutic programs aimed at normalizing the behavior of impoverished women in prison and lucidly describes how such programs are perceived by the women as instruments for coercion and humiliation.[5]

In other words, the distinctive patterns of personal interaction among impoverished and racially distinct people are partly shaped by the adversarial character of interactions between clients and service providers in government agencies and by poor people's responses to bodies of regulation that stifle their sense of independence and capacity for agency.

Such exchanges mold what Pierre Bourdieu (1979/1984) calls *habitus*, that is, a system of dispositions flowing from embodied knowledge. A specific habitus provides social actors with the practical skills and orientations necessary to navigate in fields that range from employment and sexuality to domestic relations and artistic expression; it directs behavior without the need for formal rules and mediates between social structure and individual practice. A focus on the habitus reveals nondiscursive knowledge deployed by social actors as they adapt to and modify particular environments. The concept forces us to interpret culture as an ever-permeating aspect of economic and political adaptations.

The nondiscursive character of the habitus is central to an explanation of behaviors and ways of life found in groups distinguished by nationality, historical trajectory, race, gender, and ethnicity. In America's inner cities, where mainstream institutions are nearly absent, the collective habitus is further buttressed through the enactment of physical and symbolic force. I turn to that subject next.

Accounting for Violence

Repression, coercion, and intimidation against impoverished populations have been the subject of an enduring body of research. In particular, the disproportionate representation of poor African American men among incarcerates continues to attract the attention of scholars, politicians, and public advocates. Work by Wacquant (2008), Western (2007), Pager (2009), and Alexander (2010) leaves little doubt about the extent to which extreme forms of physical containment are enforced on vulnerable Blacks, men in particular, as part of the routine actions of the state.

As described by such authors, incarceration and other forms of extreme supervision—including parole, detainment, and repeated arrests, not to mention stop-and-frisk policies as enacted in New York during the administration of Mayor Michael Bloomberg—function to level punishment but also to create a clime of intimidation in inner-city neighborhoods. Such activities are part of a wide spectrum of punitive measures, but they also contribute to generalized conflict in destitute urban areas, as several research projects and filmed documentaries now show (Geller and Toch 1996; Kennedy 2011). In addition to raw physical containment, symbolic violence is a major factor defining urban poverty.

Pierre Bourdieu, arguably the world's most prominent sociologist at the time of his death in 2002, used the concept of *symbolic violence* to highlight processes of social and cultural dominance that depend on language and other virtual imagery (Bourdieu 1991; Calhoun and Wacquant 2002). In his view, symbolic violence is the naturalized and semiconscious exercise of aggression anchored in daily practices. Because it is part of internalized worldviews, symbolic violence eludes analysis, concealed by seemingly benevolent notions. With respect to the poor, such notions include "aid," "charity," "relief," and "the helping hand," all terms that evoke compassion but also distance and verticality.

Vertical charity expects gratitude but is often met with resentment. Within its range of vision, the poor are not solely perceived as broken and in need of repair but also as beholden to the munificence of people more powerful, and therefore more virtuous, than they. The poor are vessels into which the righteous pour the fruits of their generosity. Acts of benevolence stemming from such positions exude dominance and control; they are permeated with unintentional cruelty. Vertical charity is the antithesis of solidarity.

Similarly, the sanitized language used by public agencies in their dealings with the poor often contributes to enlarging division and eliciting anger and antipathy rather than appreciation. Elements in the much-touted "attitude" imputed to poor people originate in that misunderstanding. Social workers in Baltimore, for example, face ordeals compounded by the absence of gratitude on the part of their clients. Having pursued careers in service, most of them work hard to reconcile bureaucratic requirements with the needs of claimants. Their efforts are often greeted with surliness and discontent. The structure within which they operate makes it virtually impossible to establish caring human connections or to evoke in clients feelings of recognition or mutual appreciation.

Symbolic violence pervades the stigmatizing speech used with respect to groups undergoing systematic exclusion, residential segregation, and the effects of disinvestment. Even the term "poverty" appears as the label for a disease befalling hapless individuals, not as a descriptor of effects caused by economic and political aggression. Words like "less fortunate," "underprivileged, "underserved," or "disadvantaged" project the incorrect impression that the conditions endured by residents in destitute neighborhoods are simply the result of an imperfect distribution of benefits or services—they say nothing about qualitative differences between the experience of poor and affluent populations; nor do they reveal the sequel of historical events that produced them.[6]

Bourdieu saw symbolic violence in close relationship to social class, highlighting both material *and* virtual dimensions of inequality, a point of deviation from canonical authors like Emile Durkheim, Max Weber, and Karl Marx for whom social class was mostly about economic position, not symbolic exchanges. Instead, Bourdieu distinctively underscores binary systems of classification that rely on contrast to distinguish the tastes and manners of affluent and educated populations and those of the subordinate masses. In that spirit, Bourdieu notes the opposition between the outspokenness of the populace and the highly censored language of the bourgeois, which finds echo in the political economy of bodily management. He observed that "agitation and haste, grimaces and gesticulation are opposed . . . to the restraint and impassivity which signify [social] elevation" (1979/1984: 175–176). Almost identical words may be applied to the comparison between inner-city residents and members of more affluent populations in the United States.

Symbolic violence, as analyzed by Bourdieu, depends on a variety of instruments used to impose discipline and wield punishment. This is consistent with the workings of liminal institutions, which stem from class hegemony but become naturalized terrains for the interactions between dominators and subordinates. In everyday life, communication in those settings is subject to what Bourdieu called *misrecognition* (Schiff 2009).

Misrecognition allows symbolic violence to retreat from view to become part of conventional wisdom and established social arrangements. Thus, impoverished people are said to need self-restraint, inducements to work or marry, and instruction to be better parents or fix their broken families, all of which are not expected of more affluent populations but point to seemingly obvious deficits in the case of the poor. It is the assumptions beneath such language that enable liminal institutions to act as instruments of virtual aggression.

Misrecognition is, in that sense, a blurred representation of the true aims of violence. As part of political dominance, it is blind to its own existence; hegemonic power is, by definition, innocent and unreflective of its own history and consequences. Every established order, Bourdieu insists, tends to produce to very different degrees and with very different means the normalization of its own arbitrariness. Misrecognition naturalizes existing hierarchies so that they are taken for granted rather than questioned; it thus reinforces social estrangement from impoverished people.

Put differently, misrecognition entails a forgetting of history in which the social and political worlds take on the appearance of nature and are thus imagined as a terrain impervious to the passage of time and its unfolding events. As a result, the source of social vulnerability and its relationship to current situations is obscured. Distance enables us to perceive structures of dominance as facts of life and not as contingent situations with a past and present that are susceptible of future transformation (Schiff 2009).

Bourdieu borrowed the notion of misrecognition from Jacques Lacan, using it to describe the ways in which social agents and institutions conceal and respond to the origins of inequality. Lacan (2007a), on the other hand, used misrecognition as part of his psychoanalytic theory to investigate the defensive operations of individuals as they struggle against dependence and fragility (Schiff 2009; see also Steinmetz 2006).

People of all ages depend for their sense of self on the image reflected to them by concrete others with whom they interact. In Lacan's framework, misrecognition is not solely an instrument of domination; it also involves defensive postures and attempts at correcting persons' perceived discordances between their own reality and the reality others attempt to impose on them (Lacan 2007b: 75–81). The emphasis here is on the ego and its capacity to respond and refashion oppressive pressures.

In other words, misrecognition from above fuels defiance and readjustment from the ground up. Those are the dynamics underlying the relationship between liminal institutions and impoverished clients. The former impose a series of definitions on the latter, which the poor often reject in order to salvage a modicum of agency and dignity.

Misrecognition is integral to symbolic violence. It is also the focus of psychological analysis directed at powerless populations such as children, women, and the poor, some of whose behaviors tend to be diagnosed as sicknesses or dysfunctions, not as logical responses to abnormal conditions. Some forms of misrecognition operate upon the body, leading individuals to use their physical being as a canvas for aggression. Self-hatred and attempts at re-forming bodily features are common among stigmatized populations, including those in inner-city neighborhoods. An abhorrence of nappy hair, a desire to lighten skin color or modify other physical features is part of the common experience among impoverished African Americans.

My years of research in West Baltimore yielded multiple examples of misrecognition. I remember being surrounded by children as young as three who wanted to caress my hair—they were already aware that their own was less than acceptable. "They love you hair," said Sarah, the mother of seven-year-old Taniqua. "I love their hair too," I responded, realizing immediately how my words sounded to their ear; a courteous but not credible riposte to their desire.

Clarise Twigg, whose story is included in chapter 9, was a carefree child, full of energy, who loved swimming as a young girl. By the time she became a teenager, she had learned though peers and adults that swimming made her hair kinky and therefore repugnant. She gave up competitive swimming to preserve an acceptable self. That retreat was a preamble to other defeats that further disconnected her from mainstream society.

Big Floyd, whose life was chronicled in chapter 3, saw himself as a father seeking resources to recover his three children from foster care but was seen by people in his circle, and by police officers and judges, as a rogue bent on shirking his responsibilities. Lydia Forrest, the protagonist of chapter 10, repeatedly confronted the nightmare of misrecognition. She fought to elevate her moral standing by becoming a Jehovah's Witness but was seen by child protection agents as an inept parent. When the authorities included her name in a statewide roster of alleged child abusers, she was unable to secure legitimate employment—this after years of trying to escape the dreaded welfare system. Towanda Forrest, her daughter, aimed at being a mother and respected adult but was treated as a delinquent. Such examples show how symbolic violence disfigures social interactions and brings about unintended consequences.

Because of their vulnerability, children are especially susceptible to misrecognition, and although there is a paucity of research on this subject, they too are capable of wielding alternate identities to resist the pressures wielded by powerful individuals and institutions. Little Floyd Twigg is emblematic of that process. I turn to his story in the next chapter.

7 LITTLE FLOYD

IN MY MIND'S EYE I CAN STILL SEE HIM: A SMALL BOY OF ABOUT SIX, peeking out from behind his great-grandmother's legs, smiling, his green eyes flashing. On the evening of August 20, 1990, when I first met him, Floyd Mitchell Twigg Jr. was attending a birthday party at 952 Callow Street in honor of his cousin, Towanda. The scent of fried chicken and collard greens filled the tiny room where relatives laughed and chatted in a vibrant cadence. Among the faces in various shades of brown, Little Floyd stood out for his golden complexion and light brown hair. His features were those of a blanched Benin sculpture. There was an air of sweetness about him. I had never seen such an exquisite child.

Little Floyd Twigg was the youngest of three babies delivered in rapid succession by Benita Wallace, herself only nineteen at the time of his birth in March 1984. For several months she had ignored her latest pregnancy, preoccupied and worn out as she was by the care of her two girls—Melinda, then three, and Clarise, who had not yet celebrated her second birthday. Big Floyd Twigg, the children's father was almost a year younger than she was, and although he would shortly receive a high school diploma, he had no stable job or means of support. Benita didn't know whether she wanted to stay with him. Three years earlier it had made her proud to think that she could attract such a good-looking boy. Floyd had made her feel beautiful and important. An orphan since the age of three, she had lacked confidence and trust. For a while then, she had been happy. Now, she wasn't so sure.

Things were easier when she was still living with Missie, her grandmother. It was Missie who took care of the infant Melinda while Benita faked going to school, instead running the streets in search of free weed and bourbon. On the other hand, living with her grandma had a downside—with Missie always being on her case, checking her every step, yelling to make her behave. Shortly after Benita's second daughter, Clarise, was born, and fed up with Missie's nagging, Benita had moved into a small apartment in one of the high-rise buildings at the George Murphy complex. At first she was ecstatic. With Floyd visiting several nights a week, it was almost like having a home all to herself. But her feelings of independence had soon faded.

Being on her own was hard. Most of the time, she was alone with the children while Floyd finished school and tried to keep a part-time job at the Atlas Storage Company. Increasingly, she sought respite outside the suffocating enclosure of the projects. She yearned for the carefree days when she had roamed about without worries. She wanted to recover the joyous sensation, to "keep the party going." And the means to do so were readily available. It only took a moment to leave the rundown apartment and arrive at one of many street corners where pleasure awaited for a small price. Pleasure, however, lasted but a brief moment, spinning her life out of control. Perplexed and sullen, Big Floyd was left alone in the apartment, changing diapers and complaining bitterly about Benita's escapades. Often, Melinda and Clarise had to fend for themselves without food or supervision.

By the time Little Floyd was born, Benita had ceased to care. Indifferent to her pregnancy, she hadn't sought medical attention. She dialed 911 only when the pangs of labor roused her to consciousness. Minutes later she was rushed to the emergency room of a local hospital. Booze and drugs had numbed her senses, yet she had something to say at the time of her son's birth. It became part of the family lore that when she first saw the newborn Floyd, Benita had flung her head away in revulsion. The boy was too pale for comfort: "Who that child?" she had demanded, "He too white, he not mine, get that boy out of my face!" Her aunt, Lydia and Missie, her grandmother, had laughed out loud, understanding that Benita was joking. All the same, her words set a tone for the boy's life with consequences they would have to confront years later.

After giving birth, Benita returned to her apartment and to three more years of struggle in pursuit of normalcy. In the mornings she would wake up, restless and weak, and drag herself out from under the soiled blankets to make sure her babies were still breathing: "I was scared, you know, they was goin' to die in my sleep." She then inspected the cupboards and refrigerator hoping to find something to feed them. Once a week, she walked down to the corner store, where the patient Korean owner let her have a few groceries on credit. Her children's diet consisted mostly of dry cereal with or without milk, soda pop, and potato or corn chips. Now and then, Missie brought her leftovers. Hungrily, the children ate whatever was available, and although there was little dignity left in Benita's life, she made sure they had plenty, even if nothing remained for her. It was a small but meaningful gesture. "I try to be a good mother," she said, "even if no one pays no attention."

Most difficult was the end of the month, after the welfare check had been spent and the days ahead stretched out desperately. She would then walk over to her Aunt Lydia's home. Although she didn't approve of Benita's behavior, Lydia could always be relied upon for a few emergency dollars. After all, Benita was family, and Lydia was the self-appointed matriarch of her extended kin network.

Lydia lived at 19 Goodyear Street with her husband, James, and three of her five children. Her home was a small two-storied structure wedged between identical boarded-up houses whose fronts were overlaid with graffiti. She knew that local gangsters used one of the abandoned buildings as a safe haven and shooting gallery. She kept her mouth shut for fear of reprisal, but she thought the whole thing was a damn shame—many youngsters, including her own, lived on the same block. It terrified her to think they were in constant danger.

With dogged resolve, Lydia had done wonders with her rented quarters. The paint was peeling off the walls and the heating system didn't work properly, but her immaculate living room bore evidence of middle-class yearnings. It was there, sitting on the floridly upholstered sofa, that Benita would wait for her aunt to rescue her yet again. In due time, Lydia would open her purse, lips clenched in disgust, to dispense the twenty-dollar bill that allowed her niece to live for a few more days.

Little Floyd lived with his mother and father in the Murphy Homes less than four years, but he had many memories of his early days. Those recollections may not have been entirely his own but the product of repeated conversations with his two older sisters, Melinda and Clarise. He would giggle and twitter upon recalling his childhood adventures.

Left to their devices, the three children concocted dramas in which relatives and acquaintances unknowingly took part. Television offered a bounty of ideas. They liked cartoons and *Sesame Street* and *Mr. Rogers*, but mostly they enjoyed making up stories and reenacting them for the benefit of the unsuspecting bystander.

Because Little Floyd was so pretty and so young, Melinda and Clarise thought it was fun to dress him up as a girl and introduce him to people as their half-sister, Lisa. Even Mrs. Johnson, the kindly neighbor who regularly looked after the three siblings, hadn't caught on at first. "My, oh my! Don't you look fine," she had exclaimed one Sunday morning upon seeing Lisa all decked up in cheap organza. "We goin' to church," Melinda had explained. That had bewildered Mrs. Johnson who knew churchgoing was not a regular practice at the Wallace household.

In truth, the children were headed for the playground where they were planning to test their ploy on other youngsters. Days later, when asked whether Lisa would be back, they had lied again, zealously guarding their secret. "She be back soon," Little Floyd answered. He felt very close to his sisters when he became Lisa.

Every now and then, life took a menacing turn. Once, Little Floyd and the girls had watched through a door slightly ajar how Marvin Cook, who occupied a nearby apartment, was arrested. He had been thrown up against a wall with arms akimbo while an officer patted down his sides looking for evidence. After that, Floyd and his sisters would play a game of hide-and-seek that always concluded with a police-like search of the loser's body. Even years later, the boy thought that the verb "to search" had everything to do with police activity. He had never heard the word used in any other way or context.

Another time, while he was in the playground, Floyd had seen an older boy being chased and then shot repeatedly. "It was so funny," he recounted, "Every time he took a bullet, he shook and bended, jus' like he was dancin'. We was all laughing." The event was horrifying, but his humor was real. He laughed also when recalling a night when he decided to heat up some soup. His parents and sisters were asleep so he went to the kitchen alone. He lit up a match and turned the gas pilot. The match went out and he lit another one, unintentionally setting the stove ablaze. He could still see Big Floyd running naked out the door. It had been a thrill!

Occasionally, he had been overwhelmed by fright, like the day when he and his two sisters couldn't get back into the locked apartment and almost got caught in gunfire along the narrow corridor, before reaching Mrs. Johnson's door. Little Floyd had been so terrified that he had wet his underpants. It had been his sisters' turn to laugh.[1]

As with other publicly subsidized housing projects throughout the nation, the George Murphy Homes were erected in the aftermath of controversy.[2] Originally envisioned as places to host moderate and low-income families, they were rapidly compromised by political pragmatists and became the redoubt of concentrated poverty. Funding was further restricted by conflicts over the use of public land and disagreements over wasteful handouts to unproductive families. Built in the heart of the ghetto, the George Murphy Homes absorbed and intensified every problem found in the adjoining streets.

With reduced acreage on which to board the poor, developers used the designs of visionaries like Le Corbusier, the French architect who perfected the skyscraper in the 1940s and '50s. In affluent neighborhoods, towering structures of steel, mortar, and glass reflected a taste for aesthetic simplicity. In America's inner cities, similar designs produced vertical constructions to warehouse the poor. Unable to expand laterally, the buildings went upward. Crowded and meagerly financed by housing authorities, they fell into disrepair soon after being erected. Inhabited by a majority of families with children, the high-rises gradually became contested territories for youthful gangs. Small apartments, some of them vacant, turned into points of refuge or danger. Rickety elevators were at the mercy of inventive adolescents who crippled them as part of their tactical moves. Drug dealers occupied the playgrounds. In Baltimore, when the summer heat became stifling, children of all ages poured out from the Murphy towers into the backstreets in search of respite and excitement. It was then that conflict was most likely to erupt.

In the 1980s, the Murphy Homes were commonly dubbed "the Valley of Death." Between January and December 1987, more than fifty tenants met a violent end, mostly as a result of gunshot wounds—the highest incidence of violence in public housing projects throughout the nation. Tenants living in the lower floors of the high-rises or in the small brick houses along Edmondson Street faced special threats. Fearful mothers slept on the floor with their small children close by, hoping to evade errant bullets. No taxi driver in his right mind accepted calls from residents in the area. This avoidance created opportunities for a small but burgeoning industry of gypsy cabs. In the evening's dark hours and in the summer months, however, even those were hard to find. Most people stayed home at night, except for the urban warriors, youngsters in bands and crews, whose powerful presence reverberated in the dark. The horror of it all was quietly captured in stickers pasted on many windows and doors at the Murphy Homes; they read, "guns killing us = genocide."

Still, like most children, Little Floyd and his sisters took their surroundings for granted—the boarded-up houses, the winding alleyways, the empty lots, the potholes, the severed tubing left unused along the sidewalk, the leaking water pumps, the graffiti-laden walls; all presented creative possibilities. They explored and reimagined their environment and turned it into a set for their youthful dramas. Little Floyd had no other points of reference: those landmarks represented normality. With his sisters he stood apart, sharing secrets and memories, reinterpreting chaos as adventure and mistaking physical decay for theater.

In the winter of 1987, Little Floyd was separated from his older siblings and declared a child in need of assistance by the Department of Child Protective Services. He remembered the event vividly. Benita, his mother, hadn't been around for days. Big Floyd was working late. The heating system was on the blink, and it was snowing. Then, the lights went out. In the dark, Little Floyd and his sisters pushed a mattress against a corner, where it felt warmer, and hid under the blankets hugging each other. It must have been around eight when they heard Felicia Forrest, their cousin, banging at the door. Next thing they knew, they were all in their Aunt Lydia's house and she was calling the authorities. The following day, a social worker had shown up to discuss new living arrangements. Melinda, Clarise, and young Floyd never went back to the Murphy Homes. In fact, they never again lived together for any length of time.

Margaret Forrest, Lydia's younger sister, a sweet widow with a drinking problem, wanted Melinda to come live with her in Prince Georges County. Her children were older now and living away from home. She wanted to take care of the girl, see to her every need, send her to school, making sure she wore nice clothes. Melinda had suffered enough, she thought. Margaret's yearning, however, was the fruit of loneliness, and she would soon regret her decision.

Lydia, who had taken care of Clarise before, was willing to assume custody of the girl now, but no, she would not be responsible for Little Floyd. Her house was small, and besides, she wasn't sure about the boy. That pretty smile of his had never fooled her, no sir. "He sneaky," she complained. "Never done tell the truth in his whole life. He's poison." Little Floyd smiled ruefully at his great aunt's disapproval. For a long time, he remained in limbo.

For the first month after his hasty removal from the only home he had known, Little Floyd stayed with Missie, his great-grandmother. She was a soft-spoken woman, originally from Greensboro, South Carolina, who never missed a religious function. Although he missed his sisters, Little Floyd just loved his grandma's cooking and the way she fussed over him, especially on Sundays. He didn't appreciate the long services but he liked the choir's singing and the rousing sermons. Maybe, he said, "some day I grow up and become a preacher."

If she had been younger, Missie could have been persuaded to take permanent care of Little Floyd, but she was getting on in years and, with her sciatica flaring up, she couldn't imagine becoming a mother again. She had already raised her three children and two of her grandchildren. She was tired. She therefore tried to keep her distance from the little boy who lit up when he saw her and seemed forlorn when she was absent.

Two months later, a social worker arrived in Missie's house: a foster home for Little Floyd was now available. He went to live with Ramona Brown and four other children, two of whom were her own. Alysia Cardigan, Floyd's case manager, thought this was a happy arrangement because Mrs. Brown lived in the same neighborhood. Relatives would be able to stay in touch with the boy. That, unfortunately, didn't work out as planned. In the months ahead, the boy faced isolation, boredom, and occasional mortification. Mrs. Brown was less than hospitable to visitors, especially on those rare occasions when Benita Wallace, high on crack and whiskey, arrived unannounced. By then Big Floyd had left her and moved in with his sister, Boo, who lived on the 1700 block of Ashburton Street. It wasn't often that he could find a ride to visit his son.

Abandoned, the boy became restless and hungry for attention. At first, Mrs. Brown didn't understand what was going on: things were getting lost; small amounts of money were disappearing. Tyrone, one of the older boys, thought Floyd was a thief. Floyd denied all accusations, developing, little by little, an oddly confrontational style. His excuses were not convincing but he stuck to them, building on a simple idea, incessantly contradicting every imputation, drowning the accuser's voice in his own nasal dribble, which may or may not have been a symptom of fetal alcohol syndrome, the result of his mother's drinking while she was pregnant with him.

The boy, Mrs. Brown concluded, was unmanageable. She began to negotiate his transfer. That was how, a few months later, Floyd went to live with Lucille Enfield, whose home was situated on Carlisle Avenue in Lower Park Heights, farther than ever from the Forrest, Wallace, and Twigg families. Little Floyd occupied a large room with two bunk beds where three other youngsters slept. At thirteen, Maurice Thompson, the oldest of the group, had been in Mrs. Enfield's care since he was five. Jarred and Culver Pentwood, nine-year-old twins, had been assigned to her as toddlers. Lucille Enfield was a no-nonsense disciplinarian. The boys had fared well under her observant eye and they were sure to set a good example for Floyd. Yet it may have been at the Enfield home that Little Floyd was sexually molested for the first time.

Nothing was ever confirmed. Years later, when his behavior led many to wonder about his childhood experiences, Little Floyd would change his story every time he was asked. He told his mother, Benita, that Maurice had teased him, saying he looked like a girl, and that he had fondled his private parts to make sure he was a boy. He told his sisters all that was a lie; he just didn't like Maurice "'cause he was too bossy." He may have fabricated the story, or, having told the truth at first, he may have wanted later to protect the older boy and himself. He may have been ashamed to admit his weakness or eager to gain sympathy. There was no way to know.

Little Floyd lived in the Enfield home for almost two years, during which he rarely saw his own family. He remembered attending a birthday party at the house of his great-grandmother, Missie, on Callow Street, the day I first met him. Most of the time, he was lonely. The Murphy Homes had been scary, but in the company of his two sisters, he had known safety. He didn't feel safe anymore. "Miss Enfield was awright," he told me once, "but I din't care for the place, it was borin." Boredom may have concealed his fear and disappointment.

By the age of seven, Floyd had lived in three different homes and attended even more schools. Always the newcomer, and striking in appearance, he endured other youngsters ganging up on him. He had been called every derogatory name in the book: "high-yellow dog," "half-breed," "quadroon," "mongrel," "White devil," "milky way." It was painful always to be cast as an outsider, neither Black nor White.

Under such circumstances, Little Floyd refined his survival strategies. He would smile gently at the hurling of insults and pretend the ugliness wasn't there. He didn't mind, anyway; it was all a joke. If the assault persisted, he repeated incoherent sentences in an endless monotone to dim the voices until there was silence. When there was silence, he knew he had won.

He said he didn't care if people didn't like him. With his need for acceptance set aside, Floyd didn't have incentives to do anything in particular. He reacted on impulse, without fear of consequences. Feeling betrayed, he did not develop honor or loyalties. For amusement, he played tricks on his foster brothers, taking their things and hiding them. Tyrone's money would magically appear in Culver's pockets, and trinkets that belonged to Culver found their way into a box where Jarred kept his property. No one was fooled. When reprimanded, Little Floyd offered ingratiating smiles and feeble explanations. He never admitted to anything but he thrived when he was the center of attention.

In 1992, shortly before the beginning of the new academic year, Big Floyd, who was now living with Iliad Hardwick, his pregnant girlfriend, finally obtained custody of his son. He also made plans for the boy to attend the Community School of the Holy Spirit, a parochial school in the Waverly District, where Clarise, Little Floyd's older sister had been enrolled for the past year.[3] The building was nice and clean, and he liked the uniform. Little Floyd was filled with anticipation about seeing his big sister every day. It didn't matter that, having been held back the year before, he would have to start the second grade well past his eighth birthday

For the next four years and despite daunting obstacles, Floyd persisted at the Holy Spirit School. On the term's first day, he looked grand in his navy-blue trousers, azure polo shirt, and patent-leather shoes, but from the outset, the teachers noticed his lack of basic skills. By midday, he looked rumpled. His shoelaces were never properly tied. Most of the time, he couldn't remember where he had put his knapsack, or his pencil, or his notebook. The other children made fun of him. Kisha Roberts, a pugnacious little girl, complained that she had caught Floyd rubbing his genitals. He made noise when he ate and never left the lunchroom without stains on his shirt. He sought comfort by humming softly while Mrs. Rivers, a humorless biddy, tried to teach her spelling class.

From the teachers' vantage point, the most disturbing aspect of Floyd's behavior was what they saw as his refusal to do homework. They complained bitterly to me, interpreting his conduct as insolence. Maybe he didn't belong at Holy Spirit, they said. Yet every morning, the boy swore he had completed his assignment. His green eyes filled with tears when scolded. Why didn't Mrs. Rivers believe him? He was trying as hard as he could. Really, he was.

It took only a couple of long visits to Floyd's classroom to realize what was happening. Before attending Holy Spirit, the boy had been enrolled in public schools where expectations were low and variable . In those settings, homework consisted of mimeographed sheets with printed questions that the students answered in the classroom before the end of the school day. Teachers knew that assignments taken home were almost never completed. Parents were seldom available to provide assistance to their children. Under such circumstances, homework was a simple operation. You answered the questions, raised your hand, gave your sheet to the teacher, and you were done.

At Holy Spirit, homework involved multiple tasks. While giving instructions, teachers wrote questions on the blackboard for pupils to copy into their notebooks. Students needed strong motor skills and coordination to write down questions and good auditory faculties to capture nuance and detail. After that, they had to remember which of several notebooks to take with them at the end of the school day. At home, they were expected to ask for help from a caregiver and to make sure that he or she initialed the completed homework before placing it, the next morning, at the right spot on the teacher's desk.

In other words, at Holy Spirit, homework entailed a minimum of seven decision-making points and actions. Newly arrived and relying on past experience, Little Floyd thought that he had finished his assignment after copying the questions from the blackboard into his notebook. Even that was difficult. Not having been exposed to equivalent tasks, his hand-eye alignment was deficient. He wrote at a slow pace and awkwardly. The results were unintelligible. He simply hadn't learned what it took to succeed at such a simple exercise. We forget how difficult it is to master efficacious school habits at an early age. Little Floyd's teachers had misrecognized the problem, assuming that the boy was lying.

Schools in Floyd's past had been little more than custodial operations. At Holy Spirit, academic standards were high and the moral impulse was strong. If students didn't do a proper job, teachers concluded it was because they were morally deficient, weak-minded, or both. Little Floyd had migrated from the instructional netherworld into educational purgatory. He tried anyway, addressing constant criticism with forbearance.

Early in the school year, he was happy to learn that a new sibling was on its way. Big Floyd and Iliad were going to have a baby. When she arrived, Shatyria Twigg-Hardwick turned out to be a big girl with a noisy chortle. The day of her birth, Little Floyd had spent several hours practicing spelling. Even on his way to the hospital, for a first visit, he kept repeating the word buffalo. It had taken him a week to remember the proper order of the letters but he beamed with new joy as he handed over the balloons and box of chocolates to the infant's mother. B-u-f-f-a-l-o, he recited proudly. Small victories like that mattered to Little Floyd in those days.

Iliad Hardwick and her daughter left the maternity ward on November 10, 1993. All at once, the small flat on Rosedale Road became a home. The baby slept with her parents. Young Floyd took over the living room. They lived on the top floor of what once had been a detached family house. Although small, the flat had large windows that flooded the interior with sunlight even in the late afternoon. There was a television, and Floyd could get lost in reverie while watching his favorite programs. He liked *The Simpsons* best.

He longed for attention more than ever, but Iliad, who had initially supported Big Floyd's efforts to reclaim his son, now found the boy irksome. He was always in the way, looking silly, asking to have dinner, calling for help with his homework. With growing regularity, Little Floyd was sent away to other places. The situation worsened when, unable to meet rental payments for three consecutive months, Big Floyd and his family were evicted.

Shuffled about, the boy stilled his desire for personal belongings and tenderness. He had been just another passing shadow as a foster child. Limited by bureaucratic regulations and indifference, the women in charge had kept their distance from him. Moving back and forth between his father, Aunt Boo, and Lydia Forrest, who disapproved of him, he never acquired a feeling of place or connection. His toys and clothes were as scattered as his spirit. Often, he could not find what he wanted to wear or play with. Adrift, he disguised frustration with apathy. When offered a present at Christmas, even one he had claimed to want more than anything else in the world, he accepted it cheerfully only to abandon it permanently moments later. He assumed that nothing and no one belonged to him. Once in a while he would tell me, "See, if you don' want somethin', then you don't miss it when it's not around." His logic broke one's heart.

And yet he forged ahead. When he was first tested at his parochial school, Little Floyd's scores placed him in the lowest fourteenth percentile of his national cohort. Within the next year, he had gained twenty points. He learned to spell properly and write clearly, and he knew the names and capitals of the fifty states in the nation. His favorite subject was math. Mrs. Rivers, the teacher who had tormented him in the second grade, was impressed by the boy's progress. "He reads beautifully now, and he does his homework," she admitted.

Best of all, Floyd was beginning to make friends. On his ninth birthday, he even had a party. Nearly twenty boys and girls came. No one other than his relatives had ever brought him presents or well-wishing cards. He waltzed around musical chairs, pinned the tail on a cardboard donkey, and bobbed for apples like all the other children. When he blew out the candles on his birthday cake, Little Floyd almost seemed happy.

Now, he experienced bouts of creativity. At his Aunt Boo's, he tried to enlist other youngsters into his playacting. He needed them for a congregation when he stood behind a toy microphone pretending to be Reverend Twigg delivering forceful sermons. His cousins didn't care for his antics, but they humored him. Mostly, Floyd preached by himself in the living room. In his aunt's closet, he found a veritable mine for the imagination: makeup, two wigs—one the same color as his hair—a leather skirt, blouses and slacks, stiletto heels, and the gown and veil that Boo had worn at her wedding, almost twenty years earlier. Her marriage had ended long ago, but she hadn't had the heart to toss out the ceremonial garments.

It took Floyd no time at all to transform his appearance with bits and pieces of the newly found treasure. He could become a bride or pretend he was the gorgeous Whitney Houston, his favorite singer. That was a way to recall the comforting games he had played with his sisters when he was small. When he turned into beguiling Lisa he had no problems and was loved by everyone.

Despite such attempts at coping, his life remained hazardous, especially after school hours. Little Floyd was never sure where he would end up on weekends. Boo's house was the haven of last resort. On Friday afternoons, he would climb up the front steps of her home and, upon entering the house, he would drop his knapsack on the floor, forgetting about it until the following Monday when he picked it up again on his way to school. His aunt, who had problems of her own, placed no demands on him and wasn't always around. Although spacious, her place was old and grimy.

One Monday morning, the teachers at Holy Spirit had been horrified to see hundreds of cockroaches crawling out of Floyd's book bag. A stale sandwich had attracted them over the weekend. The other children had been agog with contempt and laughter. Floyd was mortified. Jason Clark, a boy who had been his friend until then, taunted him with nonsensical tunes in the days ahead: "Roach Boy, Roach Boy, you mother is a crackhead and you father, he's a rat." Feigning disinterest, Floyd retreated again into a world apart where the judgment of others wouldn't touch him.

By the beginning of the fifth grade, he was better organized and his vocabulary had expanded beyond every expectation. After school, he would sit at my kitchen table to do his homework or read a book—the two middle fingers of his right hand reflectively touching his forehead. Taller now and slender, he turned heads as he walked down the street. One winter day, while we were shopping for tapes along Greenmount Avenue under heavy clothing, a clerk complimented him loudly thinking Floyd was a girl. He apologized in flustered embarrassment after realizing his mistake, but his glances revealed lingering doubts.

Then, shortly after Floyd's eleventh birthday, calamity struck again. He was at Boo's house over a weekend when Marcus Campbell, an adult neighbor, lured him to a nearby park. He first showed him photographs of naked boys. He then exposed his testicles and asked Floyd to feel them. He stroked the boy's body and kissed his lips. All this, Floyd claimed, had happened very quickly. He pushed the man aside and rushed back home to tell Boo. His aunt called the police. Several times, the boy repeated the story in the presence of social workers, counselors, and the police officers assigned to his case. For a change, he was the center of sympathetic attention. When he saw the police dragging Marcus Campbell away in handcuffs, the boy knew he wasn't completely powerless.

The frightening incident at the park temporarily filled Floyd with a sense of self-importance, but that didn't last. Soon afterward, his teachers noticed a change in behavior. He was regressing to the state of his early days at Holy Spirit. His attention span became shorter, his humming resumed, his grades declined. Even more alarming, he now took a hostile attitude toward other children. One day, while waiting for her mother, a girl had dashed back into the school with fear in her face after being hounded by Floyd. The teachers suspected he was stealing money from his classmates. In response to his acts of quiet disruption, the principal separated him from the other youngsters. He spent the last few weeks of the academic term sitting for several hours alone, behind a desk outside his classroom.

At about the same time, and after a long period of residential instability, Iliad Hardwick was authorized to occupy a unit in Flag House, a publicly subsidized building on the margins of Little Italy. Little Floyd went back to live with her and his father. For a while, the family achieved feelings of normalcy despite the inhospitable environment. At night, the shouting of brawling neighbors kept Iliad awake. Even if the guard at the gate knew your name, she would not allow you to enter the building without first demanding to see proper identification. Loaded with grocery bags one Saturday morning, Iliad had to wait for Little Floyd to bring down her driver's license, which she had forgotten at the last minute. The elevator was not working. It had taken the boy more than fifteen minutes to find the card and walk down the stairs from the twelfth floor.

At home, Little Floyd strove to be unobtrusive and helpful. Iliad relied on him to babysit for little Shatyria, but her trust was shattered one day when she unexpectedly returned from a trip to the corner store to find the boy pulling down Shatyria's underpants on the living room sofa. Terrified by her anger, Floyd swore he was only trying to help the baby go to the bathroom. Iliad did not believe him. She hit him hard with a belt. A month elapsed before the boy was allowed back into her apartment.

Despite every setback, they stuck together, and in the summer of 1995, Floyd Mitchell Twigg Sr. and Iliad Hardwick were married. They were expecting their second child, and best of all, after years of perseverance, Floyd had secured custody of his oldest daughter, Melinda, who was now past her fourteenth birthday. He was also holding two jobs, one as a janitor at the Johns Hopkins University and another one as a security guard. The family was about to move into a newly built house on the 1100 block of Pratt Street, close to the Baltimore & Ohio Museum. This was still public housing, but the place had three floors, including a basement, two bedrooms, a backyard, and a charming wrought-iron gate. It felt like a real home.

Melinda Twigg, who had been living in Prince Georges County with her Aunt Margaret, rejoined her father and his new wife in Baltimore. Despite Margaret's early intentions, the girl had turned out to be a big disappointment. By the age of ten, all that she wanted was to become pregnant and have a baby. She regularly disappeared in the middle of the night. She was disrespectful and had no interest in school. It hadn't helped things that Margaret, although sincere, was inconsistent in her demands and quick to still her own pain with whisky.

None of this mattered to Big Floyd who was elated to have his daughter back. Iliad was the first to suggest that the two older children occupy the basement of the new house. The bedrooms in the top floor would belong to the couple, their daughter Shatyria and a new baby girl whom they named Persia. This made sense, Iliad pointed out, because the basement was spacious. It had room for the sort of things that teenagers like—stereo systems and play stations. Melinda and Floyd could be as noisy as they wanted without disturbing the neighbors.

Little Floyd and Melinda saw it differently. They interpreted their confinement to the basement as a machination to keep them out of sight. It was clear to them that their father loved the new babies more than he loved them. That led them to conspire, subverting their diminished status and vying for protagonism. Late at night, after the lights were out, they would don their finest garments and quietly dash out the back door on their way to Chuck E. Cheese, at the Inner Harbor, to see friends and meet new admirers.

Melinda took the lead. She favored casual wear: T-shirts, tight jeans, and, instead of sneakers, high-heeled pumps. Little Floyd, who was thinner, thought he looked best in short skirts, tank tops, and sandals. Both became experts in the use of makeup. They polished each other's fingernails. In Floyd's case, the final touch was one of the wigs stolen from Aunt Boo's drawer. He used different names when giving out his phone number to new acquaintances. That way he could always tell who was calling him back.

It had dawned on him that he was not a boy but "a girl trapped in a boy's body." For the past year, daytime television had been replete with discussions of sexual indeterminacy; that may be how he acquired the words to make sense of his circumstance. He wanted to fit in, to be more like his older sisters, to mute the discordance between his body and those of the women around him. He also wanted to shock his father into awareness. Most important of all, he had arrived at a new realization: as a boy he had no power, but as a gorgeous girl he could have men at his beck and call.

Already in the throes of early adolescence, Floyd reviewed his options: "I'm not gay," he told me emphatically, "I don' wanna grow up an' be gay 'cause nobody's gonna love me. I'm a girl and then I be a woman." To be truly feminine removed the edges of an ambiguous identity. He would thus erase the hurts of the past and move into a space of clarity and acceptance.

Iliad was indifferent to Floyd's and Melinda's infractions. The two babies took up most of her time. She planned to go back to school and hoped to get a job with the Housing Authority. The older children, she told herself, were Big Floyd's responsibility, not hers. Big Floyd found the new developments hard to understand or manage. The nightly escapades worried him the most. He knew the route to the harbor was filled with danger. What were those crazy children thinking, anyway?

Then again, he was aghast at his son's changed appearance: "There never been faggots in my family, and tha's the truth." he protested, "That boy better come back to his senses before he gets hisself killed." The words rang cruel in Little Floyd's ears. He wanted his father to love him like he loved his other daughters.

By then, young Floyd had virtually dropped out of school. Plotting with his older sister consumed most of his days. Of the two, he had the larger number of boyfriends. He could spend hours at the shops in Mondawmin Mall, trying on clothes and riffling through custom jewelry. He was planning to have his ears pierced as soon as he got some real money. His hair had grown out and, with the help of extensions, it touched his shoulders. He wore it braided with beads for adornment. How comforting to at last be the receiver of men's gentle favors. He found out that boyfriends could be generous.

It is not clear how or when Little Floyd slid from flirtation into prostitution or whether he ever engaged in deliberate solicitation. He took the position that the presents and cash he received from men were testimonies of admiration, not payment for services rendered. As he said, "There's nothin' wrong by me getting gifts. It makes them happy to make me happy. They jus' boyfriends."

Throughout the summer of 1995, Baltimore had been abuzz with the impending visit of Pope John Paul II, scheduled to occur in early October. He was the first prelate of his stature to pay the city such an honor. A vapor of pieties filled the air. Down in the material world, Big Floyd wrestled with torn feelings about his child: "He my only boy, you know; he look more like me than the other children. I care for him no matter what." The day that the Camden Yards Stadium filled with multitudes of Catholics seeking a glimpse of the Pope, Big Floyd was trying to make sense of his son's life.

In search of professional help, he eventually found it in the office of Stephen Peters, a therapist who specialized in family dysfunction. Iliad and young Floyd joined him on his first visit. After a short interrogation, Dr. Peters concluded that Little Floyd's problems were being caused by a breakdown of patriarchal control. "What I see here," he disclosed, "is a youngster who thinks he can do anything he wants. What are you going to do, dad, so that your son will obey you?" Big Floyd didn't know what to say. He sat paralyzed, trying in vain to find the right words.

The consultation yielded no useful results but Little Floyd had an instructive postmortem:

> That doctor, he don't know what he's talking about. . . . Like when he aks my father what he's gonna do; he can't do nothin', but Big Floyd, he thought the doctor was tellin' him to beat me up.

Differences in status and experience had led to misunderstandings. Hitting was not part of Dr. Peters's therapeutic repertory, but he could not make sense of the situation at hand. He believed that parents retain authority over children by creating incentives and enforcing penalties. If young Floyd was acting up, it was because his father had been too lenient. Let Big Floyd now curtail the boy's privileges to extract from him greater compliance.

All this had little to do with the circumstances surrounding Little Floyd's family. His father was not in a position to enforce a code of behavior. Corporal punishment was an option, but Big Floyd had a gentle disposition; he would have never struck his son, no matter who told him to do so. The unacknowledged problem was that he didn't have the means to implement incentives or withdraw recompense. Even the boy knew that his father was no suburban "dad."

There were few more opportunities for psychological exploration. The conflict between father and son escalated. Late in 1996, Little Floyd left the house on Pratt Street and moved in with Lester Moore, a twenty-four-year-old man who did not have a job but was never without cash. "He adores me," Floyd told me, relishing the newly found expression. Lester indulged his every whim and, mysteriously, made hormones available for Little Floyd to grow breasts. In bliss, he changed his name to Jasmine.

A few months later, he showed up at my door with a bruised face. Lester had punched him in a fit of jealousy. No, he wouldn't go back to him, but he didn't want to stay with Benita, his mother, either.

He moved around from place to place, recording loving messages on the voicemail devices of relatives and friends; I contorted in pain every time I heard his voice filtering out of my telephone. Mostly, Floyd ran the streets. After all, he had never had a home to call his own; bouncing about was all he had known throughout his young life.

Things weren't going well for his father, either. It had taken Big Floyd several years to reunite with his children. Even as he was beginning to succeed, his family was splintering again. Shortly after his son's departure, he had discovered that Iliad, his wife, was involved with the man who had hired her to clean offices at the Housing Authority. Desperate and angry, Floyd had threatened her and her lover with a knife. In retaliation, Iliad threw him out of the house. He had gone around in a circle and was back where he had started.

Little Floyd heard about his father's latest misfortunes while visiting his Aunt Lydia one Sunday afternoon. "It's a damn shame," the woman said, "Big Floyd never knew how to keep a woman. He gone for good now, leeching off his sister Boo, as usual." Melinda was back with Aunt Margaret. Sitting at Lydia's kitchen table, eating scrambled eggs and sausage, Little Floyd felt pangs of guilt and a renewed caring for his father. Perhaps if he and Melinda had behaved better, Iliad wouldn't have been so mad at Big Floyd. Now he wanted to make his father feel better, to ask in his own way for his forgiveness.

That night, he roamed the streets looking for a place to leave testimony of his feelings. From an acquaintance, he borrowed a can of spray paint. Big Floyd was amazed the next morning when, in transit to a new job, he saw several walls along Pennsylvania Avenue overlaid with large yellow letters that read

Big Floyd I love you.

You son Little Floyd. Remember me always.

    I AM I AM I AM

At least for the time being, the boy had had the last word.

8

DOWN THE RABBIT HOLE: CHILDHOOD AGENCY AND THE PROBLEM OF LIMINALITY

LITTLE FLOYD WAS STILL LIVING IN WEST BALTIMORE IN 2014. HE WAS then twenty-eight and had never completed high school or held a regular job. He runs the streets and hustles, but he has never spent more than a few days in jail, once for disturbing the peace and once for trespassing. "That was a mistake," he tells me. It was his friend Lamont who invited him to enter the house in question while the owners were on vacation. Floyd was unaware that Lamont didn't have permission to be there. As for disturbing the peace, Floyd swears that too was a misunderstanding. He was just high one night and apparently singing and screaming too loudly for one of his neighbor's comfort; she had called the police. Floyd is never responsible for anything that happens to him. He always has an excuse. Someone else is always to blame. That's the way he copes.

Floyd lives off the generosity of strangers, relatives, and friends. He likes weed but doesn't buy other drugs—they're too expensive. He often crashes at the flat of his older sister, Melinda, who is now thirty-two and has four children. At the moment, Floyd and his current love, T-Zee, form a household with Melinda and her brood. T-Zee, a large and gentle soul, works as a butcher and supports Floyd. Melinda takes care of the kids and receives public assistance. Floyd has some fond memories, like the savings account I once opened on his behalf, hoping to steer his dreams in the right direction. He's sorry that didn't work out.

Little Floyd's story illustrates how children, even the most vulnerable, seek to create meaning by using whatever resources are available to them. Buffeted around, criticized and mistrusted, rootless and repeatedly molested, Little Floyd built himself a life out of his only asset: physical beauty. I will leave it to psychologists and psychiatrists to speculate as to whether Floyd's sexual orientation was biologically determined or not. What is relevant, from a sociological point of view, is Floyd's deliberate move to use gender identification: first, to bond with his two older sisters; then, to perform for others in confabulation with the girls; and finally, to form alliances with more powerful men who could confer protection and a means of support.

By using gender identity as a tool to correct external misperceptions, Little Floyd aimed to redefine his own circumstances and gain a measure of control—he tried to adjust a discordance between his own reality and the reality others imposed on him. Little Floyd's story is one of personal agency in a context of severe and multiple destitutions.

Young Floyd's trajectory also illustrates the workings of what Pierre Bourdieu (1991) calls *misrecognition*. Unable to connect with experiences so far removed from their own, teachers at Holy Spirit, Floyd's parochial school, attributed the boy's inability to complete assignments to disobedience. In fact, he was disoriented by his relocation from a public school to a new environment marked by unfamiliar rules and conventions. The teachers at Holy Spirit were White and middle class; their tendency was to naturalize norms and behaviors forged by their own socioeconomic and racial background, and to interpret deviations from those standards as willful malice—a vintage illustration of misrecognition.

Similarly, an encounter with a family therapist, at the request of the boy's father, revealed multiple counts of symbolic violence—the therapist could not apprehend the difficulties faced by impoverished fathers when attempting to discipline their children. Like most of us, he underestimated the extent to which middle-class and affluent families depend on material incentives to shape the attitudes and performance of their offspring. He could not see that the main problem at hand was not just diminished parental authority but a context bereft of resources. Trapped in the moment, interactions between parties endowed with unequal power—like those between the therapist and Big Floyd—erase history and accumulated disadvantage, relying instead on platitudes.

Finally, young Floyd's early biography illustrates the extent to which policies meant to safeguard the integrity and well-being of children often fail to meet their expressed goals. Understaffed and underfunded, laden with regulations, and saddled with suspicions about the ill-conceived intentions of grown-ups, agencies charged with the protection of children are unable to prevent egregious crimes, but they harshly penalize less-serious transgressions.

In this chapter, I explore uncharted territory: the ways in which African American children growing up in segregated neighborhoods process information produced by social service agencies and wield that knowledge to reshape their circumstances. I examine how youngsters interpret and use notions of child abuse. My analysis is positioned at the confluence between personal agency and social structure, between biography and recent history. It shows that children, far from being passive agents, sift through meanings to manage and redefine their status. Many see imputations of child abuse as a way to check adult dominance.

In poor neighborhoods, the underpinnings of parental authority are fragile. When grown men and women have to compete for entry-level jobs barely suited to adolescents, they have a hard time explaining to their children why they should obey them. As youngsters test their wings, often in opposition to parental dictates, mothers and fathers sometimes resort to physical force, a course easily misinterpreted by government agents in liminal institutions.[1] As a result, in areas like West Baltimore, parents fret constantly about the extent to which government measures aimed at protecting children undermine their ability to shelter and discipline their own kids. Beyond the vexing reality it designates, child abuse has become a code for anxieties surrounding the balance of power between children and parents.

The tension between parental intentions and children's interpretations is partly the result of ambiguities surrounding legal concepts wielded by government bureaucracies. At first intended to shield minors from gross injury and patent harm, child abuse has expanded to include an increasing number of conducts. That process mirrors a larger problem of sociological import: the tendency for concepts to spin beyond their original boundaries as they experience diffusion and popularization.

Whether in the legal or academic fields, conceptualization entails the use of familiar terms to designate insufficiently recognized realities. The gradual rupture of consensus about meanings assigned to concepts virtually guarantees that they will lose precision as competing groups vie to fit them to their own situational logic. In the case of terms like "child abuse," deployed by liminal institutions to regulate agency, the results can be contradictory at best and disastrous at worst. Child Protective Services boasts limited results in its attempts to protect children from extreme brutality, but it often trounces parental authority in the name of high-minded principles.

Left to wander without rein, concepts like child abuse mischievously beget multiple meanings, only some of which bear correspondence with actual events and many of which depend exclusively on subjective judgments. In the absence of tight definitions, a wide constellation of behaviors can be construed as child abuse, including spanking, a form of corporal punishment that is legal. The vacuum created by a lack of agreement between intent and attribution is then occupied by concessions to the views of accusers, in this case, teachers, counselors, social workers and, of course, children themselves. Victims, real or imagined, multiply.

Government agencies are left with no alternative but to implement cumbersome administrative procedures and to pursue investigations that interfere with the privacy of individuals and families. This new inquisition inverts normative understandings: the accused are presumed guilty until proven innocent; imputations are transformed into evidence. Parental loss of status, a growing reliance on judicial means to resolve conflict, and the surrendering of an already encroached personal space are the result.

That youngsters endure great suffering, often at the hands of those entrusted with their care, is indisputable as illustrated by Little Floyd's story and a long string of nauseating incidents reported by the media. It is also true that government has a legitimate role in determining the limits of parental privilege and safeguarding the physical integrity of minors. The question is whether existing policies and perceptions of endangerment promote or betray children's interests.

While child abuse designates a harrowing reality in search of better grasp and remedy, I focus here on the way notions of child abuse are understood and used by social workers, parents, and children to signify related but distinct realities. My interest is the figurative meaning of child abuse, especially in relation to the ways children use that term to resist parental control, and the manner in which parents and social workers interpret the same concept to advance their own objectives. My analysis suggests that definitions of child abuse have expanded over time, confounding loyalties and dividing families. I see this as a classic instance of unintended consequences caused by contradictions inherent to the structures and procedures of public service agencies, not by the principles underlying protective legislation.

First, I present a minimal framework highlighting situated knowledge. I provide a sketch of varying outlooks regarding children and abuse over the last century and complement that historical account with a discussion of ambiguities embedded in family law. I also discuss ethnographic data derived from interviews with African American parents in West Baltimore, and supplement them with a few cases drawn from a sample of immigrant parents residing in South Florida.

ALICE IN WEST BALTIMORE

Few writings inspire contemporary musings more often than *Alice's Adventures in Wonderland* (Carroll 1865). Like all tales of enduring power, that story resonates with alternative interpretations of familiar realities. Most of all, *Alice* is about inverted logic and the treacheries of language. In that respect, it offers a parable for our times. As the new century advances, new narratives are emerging about the essence of collective experience in relation to institutional practices. In America's inner cities, institutions tend to be government agencies nearly always interacting with members of racial and ethnic minorities. Offices charged with the protection of children face a nearly impossible mandate—to protect youngsters while facing multiple ambiguities in the language surrounding child abuse.

The lack of linguistic precision matters because, in those settings, child abuse is not defined by a single identifiable deed; it comprises a range of behaviors, from extreme crimes to severe, moderate, and minimal instances of corporal punishment and neglect. Varying interpretations of child abuse are therefore toponomical, that is, they are contingent on the information stored in specific physical locations. Practical knowledge is, for that reason, discontinuous; like Alice moving on the imaginary chessboard, it does not cross bounds without spawning new meanings. The signification of concepts changes according to social and spatial position.

To say that fragmented material spaces affect cognition is not new. Early in the twentieth century, William I. Thomas and Dorothy S. Thomas (1928: 571–572) wrote: "If men define situations as real, they are real in their consequences." Since then, the Thomas Theorem has been central to sociological analysis. Works by Becker (1997), Garfinkel (1991), and Merton (1987) attest to the durability of that insight. What social actors see as real largely depends on where they stand actually and figuratively. So it is with notions of child abuse.[2] Relevant in that respect is to understand how repeated contact with agents of the state gives children new avenues to interpret realities around them and to construe their relation to adults.

Although youngsters have been the subject of developmental psychology and, less frequently, of social psychology (Piaget and Inhelder 1969), they have not been examined until recently for their theoretical import to sociology (Corsaro 2010; Lareau 2011). Writings in the sociology of the family tend to portray children as passive recipients of parental action. That surprises for two reasons. First, children are a main focus of institutional practices and therefore represent what Robert K. Merton called "a strategic research site" (Merton 1987). In my work, children emerge as vital actors processing information and reconstituting positional knowledge.

Second, the conventions and outlooks articulated by social service agents influence children's sense about limits and possibilities—the two-pronged buttress of agency and power. A focus on children and institutions can thus expand our understanding of basic sociological processes.

UNIVERSALIZING CHILD ABUSE

Concerns about the protection of children have fluctuated in agreement with varying definitions of childhood. In the nineteenth century, children were understood to have rights only to the extent that those rights did not interfere with parental privileges. A relatively weak state, the absence of formal welfare programs, and the conceptualization of minors in proprietary terms created conditions in which there was little recourse against maltreatment.

The New York Society for the Prevention of Cruelty to Animals (SPCA) was founded several years before the New York Society for the Prevention of Cruelty of Children (SPCC) (Myers 2006). In a precedent-setting case dating back to 1874, local authorities seeking the removal of a young girl from a dangerous home had to resort to ordinances mandating the protection of horses, given the absence of equivalent legal means to safeguard youngsters (Currie 1997; Wheeler 1991).

Early efforts to protect children centered on labor legislation, gradually checking the excesses of employers regarding compensation and working conditions (Gorn 2002; Hindman 2002; Mufford 1970). During the Progressive era, social workers acting on behalf of children tried to correct dangerous community conditions by engaging culpable or suspect parents in social casework. Government interference in family matters was rare, however, and grounds for intervention required the demonstration of extreme brutality. Concepts concerning emotional or mental injury were nonexistent.

Moreover, corporal punishment did not entail an assumption of violence on the part of parents or other persons fulfilling care-taking, educational, or supervisory functions in loco parentis. That included teachers and employers. At the time, there was no basis on which to cast the relationship between related adults and children in adversarial terms. The belief that sparing the rod spoils the child dates back to the eighteenth century and was part of common beliefs inspired by Judeo-Christian traditions (Proverbs 13: 24). Corporal punishment as a parental entitlement was not seriously challenged until well into the twentieth century.

New ideas about childhood and the limits of parental power were forged in the post–World War II era. A thriving manufacturing economy paralleled the establishment of public agencies dedicated to the promotion of specific interests, including those of minors. During the nineteenth century, moral philosophers had described childhood as a brief stage in the life cycle with the advent of *reason* at about seven years of age—a legacy of clerical thinking in the Catholic Church. Youngsters were conceptualized as diminutive adults in need of humanizing action (Aries 1965). By the 1950s, however, childhood was viewed differently, as a phase extending well beyond the onset of puberty. Under the influence of Sigmund Freud (1920), Anna Freud (1966), Erich Fromm (1941) and Jean Piaget (1928)—and largely thanks to the popularizing efforts of Benjamin Spock (1946/2012)—the child was constructed anew as a tabula rasa upon which society imposed its imprint through the actions of parents, especially mothers. Psychology emerged as the wellspring of expertise in implementing a civilizing endeavor.

This understanding of childhood combined an assumption of undefiled innocence with an enlightened faith in individual potential. The family was required to provide a flexible environment conducive to children's intellectual and emotional development. Parents were discouraged from taking authoritarian stances and urged to act as guides and friends. The family was reconceptualized as a location for democracy and consensus building.

It was also during the post–World War II period that even benign forms of corporal punishment were recast as part of a continuum leading to manifest violence. During the 1960s, other ideological currents further contributed to reshaping notions of childhood. The civil rights movement and the youth revolution brought about the recognition of children as individuals and likely casualties of adult incompetence (Greven 1992).

In short, concerns over children's well-being evolved gradually: first, as part of efforts to protect minors from exploitation in the workplace and, more recently, with a growing focus on the personal rights of children as family members. The tendency has been toward increasing individuation and the framing of parent-children interactions in potentially adversarial terms. The word *abuse* has grown over time to encompass actions, feelings, and collective anxieties, not all of which bear correspondence to the reality that the term seeks to designate; that includes behaviors formerly understood to be legitimate expressions of parental authority, such as corporal punishment.

THE LEGAL PROCESS EXAMINED

Heightened awareness about the plight of children has been reflected in new legislative bodies. In the 1980s, partly as a result of a string of notorious cases involving sexual assault and molestation, definitions and procedures were introduced in public service agencies to systematize intervention. Family law was implemented through administrative channels under the authority of the Department of Social Services and, specifically, through the Bureau of Child Protective Services. Four characteristics distinguished the new laws: (a) an expanded list of punishable actions and related ambiguities in the definitions of abuse and neglect; (b) a guarantee of confidentiality and immunity from civil and criminal prosecution to denouncers and public officials in charge of child protection; (c) the treatment of information collected through interviews as evidence; and (d) the requirement for investigations during limited periods of time to substantiate findings of abuse. I review these features below.

Official definitions of physical and sexual abuse typically begin with an attempt at precision but include clauses that leave ample room for discretionary interpretation. For example, the Annotated Code of Maryland (2012) characterizes abuse as "The physical or mental injury of a child by any parent or other person who has permanent or temporary care or custody . . . under circumstances that indicate that the child's health or welfare is harmed or at *substantial* risk of being harmed" (Title 5, Subtitle 7, § 5–701; emphasis added). Sexual abuse is "any act that involves sexual molestation or exploitation . . . [including] incest, rape, or sexual offense in any degree; sodomy; and *unnatural* or perverted sexual practices" (§ 5–701; emphasis added).

The vagaries of language are not exclusive to the legal field, but in this case, the problem derives from the use of adjectives like "substantial" and "unnatural" which cover a spectrum of actions about which there is reduced consensus. A mother thrashing a recalcitrant daughter may be accused of substantial abuse by some or understood to be exercising her parental rights by others. A father photographing his six-year-old daughter in the nude and sharing the photo with others may be accused of a lewd and unnatural act, although his intentions may have been simply to celebrate the child's beauty.

Family law also reflects a lack of agreement regarding proper behaviors and means of discipline toward children. For example, the Maryland code states that "nothing [in these regulations] shall be construed to prohibit *reasonable* corporal punishment" (§ 5–701; emphasis added). This entails a double maneuver—sanctioning physical discipline while remaining vague about what constitutes acceptable action.

Among ordinary folks in West Baltimore, the resolution to such quandaries hinges on whether the effects of corporal punishment are visible or not. "Bruising" crosses the line of acceptable behavior; without marks, a child cannot be said to be abused. "They're after Marsha Cummings now," a woman living in the Murphy Homes told me, referring to a neighbor who had struck her daughter, "but that ain't right cause she didn't bruise the girl."

As that instance shows, many parents like Marsha Cummings are accused of and investigated for child abuse whose children never showed any physical evidence of maltreatment; the social workers involved have a broader interpretation: "We can't take risks in these matters," one of them told me, "my job depends on making sure children are not harmed." In other words, administrative procedures designed to manage the protection of children demand less rigor than those in criminal justice. A single testimony may be enough to begin an investigation. For that reason, it is not only the actual punishment of alleged abusers and molesters that carries weight at the community level but the very danger of being investigated. That, in turn, limits autonomy and curtails parents' capacity to act in accordance with their own sense.

Other ambiguities are apparent in the printed materials distributed by public service agencies, nonprofit organizations, and schools as part of programs whose purpose is to alert children and their families to risks of sexual misconduct and physical abuse. In Baltimore City schools, for example, the Child Safe Program distinguishes between "different kinds of touch." Under "Confusing Touch" are listed "tickling *too long*, a hug that is *too tight*, a kiss that is *inappropriate*" (emphasis added). The inclusion of spanking under "Touch We Don't Like" de facto suggests that it is a form of abuse, although there is no legal prohibition of that action. Guidelines of that kind are fraught with the potential for equivocation. Child Safe recommends that parents "immediately believe" their children's claims of mistreatment. That presents a thorny dilemma because not accepting the claims of a child in distress is a tragic possibility. On the other hand, and contrary to a common misconception, children *do* lie at times. Even more importantly, some children are highly susceptible to suggestion. A tendentious interview can extract from them unintentionally damning statements (Ceci and Friedman 2000).[3]

Finally, administrative rules (a) grant immunity to accusers and social workers to shield them from possible retaliation and (b) require that suspected cases of child abuse or neglect be reported to the authorities without consultation with those suspected of infractions. Both provisos seem reasonable because without reassuring potential witnesses that their names will be kept in confidence, many would not file legitimate complaints. Those measures, however, are not designed to detect fraudulent or exaggerated reports. Any suspicion, no matter how slim, can serve as the basis for an investigation. As a result, in most cases, neither denouncers nor public servants have to face penalties for unfounded allegations or the mishandling of cases. The absence of checks and balances is likely responsible for the rapid inflation of figures on child abuse over the last two decades (Ceci and Friedman 2000).

Investigations concerning abuse and neglect are conducted by licensed social workers required to question children in danger as well as members of their family and other caregivers. To afford youngsters a right to speak on their own behalf is appropriate and necessary, especially considering past disregard of children's rights. Problems arise, however, from sources not contemplated by the law. One is the absence of requirements for corroborating evidence. Hearsay and personal testimony are all that is required in most cases of child abuse.

It is at that juncture that words become proof because to do otherwise would challenge the veracity of children's testimonies. Yet an intense line of questioning by a zealous, biased or incompetent practitioner can yield spurious answers. In other words, the effectiveness of an investigation depends on the competence of the investigators, but many licensed social workers are inadequately trained. Meager salaries and stressful working conditions—it is not uncommon for a single social worker to be in charge of fifty cases or more—reduce efficacy. Inadequate funding and flaws inherent in the bureaucratic process further diminish the ability of child protective agencies to conduct effective probes.

Among inner-city residents, these problems are complicated by race and class. Social workers tend to be members of the same racial minorities as their clients. That shared identity plays in two opposite directions: On the one hand, Black social workers tend to see themselves as allies of the families they come in contact with and stand in solidarity with them against outsiders.[4] On the other hand, social workers are required to enact practices often perceived by their clients as repressive and unjust. Mothers and fathers accused of abuse or neglect are what Lipsky (1980) calls "involuntary clients," prone to protesting the verdicts of therapists, counselors, and case managers. Social workers, as well, tend to come from somewhat higher-class backgrounds than their clients. In some cases, they display antipathy toward parents whose behavior they see as a negative reflection on the Black community. They thus occupy a contradictory position vis-à-vis the families they are charged to investigate, and their judgments tend to mirror that conundrum.

How do parents and children manage and resolve the inconsistencies surrounding allegations of child abuse? In the next section I address that question.

INTERROGATING CHILD ABUSE

I draw from testimonies of parents and children living in West Baltimore and supplement those narratives with a few instances from a separate research project focusing on immigrant families (Fernández-Kelly and Konczal 2006). In both cases, my research did not specifically focus on child abuse and neglect; the subject surfaced spontaneously during structured and unstructured interviews.

The data collected represent a first approximation to a series of critical issues about which very little is known. Three main features emerge from a review of the relevant facts. Impoverished African American parents express misgivings about what they perceive as excessive infringement on the part of bureaucrats in family matters. Second, they have at their disposal few symbolic, human, and collective resources to resist the unanticipated effects of state control. Third, immigrant parents appear to have a larger cultural and material stock to withstand state interference than native-born African Americans in poor neighborhoods have.

Children's views about abuse and neglect, on the other hand, reflect a yearning for autonomy, a desire to improve their negotiating capacity vis-à-vis parents, and a belief that adults are unable or unwilling to understand them. A focus on abuse and neglect provides children with an opportunity to rethink their identity in increasingly individuated and potentially antagonistic terms. Children display an accurate perception that parental authority can be effectively subverted through appeals to public servants. I present here a few selected cases.

I sit with Kareen Davis outside her small living unit in the late spring of 1993. A few plants grow inside a rubber tire that she has turned into an orchard of sorts. We are discussing life in the projects and the effect it has had on her children:

> I never thought I would git on welfare. I jus' wanted . . . to be real grown up, you know. So I got married, but that din't last long 'cause he [her former husband] got into drugs . . . an' I was only seventeen. Then he left me, but I still kept my job at the [convenience] store; that's where I met Marcus. He was a good man, drove a truck for a construction company; he loved Latricia [her daughter] like his own flesh 'n' blood. We had the two children of our own. . . . He was jus' twenty-five when he had the accident; never came conscious again. After that, I couldn't support the chil'ren by myself. Latricia, she lived most of her life in the projects, so now she fifteen and she thinks she's all growed up herself!

Only three years earlier, Latricia had been a model student. She was bright and funny when I first met her, in 1990; she wanted to be a pediatrician, but making claims on adulthood in poor neighborhoods means renouncing childish illusions. Before turning fourteen, Latricia was already attending school irregularly, and "staying" with friends without her mother's permission. I asked her once about the sudden change in her behavior. "I just grew up, that's all," she said, a steely glance cast in no particular direction.

It was after one of several escapades that Kareen gave her daughter a memorable beating. Then, she chased her around the house with a towel in hand, ready to snap it against the girl's flesh but, in the end, she relented. Without hesitation, Latricia called the cops on her mother. Kareen was investigated. She had to face an administrative judge and was cited as an abusive parent. The blot went on her record. Her name was included in a roster of "alleged" child abusers for seven years.

Latricia was not contrite. She had taught her mother a lesson: she was not going to be treated "like no dumb child." As if I had not fully understood what she meant, she added, "Mama don't get it; I'm gonna do what I want to do, *when* I want to do it; it's my life."

Kareen was hurt and baffled by the incident. She didn't believe in spanking children regularly. Frustrated she told me:

> [Latricia] jus' gone way over the line and I warned her three times, too. Tha's the way my mama and her mama used to do: you get warned three times and if you don' pay attention, you get whipped. So now, on top of everything, I'm accused of child abuse. Where did she learn to treat her mother that way?

Childhood is marked by dependence and feelings of impotence. The desire to please often collides with equally strong feelings of anger and fear. Youngsters of all kinds engage in fantasies about role reversal, seeking to alter the balance of power vis-à-vis adults through manipulation, persuasion, and sometimes overt hostility. Affluent families can resort to material means of comparatively high quality to extract compliance from the young—a benevolent quid pro quo that resounds well with the interests of the larger society. Poor families, by contrast, are ill equipped to do the same. Children have a hard time accepting adult commands in environments where a large number of men and women are either unemployed or holding unstable, poorly paid jobs. "My daddy can't do much for me," ten-year-old Jamir told me. "Most of the time, he don't got no money or nothing. So why should I do what he tells me?" Jamir's father struggled to improve his financial situation, but he lacked skills. His yearning for Jamir's respect and the latter's longing for an authoritative father were equally bereft of a material foundation.

In other words, one of the effects of what analysts call low labor-market attachment is the reduction of social distance between parents and their children, a weakening of the basis for intergenerational domination and accommodation. Popular psychology, with its inattention to class and racial demarcations, celebrates the abridgment of social gaps between parents and children in agreement with antiauthoritarian philosophies, but families living in poverty do not have the resources to moderate the negative consequences of social equivalence between adults and minors.

Especially in the transition to adulthood—which arrives early in tough neighborhoods—parents compete at great disadvantage with the allure of the streets. In publicly subsidized housing, living quarters tend to be small and crowded. Searching a sense of belonging, kids gravitate toward corners and playgrounds where a certain form of power resides. It is there that young men in their mid- and late teens conspicuously exhibit the profits of drug transactions and other illicit activities that represent adventure and excitement. As fleeting as their success often is, their signs of achievement tend to be irresistible to younger children. To a greater extent than many parents, older adolescents hold the means to influence boys and girls.

Thus, when attempting to discipline their sons and daughters, impoverished parents see themselves engaged in a fierce battle against a diffuse but mighty force: the neighborhood—the place where older, transgressing youths lure their offspring. "Don' tell me I'm an abusive mother if I slap my daughter," Moira Simpson told me emphatically, "better to be slapped by yo' mother who loves you than to be raped or killed by some good-for-nuthin' son-of-a-bitch!" Taresha, her daughter, did not agree.

Taresha turned thirteen in May 1995, the same month that she met Davon Taylor, who was five years her senior. Davon had been running crack for nearly as much time. Lately he was pushing amphetamines. He had several neighborhood children under his command and wore only the trendiest clothes. Taresha thought he was "fly." She began hanging out with him to her mother's distress. The girl crossed the threshold of minimal decorum when, without permission and late at night, she attempted to leave the house headed to a party that Davon was attending.

A heated argument erupted when Moira tried to intercept Taresha. The girl swung the front door open and tried to exit. Moira caught her daughter by the hair and pulled her inside where she proceeded to slap her across the face several times. Taresha shrieked, threatening to call the authorities. Next day she did, with the expected response: her mother was questioned by a detective who kindly suggested there were better ways to teach children than through violence. "Ain't no kind of violence," Moira replied, "if you mother tries to teach you right from wrong. Can't you tell the difference?" Taresha was unrepentant:

Mama don't understand that I'm old enough to know what I want, what I need. I don't need no one hitting me. . . . But Davon, he's my homey, he be nice to me; he know what I'm about, and he likes me best, so the other girls have respect for me.

Taresha's words were layered with meaning. At one level, she was expressing a common misgiving among youngsters of all kinds: parents do not understand them. More importantly, she was identifying Davon as a conduit to status and recognition. In exchange, she offered the symbolic and actual rewards of her budding sexuality. From her vantage point, it was a fair deal. Her mother's restraining attempts were not just a barrier to her claim on adulthood but also an interference with an obvious good.

Sexuality enters the power equation in other ways. In the summer of 1995, Melinda Twigg, Little Floyd's fourteen-year-old sister was removed from the home of her aunt Margaret, with whom she had lived for five years, and sent back to her father, who had never given up the hope of reuniting with his children. The reason for the transfer, however, was troubling. Melinda claimed that she had been sexually molested by her aunt's boyfriend. "Did you hear about Melinda?" Clarise asked me one clear afternoon as we were nearing the Baltimore Harbor. Little Floyd sat next to her in the back of the cab. "Yes," I replied from the front seat, "it's awful!" After hardly a pause, Clarise's rejoinder surprised me: "It never happened, you know; she just wanted to get away from Aunt Margaret 'cause she don't treat her right." Little Floyd agreed; he had heard the same line from Melinda during a phone conversation.

What explains Melinda's inconsistent account? She may have been adjusting her version of the events in search of her siblings' admiration. They thought her ploy was clever. Alternatively, she may have wanted to minimize the magnitude of her ordeal out of shame. She may have had a dim grasp of the distinction between reality and fantasy—it is impossible to say. What is clear is that she knew how to alter her circumstances. She understood that an accusation of such gravity would mean leverage and empowerment. Little Floyd had reached the same conclusion when reporting sexual abuse. That he had endured suffering at the hands of those charged with his care is unquestionable; that he embellished some of his accounts in search of recognition is also true.

The shadowy world created by youthful desires, equivocal meanings, and reversals of power is further complicated by simple-minded interpretations on the part of adults. The idea that children never lie about physical or sexual abuse, for example, inadvertently turns children into passive victims without a capacity to fight back, sometimes through the manipulation of ambiguous information.

The vulnerability of poor African American parents and their children may be seen as the result of their lengthy and intense relationship with government agencies. Through repeated contact with the court system, police departments, and social service agencies, families have learned that the state is, in a sense, part of the family; it sits at their table. They cope and resist with limited efficacy because they do not have virtual or material resources to create distance or contest its domination. Their weakened capacity for negotiation is a function of deep assimilation. This becomes all the more apparent when comparing the responses of impoverished African-American parents with those of recently arrived immigrants.

In a study focusing on the life trajectories of children of immigrants, I interviewed numerous parents who worried about bureaucratic intrusions and fretted about potential loss of authority like many native-born Blacks. Yet they had at their disposal ideational repertoires and social networks that gave them some protection vis-à-vis liminal institutions. In addition, the encroachment of government agencies in areas of immigrant concentration is less pronounced than in Black ghettos. Marisa Guzmán, a Nicaraguan mother living in South Florida, in 2004, illustrated a common situation:

> As a Christian mother, I do not condone the mistreatment of children, but children need discipline, and all children are different. Some will respond to a strong stare, others need spanking. In every case, children must respect their parents. . . . It is best for them when parents are in a superior position.

Alex, Marisa's fourteen-year-old son, agreed. "I never thought I could trifle with my mom and dad. They are the bosses. They almost never hit me when I was younger but when they did, I didn't challenge them; they know better." Alex did not have enough information about American ways to contest his parents' power.

Helen Moore, a mother of two living in West Baltimore, held views identical to those of Marisa Guzmán. In her case, however, Child Protective

Services had placed her nine-year-old daughter, Chantal, in foster care after the girl called 911, claiming that her mother had hit her in the eyes with a high-heeled shoe. The implausibility of that report did not keep a concerned social worker from removing the child from her mother's home for nearly four months while the case was being investigated. After that, Helen was reluctant to discipline her daughter in any way.

Especially revealing, among immigrants, is the case of parents who attempt to adjust their children's attitudes by sending them back to their countries of origin where they can be properly resocialized by family members and friends. Wearing his working apron and standing behind the front desk of his tiny restaurant in Hialeah, Florida, Fidel Contreras, originally from El Salvador, described his recent decision to exile his sixteen-year-old son:

> To tell you the truth, I've been working so hard since I came to this country that I wasn't paying enough attention to my children. . . . Carlos was turning too American. He was beginning to say that school is for geeks; that sort of thing. One day I shoved him against a wall. . . . He said he was going to call social services. I didn't believe it but that convinced me drastic action was needed. I booked him a flight back to San Salvador where his uncle saw to it that [Carlos] was admitted to a military academy. He didn't like it at all; said he missed his mother; came back a different boy.

Their recent arrival in the United States and the availability of cultural and human resources originating in their countries of origin provide immigrants with tools to discipline children that are unavailable to impoverished African Americans. In addition, immigrant parents find it hard to believe that the government would interfere with their parental rights, and not knowing what they don't know gives them an advantage that urban Blacks, accustomed to the invasive practices of liminal institutions, simply do not have.

ASSESSING THE FACTS

The convergence between situated knowledge and institutional practices yields various preliminary conclusions. First, the multiplication of meanings surrounding child abuse has led to unintended consequences, the most haunting of which is the continued erosion of parental authority among families living in poverty. Flaws in the bureaucratic process, ambiguities embedded in family law, the construction of childhood along progressively individuated lines, and the casting of the child-parent relationship in adversarial terms threaten to subvert the very purpose of protective legislation. While egregious cases of child victimization seem to resist state intervention and treatment, less serious infractions bring about intense bureaucratic interference.

Child abuse is rapidly becoming a lightning rod for constituencies with overlapping but not identical interests: bureaucrats, parents, and children themselves. Max Weber (1912/2002) aptly showed that the iron law of bureaucracies is self-perpetuation. Agencies charged with the protection of children are a case in point; they justify their existence through the demonstration that the ills they seek to correct are even more plentiful than suspected. Entering the names of "alleged" child abusers in state-wide registries, even when the charges are weak, corresponds with that bureaucratic logic. Those names become part of the statistical evidence that justifies further state intrusion. Although most of the people investigated by the authorities for physical and sexual abuse against children do not endure severe penalties, the process of inquiry itself produces intimidation and loss of both privacy and authority. Paradoxically, children suffer the greatest disruption when their elders are deliberately or unintentionally humiliated and infantilized.

Third, it may be argued that the flaws associated with child protection are inevitable, a small cost to pay for the physical and mental integrity of a vulnerable population. Neither the right to personal privacy nor the inconvenience of an investigation should be held in higher regard than children's welfare. That would be a valid claim if there were no alternatives to existing policies. Yet alternatives in conceptualization, process design, and organizational capacity do exist. Community-based initiatives with a comprehensive focus on families rather than on individuals have proved effective in experimental situations (U.S. Department of Health and Human Services 2009). A non-adversarial presumption surrounding the relationship between children, parents, and other care providers would not create more havoc than exists at present. Urgently required is the inclusion of checks and balances in administrative processes to diminish their star-chamber quality. Finally, if children's well-being is a genuine pursuit, it cannot be left in the hands of poorly trained, overburdened, and inadequately compensated public servants.

From the vantage point of sociological theory, my exploratory research has three significant implications. One relates to the role of state agencies as producers of concepts and definitions that have unexpected effects among populations differentiated in terms of age, social class, race, and ethnicity. My analysis also suggests that the vulnerability of impoverished African Americans to state intrusion is largely a function of their deep social assimilation. By contrast, the capacity of immigrants to resist government intervention stems from their comparatively low levels of integration into the larger society.

The relationship between social class and state control is also worth noting. Although laws centering on child abuse make no distinctions with respect to socioeconomic standing, they have had a disproportionate impact among the poor. In 2012, nearly 257,000 cases of alleged child abuse were filed at the national level. Of those, 61 percent involved Whites and close to 40 percent were either African Americans or Latinos (National Children's Alliance 2013), though the two latter groups combined represent about 25 percent of the nation's residents. In other words, as a proportion of their respective groups, members of minority populations are overrepresented among those denounced for child maltreatment.

It is true that working-class and low-income families tend to be less skittish about corporal discipline than their more affluent counterparts (Lareau 2011). It is not self-evident, however, that impoverished African-Americans or Latinos are more violent toward their children than people in other social categories. All in all, two main reasons for their overrepresentation in investigations of abuse may be their preexisting and intimate relationship with state agencies and their vulnerability. With existences narrowly framed by their interaction with public officials, poor African Americans are more likely to be reported to the authorities than other populations.

Deserving of reiteration in this analysis is the reconceptualization of children not solely as members of a victimized population but as social actors. Youngsters should be of special interest in sociological theory because as they endure objective conditions of subordination, they also seek avenues to strengthen their position with respect to parents and other adults. That presents an invaluable opportunity to understand raw power dynamics. Children's use of ideas surrounding abuse illustrates their capacity for agency.

On the other hand, risks emerge in attempts to recover children's ability to transform their own circumstances through accommodation, enticement, and confrontation—the possibility of representing youngsters as responsible for their own mistreatment, minimizing the gravity of the ordeals they often face, or absolving adults from injuries perpetrated through omission or commission. Nothing of that sort is consistent with my analysis. Instead, my objective is to replace a maudlin, overly sanitized view of childhood with a more precise portrayal that acknowledges youthful longings and passions. The image of children who appropriate the ambiguous language of adults to act upon their world is vastly more interesting and plausible than their characterization as inert, unthinking victims.

Finally, attention must be drawn to the unforeseen effects of ambivalent benevolence. Neoconservative ideologues are not immune to the corruption of language, but it is largely in the liberal camp that ideas informing public policy originate, especially those aimed at the protection of exploited and oppressed populations like racial minorities and children. It is intellectually sobering and politically disconcerting to uncover the extent to which progressive objectives have been disfigured in the process of implementation. The original purpose of Child Protective Services was to safeguard the young; its actual proceedings entail Orwellian Newspeak, doublethink, and a profound invasion of personal spaces, especially among the poor. The problem is not with the politics of kindness but with the gross disregard for social realities.

I turn now to the operations of social and cultural capital in American inner cities, where the overwhelming presence of liminal agencies converges with high levels of residential segregation to give lived experience a unique profile. I begin with the story of Clarise Twigg.

9 CLARISE

CLARISE LATISHA TWIGG WAS EIGHT YEARS OLD WHEN SHE received a golden trophy with her name inscribed in the pedestal as recognition of her superior classroom performance throughout the 1991 academic term. The distribution of such tokens at the William Pienderhughes Elementary School was meant to elevate the spirits of students, many of whom could not read or do math at their grade level. Boosting the self-esteem of inner-city children as a precondition to improving their educational performance was all the rage in those heady days. Clarise showed off her award with eyes full of pride. Even then, she knew she wanted to become a lawyer.

For the past four years, Clarise had lived with Lydia Forrest, her great-aunt and guardian, at 19 Goodyear Street in Old Baltimore. Lydia had assumed custody of the little girl after the Department of Social Services removed her and her two siblings from their mother's squalid apartment in the George Murphy Homes. Clarise; her older sister, Melinda; and her younger brother, Floyd, were declared "children in need of assistance." She had the good fortune to go live with her great-aunt. Even when Clarise was a baby, it had been Lydia, not her mother, who had looked after her. Clarise loved being in Lydia's towering presence.

Before she became a permanent resident in her great-aunt's house, Clarise had to grow up fast. Her older sister was a passive and timorous child, and her brother was too young to know any better. It had been Clarise who had provided a sense of direction when her parents were absent; the children were often left alone in a filthy apartment without adult supervision. When there was no food, they went knocking on other people's doors while their mother, like another forlorn child, roamed the streets of West Baltimore in search of crack. "My mommy," the little girl explained time and time again, "she not bad. But when she get sick, she don't come home." There were days when Clarise had to rummage in the dumpsters at the bottom of her building in search of dinner for her brother and sister.

Things were very different in Lydia's house. Although she had been on welfare for nearly a decade, Lydia cultivated a sense of propriety. The rickety house where she lived was kept clean and organized—not an easy feat considering that six people shared two bedrooms and a small living room. That's without including the frequent crashers and overnight stayers. Lydia had a good heart and it was not unusual for her to welcome evicted relatives or neighboring children in distress. Despite the clutter of people and things, she worked at making the house reflect her yearnings for respectability. Although her oldest son, Beady, had been languishing in prison for the past six years—he would soon turn twenty-three—Lydia never lost hope that a better life was just around the corner.

On the day I met her, Clarise was wearing a pair of blue jeans, a denim jacket over a pink T-shirt, and multicolored clips in her braids. She was so tiny that I had to bend over to greet her. Her glance was trusting and her demeanor composed. She smiled grandly as we traversed the Johns Hopkins campus, with its fields of green and its severe Georgian buildings. She said she loved ice cream, and pizza, and school. Her favorite subject was reading because, as she explained breezily, "I'm good at it," but she also thought numbers were fun. The teachers treated her nicely, and she had many friends. They thought she was funny. Her only regret was that she hadn't seen her brother and sister "in a long time." She missed them. She missed her mother, too.

In the years ahead, Clarise became a wellspring of new understanding for me. From her, I obtained direct knowledge of what it means to grow up poor and female in America's inner city. In contrast to more-affluent youngsters, children like Clarise must always think of other people's needs. Because they live in crowded spaces, they learn to be mindful of the invisible lines that divide personal property. Clarise knew that her only possessions were half the bed she slept in, her nine dolls, a small section of a closet, and a few clothes. She found ways to carve out small spaces of her own without invading those commanded by other family members.

At an early age, impoverished youngsters, especially girls, are asked to assume heavy responsibilities. Their sense of what it means to be a child is markedly different from the romantic notions of more affluent people. By the age of three, most impoverished children know there isn't enough money to indulge their every whim. And because food and clothing are not always available, these emerge as a central focus of the children's fantasies. Clarise never opened a refrigerator door without asking first whether the stranded apple, glass of milk, or pizza slice that she had been thinking about for the past hour belonged to someone else. Her impeccable manners reflected an awareness of boundaries and a desire to avoid conflict.

In Lydia's household, Clarise was in awe of Towanda Forrest, Lydia's youngest daughter and the little girl's self-appointed mentor. Although Towanda was technically Clarise's aunt, twice removed, the little girl referred to her as a cousin because of the relative proximity in their ages. At thirteen, in the throes of early adolescence, Towanda conveyed an air of boldness. Where Clarise was mild mannered and respectful, Towanda was tough and knowing. At night, when they crawled together into the same bed (much to the irritation of the teenager), Clarise's eyes would widen in wonder as she listened to Towanda's tales. It had been Towanda who first gave her tips about boys and advice on the need to "stand up for youself." Towanda took no garbage from either child or grown-up. Clarise admired that.

Clarise's family and friends called her Reesee, after the popular chocolate candy, a subject that made Clarise roll up her eyes in resignation. At school, children teased her because of the odd-sounding moniker. It was bad enough to be called Twigg, a word that called to mind a stick, without also having to deal with such a silly nickname. "Reesee Twiggy," a boy who liked her sang every time he saw her. "You skinny like a willow branch, ol' Miss Reesee Twiggy pie!" Clarise tolerated the mild ribbing because she could sense its hidden compliment.

Other things she wouldn't take. Two weeks before she finished the second grade, she had her first brawl. Octavia Brown, one of her classmates, had accused her of being the daughter of a crackhead. Cheered by a throng of screaming children, Clarise had clobbered Octavia during recess. For her transgression, Clarise received a one-day suspension, but she didn't mind because, as she explained, "sometime you gotta pay a price for people to respect you mama."

And there was more to the child than family moorings. Clarise had ambition. Inspired by Olympic athletes and a recent visit to the circus, she thought she might become an acrobat. Graceful and lean, she spent her weekends pretending to walk on a high bar, doing cartwheels, or standing on her head. When invited to the Bolton Swim and Tennis Club, where I was a member, she first watched the other children from the poolside, measuring their every movement. Prolonged observation led to self-confidence. Within a week, she was at ease splashing in good company. It wasn't long before she could swim properly. She was ecstatic when invited to become a member of the club's team, the Barracudas. During practice, showing off a halo of untamed hair, she was the image of spirit and high potential.

In Baltimore as in the rest of the nation, swimming and other athletic events offer pathways for children to learn the rules of membership in the larger society. Sports foster personal achievement, cooperation, and feelings of belonging that transcend kinship, ethnicity, and race. At the Bolton Swim and Tennis Club, swim meets took place on Saturdays during the summer. Clarise would wake up very early on those mornings, eager not to miss her ride to the club. Warm-ups began at seven. Boys and girls in regulation suits swam in a crowded pool as the coaches prompted them to increase speed, watch their style, and check their errant arms. Moments later, the group of loyal parents and friends would begin to grow. Some installed food stands, others lit up the grill—hot dogs would be on high demand—and still others distributed whistles, recording cards, and stop clocks. There were always volunteers willing to serve as timekeepers under July's scorching sun.

A little before eight, the adversary team would arrive and take its place at one of the corners of the pool enclosure. The sound of young voices chanting the team's motto filled the air in regular bursts. Intermittently, the Barracudas would belch out their own mantra. At nine, everyone stood up to sing the national anthem. Water sparkled under the red, white, and blue pennants decorating the swimming-lane dividers. When the music stopped, the race began.

Youngsters made different by status, age, and ability were suddenly brought together in pursuit of a common goal. If you were a Barracuda, it didn't matter whether you were rich or poor, Black or White, friend or acquaintance. Everyone rooted for you. Even the smallest child slowly cutting a diagonal across a pool lane received accolades at the finish line. Skill levels were diverse, but Clarise excelled from the outset. The day she won her first medal, a first place in freestyle, she was exultant. Everybody patted her on the back as she emerged glistening from the pool. In the months ahead, she practiced resolutely, and by the following year, she was one of the top swimmers in her age cohort.

Soon, Clarise thought, she would be able to take part in the regional meets. In the evening's warm glow, she would skip through the park on her way back from practice, chasing fireflies and making predictions about her future. "Maybe I be a champion like Summer Sanders," she said. Sanders had captured the gold medal in the four-hundred-meter freestyle competition at the 1992 Olympic Games.

She also liked to dance. While other children were satisfied to imitate the latest fad, Clarise invented her own steps and directed her friends in complex productions. In the fall of 1993, she began to take dance classes at the Peabody Preparatory. With nearly one hundred children, she participated in three consecutive end-of-the-year performances held at the Miriam A. Friedberg Concert Hall on Mount Vernon Square.

Then, after watching *The Invisible Dragon*, a play produced by Baltimore's Pumpkin Theater, Clarise decided acting was her true calling. All the characters, including the dragon, had signed her program at the end of the show. She took a drama course at the Bryn Mawr School for girls. At the final presentation, before an audience of parents and friends, she spoke her lines with poise. She said she never tired of learning new things; her world was opening up.

In between activities, I would take her for a walk and buy her a Half Pounder with fries and a Coke at McDonald's. She talked incessantly as she gobbled up the meal. When I delivered her back to the small row house with the faulty electrical connections where she lived, my heart would sink as she sat doe-eyed at the front stoop, her expression suddenly rigid, her hands flat on her thighs, waiting for the return of her guardian. Her street was barren except for the sapless tree at the same corner where older boys gathered to sell drugs. The neighboring houses were boarded up and covered with graffiti. A vast gulf separated Clarise's neighborhood from the swim and tennis club and the Peabody Prep.

Like most children, Clarise was sharply aware of social differences, especially those based on race. She was fascinated by long wavy hair and was deeply concerned about the texture of her own. Lydia had told her she had a nappy head, and she spent a good portion of her weekends staging rituals meant to make the girl's appearance acceptable. The comb's pull made Clarise cry, but Lydia thought it was necessary to bring the girl's hair into control, especially after swim practice. On Sundays, they went together to Kingdom Hall—the holy place of Jehovah's Witnesses—and she didn't want the congregants to criticize the girl's frizzy hair. With all the fuss over her unruly mane, it wasn't long before Clarise took to wearing a cap before diving into the pool. Lydia had taught her courteous manners and a sense of deference toward her elders. She was now imbuing her mind with the proper order of things.

Clarise lived in a world of fine distinctions. It was important to know where you stood in the vast map of society. "You Black, right?" Clarise asked me one morning as we prepared for church. "No," she corrected herself. "You White." Her confusion was understandable. My friendship with her family suggested I was a member of the same group, but alas, I didn't live in the right place. My home was situated well outside the area where Blacks were confined. In the end, Clarise concluded I must be "mixed." Towanda had intimated as much, and Towanda knew best. And another thing, Clarise contended she wasn't Black either. "I'm light-skinned," she observed, making a manifest claim on racial superiority. Lydia had explained the difference between skin tones. In Clarise's evolving mental scheme, light-skinned was better than Black.

Although she was severe toward her at times, Lydia thought Clarise was the most promising of her brood. "She's a nice girl an' she willing to take orders, unlike you know who." Her oblique reference was to Towanda, who, in her search for independence, had become erratic about the time she came back from school. In Lydia's view, the girl had gone "boy-crazy." By contrast, Clarise was beholden to her approval and eager to please. Lydia seemed as proud as her charge was about the accumulation of small trophies and medals in the upstairs room, the result of Clarise's good work at school and her ability as a swimmer. As a kid, Lydia too had nurtured ambitions. Clarise's success brought back hopeful memories. Sometimes she wished Clarise could attend a better school, far from the corrosive influences of her neighborhood. She told me, "maybe you can find her—what they call it?—a scholarship."

It was the end of the Reagan-Bush years and the air exuded plaudits for volunteerism. The president had called for a legion of private individuals, "a thousand points of light," to address urban troubles. Personal, not government, responsibility was seen as the solution to social ills. It was possible in that climate to envision new ways for children like Clarise to cross from the fringes of America into its bountiful middle.

The Calvert School, a Baltimore institution with an international name for advances in basic curricula, agreed to evaluate the girl as a first step toward possible admission. Clarise was only eight years old, eager to learn and unspoiled by defeat. Surely there was a spot for her in a school renowned for its open views. Unfortunately, the girl was "losing ground fast," according to the admissions counselor. Clarise's standardized scores were well below those of students at Calvert. And no, it wouldn't be possible for the girl to repeat the second grade. That would damage her self-esteem. "We begin our work with incoming children when they are about six," the counselor made clear. "Clarise wouldn't be comfortable with students that young."

Two years earlier, Clarise's scores had been almost fifty points higher. Her performance had rapidly declined in subsequent periods—a pattern typical among ghetto children. Regardless of social condition, children in America begin the instructional race at a similar point. It is later, as the injuries of experience and the dearth of resources obstruct their capacity for intellectual advancement, that the poor get stuck at the bottom of the educational ladder.[1]

At Grace and Saint Peter, an Episcopalian school celebrated for its enlightened views, Clarise was mistakenly given a test for somewhat older students, making the results seem even more dismal. The adviser in turn suggested that she be evaluated for cognitive and auditory dysfunction. After discovering their blunder, admissions officers still refused to reconsider Clarise's application. Four other schools reached similar decisions. As young as she was, Clarise was disqualified from inclusion in the venues most able to promote her educational progress.

Private schools like Calvert and Grace and Saint Peter aim for success in the market of youthful education. Supply and demand dictate their policies. They can't risk the costs involved in uplifting lagging pupils. To attract new students, they strive to produce high graduation rates and college-bound students. Their brochures include statements about "diversity" but reliance on standardized testing guarantees that most Black and poor students will not be admitted into their halls. In that design no one is at fault. Exclusion is simply the effect of misrecognition. Concealed behind numbers and percentages, the true causes of inequality—gross racial and class disparities—remain invisible. "We can't take her," said the sympathetic counselor at the Calvert School, "but I'm so glad you're on her corner." So much for a thousand points of light.

Unfazed by disappointment, Lydia agreed to explore parochial schools. Two years earlier, she had become a Jehovah's Witness, but in those days, she thought Clarise's education was more important than religious preference. Sister Trinita, the principal at the Holy Spirit School, assured her that the daily religion class was aimed solely at instilling "broad moral values, not specific to any denomination." Most of her students were not Catholic, anyway. The school didn't even have the resources to celebrate mass regularly; there weren't enough priests to go around anymore.

Holy Spirit was far removed from the west Baltimore ghetto and Lydia thought that was good. Clarise smiled pleasantly at the prospect of wearing a uniform. It was a jumper in a pretty plaid design with a white blouse and two-tone saddle shoes as a complement. Holy Spirit didn't have a gym, a large auditorium, or a well-equipped library, but its classrooms were quiet and free of distractions. In the fall of 1992, Clarise became a third-grade student at Holy Spirit.

In its prime, the Community School of the Holy Spirit had been part of the Parish of Saint Bernard. Visible from blocks away, a cross still crowns the church by the same name. Joining the two buildings is a small courtyard covered with shrubbery where the Blessed Mother in lasting marble extends her arms in a welcoming gesture. Timeworn but dignified, the complex stands in the Waverly District behind the former location of Memorial Stadium, a major Baltimore landmark and an early attempt at urban revitalization.

Early in the 1950s, four decades before it was closed down, the stadium became the original home of the Orioles baseball team. Older residents can still remember the days when famous players intermingled at ease with their fans in the restaurants and shops along Greenmount Avenue. On weekends, en route to a game, whole families engaged in Orioles fanfare could be seen walking down the boulevard. The tradition lasted for decades but in 1994, Memorial Stadium was abandoned for the newly built Camden Yards Park, one of the city's latest attempts at resurrection. Seven years later, in a cold February morning, the old building was razed to the ground as part of a plan to build a new conference center.

Like Memorial Stadium, the Holy Spirit School was part of an era when the Waverly district attracted the hopeful middle of a working class formed by the children of immigrants, mostly Poles, Italians, and Irish. Early in the century, Waverly was built by the same enterprising company that transformed Roland Park, in northwest Baltimore, into an array of expensive properties girdled by uncultivated ravines and wooded areas. Roland Park was the residential destination for those with the clout to own summer homes. In time, it became the city's most wealthy neighborhood, the place where attorneys, physicians, and city officials resided.

The Roland Park Development Company was so successful that it next set its sights on Waverly, one of the city's northeastern districts. There it built moderately priced row houses and detached homes that were accessible to upwardly mobile families eager to partake of the élan radiated by Roland Park.[2] Waverly's pretensions were soon put to the test. The Great Depression of the 1930s transformed many of its subdivisions into slums, as owners unable to make mortgage payments saw their properties foreclosed. Populated almost exclusively by people of European descent—years before Blacks began to arrive from the South—Waverly gave testimony of the city's cyclical misfortunes.

In the mid-1940s, Waverly was the first urban area in the nation to undergo a major rehabilitation program. And it was as part of that early effort that Memorial Stadium had been raised—a prescient reflection of the motives that guided the construction, many years later, of Camden Yards Park. In Baltimore, the past is always recurring.

Waverly never had it easy, but it emerged as a solid expression of the American Dream, harvesting the benefits of a robust manufacturing economy. The Port, Bethlehem Steel, and the McCormick Reaper Company offered plentiful opportunities for employment, as did the myriad firms that rose in their shadow. The district thrived as Baltimore became a burgeoning industrial center whose mills, factories, and small businesses afforded workers of limited skills but substantial ambition the means to adopt the standards of a middle-class life.

In addition to the repute brought about by the Orioles, other virtues made Waverly a prime location. It was safe and clean. It contained all the essential services and a multitude of commercial establishments. It was also easy to reach. The now defunct A&P supermarket at the corner of Old York Road and Gorsuch Avenue used to attract customers from every corner in the city.

Sister Trinita, the principal at Holy Spirit, who stood firm in her post for over thirty years, recalled the times, well into the 1970s, when enrollments never dropped below five hundred. Holy Spirit saw several generations of Baltimore children in uniform pass through its hallways. They endured a kind of teaching that was resolutely devoid of artifice, one in which basic instruction, religious fervor, and discipline were considered to be all that was needed to civilize the young.

According to the U.S. Census, over 90 percent of Waverly's population was White in 1970. But it was during that decade that the neighborhood began to change. Large numbers of African Americans, many of them from the Carolinas, began to settle in Waverly searching opportunities even as the industrial base was yielding to the pressures of globalization. Bethlehem Steel, once the city's largest employer, hired upwards of 34,000 people as late as 1975. Two decades later, its labor force had dwindled to fewer than 10,000. The McCormick factory building, a major benchmark in U.S. labor history and a distinctive Baltimore landmark for most of the twentieth century, was gradually stilled during the same decade and finally demolished in 1993, marking the end of an era.

As in many other instances throughout urban America, the combined effect of industrial decline and the mass arrival of Blacks from the South accelerated White flight. By 1980, Waverly's White population had shrunk to 65 percent, and twelve years later, when Clarise first entered the Holy Spirit School, 59 percent of the neighborhood's residents were Black. Only two hundred children were enrolled in the school; most were African American and most of them were not Catholic.

White families had long deserted the Church of Saint Bernard. They had moved away to more insipid environs, far from the racially distinct population that now occupied Waverly. Signs in Korean now hung from the church's entrance. That was because Saint Bernard had become a shrine for the fastest-growing Catholic community in Baltimore: Koreans. Members of that group, however, did not live in Waverly. They traveled long distances from Timonium and Pikesville to attend mass during the weekends. Local residents watched their comings and goings with guarded resentment. In older times, immigrants had stayed in the city. The most recent arrivals saw Baltimore with the same distrust that guided older Americans in their exodus.

Holy Spirit was rare in its determination to remain in the Waverly neighborhood. Other Catholic schools had closed down or relocated to the suburbs in pursuit of prospering families who were able to pay the rising tuition. Left behind, Holy Spirit had become an invaluable resource for Black families seeking educational alternatives for their children. Many of the parents who sent sons and daughters to the school struggled to make regular tuition payments. But even when they were in arrears, Sister Trinita refused to press them. She knew their strife. "It's not that they don't want to pay," she told me, "Times are always hard."

Unaware of the school's melancholy past, Clarise arrived at Holy Spirit for her first full day of classes immediately after Memorial Day. She was giddy when Sister Trinita greeted her at the door. A satisfying dose of trepidation tinged her enthusiasm. "Here they give you green slips if you don' do you homework right, and pink slips if you get into some trouble," she announced. "Then your mother has to sign them, and it's embarrassing. I never get one of them slips!"

Clarise rapidly became known as a hardworking and reliable student. Following Lydia's direction, she was trying to build a good reputation. "What other people think can build you up or bring you down," her guardian told her. Her plaid uniform grew into a source of pride. Boasted the girl, "That's how people respect you, because when they see the uniform they know you go to a good school." Her desk and locker were well organized, and she was especially thorough about homework. She was hoping to make a good impression on Mrs. Mary Wulff, her favorite teacher. To impress her, Clarise developed flawless penmanship.

Clarise's progress during that period was nothing short of astounding. Attentive and cheerful, she was often the first to raise her hand to answer questions. She volunteered to help the aging librarian and was selected by her classmates to lead the recess line. In the afternoons, adding to the customary list of sports and extracurricular activities, she pretended to be a teacher, displaying her books and pencils on Lydia's kitchen table, while addressing an imaginary class. She developed a polished deportment and made a point of delivering her assignments on time. Within twenty months, her standardized test scores climbed from the eighteenth to the fifty-first percentile. She concluded the third and fourth grades with a B average. At the end of each term, she couldn't wait for school to begin again.

Yet Clarise's academic improvement was not free of troubles. Other children made fun of the way she spoke. When asked to read in public, she faced constant correction from her teachers. This was disconcerting because school demands were in contradiction with private expectations. At home, everyone spoke like Clarise. "I talk country," she declared, "like Lydia do." Other people in her neighborhood spoke "street" or "slang." Whether at home or in the playground, assuming airs through the use of "proper" English could peg you as arrogant and pretentious. The same was true about fancy words and ideas. "Don't get smart with me!" Lydia exclaimed one day when Clarise tried to explain that a kid is not only a child but also a goat. "I done full know what a kid is, and you don't have to teach me!" The girl was taken aback by her guardian's strong reaction and careful in the future not to use the wrong expressions. At school the word "smart" meant "intelligent," but at home it mostly meant "uppity." Linguistic variations reflected differences in class and race.

Made aware of her verbal deficiencies, Clarise became quiet at school. Noticing her worries, Mrs. Wulff took the girl aside. "It is like knowing how to speak two languages," she told her. "The way you talk to your family and they talk to you is your private way of communicating. When you're not at home, you speak differently; that's your public speech, so that other people can understand what you're saying." After that Clarise tackled public speaking with renewed zeal. She was not convinced, however, that the Black vernacular was as good as White English.

Despite setbacks, Clarise's progress was striking for several reasons. When she was only six, about to begin kindergarten, she had obtained above-average scores in standardized tests. That was not rare; at a young age most children perform similarly throughout the nation. Regardless of social condition, youngsters begin the educational contest with a similar potential and endowment. At the end of the first grade, however, the gap between various groups begins to widen as a result of what researchers call "the summer effect."[3] When they are tested toward the beginning of new school terms, children in affluent families gain points. Youngsters living in poverty lose them. Gains and losses accumulate over time as children sort out by social class, ethnicity, and race. Such had been the case with Clarise, whose scores had plummeted from the sixty-eighth to the eighteenth percentile in little more than two years. Her reversal of the downward trend at Holy Spirit left no doubt about the importance of situational factors in educational performance.

Context also affects the rapid bifurcation of communication skills. Mastery of reading and writing is essential, not only to increase the probability of academic success, but also to move up in the occupational ladder. "Your vocabulary is the yardstick by which other people measure your background, even your intelligence," observes a radio commercial. But children hone linguistic skills only partially from books or through school interaction. An expanding vocabulary also depends on youngsters' daily contacts outside instructional settings. High levels of urban segregation create verbal barriers between rich and poor, insiders and outsiders.

Youngsters in well-off families expand their vocabulary throughout the year. During extended summer vacations, they are more likely than impoverished children to benefit from participation in summer camps, field trips, holiday excursions, and even international travel. Within the hardened boundaries of the ghetto, impoverished youths have few opportunities to intermingle with people outside their own group. Lacking connections to the larger society, they are exposed to highly expressive linguistic forms that are, nonetheless, limited in their external applications.

Language is not the only domain affected by social and spatial seg-regation. Even games assume divergent meanings, depending on where they happen and who the observers are. In Clarise's neighborhood, the highest form of entertainment during the sweltering summer months was to pry open a fire hydrant to create a fountain under which chil-dren could bathe. In neighborhoods devoid of resources, this is con-sidered play. Moralists see the same behavior as a manifestation of a decaying civic spirit.[4] What with the miscreants infesting the streets with disregard for public property! The sight of half-naked youngsters shouting in public spaces under a pilfered water jet can be disturbing to those living by abstract principles. Context, however, matters in ways that philosophers cannot suspect.

At times, Clarise's divided life was further complicated by unforeseen events. Sister Trinita, whose own family had come from Italy in 1915, presided over the Holy Spirit School like a combatant under siege, proud to point out that the school operated "in the black" despite the diocese's stinginess and the ebbs and flows of tuition payments. The school even had a small surplus. At the beginning of 1994, she intended to use a portion of that reserve to fix the school's ceiling and make other capital improvements. Sister Trinita was willing to spend the money, "provided [it was] for the benefit of the children." If she sounded cranky while uttering that statement it was because she had been in a tiff with the Catholic bureaucracy. The superintendent of schools had informed her that Holy Spirit was targeted for closure. Its building was being ceded to the Korean community, whose parishioners needed room to expand. It took rapid footwork and an appeal to the local television stations to arrest the tidal wave that would have obliterated the little school.

In the end, it wasn't just the fear of negative publicity or the scandal of a confrontation between Koreans—a "model minority"—and strug-gling Black families that had led Catholic officials to reverse their deci-sion. On a frigid February night, just after Martin Luther King Day, more than one hundred parents had gathered in the tattered school auditorium to protest the plans to shut down Holy Spirit. They spoke eloquently, those mothers and fathers in worn-out overalls, sweatshirts, and denim caps. They reminded a sober superintendent of schools of the church's commitment to the poor. They publicly praised the same teachers with whom they had often quarreled in the past. In crisis, they presented a united front. Not even Sister Trinita had realized how much the school meant to so many. Holy Spirit remained open, but Clarise's confidence was shaken. "What if they close my school?" she asked. "Then maybe I can't get a good education no more."

For four consecutive years, Clarise made steady progress. The diminutive eight-year-old grew into a stately young girl, almost a teenager. Her aspirations did not wane. She still wanted to be a lawyer. In 1995, at the end of the fifth grade, her overall test scores placed her in the sixty-fifth percentile of the corresponding national cohort. Those results were even higher when reading comprehension was excluded from the calculation. Her score in math was 76 percent. An evaluation of her phonics capacity yielded an extraordinary 96 percent. It was the absence of a rich vocabulary and adequate reading skills that depressed her average. Even with those limitations, Clarise took college for granted. She was excited after attending an informational assembly where various high schools had been represented. "I want to go to Mercy," she said as she handed over the colorful brochures, "It's a small but selective girls' school." She had picked up the phrasing from the counselors present at the meeting.

Shortly afterward, Lydia shared a bit of good news. Her second son, Lorenzo, whom everyone called "Weedy," was coming back from Washington to be with his mother after four years of absence. He had left home when Lydia married James Culver, an itinerant mechanic who spent his weekends drinking cheap liquor. Weedy, who was then seventeen, couldn't stand his stepfather. In addition to other failings, James thought that his new role involved bossing him around.

Rather than live in conflict, the young man had fled to Washington, DC, where he had first tried his hand at drug dealing, and later, seeking an honest life, he had taken a job as a limousine driver. Every now and then, to everyone's delight, he would show up in Baltimore in the black stretch limo that he drove as part of his job. Clarise thought Lorenzo owned the car and was therefore ecstatic when he would offer her a ride and buy her an ice cream cone. Then he would disappear, only to return months later. Now, Lydia explained, Weedy was back for good. He wanted to help his mother. In fact, Lorenzo had changed his ways so much that, in solidarity with her, he was to become a Jehovah's Witness.[5]

Throughout Weedy's absence from Baltimore, Lydia's religious convictions had not stood in the way of support for Clarise's attendance at the Holy Spirit School, a Catholic institution. For Lorenzo, on the other hand, conversion was more than a matter of faith; it was also a play for manly pride and muscle. He had come back to Baltimore to regain his position as the head of the family and show he could take care of his own. It was for that reason that his first authoritative resolution was to oppose Clarise's enrollment at Holy Spirit. Neither prayer nor the principal's entreats could convince him otherwise. It was not fitting for a Jehovah's Witness to attend a Catholic school. He was especially put out by the requirement that Clarise participate in the daily religion class.

Emboldened by her son's backing, Lydia now changed her views. Clarise was getting older, and it was about time she became a faithful Witness. The girl received the news with quiet unease. Sister Trinita, on the other hand, was visibly upset. She had seen Clarise make unexpected strides at Holy Spirit. "You'd better think it over," she told Lydia, "because transferring the girl could threaten everything she's accomplished here." Her words rang in deaf ears: "It is not the school that makes any difference," Lydia replied. "It's the individual. If she gonna make it, she gonna make it anywhere." Lydia had been on welfare a good part of her life—beaten down by circumstance and seen with contempt by others—but she spoke in accordance with the values of individualism that dominate America. Once she had thought an education in a better school made a difference. Now she realized it was personal character that made or broke you. Context was incidental. A flock of conservative thinkers would have applauded.

The moment was fraught with other ironies: "We don't focus on Catholic doctrine," explained Sister Edith who taught the daily religion class, her words echoing those of Holy Spirit's principal years earlier. In her seventies, Sister Edith was one of only three nuns left in the school. "We go for universal Christian values because most of our children are not Catholic," she explained, offering Weedy a copy of the text used in her class. There was nothing in it that contradicted the beliefs of Jehovah's Witnesses.

For an instant, Lorenzo seemed about to relent, but he felt that during the religion class, Clarise should be allowed to read from the *Watch Tower*—the Jehovah's Witnesses' official publication. Sister Trinita thought that would be a reasonable compromise but the superintendent of schools vetoed the idea: "We would lose our Catholic identity if we approved such a thing," he said. Sister Trinita had thought Catholic identity had more to do with service to the needy than with a watered-down religion class. She was crestfallen.

In the end, there was no agreement. In the fall of 1996, a few months before her thirteenth birthday, Clarise began the sixth grade at Public School no. 58, the Barclay School. Accustomed to the quiet halls of Holy Spirit, its small classrooms, and personal interaction with the teachers, she was ill prepared for the din in her new environment. Throngs of youngsters gathered at the gate every morning, loudly making their way into their respective homerooms. Teachers spent a good portion of their time trying to keep students quiet and negotiating with them for attention. As soon as you entered the classroom and sat down, there was always someone raising his or her hand wanting to go to the bathroom. Subversion, not compliance, was the order of the day.

At first, Clarise was shocked by such antics: "There ain't much studying going on here," she said. "You can't concentrate with all the noise." But, soon, she began to explore new codes of conduct, reinventing herself.

At Holy Spirit everyone had known her name. Now she was just another anonymous face lost in the crowd. Recently arrived and unfamiliar with prevailing norms of interaction, she became a target for bullies. Because she was tall and attractive, boys made a point of talking to her. Other girls were jealous. Things came to a head when Tommy Williams, who everyone thought was "da bomb," plainly stated that Clarise was the best-looking girl around. His words brought no peace of mind to seasoned members of the youthful circle.

Within the first quarter, Clarise was "jumped" twice by contending girls. They hated her, she claimed, always whispering words like "slut" and "ho" or laughing out loud in her face as she walked down the school corridor. "Gotta fight them," she said, "I can't hold up my head any other way." At Holy Spirit, Clarise had been known as a peacemaker, now she became notorious for her scrappy ways.

Equally vexing was knowing that other youngsters disliked the way she dressed. As a little girl, Clarise had been more interested in jumping rope barefoot by the poolside than in buying clothes at the mall.

Later, at Holy Spirit, uniforms had muted the extent to which students engaged in appearance competition. It was different now. She became acutely interested in fashion. Every penny she could scrape went into buying the accoutrements of acceptability. She learned that looks, not educational achievement, were a top priority in her new school. Only "geeks" and "nerds" spent their days with noses glued to the books. It wasn't "cool" to reach far and high anymore.

In time, Clarise found new allies and a fresh attitude. Left behind was the openness of childhood. Now you stood strong in the school-yard with your home girls, chewing gum, striking a pose, indifferent to anyone else's requirements, especially those of adults. You held your body taut and vacantly stared at nothing in particular, lost in thought. Others watched you, how fine you looked with your hair all done up in finger waves or made long by extensions, wearing the latest style, "struttin' you' stuff," and they understood: you were a real "chassis," a "fly girl." The boys, they wanted you. You "talked the talk and walked the walk," competing for their attention even if it entailed the prom-ise of sex. "Booty duty" was never far from their mind. And because the other "bitches" knew you were strong, they respected you. "No one messes with me no more," Clarise reported toward the end of the aca-demic year.

At home, the girl's new demeanor was receiving mixed reviews. Towanda thought her cousin was finally coming into her own, but Lydia was appalled. She feared that Clarise was following in Towanda's steps. The younger girl was increasingly out of sight: "She come back from school and jus' take off in a flash! You can hardly tell she there before she gone." Most of Clarise's afternoons were now spent at the corner store adjoining the Diamond Social Club, where local residents gathered in search of easy highs and indeterminate cordiality.

It was there that Clarise was offered pot for the first time. Next and far of kin had warned her to stay away from drugs, but she was curious just the same. Besides, the people at the Diamond Social Club were older and knew more. She thought she could learn something from them. Being pursued by the men who frequented those quarters was all the more enticing because she knew they were risky. One day, in the spring of 1997, Jovan McCullough, a local "gangsta" trapped Clarise in one of the club's back rooms and tried to rape her. She escaped with a ripped blouse. Clarise was frightened but also flattered. She thought Jovan's actions reflected her own sensual power.

Bothered by the girl's behavior and firm in his conviction, Weedy insisted that Clarise join him every Saturday morning as he went through the West Baltimore streets trying to convert neighbors. Clarise acquiesced because she liked showing herself off in public. At Kingdom Hall she was bored and often dozed off, much to Lydia's chagrin. She didn't raise her hand anymore to deliver the rote answers from the *Watch Tower* booklet, ceremonially demanded by the elder in turn. Knocking on doors, on the other hand, was always filled with surprise and conversation. She didn't mind that part of her life.

The new routine put an end to Clarise's swim practice and dance classes. It was all right, she said—Weedy thought there were more important things than modern dance, and she didn't like swimming as much anymore. It ruined her hair; the water brought out the kinks. It wasn't worth the pain. Lydia had been right all along.

She still went to the Bolton Swim and Tennis Club, but now she sat by the poolside looking jaded; gummed up hair crowning her head, acrylic nails at her finger tips, a delicate sundress intentionally exposing deodorant on her chest and underarms. She wanted the white powder to show over her cinnamon skin so that people could tell she was clean and didn't smell. She had seen Lydia do the same.

Shortly after her fifteenth birthday, Clarise decided she didn't want to be a lawyer, after all. "You don't need college to be happy," she said, waving away the unhappiness about her. Besides, she didn't know anyone who had finished high school, let alone gotten farther. What she wanted was a real job so that she could dress like Candy, the rapper in vogue. Because Clarise was not old enough to be fully employed, she spent much of her time hitting up relatives and friends for money and smoking cigarettes and marijuana blunts with her homies. For all practical purposes, she dropped out of school. "It's not like I'm learning something," she said. Most of her day was spent at home or on the street.

Once in a while her flame would flicker back, and she would show signs of a renewed interest. "At least I want my high school diploma," she said, "I want to go to a school where there are Blacks and Whites and Chinese, all kinds of folks, you know." Full of laughter and verve, once she had been at ease everywhere. Her world had shrunk, and she didn't know how to recapture the connection. Discouragement took over.

Clarise never went back to school for any length of time. She stayed close to her guardian's home. She had lovers, quarrels, disappointments, and some fun. At sixteen, a miscarriage put her in the hospital for a week. At eighteen, still without a job, she gave birth to a son, Little Otis. "The baby father," said Lydia with bile, "he din't even show up to see the child a single time, not a single time, I tell yah!" That's men for you, she implied, you can't depend on them.

Clarise nodded, gazing fondly at her aunt. She knew that, no matter what, Lydia would always be there. After all, she was family.

10 PARADOXES OF SOCIAL CAPITAL: CONSTRUCTING MEANING, RECASTING CULTURE

A LARGE BODY OF RESEARCH CARRIED OUT SINCE THE 1980S POINTS to the importance of social capital as an asset commensurate to material wealth. Relationships based on trust and reciprocity can be parlayed into educational and occupational advantages, and their absence—so the account goes—portends deficits like those found in poor neighborhoods. Clarise's story, reviewed in the previous chapter, suggests otherwise, revealing a more complex reality: it is not the paucity of social capital but the absence of material resources and external links that produces destructive effects in impoverished urban settings. The lacks are caused by disinvestment, predatory commerce, and bureaucratic intrusion, not the absence of mutuality and reciprocal exchanges.

Concerned about Clarise's future, and wanting to keep her out of trouble, Lydia, her guardian, made the girl adhere to the strictures of Jehovah's Witnesses, a religion she had adopted partly to raise her own standing among relatives and friends. Lydia's intentions were noble, but the new discipline made it unfeasible for Clarise to continue her studies at the parochial school where she had made great progress for more than four years; it also prevented her from becoming involved in extracurricular activities or participate in holidays that offered exposure to mainstream mores. Her transition to a public school further derailed the girl's ambition; she had to relearn who she was and how to integrate in a competitive setting where educational advancement was not the highest priority.

Years earlier, as a little girl, Clarise had been declared a child in need of assistance by the Department of Child Protective Services. She had seen peers and adults organize their lives in accordance with or in reaction to the terms imposed by public service agencies. At a tender age, she had experienced neglect and prematurely assumed adult responsibilities. She had searched for food in dumpsters and looked after her siblings when her mother was absent. A bright and motivated student, she nonetheless showed rapid educational decline as measured by her standardized test scores.

Despite such inauspicious beginnings, Clarise's enrollment in a parochial school and her involvement in competitive swimming and other extramural activities opened up new venues for the girl to reach outside the confinement of family and neighborhood. In a short time, her standardized test scores improved, giving testimony to the importance of *toponomical*—that is, spatially situated—factors in early educational advancement. When such opportunities dissolved as a result of her guardian's decisions, Clarise's life turned inward; her bridge to people different from those in her immediate circle was irrevocably broken.

Yet it was not for lack of familial support or trusting relationships that Clarise discarded her early aspirations and reconfigured her goals. Her guardian thoughtfully assessed available information, kinship loyalties, and spiritual convictions as she made choices that critically affected her charge's life. Like Americans everywhere, Lydia believed in the power of the individual to rise above circumstances. She was convinced that, through effort, "you can be anything you want to be," a mantra she repeated for Clarise's benefit as often as other parents do when trying to encourage their children. Despite their differences in age and experience, both Lydia and Clarise were in pursuit of similar objectives: a sense of belonging, independence, and self-respect. What made Clarise and Lydia different was neither the quality of their interactions nor the worth of their convictions but the absence of tools to convert them into educational and economic advantages. In Clarise's case, social capital led to implosion—a lesson that should give pause to those who see it as a panacea.

In this chapter, I take Clarise's experience as a point of reference to reexamine the relationship between social capital and behavioral outcomes in impoverished environments. I first revisit theoretical frameworks put in place by authors like Robert K. Merton (1938), James Coleman (1988), and Pierre Bourdieu (1979/1984, 1986) and, more recently, by Mark Granovetter (1973), Alejandro Portes (1998, 2010), and Robert Putnam (1995, 2001). On the basis of such writings, I reassert a conclusion foreshadowed in previous chapters: the quality and magnitude of tangible and ideational resources deeply affects the character of personal relationships.

Subsequently, I apply those ideas to the findings of educational sociologists regarding the so-called summer achievement gap between low-income children and their counterparts in more affluent populations. A rich and thought-provoking literature, starting with work by Barbara Heyns (1978, 1987), shows that youngsters of all class backgrounds and racial filiations begin school with similar endowments, a heartening fact about the miracle of resilience in very young children. With the passage of time, however, youngsters in poor families fall behind while those in better-off families experience gains. The cumulative impact of decline, in one case, and advance, in the other, affects the life profile of individuals and is reflected in phenomena that range from dropout rates to early motherhood, unemployment, and incarceration.

In accounting for such disparities, authors have given attention to instructional activities that youngsters are exposed to during the summer months when schools are not in session. The emphasis has been on subjects like reading and math, which represent continuity in the acquisition of formal knowledge. Richer families are in a better position to provide their offspring with access to summer camps and other structured programs. Poor children are more often left to fend for themselves in environments depleted of educational alternatives.

Here I extend that analysis to include channels, other than structured settings, that aid the acquisition of knowledge relevant to school advancement. Academic subjects are significant, but so are bits of information acquired through casual and sustained interactions with members of external networks. The capacity to forge imaginary and actual links to mainstream institutions is vital to the absorption and integration of insights from books and lessons in formal settings. That is because the meaning of words, for example, only becomes real when connected to embodied experiences.

I begin by calling to mind the work of Robert K. Merton, whose conceptualization of social action remains a foundational touchstone in sociology.

RETHINKING CULTURAL GOALS AND INSTITUTIONAL MEANS

Material and human resources may be broadly understood as mechanisms connecting cultural goals and institutional means, the subject of Robert K. Merton's classic paper, "Social Structure and Anomie" (1938). A modified version of his pathbreaking typology is presented in figure 9.

The figure is a crude attempt at conceptualizing various degrees of consonance in the jagged relationship between normative goals and social performance.[1] Greater harmony between dominant values and behaviors—the sop of neoconservative thinkers—depends not solely on access to institutional means, as Merton theorized, but also on the quality and quantity of assets at the disposal of groups distinguished by race, gender, and ethnicity.

Merton identified several types of behavioral outcomes—conformity, innovation, ritualism, retreat, and rebellion—resulting from dissimilar

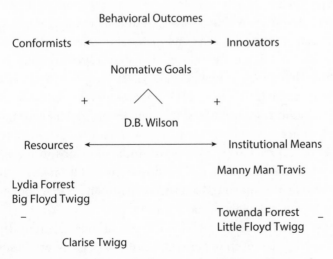

FIGURE 9. Cultural Goals and Institutional Means: Robert K. Merton Reassessed

intersections between cultural objectives and institutional means. Of those, the distinction between conformity and innovation proved to be most effective in attempts to explain common disparities in social performance between middle-class and poor people. In Merton's scheme, a correspondence between dominant cultural goals and institutional means produces conformity, that is, a capacity to align normative beliefs with personal conduct. When individuals adhere to mainstream mores but lack the institutional channels to implement them, they gravitate toward unconventional methods, thus becoming innovators. Extralegal behavior often is a mark of innovation.

In places like West Baltimore, for example, youngsters value things similar to those cherished by other Americans: family and friends, material accumulation, and self-reliance. In other environments, ordinary people realize those objectives through their involvement in functioning markets and contact with mainstream institutions; youngsters in urban settings shaped by capital retrogression, predatory commerce, and bureaucratic intrusion rely on alternative paths to achieve equivalent goals. Mediating the relationship between means and ends, as theorized by Merton, is the presence or absence of material, human, and ideational assets, which are also vital ingredients in the deployment of social capital. When present, such resources act as a cohesive agent that cements the relationship between values and social action.

Figure 9 also depicts the hypothesized position of individuals included in this book within a corresponding landscape formed by cultural goals, institutional means, and material resources. Although born poor, Donald B. Wilson, the subject of chapter 1, gained viable possessions through his employment in a manufacturing firm, and as a result, he secured the tools to implement dominant mores relevant to the fulfillment of adult responsibilities. By comparison, Lydia Forrest, whose life is recounted later in this book, held standard American values but lacked both the resources and the institutional means to make them work in accordance with generalized notions of rationality. Through the use of religion, she found alternative paths and social connections in urban spaces notable for their isolation.

Other lives narrated in this book fall into various positions depending on the triple connection between institutions, goals, and resources. Manny Man Travis, the protagonist of chapter 15, possessed greater information about and understanding of mainstream institutions than most of his peers. Nevertheless, he saw them as insufficient for securing material accumulation and upward mobility. He thus resorted to innovation by exploiting economic opportunities in his segregated neighborhood and becoming a successful drug dealer at an early age.

Affluent and educated people living in protected locations are in a better position to act in agreement with dominant mores than those residing in poor districts. Instances of true deviance—that is, individuals consciously adhering to oppositional or abhorrent principles— are rare in both settings. Depending on the material and intangible reserves available to them, people sort out into what C. Wright Mills (1959/2000) called *historically specific types*. Film stars and media personalities, for example, can engage in unconventional behaviors, including theft, adultery, and a plurality of sexual involvements, without facing the stern judgments confronted by poor welfare mothers. Similarly, working-class and unemployed men are more likely to attract severe penalties for breaking the law than their wealthier counterparts. The "common" criminal of the first case transmogrifies into the "celebrity" criminal of the second.

Thus, unconventional behaviors are not, for the most part, the result of deviant morality. Clarise's trajectory, like those of other people recognized in this book, illustrate that claim. In each case, what appear to be anomalous conducts are better described as attempts to approximate standard objectives in situations bereft of conventional means to achieve them.[2]

Individuals are born into and grow up as part of social networks endowed with concrete features. Through kinship and friendship ties they filter information, subsequently assigning meanings, classifying conducts, and yielding to or contesting authority. They make choices depending on the availability of concrete and virtual possessions but also on the way people in their midst interpret information and relate to structures of opportunity. Understandings forged through proximate contacts intersect with knowledge they obtain from external actors.

Clarise's attempt at making sense of contradictory information provides an example. Her speech patterns and limited vocabulary became embarrassing after she began attending a parochial school. She was anxious about the different meanings assigned to words and gestures by significant others—relatives, friends, and instructors—positioned in different social and physical locations. It was through the mediation of her favorite teacher that she understood the practicalities of code switching. Information offered by an external source—her favorite teacher—enabled her to create a bridge between her immediate circle and the outside world.

Clarise was also puzzled by incongruities between appearance and spatial setting. Given our close association, she wondered about my spot in America's racial hierarchy. By sorting out information through intimate connections, she was able to arrive at a satisfying conclusion, eventually "realizing" that I was "mixed." That piece of knowledge was validated by her most trusted informant, her cousin Towanda.

Jeremy Boissevain (1974) observes that a person's network is divided into zones occupied by individuals who know each other with varying degrees of familiarity (see also Bourdieu 1986; Coleman 1988; Portes 1998). For messages diffused throughout the larger society to acquire specific meanings, they must be personalized and made real through exchanges in close circles of intimacy. Thus, true learning originates in circumscribed localities. The spaces occupied by social networks provide tangible referents that buttress the signification of experience and shape the character of reciprocity.[3]

At what point did Clarise begin to relinquish early knowledge and desires? Was it when she was shamed for her singular enunciation? When she tried to reconcile the realities of two different worlds? When she sought to survive in public school?

A review of the girl's development suggests that her behavior altered in consonance with the quality and quantity of human and material assets at her disposal. Lydia's attempt to impose a restrictive code of conduct inadvertently thrust Clarise into situations that required rapid adjustment to achieve success, but in the public school, the meaning of success was different from the one cultivated at the parochial school that she had attended before.

Clarise's experience is emblematic of a process still under investigation. Attempts at elucidating youthful tendencies to drop out of school, bear children at an early age, or join gangs have been described in the past as expressions of an adversarial attitude. An indifference toward education, for example, was seen by authors like Schuman, Steeh, Bobo, and Krysan (1997) and Ogbu and Matute-Bianchi (1986) as evidence of an oppositional stance—a desire on the part of Blacks and Latinos to retain racial authenticity. Not "acting White" was seen as a cryptogram that further depressed youngsters' economic and social prospects.

Such behaviors, however, represent something altogether different— not the abandonment of mainstream goals but *a shift in the perceived locus of efficacy*. When youngsters surmise that certain goals are unrealistic or out of reach, their response is not to abandon them but to redefine them in ways that seem achievable. If advantages derived from school attendance appear false and elusive, securing a job, or at least a means of support, acquires salience. Among girls, success can be equated to having children. Motherhood entails adult fulfillment.

In other words, the propensity of impoverished youths to redefine the meaning of success may be likened to the moral in Aesop's fable, "The Fox and the Grapes." Eager to reach the tempting bunches of fruit hanging from a tall vine, the fox jumps at them over and over again without reward other than gashes in her fur. Tired and reluctant to accept failure, she dusts herself off, curses the grapes, and walks away saying they weren't ripe. Similarly, when young men and women realize that instructional settings available to them are not conducive to achievement, the response *appears to be* a shunning of education. It is *in actuality* a reorientation of effort to avoid defeat.

SOCIAL CAPITAL IN A BROADER TERRAIN

Phenomena like those discussed above are best understood from the perspective of economic sociology, a field that has grown over the last three decades, and one of whose key concepts is *social capital*.[4] As originally defined, social capital encompasses *benefits accruing to individuals by virtue of their membership in specific social networks* (Portes 1998, 2010). Social capital is often interchangeable with and complementary to other possessions—material, human, or cultural. Closure, that is, the capacity of social networks to command vital resources in the pursuit of particular ends, enables individuals connected through trust and mutuality to maximize the effect of endowments, such as education. In James Coleman's view (1988), social capital is an integrative force leading to upward economic mobility; his perspective is consistent with functionalistic traditions in American sociology.

Coleman's views were originally sketched in *Equality of Educational Opportunity* (Coleman et al. 1966)—the famous Coleman Report—where, after investigating a sample of more than 150,000 youngsters, Coleman and his associates concluded that student background and socioeconomic status, both factors critical in the production of social capital, are more important than measured differences in per pupil spending when determining educational outcomes. Teachers in parochial schools are an illustration. They earn lower salaries than those in public institutions but they typically produce better instructional outcomes. According to Coleman, that is because parochial schools are in a better position to deploy social capital and impose closure (see also Putnam 2001).

That interpretation was soon appropriated by conservative thinkers to show the limitations of government interventions and the presumed virtues of privatization. A focus on social capital informed campaigns to organize charter schools and distribute vouchers enabling low-income families to enroll their children in private and parochial schools. Such actions pivoted on the conviction that, by expanding options through deregulation, parents would be in a better position to provide children with improved educational alternatives. Competition, in turn, would force educational providers to raise their standards.

In the abstract, those ideas make sense, but when applied to concrete realities, they have limited success. That is because they do not interrogate the material and informational foundations of choice. They assume that when terrains are leveled, equivalent alternatives will be available to all competing actors. That conclusion is false; to be poor is to command information of a different scale and quality than the one available to people in control of more and better assets. Leveling competitive fields through the expansion of choices does not improve the capacity of people to improve personal options unless the fundaments of economic and racial inequality are directly addressed.

Thus, research conducted for nearly two decades now shows that voucher programs benefit mostly children in families already at an advantage, not impoverished youngsters who need them most (Carnoy 2001; Pedroni 2007). That is because in addition to lacking adequate information, poor families also lack the financial wherewithal and means of transportation to facilitate access to distant schools.

A better solution to the quandaries faced by needy children would be to expand employment opportunities for their parents, reduce levels of racial segregation, and diminish the operations of liminal government institutions in the urban areas where those children reside. As shown in chapter 5, more than two centuries of legislative action promoting high-quality education and access to real estate among mainstream populations demonstrates their efficacy. In lieu of exerting political will to implement similar measures toward the poor, policy makers continue to rely on a hodgepodge of mostly ineffectual palliative measures.[5]

Coleman's work spurred an ongoing debate about the application of social capital to children's educational advancement. Mark Granovetter (1973) revolutionized thinking in that regard with his distinction between *strong* and *weak ties*, the terms he used to distinguish between qualitatively different connections between and among social actors. In his view, strong ties are those linking individuals in intimate circles, including family members and close friends whose backing tends to be unconditional and predicated upon affective relations. Weak ties, by contrast, connect individuals to external actors, some of whom may be in a position to expand an individual's options through intermittent exchanges. Poor people tend to have a plurality of strong ties, but they lack weak ties joining them to groups and resources outside their immediate environment.[6]

Bearing resemblance to Coleman's and Granovetter's work was research conducted by the political scientist Robert Putman. In an article published in 1995, he popularized the notion of social capital by equating it to civic sense, a factor he believes to be the mainstay of collective integrity, educational achievement, and economic progress. In Putnam's perspective, group efficacy is the result of a competent use of social networks, such as voluntary organizations, to maximize the public good.

A logical implication of Putnam's views was that social capital can be employed to solve the problems associated with poverty and anomie. Largely for that reason, his ideas resonated far and wide, informing the outlooks of institutions like the World Bank and the United Nations.

Putnam's interpretation also captured the imagination of policy circles in the Clinton administration. Proposals to bolster social capital in inner-city neighborhoods multiplied, and Putnam was invited to lecture at the White House. He later developed his perspective in an extended version of the article that first drew him to public attention, a book titled *Bowling Alone: The Collapse and Revival of American Community* (2001).[7]

Despite its popularity, the focus on social capital as a remedy for poverty yielded minimal results. The absence of access to mainstream institutions and the presence of high levels of insularity—caused by negligible investment, in tandem with predatory commerce and government omnipresence—disable the poor from converting social capital into economic progress and social advance. Social capital abounds in poor neighborhoods; family and friends are mostly what the poor have (Stack 1971/1997). Without competent use of social networks, and a measure of mutuality, indigent families would not be able to survive. And, notwithstanding the fracturing effects of bureaucratic intrusion and the drug trade, inner-city residents constantly seek a refuge in which to enact or approximate normative conducts and relationships; it is largely the dearth of weak ties that keeps them stuck at the bottom of the social ladder.

The erroneous conviction that poverty results from the absence of social capital has been matched by the exaggerated belief in social capital as a tool to achieve economic success, civic participation, and political engagement. In opposition to that conceit, Portes (1998) offers a detailed account of the leveling effects of social capital in situations where upwardly mobile youngsters, including immigrants, are unable to accumulate wealth because of expectations that they should support relatives. In that case, strong ties reduce the capacity of individuals to develop weak ties. Pressures exerted by kin and friends to share the little that upwardly bound individuals have mustered can trap all concerned in poverty.

Cecilia Menjívar (2000) has given attention to similar phenomena among Salvadoran immigrants whose reduced status and means produce high levels of fragmentation. Löic Wacquant (1997) further discusses negative social capital as a factor perpetuating anomalous conditions in urban ghettos. The conclusion derived from such writings is that social capital in any setting can expand benefits accruing to individuals, but it can also reinforce the damaging effects of isolation. That fact is aptly illustrated by the interaction between Lydia Forrest and Clarise Twigg, described in the preceding chapter.

In contrast to Coleman and Putnam, Pierre Bourdieu (1986) conceptualized social capital as part of group relationships marked by conflict and the search for affirmation. While Coleman emphasized integrative features and Putman focused on civic spirit, Bourdieu noted the role of social capital in the constitution of inequities. In Bourdieu's scheme, society is formed by a plurality of fields, some of which are related to class and others are defined by factors such as gender, race, and ethnicity. From that point of view, social capital is "an assemblage of resources, actual or potential, in the possession of a durable set of social relationships with shared knowledge and level of power" (Bourdieu 1986: 242).

Like Coleman, Bourdieu notes the role of individuals as key actors in social exchanges, but in contrast, he mostly envisions social capital as a group attribute (Siisiäinen 2000). Bourdieu emphasizes the role of power in the acquisition and deployment of social capital, whereas power is nearly absent in Coleman's and Putnam's perspectives. And while Coleman stresses the role of *mutuality* and *trust*, Bourdieu refrains from using such terms, instead giving attention to reciprocal cognition and recognition as necessary elements that transform *social* capital into what he calls *symbolic capital*.[8]

CULTURAL CAPITAL AT WORK

In his "Forms of Capital" (1986), Bourdieu further defines various types of immaterial goods essential for the creation of wealth and the maintenance of collective well-being. He equates cultural capital to material assets because, in his view, it can be used and exchanged in the pursuit of economic mobility. Drawing from Bourdieu, I contend that symbolic capital may be best understood as *a series of expressive behaviors forged collectively and placed into circulation to affirm group membership and identity.* Among poor people, that is about the only capital in store and worth mobilizing.

Such a conceptualization sheds light on widespread behaviors in destitute neighborhoods. Lydia Forrest's emphasis on pulchritude, for example, and her attempt to subdue Clarise's hair acquire vivid meaning when seen from that perspective. Neither of the two conducts was a mechanical response to stigma; both actions were also part of an independent search for respectability and differentiation. Such elements of identity have multiple effects: the mystique surrounding hair in general and Clarise's hair in particular diminished the girl's enthusiasm for swimming, an activity that had connected her to a wider and more diverse social network. On the other hand, the assertion of cleanliness and respectability had positive connotations in Lydia's circle; it made her stand out as a responsible and ethical guardian.

Wacquant (1998: 27) reaches similar conclusions with respect to the use of language in racially segregated areas. Mastery of the Black English vernacular and the linguistic games it permits is highly valued in the ghetto, but its use is condemned in school; it functions as positive cultural capital in the first context but as negative in the second (see also Kochman 1973; Gilmore 1985; Solomon 1992).

Religion, as well, can be an effective resource to mark an elevated social standing among impoverished people, as I further discuss in chapter 14. Lydia Forrest and her son, Lorenzo, used their beliefs as Jehovah's Witnesses to uplift Clarise's moral status and control her behavior. Doctrinal demands, however, reduced Clarise's capacity to pursue objectives outside her immediate environment.

As a budding adolescent, Clarise deployed symbolic capital in meaningful actions towards peers and adults. In her case—illustrative of widespread experiences among youngsters—striking a pose was not a simple gesture of detachment; it was also an affirmation of independence. Marks of deodorant in her armpits were not to be confused for abandon; they were signs of cleanliness. Among her friends, wearing one's shoes unlaced or one's overall straps let loose, or hat turned backwards, or pants low enough to expose underwear, or leaving combs stuck in one's hair sometimes might have been acts of rebellion, but they always were affirmative expressions of self-distinctiveness. The same is true about aesthetic manifestations, from graffiti to hip-hop (DiMaggio and Fernández-Kelly 2010). Matters of identity are crucial in all social groups, but they reflect raw endurance among the dispossessed.

Finally, Lydia's belief in the power of the individual to overcome difficulties was not a trite slogan borrowed from preachers and politicians. She had lived out the refrain in her own life through exceptional effort to turn adverse conditions into a series of personal triumphs: securing marriage, supporting her family, and gaining respect. She saw herself as the protagonist of a morality tale in which good would eventually overcome evil. Her efforts may have had unwanted consequences, but her cultural repertory was as American as they come.

BONDING AND BRIDGING CAPITAL

In recent years, authors have made additional efforts to describe the operations of social capital. Major contributions have come from thinkers who have distinguished between *bonding* and *bridging* types (Jarret 1995; Jarret, Jefferson, and Kelly 2010). According to Aldridge, Halpern, and Fitzpatrick (2002), bonding effects are horizontal and occur among peers in a common social network, while bridging capital connects disparate communities (Dolfsma and Dannreuther 2003; Narayan 2002). Anheier and Kendall (2002) further suggest that bridging social capital is closely related to various forms of confidence involved in interpersonal transactions. From that vantage point, bridging capital relies on "thin" trust, while bonding social capital depends on "thick" layers of dependability. Bonding capital exists in lower-income neighborhoods, but bridging social capital is scarce (Sampson, Morenoff, and Earls 1999).

Thus, as Warren, Thompson, and Saegert (2001: 4) note, "the main problem for [the poor] may not be a relative deficit in social capital, but that their social assets have greater obstacles to overcome, and are constantly under assault." An illustration is provided by Edin and Lein (1997), who investigate the daily routines of mothers living in public housing; they consistently depend on cash flows circulating in networks formed by family and friends. Bonding capital enables those women to obtain bare necessities, but their efforts never transcend the limits of their immediate circle (Larsen, Harlan, et al. 2004).

Similar conclusions apply to West Baltimore, where women like Lydia Forrest and her neighbors depended on each other to function on a daily basis. Lydia, in particular, was known as a generous woman who seldom turned away children or adults in need of assistance. Her small home was regularly occupied by friends and relatives. Benita Wallace, Lydia's niece and Clarise's mother, was one of them. Although reluctant, Lydia was a dependable source of emergency cash and overnight shelter for her wayward relative. Her judgments were harsh, but there was little question that Benita could always rely on her aunt.

Women residing in the George Murphy Homes were seldom able to get to the end of the month on their meager welfare checks and food stamps; they depended on credit extended by patient store owners but also on loans from relatives and friends. Some received irregular contributions from the fathers of their children. Many played the numbers or bought lottery tickets, hoping to increase their funds. While such behaviors maximized the likelihood of survival, they did little to push them out of poverty.

SOCIAL CAPITAL AND THE SUMMER ACHIEVEMENT GAP

I met Justin L. Carson in 1995, when he was ten years old. His mother, Annette Smithson, was a soft-spoken woman whose poised demeanor concealed a nasty addiction to crack cocaine. Despite her personal struggles, she doted on Justin, an exuberant boy with a broad smile and a sharp wit. For a while, Justin had been eager to join Clarise Twigg and her brother, Floyd, at the swim and tennis club where I regularly took them. One day, Justin simply refused to stay home. Eventually, he too became a student at the Holy Spirit School and, like Clarise, he experienced remarkable academic progress over the next few years.

Justin wore his school uniform with style, but in the summer months he shed it for his favorite attire: shorts, sneakers, and a tank top. He cavorted like a goat on the Baltimore streets and by the poolside, turning cartwheels and jumping rope. Yet, despite his winning personality and love of life, Justin could hardly read or write at the time of his enrollment in the third grade at Holy Spirit. Like Clarise, he had a narrow command of English and a limited vocabulary.

Eager to keep him busy during the summer, I connected Justin and other children in his circle with a friend of mine who, opportunely, was vying for a spot on the Baltimore City Council. He was happy to take the children under his wing to serve as "summer interns" in his political campaign. They loved stuffing envelopes with leaflets promoting the candidate's virtues and tagging along with him in related activities. One evening, after picking up Justin and his crew at my friend's political headquarters, I casually asked the boy about his day. "It was a lot of fun," he replied, "we went *canvassing*."

It was the ease with which he pronounced the word that struck me. A child with his educational deficits would have found it difficult to know the meaning of the term under any other circumstances, but in this case, Justin had acquired the word through direct experience. It had become part of his embodied knowledge. He hadn't read the word in a book; he had absorbed it as part of his sociable interactions. There lay the true meaning of bridging social capital. There too resided a clue to understanding the summer gap in learning.

In 1978, the sociologist Barbara Heyns published *Summer Learning and the Effects of Schooling*, a landmark study of nearly three thousand youngsters in the fifth, sixth, and seventh grades in Atlanta's public schools. Hers was the first longitudinal investigation of children's knowledge acquisition over the summer months. She discovered that poor children and Black children come close to the performance of middle-class youngsters in cognitive advancement when schools are in session, but they fall behind when they are in recess. Heyns's research showed that in general, low-income students lose close to three months of grade-level equivalency during the summer. By comparison, middle-income students lose only about one month. With the passage of time, the gap widens.[9]

In 1982, Doris Entwisle and Karl Alexander extended that line of research through another remarkable project, the Beginning School Study, an examination of school children's progression in Baltimore City over more than two decades. They compared the school-year and summer gains of nearly eight hundred youngsters in twenty public schools from the first grade onward. They also tracked students' progress through high school and college (Entwisle, Alexander and Olson 2000). They found that by year nine, youngsters in low-income families lagged seventy-three points behind children in better-off families in reading comprehension, as measured by the same standardized test scores. About one-third of that differential, or twenty-seven points, was in place at the time children in the sample entered first grade. Subsequently, poor children fell further behind each year, with the gap reaching a plateau of about seventy points in the fifth grade. The remaining two-thirds of the seventy-three-point gap grew over the course of the elementary and middle school years.

Similar facts were uncovered by Douglas B. Downey, Paul T. von Hippel, and Beckett A. Broh (2004), researchers at the Ohio State University, who drew data from the Early Childhood Longitudinal Study to conduct a nationwide investigation of 17,000 kindergarten and first-grade children. They corroborated earlier findings concerning inequalities in performance among students beginning their school years, showing that one standard deviation's lead in socioeconomic status predicts close to a one-month advantage in initial reading skill on the first day of kindergarten. They also found that the class-based achievement gap continues to grow after schooling starts, with summer learning accounting for most of the difference in achievement between poorer children and their wealthier counterparts.[10]

A meta-analysis of thirty-nine studies conducted since 1978 further substantiated those claims: in the absence of school, students of all kinds score lower on standardized math tests at the end of the summer as compared with their performance on the same tests at the beginning of summer. This loss is more pronounced in subjects like mathematical computation, where an average setback of more than two months of grade-level equivalency has been observed among both middle- and lower-class students. In reading and language, however, more substantial differences emerge. While more-affluent children show negligible gains in reading scores, poor students show major losses: there is a differential of three months in grade-level reading skills between the two groups as a result of the summer interruption in formal learning.

Even more recently, Alexander, Entwisle, and Olson (2007) examined the long-term educational effects of summer learning differences, finding that cumulative achievement gains over the first nine years of schooling mostly reflect school-year learning. Out-of-school summer learning variations, in turn, significantly account for achievement-related disparities in college preparatory placements toward the end of high school. Such disparities are strongly correlated with school

abandonment in the case of poor children and four-year college attendance in the case of middle- and upper-class youths.

The best data thus show that the broadening divisions in achievement between low-income and better-off children depend largely on
class background. Cognitive gains during the school year remain nearly
equal between both poor and richer children but mounting summer
deficits expand the chasm between them. Moreover, research on the
summer learning gap conclusively shows that schools, even those that
are less effective, promote the acquisition of knowledge relative to periods of time without structured instruction. Schools equalize educational outcomes, not in absolute terms, but relative to the inequality
produced when schools are closed (Heyns 1987: 1156).

Schools are a main source of cognitive progress but other factors
contribute to it as well. Beyond the confines of formal instructional
settings, knowledge acquisition is significantly influenced by cultural
and social forces operating throughout the year (Heyns 1987: 1156).
Downey, von Hippel, and Broh (2004: 634) thus argue that to reduce
inequalities between impoverished and more-affluent youngsters, it is
necessary to enhance disadvantaged children's nonschool environments
or increase their exposure to schooling. All this can be reformulated as
follows: the dearth of formal educational alternatives during the summer months explains the plummeting gains of impoverished children,
but also significant is the absence of informal connections to external
groups in settings that facilitate the acquisition of practical knowledge.

MENTORING AS BRIDGING SOCIAL CAPITAL

There is a paucity of systematic research on the effects of sustained
informal contacts between children in poor neighborhoods and better-
off individuals in richer districts. That is largely because the condition
of poverty in the United States involves high levels of residential segregation in terms of race and class. On a day-to-day basis, Black children
living in poor neighborhoods are unlikely to interact with people residing in other districts unless those interactions occur as part of commercial exchanges or in institutional settings. As discussed in chapter
6, the latter often are government agencies that operate according to a

liminal logic that accentuates disconnection from the larger society (see also Massey and Denton 1993; Wacquant 1998).

On the other hand, a growing literature on mentoring programs can serve as a proxy to widen understanding about forms of sociability that enhance childhood learning through informal exchanges. The richest available source of information on school-based mentoring programs is Big Brothers/Big Sisters, a longtime endeavor that pairs volunteers with boys and girls in deprived neighborhoods (Herrera, Grossman, et al. 2007/2011). Research on such efforts and similar initiatives of a smaller scale suggest that unstructured connections between mentors and low-income children have a host of positive effects.

Gaddis (2012), for example, used data from youth and mentors in several chapters of Big Brothers/Big Sisters to assess the characteristics of mentoring relationships. As part of his research, he gave attention to the effects of social capital on academic and behavioral outcomes, concluding that the amount of time spent in mentoring and the level of trust involved have positive effects on the conduct of young people.[11] Contrary to intuitive beliefs, Gaddis found that race-matching and closure between parent and mentor have limited repercussions, and social class differences between individuals have no significant effects on youthful behaviors. In other words, what seem to make a difference in mentoring are (a) the duration of the relationship and (b) the level of trust joining the two parties, both factors defining social capital.

More generally, mentoring studies have focused on two kinds of efforts: initiatives operating at the community level and mostly depending on local resources, and school-based projects that couple students with volunteers who guide them in their academic strivings. In both cases, mentoring relationships have been found to be positive for young people in unsatisfactory relationships with parents or other caregivers (Grossman et al. 2012). Mentors can function as sounding boards, and they can casually model effective interpersonal and communication skills, helping children to understand, express, and regulate their emotions (McDowell et al. 2002).

Children can then appropriate and extend such personal experiences to achieve more effective interactions with others. As a result, durable mentoring relationships have been linked to significant improvements in youths' perceptions of their interactions with parents, peers, and other adults (DuBois and Karcher 2013). Some research also finds that more-frequent meetings (Slicker and Palmer 1993) and longer overall matches (Grossman and Rhodes 2002) lead to better academic and behavioral outcomes.

In a related project, Grossman, Chan, Schwarz, and Rhodes (2012) studied match length and rematching on the effectiveness of school-based mentoring through a randomized study of more than one thousand youngsters in Big Brothers/Big Sisters programs. The sample included youths in grades four through nine from diverse racial and ethnic backgrounds. They found that at the end of one year, uninterrupted relationships between mentors and protégées had yielded significant improvements in academic achievement. Pairings that ended prematurely showed no impact, but those that were rematched after interruptions exhibited negative effects, perhaps because of the child's response to feelings of abandonment by a previous mentor.[12] More importantly, the experience and length of time invested in the mentoring relationship increased the likelihood of continuation. Children in matches lasting twenty-four weeks or more attained the largest academic benefits.[13]

The most reliable data on mentoring programs thus suggest that it is not just interaction between parties that can bring about benefits but also the integrity and duration of the mentoring match. In other words, at their best, mentoring relationships come close to replicating weak ties and expanding strong ties. Good mentoring associations are not very different from those established between children and older, richer, and more cosmopolitan relatives who command larger stocks of cognitive and material resources. A mentoring relationship expands children's access to critical assets and enlarges their social networks. Mentoring programs thus offer a fleeting glance at possibilities that would open up through the reduction of class and racial inequalities. Such relationships diminish levels of isolation and connect children to a universe of ideas and tools not present in their immediate environments.[14]

As illustrated by the lives of children featured in this book, one of the dire effects of residential segregation is a reduced command over the dominant language and, therefore, diminished possibilities to tap higher levels of education and attractive employment options. Ultimately, language deficits represent the last bastion of class and racial inequality.

In light of these findings, it is possible to reconsider the effects of capital retrogression, distorted engagement, and liminal institutions that perpetuate isolation among impoverished, racially distinct children. If productive investment is increased and residential segregation is reduced in America's inner cities, the effects of mentoring programs would be generalized as a result of the removal of barriers that currently delay the social integration of a significant segment of American society.

In the next two chapters, I continue this line of thinking by exploring identity formation and its relationship to cultural capital. Towanda Forrest leads the way.

11 TOWANDA

TOWANDA FORREST WAS TWELVE YEARS OLD WHEN I FIRST MET her in 1990, a gorgeous woman-child with a grainy inflection and eyes full of daring. During one of our first conversations, she told me:

> Only fools get pregnant. They be thinking they so smart but they is fools 'cause you don't gain nothing by having a baby, only worries. I tell the other girls, Towanda's smart, she will never get pregnant—never! Just wait and see.

One of five children born to Lydia Forrest and the second conceived by Lydia and the man who would become her legitimate husband, James Culver, Towanda was sharp and spirited. Her two older brothers had a different father and their birth had taken place much earlier, when Lydia was young and reckless. By the time Towanda came of age, Lydia had emerged as the moral center of her extended family; gone were the days of mayhem and dissipation; toward the end of the twentieth century, Lydia cultivated dignity.

Towanda's oldest brother, named Reuben after his wayward father and nicknamed Beamy because of his cheerful disposition, was a distant memory. She could not remember him ever living at home; for nearly a decade, he had been locked up after being convicted as an accessory to the murder of a Baltimore cab driver. Once in a while, Lydia would take Towanda with her to the Jessup Prison for a visit with Beamy—her son, her firstborn, the child in whom she had invested so much hope and then seen handcuffed, carried away in leg irons as a common criminal.

When she was little, Towanda didn't know enough to tell the difference between prison and other dwelling places. She merely thought that some people, like Beamy, lived in large buildings where they spoke to visitors through bulletproof parapets. She remembered putting the palm of her hand against the cold surface of the transparent, dividing shield while Beamy did the same on his side. He had large, strong hands and he always said nice things to her. He was a good brother.

After Towanda grew older and understood why Beamy lived away from home, she was first humiliated and then angry. All along, she had been looking up to someone whom no one else respected. From then on, she refused to visit Beamy in prison. By the age of twelve, she could hardly recollect what her half-brother looked like. In a desultory tone she told me, "Maybe, if I see him in the street, I don't know him, tha's jus' the way it is."

Next in line among her siblings was Lorenzo, whom the family knew as Weedy. He had been living in Washington, DC, since Towanda was eight. There he drove a limousine for hire and dealt drugs to supplement his income. His move away from home had been prompted by an altercation with his stepfather, James Culver, whom Weedy despised for many reasons but mainly because James had usurped his place as head of the family; he was an interloper and a drunk, Weedy thought. In passionate contrast, Weedy loved his mother. He visited Baltimore regularly with presents to express his devotion.

The children in Lydia's extended family believed that Weedy owned the limo he drove. Towanda was no exception. She thought her brother was rich because he brought her gifts and cash. Once he gave her a crisp twenty-dollar bill. Towanda kept it for the longest time, until she thought about buying a "very fancy makeup set." By the age of six she knew she was attractive and hastened to make the most of her appearance. She had a honey-colored complexion and bold features. Her hair draped about her shoulders, pleated like a mantle.

Felicia, Towanda's older sister, was four years her senior; an obedient, worry-prone girl who worshipped her mother and often took her place looking after the younger children. Even at the age of seven, Felicia had been entrusted with Towanda's care. She bathed her and washed her hair, admiring her loveliness all along. Felicia didn't care much for her own looks. She abhorred her kinky hair and heavy-set frame. Not able to rely on appearance to be popular, she depended on good behavior at home and at school. People in her circle knew that she could hold her ground—as a child, she had always been treated as a short adult. She was trustworthy, like her mother. Sometimes she felt invisible but liked it that way; her reward for loneliness was respect. And Felicia had ambition: she hoped, one day, to be a nurse because she was good at taking care of others.

Towanda also had a younger brother, James Jr., known as Mush. He had been born a sinewy child and grew up to be strong and pleasant. He did well in school until the age of twelve when he was hit by a car while crossing North Avenue. He wasn't killed but suffered concussions that his mother blamed for the boy's change of temperament. He became belligerent and rebellious, confirming Lydia's newly found conviction, as a Jehovah's Witness, that evil was a real and active force in the world, entering bodies and minds without warning. It was left up to people like Lydia to fight on the side of good, awaiting the Second Coming of Christ, and looking after the fallen angels whose lives Satan was always trying to ruin.

Towanda thought differently; she didn't think her younger brother was so much evil as willful. He did what he wanted to do without regard for other people's opinions. In this, Mush was like Towanda; she too was keenly aware of the turmoil engulfing youngsters in her crowd but didn't worry about the causes—her main goal was survival.

In addition to her siblings, Towanda thought of Clarise Twigg—who was five years younger and shared her room—as part of her immediate family. Clarise was the daughter of Lydia's crack-addicted niece, Benita Wallace. The child had been living with her since the authorities declared her a child in need of assistance . Clarise was Towanda's niece twice removed, but Towanda thought of her as a sister or cousin. Kinship nomenclature in extended families where women become mothers in adolescence assigns all children in the same cohort a similar status and label. Lydia had been appointed as Clarise's guardian and, as a result, the child had become her daughter for all practical purposes.

The same was true among the growing number of families in West Baltimore, where middle-age women assumed responsibility for grandchildren after their own sons or daughters became parents at an early age. In West Baltimore, adolescent pregnancies have been the norm, not the exception, for nearly four decades. In 1995 more than 40 percent of all girls nineteen or younger living in Upton and Sandtown-Winchester had given birth to at least one child. With small fluctuations, that trend has continued in the second decade of the twenty-first century.[1] Young mothers are seldom equipped to care for their children—some are too inexperienced, and others, like Clarise's mother, are impaired by dangerous drugs that consume their time and energy. As a result, older women end up caring for babies.

Clarise, who thought of Towanda as her big sister, looked up to her in ways that no one else did. The two girls shared the same bedroom in the broken-down house on Goodyear Street that the family inhabited before moving to a low-rise in the projects. As Clarise grew older, she increasingly depended on Towanda to organize her sense of the world. It was Towanda who explained to Clarise who was who in the neighborhood. It was Towanda who shaped Clarise's taste in clothes and eventually told her about boys and sex.

According to her mother, Towanda was tough even as a small child. Lydia could remember the look in her daughter's face when, as a toddler, she confronted parental authority, or was asked to do anything she was unwilling to do. Said the mother, "[Towanda] just stood there, doing nothing, sayin' nothing, looking at you like she was all growed up. . . . I jus' wanted to slap her face."

And Lydia often did, in a futile attempt to bring the girl into compliance. She did not succeed. The girl always fought back. She was six when her neighbor's seven-year-old son, Rudy Price, tried to steal a piece of food from her plate while visiting Lydia's home. Towanda stopped him with a fork. The boy suffered no serious damage but the gesture spoke volumes about Towanda's disposition. Lydia protested the girl's ways but she also respected her. She concluded that it was her daughter's nature to be contrarian. Towanda was strong and clear-minded. She took guff from no one, not even her mother.

It was therefore not surprising that, as she grew older, Towanda became a mighty presence in her neighborhood. She vividly remembered her first day at the Gilmore Elementary School, its clean corridors and the large bulletin board framed in green crepe paper, featuring signs that read in large yellow letters, WELCOME STUDENTS! It still gave her a thrill, at the age of twelve, to remember her first classroom, filled with light and the sound of children ready to learn. "I sometimes wish that day didn't end," she told me wistfully:

Because it was one of the happiest [days] I ever had. I wasn't afraid; it was good to be out of the house. I jus loved those nice books where we could put numbers and write words. I love the way they smelled. And the teachers, they was nice. I was only seven but yeah! I wanted to learn so bad. . . . I loved that school!

First impressions gradually faded as Towanda noticed the scrawls in textbooks that had been used before, the indifference shown by some teachers, and the broken gym with its boarded-up door, but in the beginning, like most young children, Towanda was filled with expectation. According to her teacher, Paula Robinson, who took an early interest in the girl and remembered her well, "[Towanda] was a pistol. All the other kids wanted either to be near her or really far from her because, if she liked you, she really did, but if you got on her bad side, she could be a force." Towanda agreed:

Right away I knows who need to be my friends. But it's the same everywhere—you start makin' friends and that means other people get left out, and they get other friends too; so now you have crews that don't like each other. They act nasty to each other. They don't know much about each other, but they know they don't like each other because they in different camps. So you end up fighting for no reason at all, just because you have different friends. It's crazy but it's real, and you learn that right away.

Given her outgoing personality and good looks, Towanda soon became a leader, popular and skillful at bringing people into her sphere of influence, and rejecting others to show her power. At the age of nine, she had her first big fight. Her motives, she said, were legitimate:

There are people that just annoy you all the time and Lavinia [Thomas] was one of those people. She din't know how to behave. She was always out of line, laughing when she shouldn't, mouthing off all the time. So this one morning, she bumped into me, right? And I knows she's not intentional, but I still pretend she was, 'cause it was about time she got her ass kicked for being stupid. So I shoved her back an' she come back to me and we fight. The principal suspended us for a couple of days. When I went back to school, it wasn't the same no more; maybe people thought I was a troublemaker. I started feelin' bad; like I didn't belong.

Then, when Towanda was a sixth-grader, her body began to change. She got her first period, a development that filled her with a renewed sense of self, and she grew breasts and hips. Lydia, her mother, was concerned at such a rapid transformation in a child so young. Only yesterday, Towanda had been one more little girl in the neighborhood; now, according to her mother, she looked like "a half grown mare that needs reining-in real good."

Lydia bought Towanda her first brassiere and soon found herself in perpetual conflict with her daughter over what kinds of clothes the girl was allowed to wear. Towanda favored garments that displayed her physical assets, while her mother tried to conceal them. Such conflicts are common beyond impoverished areas in American cities. In tough neighborhoods, however, children soon learn that mothers lack the wherewithal to impose control, given their humble economic and social stature. And so it was that Towanda, smart and pugnacious, began to test limits to her actions, defying Lydia at every step of the way.

At first, she felt guilty when yelling back at her mother in bursts of emotion that left both of them disgruntled and limp. In time, feeling gave way to numb habit. Whatever the mother dictated, the daughter opposed. According to Towanda:

> It's because my mother, she can't understand. She tries to make things right, but wha's right about our life? My father a drunk, my brother in jail, never enough money to pay for nothing, everybody always screaming. There's never peace. Sometimes, I wish I could just go somewhere far away where I was not myself. I feel bad to say [these things] but it's true. It would be best if I was someone else.

As Towanda grew older, and home grew more difficult to endure, public spaces offered endless opportunity. Under Lydia's relentless watch, Towanda felt trapped, angry, and always at fault. Slamming the front door behind her, she could breathe an air of independence; she could step into places where she was not a child anymore but the main character in an unfolding adventure.

School became a terrain for sociability where gossip, intrigue, and potential romance vastly outweighed the benefits of formal learning. Towanda may have been poor, but she was not stupid; like other children in her circle, she could tell that success through education is a lie when schools have fallen into disrepair, books typically have pages missing, and teachers, perhaps once hopeful and bright, now show hermetic indifference. Few if any in Towanda's circle had completed high school. She knew no one able to hold a better job by staying in school.

By contrast, the street with its variegated landscape of corners and alleys, stoops and doorsteps, parks and playgrounds, presented a platform for experimentation and pleasure. Now thirteen, Towanda attracted more than compliments for her pretty face; boys in the neighborhood went giddy when she walked by. At school, envious girls began to hate her, and at least one of the teachers, Clara Lancy, made plain her contempt for Towanda. Lancy thought the girl was a cockteaser and didn't hesitate to tell her. It was a grossly uneven confrontation— the grown-up bullying a young child—but the teacher didn't see it that way; she thought that by talking straight, she was exercising her right to correct the girl. Her insult paid off, bringing tears to Towanda's eyes. Few people could make Towanda cry, including her mother. She also knew that some of her peers called her names behind her back. Now, the teacher was siding with her enemies.

At an age when children in more affluent families are preoccupied with extracurricular activities and athletic pursuits, Towanda was involved in an elemental political struggle defining territories and loyalties. Divisions were clear: her friends were devoted to her, imitating her gestures and manner of dress; her opponents tried to find every opportunity to trip her and make her fall. She told me:

> It wasn't like I planned it, 'cause I wasn't messin around with boys or nothing like that, but when that bitch [Clara Lancy] call me a cockteaser, I just decided to show her and the others. You never think a teacher [who's] supposed to set an example would call you names. But she wasn't goin' to make me cry again. No way! It was OK by me if she thought I was a slut. There's no way anyone would call her [Lancy] a slut—you know why? 'Cause no man would want to fuck that ugly cow!

It was about the same time that Towanda intensified her confrontations in school as part of an attempt to strengthen her top position in the youthful pecking order. When Lucinda Martin, one of her rivals, a girl with a slender body and a filthy mouth, told Towanda that Dionne, the most popular boy in their class, thought she was a ho, Towanda didn't flinch. She stood tall in the school yard chewing gum, looking at her fingernails with a cocked head and a desultory gaze. When Lucinda turned her back and was about to walk away, Towanda leapt forward like a cougar pouncing on a rabbit. She pulled Lucinda's hair, forced her to the ground, and punched her in the face.

This brought delight to the gathering crowd until the gym teacher, Mr. Johnson, stopped the fight. Lucinda was bloodied. Towanda was suspended for a week, continuing a troubling trend. That didn't matter to her; she had salvaged her pride and knew that other youngsters admired her for her courage.

With her attention now fully focused on containing anger, responding to insult, and courting favor, Towanda relinquished her last bit of interest in academic subjects. She wrote and read with difficulty, and once, in my presence, she confidently stated that New York was the capital of Africa. She wasn't joking. She could add and subtract a little, but her knowledge remained rudimentary into adulthood.

On the other hand, her warring instincts were superb. Now the center of her social network, she thought of school mostly as a setting for display and competition. Her life was full of trickery and drama. She bargained and made alliances, and soon she began to sample the elements of young adulthood in deprived neighborhoods. At fourteen, she tried her first joint of marijuana. Her friend, Deiondre Garrett, a muscular boy in dreadlocks, sixteen at the time, knew how to get it and where to find the money to pay for it. He was the local procurer, an apprentice of Calvin Cooper, who was known in the streets as Blackjack. Blackjack knew Jamaicans who regularly dumped a variety of controlled substances throughout West Baltimore. Deiondre looked up to Blackjack, and from him he obtained small amounts of crack and grass to peddle among his friends and acquaintances. Towanda was one of them.

Before the age of fifteen, Towanda had virtually dropped out of school but not out of sight. She kept up the pretense for the benefit of her mother, who still thought that her daughter was headed for Marshall Middle School every morning when she left home. Instead, Towanda often met with her crew outside the school to chat and take in the news of the day. Sometimes, she followed Deiondre and the others to a nearby townhouse where the boy lived with an older sister. Because the sister worked long hours at a fast-food place, she was seldom home.

Unbound by the strictures and obligations of school, Towanda found a freedom and status seldom available to middle-class youngsters, whose lives are overscheduled and tightly regimented. Independence, she thought, was the mark of adulthood. Having become a nodal point in her circle, she could exchange critical bits of information that resulted in the mobilization of scarce resources. She knew, for example, the secrets of kids who didn't speak to one another and could persuade them to combine forces to reach mutually beneficial goals. "It's like this," she explained:

> Oscar Miner, you know? The kid who lives at 110 Mosher? He gets money from his granny. Deiondre don't like him 'cause he say [Oscar] is a faggot but I know that's not true, and it don't matter anyway, so I told Deiondre to give a break to Oscar and now Oscar cuts him half of what his grandma gives him every Sunday. I get my piece, too.

She needed money to purchase the sorts of clothes that made her into a unique presence in the neighborhood. When she had cash, her favorite point of destination was Mondawmin Mall in Liberty Heights. She could spend hours trying on garments and costume jewelry and imagining where she would wear them if only she were rich. She aspired to have the style that made Tina Turner an icon. After watching *What's Love Got to Do With It* (1993), the film about Turner's tumultuous life, Towanda arrived at two conclusions: first, "Men are trouble"; and second, "You can survive if you strong and look good." It was for those reasons that, although Towanda dabbled in the perilous consumption of beer and weed, she kept to herself as far as sex was concerned. She thought only fools get pregnant. Her friends admired her determination not to fall prey to the lure of the older boys who seemed to want only one thing. Towanda had the skills to keep them interested without giving her young body away.

Within the tight confines of her home, Lydia struggled to keep Towanda out of trouble, but she confronted daunting obstacles. For one thing, she couldn't keep the girl inside. Crowded and damp, the house offered no refuge from external dangers, especially during summer when temperatures reached suffocating levels and youngsters, hungry for sociability, took to the streets. Mothers like Lydia fought a constant battle with the nearby playground, where children congregated in search of recreation but where older boys sold drugs and negotiated turf control. The playground was a living force luring away sons and daughters, sucking them in, and transforming them. It was an uneven battle in which mothers faced overwhelming odds. Trying to keep a teenager like Towanda at home, away from the colors and sounds of the street, was nearly impossible.

Parental authority was also eroded by factors other than the bricks and mortar of physical context. Towanda loved her mother but felt no pride in her. Lydia depended on public assistance and cleaned other people's houses to supplement her paltry income. She suffered from a credibility gap. When competing for her daughter's attention, she was unable to buttress sensible advice with better assets than those used and controlled by Towanda's peers. The girl felt free and powerful only away from home. When I asked Towanda about her new friends in the neighborhood, she said:

> They's nice kids no matter what mama says. They like me and I like them. They cool, not like the other people. . . . They don't like me in school, always calling me names. I don't have to take their shit 'cause I can take care of myself and my friends take care of me.

In other words, her membership in a youthful social network afforded Towanda protection in an environment bereft of material reserves. In poor neighborhoods, family integrity and parental authority are threatened on a daily basis by decrepit physical structures, a lack of means to secure children's compliance, and the absence of status distinction between youngsters and adults.

Only weeks after her fourteenth birthday Towanda decided to leave home in the middle of the night to attend a party with her homie, Deiondre. She felt pressure to do so because almost everyone that meant anything to her was planning to go; she just couldn't miss the event, but when asked for permission, Lydia resolutely said no, citing concerns about her daughter's safety and the reputation of Deiondre and his crew, whose dubious record was well known in the neighborhood.

Towanda rebutted her mother's objections without success. Lydia held her ground. Towanda then retreated to ponder her options. She could not miss the party, and given Lydia's unbending position, all she could do was to leave home surreptitiously. Lydia suspected as much; knowing that Towanda was headstrong and sly, she had been surprised to watch the girl submit so quickly to her authority.

On the night of the party, several things happened in quick succession. Around nine, Lydia locked up the front door to her small house and waited in the darkened living room, her eyes heavy with exhaustion. More than one hour later, she heard Towanda quietly tiptoeing down the narrow staircase, walking over to the right wall and opening one of the windows that led directly onto the street. The girl straddled the window sill and was about to touch the sidewalk when her mother, bolting from a corner, pulled her forcibly into the room. Towanda squirmed, trying to get away from Lydia's grasp, but the woman dragged her further, slamming her against a wall. She then dashed into the kitchen to fetch a broom, and on her way back, she grabbed Towanda as she climbed over the window sill for the second time. Striking her with the broomstick, she chased her all the way upstairs into her bedroom, where Clarise, awakened by the racket was sitting up in her little bed, eyes wide open with surprise and fear. Towanda fell over crumpled sheets wailing loudly, feeling more rage than pain. Lydia left without a word. Gradually, the girl's crying diminished, and silence befell the home.

Worn out, the mother went to bed expecting to sleep less than six hours. She had planned to leave early the next morning to fit in two house cleanings, one in Towson and the other in downtown Baltimore. But even a small respite was denied to her; the new day had not yet dawned when she was awakened by a loud banging on the door. As she responded, two police cars flashed their lights in the poorly lit street. One of the two officers in charge informed Lydia that they had received a report of a domestic altercation and possible child abuse.

Rushing out of her room and down the stairs, Towanda, still teary-eyed, hastened to fill in the details, giving little attention to her stupefied mother, who stood by in disbelief. By the next evening, the case had been turned over to Child Protective Services and, shortly afterward, Lydia was confronting a social worker appalled by Towanda's complaints. The mother was cited for child abuse.

A week later, Lydia had to appear in court to explain her behavior and give proof that she was not a danger to her daughter. The girl sat in the front row of the court room, right behind Lydia, with a satisfied expression on her young face. She had said she didn't take guff from anyone—not even her mother—and, by God, she had kept her word. For the next twelve months, a social worker visited the family regularly to make sure that Towanda was not being harmed. Filled with frustration, Lydia confided:

> Those peoples [the social workers], . . . they think our kids will listen to us when not even they [the social workers] have respect for us. . . . What could I do? It was a lot more dangerous for [Towanda] to be alone at night at that party than for me to chase her around with a broom. And I didn't even bruise her! But they [Child Protective Services] don't see it that way; they think they can come between a mother and her children.

Lydia's sentiments were not atypical. Most of the women that she knew feared and tried to avoid Child Protective Services, whose agents they saw as intruders imposing control and surveillance. "I knows they tryin' to keep children safe, their intentions are good," reflected Lydia, "but the fact is they mess up things more than they improve them."

Especially galling was the perception that, because they were poor, women like Lydia were unfit to be parents. When she had a little time to herself, Lydia read the popular tabloids. She was especially fond of the *National Enquirer.* In its pages, she regularly found the stories of women whose lives appeared to be even more chaotic than her own. But those were celebrities who could pay nannies to take care of their children. Most of them averted suspicions of child abuse.

Lydia's case was emblematic: in her thoughts and behavior, she sought to inspire her family and small community. In the eyes of the world, however, she was little more than an uneducated woman, on welfare for nearly a decade, who cleaned houses to supplement her meager income; a woman who countenanced a drunken husband and possibly abused her children. The two conflicting images—one of a

God-fearing mother, another of a danger to her children—aptly sum up the quandary faced by poor women in American inner cities. After Lydia's court hearing, and subsequent to a yearlong investigation, her name was included in a state-sanctioned list of alleged child abusers for seven years, a fact that would soon make it impossible for her to become a teacher's aide.

To secure a job, any job, had been Lydia's goal throughout the period during which she had depended on public assistance. She took resigned pride in the work that she did as a house cleaner but yearned for more. She often wished that she had stayed in school and become a teacher, because she felt that she had the temperament to benefit youngsters. In the 1990s Lydia's aspirations finally dovetailed with changes in welfare policy. Since its inception, the Clinton administration had made clear its intention to dismantle welfare programs. The rallying cry of government was to get people like Lydia "off welfare rolls into payrolls." Critics saw the slogan as a veiled attempt to bolster Clinton's reelection odds and to use welfare mothers as fodder to satisfy public demands for accountability. All the same, women like Lydia were eager to find new lives of dignity by accepting jobs, even if those jobs paid low wages.

That was the reason why she had risen to attention when one of her friends encouraged her to apply for a position as a teacher's aide at the Gilmore Elementary School. With some difficulty but high hopes, she filled out application forms and submitted them to the school's office of human resources. Some of the teachers knew and liked her. There was a good chance that she would land the position. Only two weeks later, her application was denied. Her record showed the blot of "alleged" child abuse. The term was doubly confounding because, not affirming beyond doubt the commission of a crime, it nonetheless pointed to it as a distinct possibility.

Lydia was in earnest to plead her case before the court of public opinion, but it was all for naught. In compliance with the law, she was ineligible for jobs that put her into contact with children. A teacher's aide position would not have paid more than what Lydia already made as a cleaning woman, but her sense of self-worth would have been uplifted. Chasing a rebellious daughter with a broom had put her within the same category as individuals who torture, rape, and kill minors.

"There's no winning here," Lydia said dejectedly, "I keep tryin' and tryin' and they's always knockin' me down. You wonder if the government knows what they doin' when they hurt mothers like me."

Yet in 1993, when Towanda was nearing her fifteenth birthday, Lydia fulfilled a long-held dream: to move her family into a low-rise unit within the George Murphy Homes, one of Baltimore's housing projects.[2] The transition was auspicious and filled with hope that a break with the past would usher in a new life. As Lydia settled into her new home, she was encouraged to see that Towanda was changing her ways. She tried to be more helpful at home and was making an effort to resume her studies at Marshall Middle School. Such hopes were short lived, however. After a few weeks, the girl's behavior began to deteriorate again. A newcomer in the projects, she received a far from hospitable reception from some of the neighbors. She acquired some new friends, but not the kind that would encourage her to stay in school.

Soon, Lydia started receiving warnings of eviction stemming from Towanda's transgressions. The girl was caught breaking curfew and shoplifting. Less than six months after the move to the George Murphy Homes, she was sent to the principal's office, not for the first time, by a dispirited teacher whose class Towanda often disrupted. In frustration, the principal had raised her voice at the girl. Towanda had advanced menacingly towards the woman with a clenched fist. She didn't strike her but the gesture sealed the girl's fate. She was permanently expelled.

Sullen but relieved, she returned home and plopped on the sofa of the tiny living room. I asked her whether she realized how difficult she was making life for her family:

> I don't mean to be bad. But a girl has to take care of herself; in a 'hood like this, you can die if you don't fight for your rights. I wanna make something of myself, you know, to have a family, my own home. I want to be with people that think I'm something.

It was about that time that Towanda renewed her acquaintance with Reggie Brown. He was one of two children born to parents who had been married but divorced when Reggie was ten. His mother, Regina, worked as a clerk at the Motor Vehicles Administration, trying to set a good example for her son and his younger sister, Dalia. In the 1940s, Regina's maternal grandfather had migrated from Spring-field, South Carolina, to Baltimore. Two generations later, she exemplified the extent to which the code of the street alters the intentions of parents.

Like other women in West Baltimore, Regina had seen her two children evolve from enchanting tots into voluble youngsters whose behavior she could not control. She too had been rebellious and filled with desire for a better life. Now in her mid-forties, and afflicted with diabetes, she was completely dedicated to Reggie and Dalia. A devout member of the Bethel AME Church on Druid Hill Avenue, she combined paid work with work as a volunteer in the neighborhood.

Regina remembered her son as a happy and docile boy. He had grown into a somber adolescent who worried about the well-being of his mother and sister. He thought Regina worked too hard. By the age of sixteen, he had dropped out of school and begun to make significant contributions to the family's income. He worked part-time jobs, but mostly he sold drugs. That he did with discretion, never taking unnecessary risks and toning down the taste for exhibitionism that had doomed some of his friends. As a result, he commanded a rare kind of respect.

Reggie was only nine when he and his friend Manny went out to have fun at the local park. On their way, they stopped at a local store to get a Coke. As they were leaving, Manny gingerly took some cookies from the store's counter. The owner reported the incident to the police, and Manny was detained. For two weeks, he was confined to a juvenile center, where he underwent observation before being returned to his anxious mother. That experience had caused an indelible impression on both youngsters, partly because they had seen it all happen before—it was not uncommon for the police to pick up boys whom they saw as potential risks. According to Reggie:

> When you little, you don't really know [that] the police are always watching, but then, when you's bigger, you realize everything you do can be turned against you. Manny and me, we was just havin' fun; he didn't mean nothing by taking the cookies. . . . But when you get treated like a criminal, there's no way out. You begin to think of youself as a no-good criminal.

Manny's life was changed by the incident; it strengthened and embold-ened him. Filled with anger, he formed a posse and became one of the most successful drug runners in West Baltimore. I review his life in chapter 15.

It was different for Reggie. He did not aim to be a gang leader or to make a fortune by selling large amounts of drugs. Mostly, he wanted to be a family man. He felt a sense of responsibility toward his mother and sister. A boy can't become a man without looking out for his own, right? At first, he took part-time jobs in downtown Baltimore. He worked in kitchens, waited on restaurant tables, and swept the floors of several commercial establishments. For his efforts he was paid small sums of money, most of which he gave to his mother. Wanting to earn more, he dropped out of school in the eleventh grade, hoping to get a full-time position, but the sort of employment that would have enabled Reggie to support a family was unavailable to a high school dropout. It was then, upon realizing his limitations, that Reggie started peddling ice—small plastic bags filled with crack cocaine.

Not lacking talent or drive, Reggie soon became a figure to be reck-oned with, an entrepreneur of sorts and, by the standards of young peo-ple in the neighborhood, "a really cool guy." Before the age of eighteen, he had risen to become a local kingpin, always with cash in his pockets. "It's all drug money," Lydia proclaimed in disgust.

By contrast, Towanda, tough and street-smart, believed that Reggie was about the only boy who might understand her. He too had fought to gain respect and independence. That's why he had dropped out of school and looked for means to help lift the heavy burden that his mother shouldered. He was as hard as nails and had honor; kids in the neighborhood looked up to Reggie because he was generous and funny, and he never let the younger children be bullied.

Towanda thought that "a boy like Reggie, he looks a bomb, he knows the ins and outs; he knows everything." To be his friend was to hold a firm position in the hierarchy of youthful status. Although she feigned indifference, Towanda was secretly thrilled when Reggie began to show interest in her. They had known each other for most of their young lives, but now, in Reggie's eyes, Towanda seemed new and attractive. She had a wild reputation and knew how to dress smart. She had kept other boys at bay and thus presented a challenge. He kept showing up everywhere Towanda went. For hours, he waited for her at Mr. Kim's grocery store, one of the few commercial establishments in the neighborhood, where youngsters often purchased candy. Once, when Towanda was walking down the street with her homies, Tyrella, Margaret, Latoya, and Lucy, Reggie came directly at her and blew her a kiss. The girls laughed loudly at the gesture while Towanda cast a vague glance in Reggie's direction. For the first time in her turbulent life, Towanda thought that it might be wonderful to have a partner like Reggie Brown.

She was nearing fifteen, and in her imagination, that was not a young age. She had seen life; she was not like those characters on TV family shows that speak in little-girl tones and pretend to be weak so that others take care of them. In Towanda's world, you grew up quickly and assumed responsibilities that even some adults might find overwhelming. Hadn't she helped find her father when, under the influence of bourbon, he fell in the back alley and almost lost his life? She had been only eight at the time. James had to be rushed to the emergency room of Mercy Hospital.

While Lydia stood by the man's side, Towanda stayed home, helping Felicia, her older sister. When they ran out of food, it was Towanda who had gone to Kim's store begging to have some cans on credit. Hadn't she taken care of Mush and Clarise when Lydia was out working? Didn't she cater alone to her younger brother after he had the accident while crossing North Avenue? She knew how to cook and clean a house. And she could take care of herself. Didn't she have to hold down her turf and earn the respect of kids who carried knives and guns to school? She wasn't helpless. She wasn't a child.

In other words, although she was very young, Towanda thought of herself as a woman. Poverty, violence, and isolation telescope time in ways that are incomprehensible to people living in gentler environments. Having resisted the temptations of sex "for a long time," she was now ready to join forces with Reggie Brown:

He aks'd me to be his woman. Well, you can't trust the men, but to be his woman, yeah, he all right. . . . But I wouldn't marry him 'cause men, they wants to be on top, and no one's on top of Towanda—not even Mama.

Throughout the summer of 1993, Towanda Forrest and Reggie Brown attained a kind of neighborhood notoriety seldom achieved by youngsters in different environments. Their lives were full of commotion, alternating quarrels and passionate moments. Their romance was watched with interest by other young people. After all, Towanda and Reggie were well matched—she was beautiful and strong; he never lacked money and was loyal to his family.

Towanda's association with Reggie Brown consolidated her position. Many of the girls in her group had become mothers as young as age thirteen. Some in their late teens had two or three children to support, although most of them relied on public assistance and the help of their own mothers. Many women in the projects were still taking care of their own children when suddenly confronted with the need to shelter grandchildren. Each new arrival became part of the same young generation. Babies born to adolescent mothers were more like little brothers and sisters to them than offspring. As their families grew, grandmothers and sometimes grandfathers assumed central positions and cared for children of widely different ages.

Towanda had been unusual in her determination not to fall prey to motherhood too soon. She wanted her independence, but Reggie countered her desire. He thought the mark of adult masculinity was a clear demonstration that he could father a child. This is part of the condition of masculinity in deprived environments. In lieu of material wealth or access to meaningful levels of education, young people build a reputation in reference to the efficacy of their bodies. Having sex is not mostly about pleasure but about the appropriation of vicarious power; it is like defending or conquering turf.

Two months shy of her fifteenth birthday, Towanda was delivered of her first child, a boy named Reggie Shantell Brown. She had pondered the baby's name for several months, but sadly, she couldn't spell it. Towanda was then, and is now, almost illiterate. By the time Reggie Shantell was born, she had abandoned school. When I reminded her about her earlier resolve not to become pregnant, she retorted, "Some things are just meant to be." In the spring of 1996, Towanda was expecting her second child. She was then seventeen.

Shortly after Reggie Shantell was born, I found myself engaged in a conversation with Lydia Forrest in her small but tidy living room. She was inflamed by Towanda's behavior:

Dem children coming up have no sense. They's always thinking they know better. Towanda, she got an attitude, always got an attitude. I don't know how she came by that attitude!

I was preparing for a barrage of moral invective when Lydia's expression changed suddenly. She asked whether I wanted to see the baby. Of course I did. Like a commander deploying her troops, she raised her voice to call Reggie. "Ma'am," was the courteous response from the second floor. "Bring the baby down!" Obediently, the young man came down the stairs with his son in his arms and his eyes gleaming with pride. Moments later, I asked Reggie how he felt about the birth of his son:

It's good; it's good, ma'am. And I was there when he was born—right there in the hospital. I 'bout fainted with all the blood and that, but I was there; I sure was there. Now, I have someone to really live for, someone who needs me and who'll look up to me.

I could not help but wonder whether James, Lydia's husband, had felt the same way when his first child, Towanda, was born, and whether Reggie would replicate James's defeats in the years to come.

Those thoughts were interrupted by the chatter of family members and friends who joined in with admiring exclamations. What ensued was a collective demonstration of genuine delight that dissipated any doubt about the extent to which Reggie Shantell was welcome. This was family; this was a reason to celebrate; this was a time to rejoice.

Sitting in a corner, Towanda chewed gum in contentment. Hers was the moment of triumph.

12 CULTURAL CAPITAL AND THE TRANSITION TO ADULTHOOD IN THE URBAN GHETTO

How did Towanda Forrest move so quickly from a determination to stay away from motherhood to two pregnancies by the age of seventeen? Was she, with other impoverished girls in the nation's ghettos, taunting the values of the larger society? Was she confirming the suspicion that welfare programs encourage dependence and sexual misbehavior?

In this chapter, I consider these questions and return to the field of economic sociology to investigate phenomena that continue to elude scholars and policy makers. I give attention to the interplay between cultural and social capital, now as a way to gain a better understanding of early motherhood and its meaning in inner-city neighborhoods.

As stated earlier, the concepts of social and cultural capital designate forms of noneconomic knowledge, derived from sources other than formal learning or instruction, which directly impinge on the economic practices of individuals and groups (Smelser and Swedberg 2005; Bourdieu 1979/1984, 1986; Coleman 1988). Although both phenomena result from interactive processes, the main distinction is in their location. Cultural capital consists of symbolic repertories; social capital depends on relations of reciprocity among individuals and groups. Cultural capital brings forth expressive behaviors; social capital hinges on connections of trust and cooperation, which facilitate access to scarce resources (see also Zelizer 2011).

The form and effects of cultural and social capital are defined by spatial and temporal factors and by collective constructions, such as social class, race, and gender. The fragmentation of experience along those lines leads to behaviors whose meaning varies from context to context. The task to be accomplished, then, is to examine the ways in which people in impoverished settings both talk about values and support their talk with action or inaction.

Because people acquire practical knowledge in the locations where they live, they also expect what is probable in their nearby environments, and they recognize as reality that which is defined as such by members of their social networks (Thomas and Thomas 1928). This is true for affluent children as well as for impoverished youngsters, many of whom become parents at an early age.

One of the implications of this insight is that lived reality structures the meaning of social performance to a larger extent than disembodied notions of morality (Swidler 1986, 2001). Impoverished people in racially segregated neighborhoods express adherence to mainstream American mores; hard work, family loyalties, and individual achievement are all part of their cultural repertoires. Nevertheless, the translation of values into actions is shaped by the tangible milieu that encircles them. So, incidentally, is the ability of affluent families to actualize values into behavior.

ADOLESCENT PREGNANCIES AND POVERTY

West Baltimore—especially Upton and Sandtown-Winchester—stands out for its incidence of adolescent pregnancies and early motherhood, surpassing even that of the city at large, whose rates triple the national average and are among the highest in the nation (Healthy Teen Network 2010). In 1990, nearly a quarter of Baltimore's 13,000 births were to teenagers. The same year, almost one-third of girls between the ages of fourteen and nineteen living in West Baltimore became the mother of at least one child. Many of those girls had grown up in female-headed households receiving government aid (see also McLanahan 1985; McLanahan, Donahue, and Haskins 2005).

The landscape had not changed substantially by 2012. In the early years of the twenty-first century, Baltimore experienced slight decreases in the high incidence of teen pregnancies and births, but by 2009 there were new upticks in a city where such phenomena are almost two times the rate for Maryland and almost three times that of the United States (Baltimore City Health Department 2008; Hamilton, Martin, and Ventura 2011).[1]

In 2006, the total number of births to women under age twenty in Baltimore City was 1,739. Of these, 65 percent were to young women aged eighteen to nineteen; 33 percent were to girls and young women aged fifteen to seventeen, and 2 percent were to girls under age fifteen (Terry-Humen, Manlove, and Cottingham 2008) Of the total number of births, 92 percent were to unmarried girls and sixteen percent were repeat births. Births to Baltimore girls younger than age twenty represented 9 percent of all births in the state of Maryland.

The rate of adolescent births varies in terms of race and ethnicity. Hispanics, especially immigrants from Central America, are currently the fastest-growing minority group in Baltimore. They also exhibit the highest incidence of births to adolescents, although judging from similar phenomena in other parts of the country, that may be related to higher levels of early marriages among Hispanics than among members of the population as a whole. At the national level, Hispanics have the highest rate of teen births (81.7/1000 females aged fifteen to nineteen), followed by non-Hispanic Blacks (64.3/1000) and non-Hispanic Whites (27.2/1000). In Baltimore, where Hispanics represent 2 percent of the population, they had the highest rate of adolescent mothers in 2007 (149.8/1000 females aged fifteen to nineteen) compared with non-Hispanic Blacks, who represent 70 percent of the teen population and had a birthrate of 80.2/1000, and non-Hispanic Whites, with 24 percent of the population and a birthrate of 32.7/1000 (Centers for Disease Control and Prevention 2011).[2] Figure 10 shows Baltimore teen population by race and ethnicity.

Both non-Hispanic Blacks and Hispanics significantly exceed the overall city rate in teenage pregnancies and births. The reasons for disparities across race and ethnicity are not fully understood, but socioeconomic status plays a significant role. Poverty increases the risk of a teen pregnancy and birth, and minority populations are disproportionately represented in lower socioeconomic strata.

In Baltimore, as in the nation at large, adolescent mothers are likely to have been born to women who became mothers themselves at an

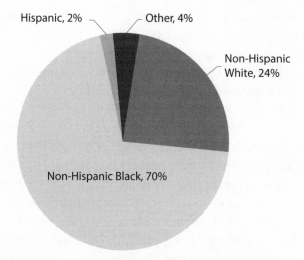

FIGURE 10. Baltimore Teen Population, ages 15–19 years by Race/Ethnicity. Source: Baltimore City Health Department. (2008). Baltimore City Health Status Report.

early age, and for whom public assistance is often a permanent source of livelihood. The odds are staggering in that respect: one out of two girls born to adolescents receiving public assistance become mothers before completing their teenage years (McLanahan 1985; Tienda and Stier 1991).

DEBATING TEENAGE MOTHERHOOD

The widespread birth of children to adolescents has become the fulcrum of a controversy about the causes and perpetuation of poverty. Conservatives see teen pregnancies as a symptom of moral decline, permissiveness, and the failure of the welfare state (Murray 1984). Early motherhood, they argue, causes poverty; they thus demand stricter eligibility requirements, increased accountability, and limited access to government support.

In the 1990s, conservative interpretations of adolescent pregnancies and early motherhood translated into legislative measures. In some states, including Maryland, women receiving Aid for Families with Dependent Children were denied welfare payments if they became pregnant while receiving government assistance. In accordance with long-held philosophical views, critics of the welfare state believe that public support unwittingly rewards promiscuity and dependency. Images of lustfulness at the expense of the public simmer below more-serene enticements toward personal responsibility.[3]

Considering the vigor of the debate, it is sometimes difficult to remember that, as Constance Nathanson (1991) and Kristin Luker (1991) have shown, the vast majority of babies throughout history have been born to adolescents, largely because life spans used to be shorter and because the inception of puberty coincided with the expectation of motherhood within or, in some cases, before marriage.[4] The stigma attached to adolescent pregnancies is a recent phenomenon that pertains mostly to single mothers, especially those in racial minorities.

At the aggregate level, the trend has been for fewer women to have babies across their life cycle and in their early years. Pregnancy rates among adolescents declined sharply, falling by about one-third, from the mid-1960s until the late 1980s. This was partly as a result of the dissemination of oral contraceptives in the second half of the twentieth century. Teen-age pregnancies dropped again after abortion became widely available in the 1970s. The rates continued to decline slowly, with adolescent pregnancy rates among Blacks remaining higher than Whites but declining faster.

To put it succinctly, in 1966, a random sample of one hundred Black teenage girls could be expected to have eighty babies by the time they all turned twenty. For White girls, the equivalent number would have been forty babies. By 1986, those figures had dropped to fifty-one for Blacks and twenty-one for Whites (Jencks and Peterson 1991). When socioeconomic status and level of education are taken into account, the rates of pregnancy among Black and White teenagers converged even more noticeably, although the former remained higher. The birthrate for all teenagers aged fifteen to nineteen fell to another historic low in 2011, to 31.3 births per thousand, down 8 percent from 2010 (34.2). The rate in 2011 was the lowest recorded in more than seven decades (Hamilton, Martin, and Ventura 2011).

In other words, the panic over adolescent pregnancies often disregards facts. If there is such a thing as an epidemic, it is concentrated among the members of a comparatively small population formed by the rural and urban poor. The latter, clustered in areas like West Baltimore, have captured the most attention.

Teen pregnancies stand in the public imagination as a proxy for a variety of problems, ranging from idleness and poverty to incarceration. Some see high crime rates as the result of early motherhood and single-parent households. The heated debate over "makers" versus "takers" during the 2012 presidential campaign was but the latest episode in the American concern over the perception of less-affluent populations as burdens on society.

Beyond ideologically motivated arguments, the growth in the number of unwed teen mothers is of interest to the study of poverty, since female-headed households constitute a large percentage of all impoverished people. Poverty's associated problems make it difficult for single mothers to supervise their children who, as they mature, seem more likely to drop out of school and face other troubles, spinning a cycle of destitution down through the generations (McLanahan 1985; Taub 1991).[5]

Starting in the late 1980s, a new wave of scholars and policy thinkers began to focus on the reconstruction of the husband-wife unit in poor areas as a possible solution to poverty. Such efforts came to fruition under the George W. Bush administration when several initiatives were implemented to stimulate marriage among low-income people (U.S. Department of Health and Human Services 2013). Such ideas were based on a simple observation: married couples tend to have more wealth and education than unmarried people. Yet supporters of marriage as a remedy for poverty have the equation backwards: in the past, more affluent men and women have been likely to marry because pooling resources, educational as well as financial, can bring them shared benefits. In those conditions, to marry is to maximize preexisting advantages, but that is not the case among impoverished people. In other words, marriage does not cure destitution; more-affluent and better-educated people gravitate toward marriage because they have larger material and educational reserves in the first place.

Underfunded and restricted by this erroneous logic, efforts to promote marriage among the poor have notoriously failed. In addition, there are now more unmarried than married people of all kinds living together in the United States. The reasons for that development are complex—changing cultural norms and the severe impact of the 2008 Great Recession may be among the causes—but drops in marriage rates per se have not contributed to the growth of poverty. Similarly, single mothers with high levels of education and income have lives and children not significantly different from those who are married. The problems that so fervently preoccupy conservatives and liberals alike do not stem from single motherhood itself but from dispossession, and not surprisingly, those problems are more pronounced among impoverished minority groups.

WELFARE, CULTURE, AND ECONOMICS

The original debate over the intergenerational transmission of welfare dependence has taken two forms. A cultural version emphasizes values and attitudes. Oscar Lewis (1961/2011), whose influence spanned several decades, noted structural constraints but emphasized beliefs and behaviors that once established are assumed to perpetuate the diffusion of poverty from parents to children. Consistent with that view is the idea that daughters reared in homes receiving public assistance adopt values that denigrate work and make reliance on government aid an acceptable means of support. Economic dependence is thus maintained by acquired *tastes* for public aid and the development of a way of life pivoting on welfare (Jencks 1993).

An alternative perspective emphasizes social and economic factors that limit options available to children who grow up in impoverished neighborhoods (Hannerz 1969; Fernández-Kelly 1984). From that viewpoint, daughters growing up in poverty are more likely to be poor than daughters brought up in affluence, not because of deviant values and attitudes, but because of limited opportunities.[6]

In an analysis that created widespread interest during the 1990s and beyond, William J. Wilson (1987) further emphasized *concentration effects*, which he defined as systematic "differences in the experiences of low-income families who live in inner-city areas [in comparison with] the experiences of those who live in other areas of the central city" (Wilson 1987: 58). Wilson argued that spatial and social isolation from mainstream norms was partly produced by the exodus of working- and middle-class families from inner-city neighborhoods.

In other words, situational and cultural explanations of the relationship between poverty, government aid, and adolescent pregnancies hinge on opposite chains of causation. In one case, culture is said to explain economic outcomes; in the other, economic factors are seen as determinants of norms and values. In the first instance, adolescent pregnancies and their byproduct, poverty, are depicted as a function of welfare culture; in the second, the uneven distribution of resources and residential segregation explain poverty and, indirectly, teen pregnancies.

A closer look shows that cultural explanations, like those advanced by Murray (1984), correspond with the outlooks of neoclassical economists: adolescent women are said to choose motherhood as a way to maximize benefits derived from public assistance, and reduce work effort. Therefore, dependence on welfare is not primarily about values but about the weighing of costs and benefits, an economic phenomenon. Ultimately, conservative views do not clarify the role of cultural repertories, either in the transmission of poverty or in the interplay between individual economic decisions and larger economic institutions. Yet, the contest between cultural and situational explanations allows for an examination of concepts fundamental to the relationship between economy and society.

Throughout the twentieth century, the rise of economics as a dominant field entailed what Robert K. Merton (1972) labeled *a public interpretation of reality* captured by the idea of *Homo economicus*, the purposive, calculating creature who competes for scarce resources on the basis of information and skill. The development of mathematical models based on that formulation lifted economics to its sovereign status among the social sciences, but the lofty reputation of the neoclassical paradigm also depended on persistent beliefs that greed and self-interest define the human condition and that the pursuit of personal profit translates into collective prosperity. Such convictions were conveniently suited to capitalist rationality.

In contrast, a principal aim of economic sociology is to show the extent to which sociability sustains economic action or, to put it in terms best articulated by Viviana Zelizer (2011), the ways in which economic phenomena are, in fact, social phenomena. Markets, firms, and other related structures depend on social norms of reciprocity and cooperation that would appear irrational and therefore inefficient by the dictates of orthodox economics. Economic sociologists underscore the role of *bounded solidarity* and *enforceable trust* as facilitators of economic behavior, including labor market participation and the consolidation of ethnic business enclaves (Portes 1993). Concepts derived from economic sociology add nuance to what otherwise constitutes a caricature of human conduct.

If one of the purposes of economic sociology is to clarify the social basis of economic action, then the functions and attributes of social networks must also be considered. Social networks are intricate formations that channel and filter information, articulate meanings, allocate resources, and control behavior. Individual choices depend not only on the availability of material and intangible assets in the society at large but also on the way in which networks interpret information and relate to structures of opportunity. Characteristics such as size and composition, degree of spatial concentration, and the frequency and character of transactions give social networks specific profiles (Boissevain 1974; Granovetter and Swedberg 2011; White 1970).

Perhaps a network's most important feature is the degree to which it may include persons of a differing social status, linked in a variety of ways, and playing multiple roles in several fields of activity—what Jeremy Boissevain calls *multiplexity*. A diversity of linkages and roles facilitates institutional overlap. The integration of groups of various sizes into the whole that we call society takes place via personal connections. Higher degrees of multiplexity increase the probability that information about resources (such as jobs) and knowledge (such as entrepreneurial know-how) reach individuals on the basis of their ascriptive characteristics. Mark Granovetter's classic study of the ways in which people secure jobs underscores the importance of personal contacts and qualifies the neoclassical proposition that employment is the simple effect of supply and demand (Granovetter 1995; Willis 1981).

By definition, social networks are spatially circumscribed and serve as conduits for the transmission of practical knowledge. That includes conceptions about the body—its movements, appearance, and speech—and notions about time. Finally, social networks facilitate the deployment of cultural repertories. How an adolescent girl understands motherhood depends on such factors.

CULTURAL CAPITAL EXAMINED

Culture matters in the analysis of poverty, but the lamentable tendency has been to use culture as a residual category in which disparate phenomena are indiscriminately stacked. Consider, for example, the following declaration from a leading figure in the study of American poverty:

> There is . . . fairly strong evidence that mainstream American norms of behavior exert less influence on blacks than on whites with the same amount of schooling. Blacks are more likely than whites with the same amount of schooling to have their babies out of wedlock. . . . Such differences can, of course, be seen as part of racism's appalling historical legacy. But if all whites were suddenly struck color-blind, we would not expect these differences to disappear overnight— indeed, they would probably persist for several generations. That is what it means to invoke "culture" as an explanation of such differences (Jencks 1993: 13).

Three suppositions underpin that statement. The first one concerns ways in which norms and values are translated into action. Jencks takes for granted that values explain behavior. The second assumption is that disparate outcomes in a similar behavioral plane must indicate corresponding cultural differences. Finally, the statement is grounded in the belief that culture metastasizes in a relatively autonomous field that is, for the most part, impervious to economic and social forces.

It is possible to articulate a reading other than the one offered by Jencks of the varying incidence of out-of-wedlock births among African-Americans and Whites with analogous levels of schooling. Given sharp levels of residential segregation and high levels of poverty, African-Americans have at their disposal dissimilar types of resources to realize mainstream norms and values. A seventeen-year-old White woman about to graduate from high school, living in a middle-class neighborhood, and contemplating college, even with ambivalence, is likely to defer motherhood in order not to jeopardize other opportunities. In that case, the young woman perceives giving birth to a child out of marriage not only as a breach of norms but also as an impediment to achieving realistic, desirable ends.

A seventeen-year-old Black woman about to graduate from high school in an urban ghetto faces a different set of choices. It is unlikely, for instance, that her social network will include a significant number of individuals who have pursued an education in "good" colleges and gone on to secure stable jobs. As a result, many adults and adolescents in her circle may see graduating from high school as the end point of childhood and the beginning of maturity. The young woman in question may share with men in her peer group the impression—fostered by conventional views—that parenting should be connected to adult status. In this case, motherhood has a distinct meaning: it is not a deviation from but a path to approximate dominant norms.

As with Jencks's interpretation, this second reading is based on assumptions that must be made explicit. One is that disparate behavioral outcomes can spring from attempted adherence to shared cultural understandings. The second is that the translation of values into behavior is mediated by specific resources and embodied experiences.[7] The third assumption is that seemingly identical features like "same level of education" may conceal different social realities. Finally, this interpretation is based on the claim that *cultural capital is a byproduct of social capital; it does not reproduce autonomously but only to the extent that the conditions surrounding specific forms of social capital are maintained.*

In other words, cultural capital is of interest here in three related ways: first, insofar as it creates a repertory of symbols interactively developed, placed into circulation, and tapped by individuals to "make sense" of their experience (Bourdieu 1986); second, to the extent that those symbols re-create centers of power within larger structures of domination; and third, inasmuch as those symbols affect the relationship between individuals, social networks, and economic structures.

Consider again the two imaginary teenagers described above. Whether the young White woman is celibate, using contraceptives, or pondering an abortion, she is also likely to favor certain kinds of music, attire, and gestures. Those tastes were fashioned interactively with her peers, the mass media, and the responses of adults. Because she belongs in a network connected to a plurality of external agents and groups, she is liable to engage in behaviors valued in different ways by different sectors of her broader network. She is unlikely, for instance, to interview for a job in anything other than acceptable garb, no matter how repugnant she may find it when associating with her close friends. In preparing for the job interview, she is certain not to expose a tattoo on her breast that recently drove her parents to distraction.

Her Black counterpart in the ghetto has tastes too. She is likely to be preoccupied by her hair, which members of her inner circle describe as bad, kinky, or nappy. Therefore, she goes to great lengths reshaping her tresses into acceptable, even flamboyant, displays of craftsmanship. Vulnerability is recast into power. A body feature is transformed into a canvas for recognition and individuation.

To this point, the sparkling mounds of braided hair worn by the Black teen do not differ much from the tattoo on the breast of the White teen. Both are expressive behaviors aimed at self-affirmation. But because the Black teen's network has few connections with outside people and information, she may be unaware that her coiffure can doom her in job interviews. What is wrought as an empowering symbol in an insular milieu becomes a signal that bars access to resources in the larger society.

Whether the young woman in question would modify her appearance based on knowledge obtained through an expanded social network is a different matter left to be explored in relation to issues of resistance and compliance. My point here is that intangible forms of knowledge at the disposal of the first woman are unavailable to the second and vice versa. This is what I mean by *embodied knowledge,* a term more serviceable than Jencks's use of *culture.*

With these concepts in mind, I now return to the meaning of adolescent pregnancies in Baltimore's ghetto.

THE YEARNING FOR ADULTHOOD

What do children dream about when yearning to become mothers and fathers? Among middle-class and affluent youngsters, parenting tends to be delayed because the shift between childhood and adulthood is marked by advances in education and actual and symbolic interactions with the market. Good grades, athletic ability, and conformity become assets in a competition for higher incomes, decency, and self-sufficiency. Childhood and adolescence are extended as individuals accumulate educational resources to be deployed at a later point.

Without material resources, clustered in segregated neighborhoods, and vying for entry-level jobs even as grown men and women, the poor must find other ways to define adulthood. Among them, time protocols are compressed, since even young boys and girls have to assume large responsibilities. As shown by the life of Towanda Forrest, long before puberty, impoverished girls are often charged with the care of younger siblings and poor boys soon understand the need to provide for themselves and others.

The arrival of a new baby attracts utmost interest because there are few milestones in poor neighborhoods that people can call upon to separate stages in their life cycles. Hardly any of the events that mark the passage from childhood to adulthood in wealthier areas exist in the urban ghetto. Savings accounts, extracurricular activities, hopes of getting a driver's license, prospects of finding a well-paying job—all middle-class perquisites of the journey toward maturity—are rare in poor neighborhoods. Infants galvanize attention and offer possibilities to attain a mature status. Having babies, then, is about the articulation of meaning, not necessarily the consequence of careless behavior.

Long before the onset of adolescence, children hold solid notions about the meaning of masculinity and femininity unfolding over time. "Now's the time to play," repeatedly said Towanda when she was nine, "but when I grow up, I take care of my children and make them a home." Her friends agreed that the defining feature of maturity was to become a parent. That was true for both sexes. Eleven-year-old Dante Washington, who attended the same school as Towanda, understood the difference between youth and adult status in relation to parenting: "When you little, you not a man," he told me, "You grow up and have babies; then people know you's a man."

Especially worthy of attention is the case of very young girls in segregated neighborhoods who describe their hopes for adulthood in direct relationship to government programs. At the age of ten, Melinda Twigg had mostly one goal: to have a baby and live on her own while receiving government aid:

> I can't wait to have a baby like my cousin, Tanya, she has two babies and her own apartment. She's on welfare, so she can take care of her kids; she her own woman. And her babies, they so cute! No, I can't wait to have my own child; I call her Shantell, or maybe Alyssa.

Countless Americans respond with shock when hearing very young girls like Melinda discussing plans for pregnancy, motherhood, and dependence on the public dole. Remarks like hers are seen as evidence of low moral character: not only are the poor driven by an unrestrained drive to bear children prematurely but also to live in idleness at the expense of responsible citizens who helplessly watch in disbelief.[8]

Despite such judgments, the calculations of impoverished children largely hinge on the assets and information stored in their environments. The cost of motherhood varies in terms of social class and context. Middle-class girls are less likely to give birth because motherhood interferes with the fulfillment of attainable goals in education and employment. In the case of poor girls, such goals are mostly absent, and as a result, motherhood does not entail as high a cost as it does among their wealthier counterparts—it is not easy to become poorer when you have little in the first place (Furstenberg 2010). When a girl like Melinda Twigg speaks about her urgency to become a mother, she is revealing her desire to grow up and live as a woman with greater standing and autonomy than those afforded to a child.

A longitudinal study of a randomly selected sample of impoverished girls led by the sociologist Frank Furstenberg supports such claims (Furstenberg, Brooks-Gunn, and Morgan 1987). It shows that impoverished women who became mothers as adolescents in the 1980s did not go on to have lives significantly different from those who deferred pregnancy or had no children. Most remained poor, even when holding jobs. In other words, parenting at an early age is not the cause of enduring poverty. The opposite is more likely: dispossession creates the conditions for early parenting.

Advancing from childhood to maturity interacts with gender constructions. Children hope to become men or women, not just grownups. While wealthier children grow up in close interaction with markets; impoverished children more often relate to agents of the state. Government agencies in impoverished neighborhoods, key factors in the experience of children, also bifurcate along gender lines. Public assistance touches single women and their children. The corrections and criminal justice systems deal primarily with boys and men. That split has repercussions for youngsters growing into adulthood in racially segregated neighborhoods.

Boys in West Baltimore are fascinated by the police, whom they admire and fear. Many want to become cops to "help people," but if you ask a kid in the 'hood what the verb "to search" means, one of his first responses will be to describe an officer engaging in a bodily probe. The boy is likely to recall the times he has seen men thrust against walls or cars and asked to put their arms up while the officer pats them down. By the age of sixteen, a boy may have had more than a dozen detentions.[9] Even pranks that would be dismissed in other locations can be taken as evidence of criminal leanings when the poor are involved.

Towanda's younger brother, Mush, started his delinquent career at age thirteen after he was caught running crack for an older friend. When I discussed the incident with three of his young cousins, aged seven through eleven, they agreed that it was unfair for Mush to be punished. "After all," one told me, "he was just doin' it to help his family." By age eighteen, Mush was spending most of his time in a correctional institution, although he was allowed to visit the family during holidays. In addition to a muscular frame, he boasted a gold tooth. Towanda boasted one too. Both were glittering displays of importance gained in the struggle for respect in the neighborhood.

Although it may seem paradoxical in modern times, the passage from childhood to adulthood is still ritualized today, imprinted at every stage by symbols that denote fuller approximations to maturity. In the case of affluent children, those symbols point to competition (Levey Friedman 2013). Parents push their offspring to perform in school and in extramural activities because they value their intellect but also because they *know* that credentials from *good* schools, high standardized-test scores, and behaviors learned from the *right* contacts create reserves that can be parlayed into attractive jobs. Intimations about a future filled with promise flavor the conversations between middle-class parents and their children.

Similar conversations are less likely to ensue among impoverished people because the means and personal contacts that make promises seem real to children are not there. None of the signs of success in better neighborhoods exist in the Baltimore ghetto, where the number of social service delivery programs by far exceeds that of banks. In those circumstances, children's symbolic repertory is significantly shaped through interaction with the apparatus that targets them as a problem to be solved.

Whether affluent or dispossessed, children form views of the world through direct exchanges with individuals and institutions in their proximity. It is difficult to envision options other than those *made real* by people in common social networks. Even images transmitted by television and other media remain elusive unless they can be connected to personal experience and activated by mutually reinforcing interchanges with others in the same circle. Both in prosperous and poor environments, people talk about what they know personally or about matters transmitted to them by people they trust.

In neighborhoods like those in West Baltimore, where upward of 40 percent of women take public assistance, girls understandably talk about welfare. Residential segregation and the presence of liminal government institutions facilitate that process. The young take stock of the information disseminated by adults and peers, and such ideas become part of the knowledge reserve they draw upon to make choices. Cultural capital and symbolic capital are both implicated in such interactions. In that sense, epistemology is not an abstraction.

MOTHERHOOD RECAST

At seventeen, Latanya Williams was expecting her second child when I met her in 1990. She was an outspoken girl who lived with her mother and five siblings. Her mother, a quiet, religious woman, had depended on public assistance for almost twenty years. While nibbling pumpkin seeds in the yard of a neighboring house, one hot summer day, Latanya put forth a typical view:

> I waited for a long time before I had my baby. Anyone can tell you, all my girlfriends had babies before me, and I was jealous 'cause when you don't have a child to call your own, you's nothing; you got nothing to be proud of. I couldn't wait. What's there to wait for?

When I asked whether she had considered finishing high school, she looked at me with skepticism and said:

> It's not like I don't want to get an education, but it's not so easy. . . . And besides, I don't know no one, I tell you no one, who has a good

job by finishing high school. That's a lie, just a fucking lie! So why waste time to end up at the 7-Eleven? It ain't worth it. What I want is to have my own apartment, my own place.

I ventured further; was Latanya hoping to marry the father of her children?

I don't know about that. . . . I like my independence, and you can't trust men—they go crazy on you. First, I have to see that he really wants to take care of my babies, test him, you know . . . 'cause no crazy boy's gonna boss me around, no way!

By the time we got around to the delicate subject of contraceptives, Latanya had achieved momentum:

What's yo talking about? Man, just because I'm seventeen, it don't mean I don't know nothing. Look, the pill's bad for your health, swells you all up. . . . Rubbers? They's gross; my old man don't like 'em, and abortion, that's a sin, to kill a poor baby. I love my baby. I'm gonna raise him good.

Another young woman, Latishia Marvin was facing the arrival of her first baby with trepidation in 1990. She was eighteen years old:

I didn't know I could get pregnant, you know, 'cause the doctor said I had a lopsided uterus. But I did, and I'm scared, but I can't do nothing now.

Her fears were tempered with hope. She told me the arrival of the baby would give her a "new chance." According to her mother, Latishia had held a steady job at the local food store since she was fourteen and was struggling at school. Latishia had lukewarm expectations about going to college but was having difficulty getting a passing grade in "her English subject." Close to the arrival of Byron, her first son, she was able to graduate from high school but a doctor recommended that she quit her job because the pregnancy had caused her feet to distend. In one stroke, she had completed the requirements to apply for college and moved from membership among the working poor to full dependency on public assistance.

Although Latishia's mother had mixed feelings about her daughter's pregnancy, she didn't see anything extraordinary about the event. She too had become a mother at an early age. "God sends the babies," she told me. "They are our greatest joy."

The statements above reveal mixed feelings toward education. Girls who were interviewed differentiated between educational achievement as an ideal and the reality of the schools they attended. No one saw schooling with indifference. They agreed that educated, "smart," people got all the advantages, but they didn't believe their own academic records or the schools they were attending would unlock better opportunities. Ten-year-old Belinda Twigg had suffered meningitis when she was a toddler. Shuffled between relatives and foster parents, she had ended up living with her aunt Margaret, an affable alcoholic. Her standardized-test scores placed her at the bottom of the national norm group. Eighteen-year-old Latishia Marvin had displayed excellent behavior while growing up, but she had struggled with grades all along. Towanda Forrest was almost illiterate at age twelve and a high school dropout two years later.

Most of the young women thus perceived schools as social, not educational, arenas where they participated in the small dramas that children of all types are wont to enact. They gossiped, picked friends and adversaries, defied instructors, competed for each other's attention, and struggled for self-distinction. When Towanda was ten, she started receiving suspensions for fighting in school; Melinda, who was two years younger than Towanda, was also ten when she was first suspended. Clarise too had a similar experience; she was barely eight when she received her first suspension. All three offered the same justification: "You can't let people walk all over you; you got to get respect."[10]

The quest for respect is commonplace among adolescents of all class backgrounds (Bourgois 1996; Taub 1991). In impoverished environments, it tends to focus mainly on physical force, the defense of turfs, and corporal adornment. Images of power are thus constructed where other alternatives are not easily accessible.

The young women that I interviewed also expressed mistrust about the qualifications of men as mates and parents. In chapter 4, I reviewed the clashing interpretations that impoverished African-American men and women had about each other (see also Hannerz 1969; Wilson 2010; Taub 1991). Those views are common in settings characterized by high levels of male unemployment and underemployment, where the prospects of marriage and conventional family formation are unrealistic, given men's difficulties in securing jobs. Moreover, men and women alike see differences between the jobs that are available and the jobs they deem desirable. Because male identity strongly depends on the characteristics of employment, men are starkly aware of their inability to fulfill their prescribed role as providers. Their perceptions about work and jobs influence their orientations toward marriage. Men as well as women may *say* they don't get married because they wish to protect their independence, but they also *feel* they can't afford to be married.

Similarly, the relative incomes of prospective spouses have explicit consequences for the balance of power in relationships. Those who have jobs fear exploitation while those who are jobless fear domination. Conflicting perceptions emerge from this predicament. Women see men as untrustworthy, exploitative, flighty, and undeserving of respect. Men, in turn, speak of women as materialistic hags whose only interest is in long-term financial security and who have forgotten how to be respectful.

Thus, the debasement of women by reducing them to "bitches" and "hos" conceals an attempt at redefining the locus of power in gender relations. The skepticism of women and their determination to preserve personal autonomy by shunning marriage represent the flip side of the same process.[11]

SOCIAL TIME AND ADULT STATUS

The relationship between bearing children and acquiring maturity calls into question notions about social and actual time, a venerable theme in the social sciences but one that has been undertheorized with respect to impoverished populations. In a pathbreaking essay, Robert K. Merton (1984) defined socially expected durations as collectively patterned expectations about temporal intervals embedded in social structures of various kinds. Equally important was Merton's observation that socially expected durations affect anticipatory social behavior.

Impoverishment combined with spatial segregation and government intrusiveness shapes specific conceptions of time and socially expected durations. Poverty and exclusion flatten and compress temporal rhythms. Alex Kotlowitz (1992) recounts the experience of

African-American boys in a Chicago housing project who, in response to the question "What do you want to be as an adult?" preface their answers with the conditional clause "If I grow up. . . ." *If,* not when. Familiarity with violence and death influences their perception about the probable length of life and guides behavior appropriate to fore-shortened phases.

Ethnographic research among ethnic and racial minorities further reveals the extent to which accelerated development characterizes the experience of impoverished youth (Jarrett, Jefferson, and Kelly 2010). More frequently than among wealthier groups, impoverished adolescents maintain lateral relationships with parents and older relatives not only because age differences tend to be smaller but because poor adults occupy with their children a similar position vis-à-vis labor market alternatives.

In that context, motherhood represents the extension of responsibilities assumed at an early age and expresses a specific relationship with the labor market. That partly explains why, at seventeen, Latanya Williams can state with conviction, "I waited for a long time before I had my baby." That's why she can ask, "What's there to wait for?" In poor neighborhoods, the absence of a material foundation leads to the perception of newborns as unqualified assets, rather than handicaps, in a temporal progression.

Partly for the same reason, there is a link throughout the world between poverty and early pregnancy. In most poor countries, public assistance and welfare programs are unavailable and, therefore, cannot be held responsible for providing the "wrong" incentives. Even when removed from the insular confines of the policy debate in the United States, the situational connection between adolescent pregnancies and poverty persists. Pressures exerted by predatory men seeking their own affirmation further complicate matters. Bereft of actual power, young men and women seek control over time and space through the use of their bodies.

Therefore, when very young girls speak about their desire to have babies, families and apartments of their own, they are identifying the attributes of personal autonomy and hoping for circumstances that will enhance their social position. That interpretation points to a configuration of events that make motherhood a desirable option when other alternatives to define adulthood are unavailable. The circumstances of poverty lead to accelerated development and motherhood at an early age.

Two implications of this analysis for policy are worth mentioning First, social networks matter. Meanings attached to behavior depend largely on whether a network is diversified, formed by subgroups with varying social statuses that act in various fields of activity. A diversified network makes it possible for individuals to tap a broader range of resources. To reduce pregnancy rates in areas of concentrated poverty, it is therefore necessary to expand children's social networks by bringing them into sustained contact with those who, by virtue of class and circumstance, know different, richer realities.

A second, derived implication regards the efficacy of sex education. Throughout years of research, I seldom found young women in West Baltimore who were unaware of or unable to obtain means of birth control. They attended schools where attention was given to reproductive behavior and where counselors habitually distributed informational booklets and made referrals. Yet, even in cases where pregnancy had been involuntary, girls still chose to keep their babies. This suggests that the liberal notion that births to adolescents can be prevented through education alone will always yield limited results in areas of concentrated poverty, where youngsters view motherhood as the only avenue to reaching adulthood. The expansion of the resource stockpile through which children can achieve maturity is a necessary precondition to reduce teen pregnancies.

13 LYDIA

As a little girl growing up in Greensboro, North Carolina, Lydia Forrest used to pray on her knees for her mother to come
back and take her away from the inhospitable place where she had lived
with her three sisters for the past two years. It was 1960. She was only
ten and staying with her great-aunt, Elvira, who was then in her nineties. Feeble and desiccated, the old woman haunted the small farmhouse
like a spirit. People said she had been born a slave, but it was hard to tell
because Aunt Elvira was a woman of few words. Her daughter, Sarah,
ruled the house with an iron fist. She resented having Lydia and her sisters around but saw no alternative. Although distantly related, the girls
were family. Sarah made up for her generosity by saying that Missie,
Lydia's mother, had God's punishment coming to her for neglecting her
children. According to Lydia:

> [Aunt Sarah] slapped us for the littlest thing. We knows she didn't
> like us, and it hurt 'cause before we was taken from my daddy's
> house, we was happy. . . . My sister Gertrude—we call her Gertie—
> she was the oldest and then came Deborah. My sister Margaret came
> after me. . . . There was about two years between [each of] us so we
> was very close.

Jonah and Missie Forrest, Lydia's parents had been loving and full
of laughter. By contrast, Aunt Sarah had no tenderness or patience. She
thought the way to instill discipline in the young was to make them
work all day in the fields and then saddle them with home chores in the
evening. Lydia woke up before dawn to spend the early hours of the day
picking cotton or feeding barn animals. Later she minded the hay cart,

swept the house, and did errands. After supper, it was time for prayer. When the fields were lying fallow, the girls were permitted to attend school. "It was a country school that only went to the eighth grade," Lydia said, "but we couldn't go all the time. There was always work to do at home and, besides, Aunt Sarah din't think girls should go to school. She thought the devil was in the books." When angry, Aunt Sarah could be terrifying. More than once she had tied Lydia to the bedpost through the night as a reminder that the wages of sin is death.

Before Lydia and her siblings were removed from their first home, Jonah Forrest, their father, had raised rabbits in a small plot rented from a White owner. During the planting and harvesting seasons, he had also leased his parched hands to other farmers. The family was poor but stable until Jonah broke his right leg and was confined to bed for a long while. "His bones didn't mend right," Lydia recalled. Jonah never stood up again without the use of a walking stick. He had been digni-fied and self-sufficient. Now he felt useless. After Jonah's accident, Mis-sie, his wife, left no stone unturned in her efforts to support the family, but there were few opportunities for women in rural North Carolina. Mostly, she cleaned other people's houses. "Sometimes all we had to eat was boiled flour dumplings," Lydia reminisced, "and strong coffee."

Time stretched long with food in short supply. Less than a year after her husband's mishap, Missie thought of moving to Washington, DC, where her cousin, Pearl Monroe, lived. The two women had known each other as children and had been good friends. Missie had shed tears over Pearl's departure from Greensboro, but during one of her visits back home, Pearl had told her that jobs were plentiful in the nation's capital. Now that she was the sole provider of her family, Missie was eager to try her luck away from the depleted home of her childhood. And although her main goal was to improve the lives of her daughters, she was also curious about city ways. She was still young and full of life. Yet she intended the move to be temporary. Missie left Greensboro fol-lowed by the memory of sadness in her children's eyes.

At first, things went just as she had hoped for. Gertie, Lydia's older sister, was almost thirteen at the time of her mother's departure. Seri-ous and obedient, she looked after the younger girls with a parent's devotion. Jonah found odd jobs to supplement the household's mea-ger income. Then, one morning, six-year-old Margaret, the youngest of the four sisters, tried to dispose of a pile of trash by burning it in the backyard. She only intended to do her share of the chores, but the results were disastrous. The fire spread, perilously scorching the door of the rickety house where the family lived. A neighbor who disapproved of the girls living alone with their father reported the incident to the social service authorities. Soon afterward, the four sisters were placed in foster care with Aunt Sarah, their maternal grandmother's sister. "They thought my daddy couldn't take care of us," Lydia recalled many years later:

> We was cryin', the four of us, 'cause we didn't want to leave my pa alone, and Gertie she was crying loudest because she felt responsible, and poor Margo [Margaret], the li'l one, said it was all her fault. It was nuthin' but pain from then on. I cried myself to sleep every night. I even promise God to be a good girl if my Mama comes back, but she didn't.

Immobilized and dispossessed, Jonah Forrest was left behind, waiting for news from his wife and for his leg to heal properly.

When Missie learned about her family's latest setback, she considered going back to Greensboro but soon abandoned the idea. Aunt Sarah was no pushover, but the girls were safe with her. Jonah was now absolved of childcare responsibilities. That too was a blessing. So she steeled her mind to accomplish what she had intended to do in the first place. Until she saved enough money to strengthen her family, there was no going back.

Expectant and full of hope, she had arrived in Washington, DC, in the late spring of 1958, Although she was focused mostly on survival, she couldn't help but notice the maelstrom building up around her. The nation's capital was becoming a central nerve point in the emerging civil rights movement, and politicians were abuzz with the rhetoric of social transformation. Four years earlier, following the *Brown vs. Board of Education* U.S. Supreme Court case, new legislation was rapidly passed in the name of racial justice. Desegregation was in full motion. As controversy raged, the Reverend Martin Luther King Jr. made dents in the nation's consciousness. White and Black youngsters held hands chanting together in public demonstrations of solidarity. Missie Forrest had never seen anything like that. The whole thing made her remember the way life had changed since she was a girl. From time to time, Greensboro's languor had been punctuated by violence:

> The thing I remember from when I was a li'l girl, I think three or four, was a neighbor, Mr. Thompson, and he had three sons. Johnny was the oldest—he must been fifteen, sixteen maybe. He was the smilin' kind, and polite. Then one night my papa comes home with fear in his eyes. A gang beat Johnny to death and hung his body from a tree limb. So his two brothers, they didn't stay behind for long, they went to New York. When people got scared they just left.

Now, in Washington, she was part of a tidal wave that was altering the profile of American cities. Everyone who traveled north had a reason. Some were led by terror. Others, like Missie, were spurred by a desire to prosper. Urban life was filled with excitement, but new dangers lurked in every corner. Without the support of family and community, migrants, especially women and the young, faced hazards that had been almost unknown in the countryside. Missie told of girls who had arrived in the city to work as live-in maids, only to end up selling their bodies to local passersby. In the absence of controls, a dismantling of self soon followed. Missie was appalled by the beggars who sat despondently at the street corners or loitered in the back alleys searching inside trashcans for discarded food. The raw hostility of the South had been paralyzing, but the semblance of urban equity was treacherous. Said Missie:

> [In Washington] you had to watch yo'self all the time to stay out of trouble. There were people in the street night and day. Crime was up, so you had to mind yo' property. It was worse in the winter. I had to wait for the bus in the dark, and I was always thinkin' someone's gonna snatch my bag.

The city demanded caution, but it also offered job prospects and freedom of movement along the thoroughfares and up the social ladder. Missie spent her weekends at the park surrounded by people from all walks of life. At dusk on the Fourth of July, she sat on the fields beyond the White House, with the Washington Monument straight ahead, waiting in a crowd of thousands for the fireworks. Her heart thumped a little faster under the multicolored cascade of light filling the dark skies, a taste of independence in her mouth. Then it was back to the small apartment she shared with her cousin. Rooming with Pearl had been full of rewards. Even as an old woman, Missie had vivid recollections of her life in those days:

> [Pearl] was a fine woman, she sho' was! Never married, never had childrun, and that was on purpose 'cause she didn't want to give up her ways. Lots of men was interested [in marrying her]. Sometimes Pearl didn't get home 'cause she was swingin' all night. Once in a while I go out with her, and oh Lord! We have some fun. I even got myself a couple of boyfriends, [but] I had to come clean with them. I couldn't go out much 'cause I was married, and I was putting away cash for the sake of my children.

She kept to herself most of the time, wiring money back home and sending mementos with encouraging words to her daughters. Young Lydia had a collection of postcards showing every tourist site in Washington. As pretty as they were, the cards did not make up for Missie's absence.

Back in Greensboro, suspended in time, Jonah visited the girls every weekend. On sunlight-filled Sundays, Lydia donned her only good clothes and rushed to the Genesis Baptist Church in the company of her father and sisters. The service lasted almost three hours, offering respite from the daily boredom. Lydia remembered the preacher's rousing exhortations to put aside anger and be obedient to God until death. She wanted to follow his commands, but a single thought ruled her mind—if Missie had cared for her and her sisters, she would not have left. Lydia watched with emotion as members of the congregation marched forward along the central aisle of the shrine to be healed by Jesus. She saw old men and women shout to the Lord in Heaven after suddenly recovering their sight or hearing, and people of all kinds falling on their backs overwhelmed by the power of the Holy Spirit. She wanted her anger to be wiped away by miracles such as those, but in her childhood, miracles never happened. Every time, she prayed hard but left the church with a heavy heart.

After worship, the small family would stroll about in the square until the girls had to return to Aunt Sarah's house. Lydia told of the day her father bought her a stuffed doll from a street vendor. It was a Raggedy Ann with embroidered eyes and hair made of black yarn, not much of a toy to play with but she kept it well into adulthood. Jonah said it would look after her when times were hard, and that she should always trust God for things to improve. Lydia had doubts about God but believed her father about the doll. Even as a grown-up savaged by despair, homeless and drunk, she hugged her tattered toy and felt better.

The days of her childhood dragged on slowly but, finally, in 1962, almost four years after Missie's departure from Greensboro, the Forrest family was reunited. Their coming together did not take place in their hometown, as originally planned, but in Washington, the site of Missie's progress. By then, Lydia was past her twelfth birthday. Her mother had recently secured a job as a housekeeper with a family of means. Missie couldn't say exactly what the man who owned the large house on Dupont Circle did for a living, but she knew he worked for the government. His wife was an agreeable woman who offered praise liberally. She liked Missie's courteous manner, her diligence, and even her cooking, although according to Missie, it was simple Southern fare. She felt lucky to have the lady's approval and even luckier to get a raise and a rent-free room. "Back then," Missie related, "good help always stayed. If you was honest and worked hard, the lady didn't let you go."

With renewed confidence, Missie wired the rail fare for Jonah and the girls to join her in the nation's capital. There was no going back to Greensboro where the vegetation was lush, the days dragged on, and opportunities were nowhere to be found. "She gotten used to the city ways and her own freedom," observed Lydia peevishly many years later. Still hobbling but with his faith intact, Jonah gathered his daughters and said good-bye to the familiar sights of his youth. As Lydia remembered it, the trip to Washington had been spine tingling:

> We never been away from home so Pa and my sisters, they jus' sat there real quiet [in the train], but when we got to Union Station, we was scared. I never saw a place so big. And all the rush and buzz in the street! I had butterflies in my stomach, like when you're in a Ferris wheel and afraid you's gonna fall.

For a while they huddled together in Pearl Monroe's rooms. Then they found a flat not far from the railroad tracks. It was dark and damp but it had two bedrooms, one bathroom, a nook for a sofa, and a small kitchen. Given her job's requirements, Missie saw her family only on

Sundays. That, she thought, was a big improvement over the previous years of separation, but the four sisters didn't see it that way. Now that the family was reunited, they were strangely detached and judgmental. Time and distance had taken their toll; they blamed Missie for the pain they had endured as foster children. In her heart, Lydia knew that her mother had left prompted by circumstance, not preference, but she sulked like her sisters just the same.

The climate in the small home could turn chilly as a result of the girls' resentment, but things were improving in other ways. Jonah surprised everyone, even himself, by securing a job at the reception desk of a warehouse, one of a string of similar depots near the train station. Although he was approaching his thirty-eighth birthday and walked with a limp, his resolve had impressed the manager who hired him. Jonah could read and knew a little about numbers. So great was his desire to pull his own weight that he was willing to do almost anything for any kind of pay. The job offered a decent wage, at least by Jonah's standards. After pooling their earnings, Missie and her husband no longer had to worry about covering essential needs. For the first Christmas after their reunion, they went so far as to buy a small tree and a box of plastic ornaments. Lydia and her sisters did not appreciate their parents' effort or good humor. A string of electric lights hung pitifully around the tree, thought Lydia, illuminating the squalor of their quarters more than the progress they had made as a family.

When she went out, her environs appalled her. They were vastly different from the tourist attractions embellishing Washington's core, where every structure gave testimony of the country's grandeur. By contrast, the neighborhood where the Forrest family lived was decrepit. Buildings stuck out like freaks in a barren landscape, especially during the winter. Without trees to soften it, the view was all asphalt, wire, and sharp edges. Lydia missed the verdant fields of North Carolina, where everyone knew her by name. With her mother away for most of the week and her father at work, there wasn't much time for "fun or frolickin'." The four sisters were cooped up in the rented flat, which became stifling in the winter months.

The more she lived in the city, the more insight she gained about social divisions. Back in Greensboro, differences of status and class had seemed minor. In Washington they stood large. She had never seen so many women in sable furs or so many men sleeping in the street under the pages of yesterday's newspaper. Everywhere she went, she was made conscious of the things she couldn't have. A vast gulf separated insiders and outsiders. Disparities were also visible at school, where the more-established students made Lydia feel her lowly position. Her country speech and bashful ways made her an easy target for derision. Without warning, enmity sprang up in front of her like a pop-up figure. Other children called her ignorant, and ugly, and high-yellow mule. Enduring reproach during the day, she wept at night as she had done in her mother's absence.

As time passed, however, she made friends among her neighbors. In the summer, relieved from the torment of school, she sat gossiping with them on the front stoop of her building. She taught them how to play jacks; they returned the favor by teaching her double Dutch. In that game Lydia found her only talent and reward. A rare sense of power would overtake her as she chanted in unison with other girls, all the while feeling the two jump ropes gliding easily under her feet in opposite directions. Her agility attracted compliments. She was hungry for approval, but her mother told her double Dutch was a child's game and she was getting much too old to be called a child.

At first, she tried hard in school but her marks weren't good. Maybe Aunt Sarah had gnawed a way into her inner self—she thought Lydia was stupid. The only certainty was that the academic deficiencies of childhood now made it difficult for the girl to catch up. "I jus' didn't have the mind for school," she said.

In the absence of legitimate claims to status, she was lured away by risky pursuits. Feeling like an outcast, she joined other outsiders. Her new friends knew where to get reefer and bourbon. She dozed through class periods and later congregated in the school corridors with a small crowd of acquaintances to make plans for the afternoon. Young and rudderless, Lydia "tried the pot and the whisky an' stayed out all night long, . . . worried my mother sick." To punish Missie wasn't the girl's main goal, but she took satisfaction in seeing her mother weep—let her suffer like she had suffered all those years in Aunt Sarah's dungeon. Jesus hadn't helped her then, and he wouldn't help her now. In her drunken stupor, she cursed God. When her mind was clear, she knew she had sinned. Angels wept for her lost soul. She said she had known the dark side of hell during that period. Her only consolation was the raggedy doll her father had given her years earlier.

By her seventeenth birthday, however, Lydia was bent on reform. One sleepless night, she had found one of her girlfriends in an abandoned house, unconscious and frothing at the mouth, a bottle of cheap whisky lying by her motionless body. She wasn't dead but she could have been, according to the medics that rushed her to the emergency room of the local hospital. The frightful incident had shaken Lydia to the core. In silence, she promised to be good and stay clean.

She assumed that her intentions were coming to fruition, because soon afterward she met Reuben Chapman. Six years her senior, he was good-looking and was employed as a custodian in downtown Washington. In the afternoons, on her way back from school, she would spot him waiting at a corner. Together they walked in the park licking ice-cream cones. Reuben was a gentleman; he even escorted Lydia right up to the front door of her building, making her feel like a princess. Other than her father, no man had ever been as kind.

Lydia loved Reuben so much that she thought she might marry him. That was before she found out that he had a reckless history with women and two babies by a different girl. Sadly, that news reached her ears too late. It was a little over five years after her arrival in Washington that she gave birth to her first child, a boy whom she named after his father. "He had big eyes that shined like beams of light," explained Lydia, "so we thought he should be called Beamy. Beamy was his nickname."

Despite Big Reuben's errant ways and her parents' reproaches, Lydia continued her involvement with the man. After she became pregnant for the second time, Jonah, her father, put his foot down. There simply was no space for another infant in the small flat where they lived. She would have to make other arrangements.

Oddly enough, considering his record, Big Reuben felt an obligation toward Lydia. Wishing to do right by her, he agreed to rent a place for them to set up housekeeping. Lydia saw his gesture as a good sign; maybe they would be married, after all. Their second son, Lorenzo, was born in 1970. He was a wisp of a child, so his parents called him "Weedy."

At first the couple turned a blind eye on hardship. In the small flat all to themselves, they were kept busy and amazed by their babies. Soon, however, they began to argue bitterly over money. Reuben didn't earn

enough to support a family. Lydia looked for jobs cleaning buildings
and baby-sitting, but even by combining their two incomes they were
unable to cover monthly expenses. She could have applied for public
assistance, but she shuddered at the thought:

> See, I had a rough childhood, and it wasn't much better when we got
> to Washington, but the one thing I got was pride. To me, the welfare
> was the worst fall, like being in jail and everyone thinkin' you's scum.
> I wasn't gonna do it for nothin' in the world!

Money troubles mounted, giving way to other complaints. Lydia was
enraged by Reuben's devotion to his older children. She knew he spent
money on them while Beamy and Weedy went without decent clothes
or toys. Reuben had gripes of his own. Now that Lydia had a home, she
was always sullen and angry. He didn't get credit for his efforts, and furthermore, he suspected Lydia met other men on the sly. She was tall and
eye-catching, with light mocha skin and hair that she flattened around
a pretty face. Tortured by jealousy, Reuben became dangerous. In fits of
rage he hit her, and once he slashed her with a knife. Lydia called the
police in haste. Reuben had to spend several nights behind bars. After
that, she didn't want him back as a live-in partner. She bore a three-inch
scar in her upper left arm as a reminder of the episode.

Now alone, as the sole support of her two sons, Lydia redirected
her life. Abashed by his stint in jail, Reuben visited regularly, bringing
smiles and petty cash for the children. His flame for Lydia had grown
brighter as a result of the separation. He begged and made promises,
but the woman's heart had stiffened. She would not let him sleep in the
same bed unless there was a clear advantage. "He can't stay if he don't
pay," was her new motto, which she applied liberally not only to Reuben
but to other men she was cozy with.

In her mind, this was far from whoring. Prostitutes were the women
with painted faces that strolled in Washington's red zones wearing out-
rageous outfits and exposing their bodies to the gaze of strangers. By
contrast, only friends were allowed into Lydia's rooms. Intimacy was
not assured. She set no fee. Her visitors could tell she had bills to pay.
They left money as a token of appreciation for her company; otherwise,
they might not be invited back. She was no whore. "The welfare" was at
bay and she could still hold her head high.

Missie, Lydia's mother, saw things differently. She suspected more than knew the details of her daughter's life but she feared that Lydia was tottering on the brink of disaster. She couldn't understand her troubles. Her other girls had found a straight and narrow path in Washington, after overcoming their early rancor. Gertie had finished high school on time. Now in her late twenties, she worked as a waitress to support her own little daughter, Benita. Although a single mother and a diabetic, she held a decent job and was making progress. After completing high school, Deborah, whom Missie had named after her own sister, was married and now had two babies. Her husband, Will, worked for the Social Security Administration. They lived in a small but nicely appointed house in Prince Georges County. Margo, the youngest of the four, was still living at home, and Missie had high hopes that she would attend college.

It was only Lydia, whose rowdy ways caused Missie grief; she was selfish and unwieldy. Couldn't she see how hard her mother had struggled to support her and her sisters? In the early 1970s, while Lydia floundered, Missie was still holding the same job she had when the family was reunited.

Men's contributions helped her through difficult moments, but Lydia persisted in her intent to live independently. Because she had limited skills, the best she could do was clean houses, like her mother had done before her. Times had changed, however, since Missie had first arrived in Washington. In the aftermath of the civil rights movement, hardly anyone did live-in work anymore. African Americans shunned such menial positions because they evoked slavery and the segregated past. Whites increasingly shied away from treating Blacks as servants. It was the beginning of a new era marked as much by pretense as by genuine hope for racial equality. Women now had greater autonomy, but they also had higher expenses. Lydia needed a job that paid enough for rent and child care.

In due course, she found an almost ideal position, especially given her educational shortcomings. At age twenty-four and for the next seven years, Lydia worked as a custodian at Schwitzer, Marlin and Tzabo, Attorneys at Law, a firm with a clientele consisting of private individuals and small businesses. Her shift went from five in the afternoon to midnight, and she supplemented her earnings by cleaning houses in the mornings or on weekends. For more than fifty hours a week, she toiled without much of a break and was grateful despite the back pain from the work that allowed her to support her growing children. She had sworn to keep her pride, and "So help me, God, I did jus' that!"

Holding a steady job altered her disposition. Tempered by past travails, she now perfected a sense of worth founded on honesty and attention to detail. Her employers valued her work so much that they gave her bonuses at Christmas and showed their appreciation in other ways throughout the year "They was Jewish," remarked Lydia, "but they acted like Christians should." Mr. Tzabo was especially attentive. She thought he had a crush on her—once he even asked her out for a bite. She politely declined because she didn't think that sort of behavior was proper; people should stick to their own kind. Besides, she liked her work and didn't want complications.

By piecing together the wages from her main job and two or three cleaning gigs a week, Lydia was able to meet monthly expenses. On credit, she bought a new sofa and a large television set. Even her relationship with her mother improved. Missie looked after her two grandchildren on weekends while Lydia worked as a day maid.

Only one thing marred the comparative peace of that period. Unexpectedly, at the age of thirty-four, Lydia's older sister Gertrude collapsed one day and later died, leaving behind her ten-year-old daughter, Benita. Because she had nowhere else to go, the girl was sent to her Aunt Deborah, Missie's sister, who lived in Baltimore. Bitter tears were shed on Gertie's behalf. She had taken care of her younger siblings since they were small. Like a mother in Missie's absence, she had sheltered them from Aunt Sarah's frightful temper. "Of the four of us, she was the best," Lydia reflected. "Maybe that's why she died; that way she was spared more pain." Now it worried her to see the anxious expression on Benita's face. The girl was as young as Lydia had been when her own mother traveled to Washington.

Sometime in 1972, while strolling with her boys in a park, on a clear September day, Lydia met James Culver, a mechanic who worked at a car dealership. He approached her courteously, offering to buy hot dogs for the children. He seemed gentle and sharp, so they began to see each other regularly. Almost two years passed before their first child, Felicia, was born. Towanda, a second girl, arrived in 1977. James gave as much as he could toward the support of his brood, but Lydia wouldn't allow him to live under the same roof. She didn't mind loving his children because, as she put it, "babies are always a gift." It was different with men. Now that she had attained self-reliance at great personal cost, she needed no more "man troubles." She was in her late twenties and content to be on her own. James stood patiently on the sidelines, waiting for her to change her mind.

One morning in 1982, when he was fifty-six, Jonah Forrest, Lydia's father, arrived at his job on time as he always did. Moments later, the head supervisor found him hunched over the desk he had occupied for nearly two decades. He never regained consciousness. On a gelid October morning, he was buried back in Greensboro, the place of his birth. His wife and three daughters traveled from Washington to weep at his burial site.

After that, Missie returned to Washington with a changed outlook. Now that she was a widow and the girls were living away from home, she thought it was time to give up her full-time job as a housekeeper. Her sister Deborah lived in Baltimore. She too was a widow and eager for Missie to join her.

Echoes of her lost childhood rang in Lydia's ears upon hearing the news. Her father was dead and her mother was about to abandon her again. Pregnant with a third child by James Culver, she needed Missie's care now more than ever. When her mother packed her bags, Lydia decided to tag along. Baltimore wasn't that far, and Aunt Deborah said the American Label Company was hiring. Factory jobs were scarce to come by; they paid well and carried benefits. She didn't mind leaving Washington, anyhow, because her position was not as secure by then. Hurt by the recession that inaugurated the Reagan presidency, business was down at the law firm. It was uncertain whether Schwitzer, Marlin and Tzabo would be able to afford her services anymore. Now that Missie was alone, she could look after the children while Lydia supported the family. She made up her mind quickly but didn't tell James a word until she was making ready for the move. Unfazed, the man said he would soon follow—he too had relatives in Baltimore.

Temporarily ensconced with her children in the small house that Missie now shared with Deborah and the orphaned Benita, Lydia hastened to apply for a job at American Label, but her aunt had been wrong. Stifled by bulging inventories and declining demand, the firm was cutting back on production. A nice lady at the reception desk told Lydia to come back in a few weeks. A month later there were still no openings. American Label closed down permanently less than a year after Lydia's arrival in Baltimore. Undaunted, she kept searching and felt lucky to be hired as a janitor at the Baltimore Gas and Electric Company. Her cheer lasted but a little while. She was laid off only six months after starting on the new job. The company was a public interest, and the government was cutting back on nonessential expenditures. Pregnant, with no money or a real home and four youngsters to feed, Lydia was desperate. It mortified her to admit that in those days she had gone back to the bottle seeking to quiet her unrest. Space grew crowded at Aunt Deborah's house, and tempers flared up all the time.

James Culver Jr. was born at the First Presbyterian Hospital in West Baltimore on February 10, 1982. His arrival brought Lydia new hope. She called him "Mush" because that's the way he felt when being held—just a bundle of melting tissue with big brown dots on his honey-colored face. It astonished her how much she loved her children. She would do anything for them. For that reason, she now embraced what she had previously avoided like the plague. Less than a week after her last son's birth, Lydia applied for public assistance, with the ghosts of detractors mumbling in her brain. She knew what welfare mothers were called—parasites, freeloaders, and moochers. But how dare anyone pass judgment? Hadn't she done as much as possible to stand on her own? Besides, she didn't intend to take charity forever; a job would turn up soon enough. So she stifled the voices of shame in her head and walked resolutely into the gray welfare office that swallowed her like a gullet.

From the government, Lydia received, in addition to food stamps and Medicaid, a monthly allotment of four hundred and eighty dollars to support her five children. More than half of that amount went to rent a two-storied row house located on the 1900 block of Goodyear Street, not far from the projects. The block was fraught with danger and the building was old and ramshackle, but it provided independence. Just to keep its head above water, the family required at least another five hundred dollars every month. To make up part of that amount, Lydia went back to cleaning houses and, on occasion, played the numbers with some luck. Both activities were against welfare regulations.

James gave her as much as he could. In fact, it was due to his financial contributions that Lydia finally relented, allowing him to live with her and the children. That too was a violation of government rules. Miss Hastings, Lydia's social worker, was always reminding her of this: no live-in boyfriends or gifts from men. So adamantly and so often did Lydia deny James' existence that she fell into the habit of ignoring him publicly and even when she had company. Her attitude and deportment told others that the man standing by her side was nothing but a figment of their imagination. She wasn't breaking any rules—he was just passing by. In fact, he wasn't really there. Her calculated indifference was especially marked when James drank, a condition that befell him with regularity on weekends.

Little Reuben Chapman, Lydia's first child known to everyone as Beamy, was fifteen years old when his mother first had to go on welfare. He had grown up strong; a boy of few words but devoted to his family. Lydia's new predicament filled him with guilt and a failed sense of duty. What was the point of being a man if he couldn't even support his own? Because of his lack of power, now the family had to take handouts; he could do nothing. Lydia saw his son's worries change into muddled action. He had been a studious child; now he left for school without bothering to take a book bag and came back in the afternoons with money she hadn't given him. "Beamy, he wasn't bad," said Lydia, "jus' confused because, well, he thought he should be the head of the family." The more she tried to hold on to him, the more he slipped away.

On an overcast December night, about a week after Thanksgiving Day, young Reuben and his friend, Tito Marsh, also known as Gem, stood outside the local 7-Eleven, smoking cigarettes and trying to decide how to spend the hours ahead. It was about seven-thirty in the evening, with darkness hanging like a veil over the city skyline when Gem showed Reuben the Saturday night special he had bought on the street the day before. Beamy was in awe. He was further impressed when Gem shared his plan to rob a cab driver. It would be easy; no one would get hurt. The gun was only for show—to scare the cabbie and take off with his money. Shivering with excitement and fear, they walked down North Avenue around eight in the evening, dressed nicely, just two young men on their way home.

Buford Hanford, who worked for the Sparrow Cab Company, was driving his black-and-blue vehicle when he saw the two boys waving at him at an intersection of North and Hilton. According to the official report, when Mr. Hanford stopped, one of the boys, Tito Marsh, slid into the front seat while the other, Reuben Chapman, entered the back compartment. They asked the driver to make a turn onto Hilton Street away from the traffic. Less than three minutes later, the sound of two gunshots rang out. Mr. Hanford had tried to resist the boys' demands and the gun, said Marsh, had fired accidentally. Terrifying was the sight of the cab driver slouching behind the wheel, his unblinking eyes staring into space.

The youngsters had tried to escape, but their flight was cut short by three police cars a few miles away from the crime scene. In handcuffs, they were transported to the Baltimore City Jail. Later they were tried as adults. Marsh faced life in prison. As an accessory after the fact, Beamy's sentence was yet to be determined.

Neither Missie's abandonment nor the lonesome days of her childhood nor Big Reuben's disloyalties nor even the death of her father and sister had shaken Lydia as much as seeing her eldest son in shackles at the courthouse day after day as his fate was being decided. She sat behind him, choking back the tears and reciting in silence, "He not a bad boy, not a bad boy; jus' in the wrong place at the wrong time; please give my boy another chance." Then, all was finished—the uncertainty and the hope. It took the jury only one hour to reach a verdict: a twenty-five-year sentence. It was a long stretch, but Lydia believed Beamy might be out in half the time if he behaved. Faithfully, once a month, she visited her son at the Maryland Correctional Institution at Jessup, dragging Towanda with her. Eventually, she came to realize that given the dangers skulking in the world outside, having a son behind bars was not as bad as she had imagined. At least he was safe, she told herself.

A few weeks after Beamy's incarceration, one Saturday morning, two Jehovah's Witnesses came knocking on Lydia's door. It was not their first visit, but this time Lydia invited them in. Doubt and disbelief had nagged her since she could remember. She had rolled up her eyes at the preaching of Baptists and Pentecostals and scoffed at the pious beseeches of the Alleluia People. The severity of Catholics, with their idols and incense repelled her. But now, at the lowest point in her life, here were Frances Collins and Gene Miller, two of the nicest people you would ever want to meet. Surprisingly, they were interested in Lydia; it mattered to them that she had stayed strong and endured, climbing every mountain, conquering all difficulties, even the imprisonment of her Beamy, whose tears she had wiped off as a little boy.

Lydia thought that Frances and Gene had arrived at the precise moment when everything threatened to collapse about her. It wasn't just her troubles, but the troubles of others that afflicted her. A year after waving good-bye to Beamy in prison, she had come to the rescue of her great niece, Clarise, Benita's second daughter and one of three children left stranded when Benita turned to drugs and alcohol. Only a while back, Benita had been a skinny little girl saddened by the untimely death of, her mother, Lydia's sister Gertie. Now, twenty-two, Benita roamed the streets of West Baltimore without purpose or direction. Melinda, her firstborn, was in the custody of Aunt Margaret. Little Floyd, the youngest of Benita's three children, languished in foster care. Three-year-old Clarise was now staying with Lydia—another mouth to feed with only a little more from "the welfare."

Then there was Weedy, Lydia's second son, who disapproved of his mother's involvement with James Culver. It pained Lydia to know that he sold drugs. By 1989, her twelve-year old daughter, Towanda, would show signs of ruination, balking at her mother's reprimands and staying out all night. Mush, the youngest of the brood, wound up in a correctional facility by his sixteenth birthday. Only Felicia, Lydia's firstborn, remained helpful and obedient through high school and beyond.

Finally, there was James Culver himself, usurping the privileges of marriage without having asked Lydia to be his wife. When they first met he had seemed sturdy and hardworking, a rock upon which to anchor her life. He had followed and comforted, never withholding money or affection. Lately, however, he jumped from job to job "like a grasshopper," and his drinking was getting worse. She wouldn't ask him to leave because "it wouldn't be fair"; he had nowhere else to go. On the other hand, how he enraged her with that silly smile of his and that ridiculous wobble after a binge, reeking of cigarette smoke and talking nonsense: "Hey, baby, yo' looking good, gimme a kiss—yeah baby?" Lydia felt more like tossing him out like a rotten onion: "I see the knife, " she muttered, "the big one in the kitchen drawer, and think how easy . . .

to cut his throat when he's passed out." It was just talk, but the words reflected the scale of her frustration.

She wanted something other than this blind rage and sadness to follow her around for the rest of her life. Frances Collins and Gene Miller, who trusted Jehovah God had taught her how to use the Old Testament to gain new understanding. On Wednesday evenings, in her own living room, after offering them coffee and cake, Lydia would listen to their religious instruction. They made her feel respectable. School had been a bore but now her mind soaked up knowledge like a sponge. She came to see how the Bible explained all that was happening around her—the men idling in the empty corners, the streets without trees or solace, the garbage at the curbside, the twisted words on the walls, the nightly gunshots, and the sobs heard at night. Her world was not senseless anymore.

On Saturday afternoons she marched to Kingdom Hall with Clarise, her grandniece and ward, held by the hand. Lydia loved the little girl who, at seven, was tall for her age, slender, and bright. Four of her own five children were in trouble, but Clarise, Lydia thought, would still make her proud. At Kingdom Hall, Clarise sat sweetly, waiting for the elders to begin the service. She wasn't afraid to read aloud from the *Watch Tower*, the Jehovah's Witnesses' instructional manual, for the whole congregation to listen. She was respectful and docile, as youngsters should be. Like Lydia, other people thought Clarise was special. At the end of the service, after chatting with members of the congregation, Lydia would return to the trials of her daily life renewed and expectant.

It was her conversion to the faith of Jehovah's Witnesses that gave Lydia the resolve to do two things. One was to press James Culver into marriage. "It ain't proper for a God-fearing woman to be living in sin," she told him. He had little power to resist—they had been together through thick and thin for more than a decade. Her second decision was to move the family into a better place. The house on Goodyear Street was "nasty" and the block "detestable." Two boarded-up structures flanked Lydia's front, their walls splattered with graffiti. It was no secret what went on in their murky rooms. Besides, to cut down on rental expenses, she wanted to live in the George Murphy Homes, the sprawling housing complex in West Baltimore. Achieving that goal required belief in a higher power because the wait period was eleven years. Lydia would have preferred not to live on Goodyear Street for another month.

She pleaded and argued, sat in offices for hours, got letters from her employers and many times described the fears she had for her children, both those she had borne herself and the one she had taken in, Clarise. In the end, she prevailed. Her caseworker went to bat for her, and by the end of the year Lydia's application had been approved. She had never doubted the outcome of her maneuvers. Jehovah God was finally on her side.

Lydia saw the two-story unit in the projects as a vast improvement. It had four small bedrooms, a larger kitchen, and even a linen closet— that was "mighty proper." At the same time, she couldn't help but notice the home's shortcomings: "It kills me," she observed, "it don't have a back door! This is still the worst neighborhood, for cryin' out loud! If someone comes after you through the front door, there's no escape." It annoyed her to see that architects hadn't thought about such things; they were supposed to be the ones with the smarts.

In her new domicile, relieved from onerous rental fees, Lydia could stretch income farther. Putting together cash from her cleaning jobs, irregular contributions from James, and the occasional Lotto win, she began to entertain middle-class dreams. In the tiny living room, she placed a couch and two armchairs upholstered in blue paisley fabric. They were cheap but recently bought. So were the cocktail table at the center of the room with its shiny glass top and the mirror hung on the wall between large paper fans. The fans were from Pottery Barn. Lydia knew that was where women who hired her services bought decorative trappings. Maybe she wasn't as rich as they were but, still, she had taste. With their azure background overlaid with leafy red chrysanthemums, the fans were the first thing a visitor noticed when entering the house. She thought they were elegant.

Over the next few years Lydia strengthened her position as the family pillar. Her youth had been reckless, but she had mended her ways. It was no shame to be on welfare, said those who knew her; Lydia still pulled her own weight. She was the one who friend, kin, and neighbor came to when looking for the occasional loan or piece of advice. Lydia knew how to work the system; she knew how to get things done. And she had a kind heart; countless children in distress passed through her door, never to be sent away hungry or sleepless. Benita, her niece and Clarise's mother, saw Lydia as her protector and last resort—when even food money had trickled away, Benita could rely on Lydia for a few bucks. It shamed the young woman not to be like her aunt who had some money and whose figure loomed large over her, tall and robust like a statue.

Although she had never held a job that paid more than the minimum wage and her welfare stint was nearing a decade, Lydia took pride in the way she had always supported her children. "Never had a problem putting food on the table for them babies," she boasted. Even when life had been at its most difficult, she had seen the children as a blessing. As a girl in Aunt Sarah's farm, she had earned her keep. Later she had done what was needed to take care of her family. For the same reason, she saw no moral dilemma when combining paid work with public assistance. It was her way to behave responsibly. Once I asked her whether she regretted having had five children. She was indignant, "No ma'am. Dem children wasn't the reason for me stayin' poor. It was on account of not finding a job that paid decent that I gone on welfare!"

Lydia's sense of moral purpose was expressed in other ways. Over time she developed a code of etiquette to uphold her life as a domestic worker. At the house of a potential employer, she would clutch her purse with resolve and survey the etchings on the walls, the crystal chandeliers, and some furniture with intricate designs that would demand special treatment. After stating the cost of her services as a once-a-week cleaning woman, her expression announced "Take it or leave it." Having succeeded in her bid, she would later say, "good families don't mind paying me more because I am good at what I do and I am trustworthy." In Lydia's list of desirable virtues, integrity and self-respect ranked at the top.

There were other rituals attached to her new identity. Immediately after arriving at her place of employment she would change into a pale green uniform as a way to proclaim to actual and imaginary witnesses that she held a real job. It didn't matter that she had been on the dole for so long. Cleaning houses was an honorable way to earn a living, the one thing that separated her from the lazy bums she left behind every day in the 'hood. She had learned from her religious mentors that honor did not depend on where you live or what you do but on who *you are*.

As a convert, Lydia learned that religious faith can ease the pains of scarcity. Jehovah's Witnesses reject as vestiges of paganism nearly all holidays and personal celebrations, including birthdays, and Christmas. Lydia could remember days of suffering when she didn't have enough money to buy presents for her children. She could recall their disappointed expressions, their silent tears; their resentment. Jehovah's Witnesses had taught her that holidays were worldly distractions, and so by surrendering her material desires, she had found rectitude and peace.

And something else: Baltimore's mean streets ravaged by fury and drugs could now be understood as a battlefield where supreme good wages war against supreme evil. Jehovah's Witnesses believe in Satan's real presence on earth. It had been Satan who had led Beamy to prison. It had been he who had coaxed her daughter, Towanda, into becoming pregnant at fourteen and a crack addict at fifteen. Resigned to the temporary victories of evil, Lydia stood resolutely on God's side, waiting with the other faithful for the destruction of the wicked world and for the Great Rapture, when all signs will be clear and all pain shall be forgotten.

But Lydia's religious convictions were also producing unexpected consequences. When Clarise, her charge, was eight, she began attending the Community School of the Holy Spirit, a Catholic institution. At that time, Lydia had not allowed sectarian divides to stand in the way of Clarise's educational advancement—she wanted the girl to thrive, "Let her have more than I had," she said. "She shouldn't have to go through what I've been through for lack of schooling." Five years later, her views had changed; she wanted Clarise transferred to a public school because it wasn't right for a Jehovah's Witness to attend a Catholic school. Sister Trinita, the principal at Holy Spirit, tried to persuade her otherwise, but Lydia never relented. By then she was convinced that following God's will was more important than a fancy education. Clarise was forced to leave the parochial school—an event that demolished her early accomplishments. Still, Lydia thought it was the girl's character that had been tested and found wanting.

That was a pivotal moment joining centuries of history with one woman's conviction. Lydia's ancestors had been Baptists; she had shunned their traditions to join Jehovah's Witnesses, a millenarian sect. Longing for citizenship, her forebears had sung "Carry Me Low," "Sweet

Chariot," and "Lift Every Voice and Sing," the unofficial anthem of African Americans in their struggle for civil rights and full inclusion in
American society. By contrast, Lydia had cast off secular allegiances,
including the thirst for a nation. Years ago, alone in the pit of darkness, she had turned her life around, seeking a route to salvation. She
had triumphed over self and circumstance by the power of faith. Lydia
failed to notice, however, that her new beliefs were now pulling her
back inward, away from the world at large, further down into a vortex
of distance and isolation.

She was not alone—Clarise followed, held firmly by the hand.

14 FAITH AND CIRCUMSTANCE IN WEST BALTIMORE

LYDIA FORREST, WHOSE LIFE IS ACKNOWLEDGED IN THE PREVIOUS chapter, was compelled to make decisions along a journey of sorrow and disappointment but also determination and hope. She represents countless women of African-American descent whose fates have been sculpted by internal migration, abandonment, impoverishment, gender discord, and ultimately religious faith.

The daughter of penniless sharecroppers in a southern state, Lydia spent her early years in a rural environment. Her mother's recollections were of luscious vegetation and family unity but also scarcity and fears of lynching. In such a context, every mishap had dire consequences. When Lydia's father, Jonah, lost his capacity to work as a result of an accident, Missie, his wife, had few options but to seek opportunities elsewhere. In the nation's capital, Missie found work but also dislocation and anomie. Left behind, her children, including Lydia, mistook their mother's courageous departure for neglect. Even then, Lydia's memories of churchgoing with her father when she was still a girl in foster care point to the monumental significance of religion as a way to make sense of suffering.

After the family was reunited in Washington, DC, Lydia, by then twelve years old, faced other challenges: as a recently arrived migrant from the rural South, she was the target of prejudice not only from Whites but from Black children and Black teachers as well. As a young woman, lured by alcohol and drugs, she spiraled down to near disaster but sought normality by forming a family of her own—motherhood was part of her yearnings.

After moving to Baltimore, she was reluctantly forced to accept public assistance to support her children but maintained a sense of self-respect by working as a domestic servant. In the eyes of the government, working for pay while receiving public monies was a violation. In Lydia's mind, paid work was a mark of honor no matter what welfare rules said. Hers was not an attempt to break the law but an effort to uphold her worth.

By developing rituals around her presentation of self, Lydia found multiple ways to assert an honorable identity. Donning a uniform while cleaning other people's homes expressed her constant search for respect. The uniform accentuated the separation between personal life and employment; it was an organizing tool meant to dignify work. Although she was not aware of it, Lydia's behavior held a connection with the historical past: African-American women deliberately chose to wear uniforms when working as domestics in the period that followed emancipation and desegregation (Clark-Lewis 1996). With that gesture, they too sought to elevate their status in the society. In Lydia's case, what appeared to be a trivial choice was, in fact, the legacy of collective experience—an action fraught with significance.

Even more important in her pursuit of an elevated status was Lydia's religious conversion, that is, her determination to embrace religious faith as a means to explain the unhappy events in her life. It was religion that enabled her to understand her oldest son's crime and imprisonment and her young daughter's dangerous behavior. It was religion that gave her a reason to demand marriage from the father of her three younger children. And it was religion that provided her with strong criteria for evaluating her own behavior and other people's conduct.

Here I use Lydia's religious journey as a point of reference to understand, first, the ways in which people living in poverty use their bodies as a canvas to re-present values and construct self-worth and, second, to review the multiple forms in which religion serves as a fluid narrative used by individuals to explain and legitimate personal choices and evaluate the choices of others. The paradoxical conclusion is that although religion acts as a source of strength and empowerment, it can also serve to foster passivity and to complicate the effects of residential segregation and destitution. I begin by discussing notions of downfall and redemption as I discovered them in West Baltimore.

TO BE HUMAN IN INHUMAN PLACES

"No one told me to do it, right?" Alonso Dickson states emphatically as I sit before him in a barren room set aside for visitors at the Jessup Correctional Institution in Baltimore. The year is 1995. He is twenty-seven, tall, and lean. A scar over his left eyebrow adds interest to an otherwise unblemished face. He has now served eight years of what will be a twenty-five year sentence for armed robbery and multiple charges associated with the event that led to a death, changing Alonso's life. "No one told me to get involved," he continues:

> I had free will; I could have told them [Eldon and Morris Adams, his partners in crime] that I had something else to do that night, right? But I din't; I went willingly with them into the store and I looked out while they shoot the cashier and take the money, right? So who's to blame here? It ain't like I don't know right from wrong. But I din't want them to think I was weak; I wanted to show I was a man.

Alonso's story is painfully familiar—told so many times that it has become a cliché: young men in groups playing to each other in a game of chicken that never ends well. Yet arrest and punishment is never the end of the story. States Alonso:

> I'm not sayin' it was a good thing, but there was good things that came out of that night. . . . I wouldn't have found a better way without going through what I've been through. Being in jail has taught me that I can still be good; I can still make my family proud, know what I mean? It's like everybody, not just me, has to fall low to prove they can get back on their feet.

Despite differences in age and gender, Alonso's narrative is nearly identical to that of Lydia Forrest, whose efforts as an adult had been fiercely directed at salvation. In both cases, the narrative begins with a newborn child—a blank slate. The child grows up. Endowed with free will, he or she makes the wrong choices not as a result of ignorance but because of pride. Condemned and rejected, he or she seeks a new life by rethinking options and overcoming temptation. The will triumphs over impulse; the human buries the animal; God defeats Satan.[1]

Less abundant, however, are sociological accounts that investigate the role of conversion, ritual, and redemptive behavior in attempts to normalize the experience of destitution (exceptions are Bane and Mead [2003] and Crawford Sullivan [2012]). The conventional view is that among dispossessed people, religion and other spiritual pursuits are mostly the effect of despair and marginalization (Hunt 2002). They make life bearable and are often the result of ignorance and superstition rather than the outcome of analysis and reflection. Empirical research shows, by contrast, that religious practices in poor neighborhoods are often the product of introspection and creative thinking; they are seldom a mechanical response to want.

In a secular world ruled by the market, religion provides one of the few tools that the poor can use to explain their circumstances in affirmative ways (Hirschman 2004). When confronted with the judgment of people wealthier and more successful, the poor can resort to an ample repertory of religious symbols, rituals, and narratives to ennoble their condition. That was the case of Moriah Hunter, a thirty-six-year-old mother of three who called the Baltimore projects her home:

> When you look around and see the misery of people living in this neighborhood—the junkies and the drunks; the drive-by shootings, the kids killing each other, you think this is hell! . . . But then I remember there's a reason for everything. I think God wants me to prove that I'm human even if this is an inhuman place, so I pray a lot. . . . I pray for deliverance.

Like Moriah Hunter, many women living in poverty have developed points of view and rituals, including prayer, to strengthen their capacity to survive in uncertain and hazardous conditions. Their religiosity is often private. Many do not attend church on a regular basis—some are too overwhelmed with daily routines involving the care of children and relatives. Others are afflicted by personal demons, including drug addiction, and fear the condemnation of churchgoing people whom they assume to be more virtuous than they are. Yet others find it difficult to relate to the words of preachers, whose outlooks can seem remote and disconnected from their own experience. In private, women living in poverty often resort to religious imagery to validate their experience (Crawford Sullivan 2012).

Amanda Owens, Lydia Forrest's neighbor, was only twenty-two when I first met her in 1995. She didn't attend church mostly because she suspected single mothers were looked down upon by congregants at the Divine Shepherd, the closest place of worship in her area. Although her institutional affiliation was weak, Amanda depended on a solid religious stock to inspire and push her forward. "It's not a sin to be poor," she told me:

> [B]ut it is a sin to get discouraged. Every day, I wake up and the first thing I do is pray that I will find the light. Then, when something nasty happens to me or to the people I care about, I pray and that gives me peace. Before I put my baby down to sleep I pray over her, and I pray before going to bed. I think God hears my prayers because, so far, things ain't so bad, and I believe in my heart they will get better.

Three years later, after obtaining an associate's degree from the local community college and marrying a man five years her senior who had a stable job at the Motor Vehicles Administration, Amanda attributed her success to the power of prayer. Even as she packed her belongings in preparation for a move to a different neighborhood, her conviction was that God was with her.

The same is true for those left behind. Katrina Spencer had seen her share of trouble by the age of nineteen when she had her first child, Antonio. Caught holding a plastic bag with more than five grams of crack cocaine belonging to her boyfriend, she was convicted of possession with the intent to sell and received a five-year mandatory sentence. Chastened by the loss of her son who had been turned over to the care of her own mother, Katrina reasoned:

> There has to be a reason for all this happening, you know. It don't make sense. I didn't even know there was drugs in the bag; I was jus' doing someone [her boyfriend] a favor. Now I'm stuck in here but I figure God will take care of me. . . . I hurt a lot for my mistake, and God always takes care of those who hurt, even when they hurt out of their own mistakes. I got to keep my faith 'cause without it I'm nothing.

Or, as Maggie Laughton, a forty-year-old mother of three who had spent most of her life on welfare told me:

> Jesus saves, and Jesus was poor. So you can be rich, as rich and famous as you want, but that don't make you better. Jesus died for the poor. I never forget that. Jesus had less than I have.

Almost every woman I met in West Baltimore had close relatives who had faced arrest and sometimes lengthy jail sentences. All had to wrestle with the hard reality of imprisonment. When children were involved, the experience was gut-wrenching. That had been the case with Lydia Forrest and her son, Beamy. Both saw the events that led to his incarceration as part of a universal plan in which evil confronts good and God wrestles with Satan. Reflected Lydia:

> He [Beamy] was a nice boy; all his life he's been a good boy. He was just in the wrong place at the wrong time. And it ain't like I didn't teach him proper, but the Devil is everywhere trickin' you, and when you's young you don't have so much strength. You don't stand a chance. I should know because I've failed too. So you have to understand that people just fail sometimes, but they can find the right path with the help of Jehovah God.

These and other accounts I collected in West Baltimore suggest, first, that religiosity is part and parcel of the experience of people living in destitute neighborhoods. Second, the poor often see their lives as part of a godly plan that involves sin and atonement as markers of humanity. Morality in this case does not involve fixed characteristics of temperament but a learning process by which a defeat leads to deliverance. Self-worth emerges from the individual's capacity to overcome the effects of past failures, secure absolution, and arrive at an improved state. Finally, religiosity among the poor need not depend on formal institutions or the sanction of priests and preachers; it emerges as a personal experience in which belief and trust in God are sufficient sources of justification. The accounts sketched in this section provide the raw material to better conceptualize the relationship between religion and poverty. I next place these experiences within a larger context.

POVERTY AND RELIGION IN A THEORETICAL PERSPECTIVE

Studies of religion are coterminous with the advent of modern sociology. In *The Elementary Forms of Religious Life* (1912/2008), Emile Durkheim described religion as a collective experience aimed at reenacting the central beliefs and values of social groups. He saw the difference between the sacred and the profane as religion's defining feature. People gather in sanctuaries not solely to affirm shared convictions but also to separate the banal from the significant and the mundane from the transcendent (see also Lenski 1961). Ritualized behavior—the habitual repetition of learned actions performed with others holding a similar belief system—further enhances the distinction between the sacred and the profane. Through the management of their bodies, individuals bring human existence above the realm of the commonplace.

Durkheim's insights represent a genitive moment in the sociology of religion but other authors have had lasting influence as well. Max Weber, for example, noted the significance of religious beliefs and practices in the maintenance of economic systems (Weber 1912/2002). Weber is known for his attention to Calvinism whose focus on the doctrine of predestination informed the frugal practices of early capitalists allowing for the accumulation of wealth. Even more recently, Peter Berger (1967/1990), Daniel Bell (1977), and Robert Wuthnow (1990, 2007, 2012) have extensively discussed the uses of religion in relation to political and economic action. Although sociological studies of religion waned in the 1980s, they have gained force in the new millennium, especially in the United States, a country that stands alone among other industrialized nations for its high levels of religiosity.

Given the central role religion has played as a theoretical and practical subject in sociology, it is surprising that not more attention has been given to religion and poverty in urban environments. The focus with respect to the inner city has been on the dysfunctions afflicting poor people, not on the manner in which spiritual pursuits are used by residents to explain, justify, or ennoble their surroundings.[2]

Such omissions are all the more striking given the historical significance of religion in the African-American experience since slavery. Early upon their arrival on American shores, African slaves were subjected to the evangelizing efforts of their masters (Lincoln and Mamiya 1990). To justify the egregious crime of forced migration and bondage, colonists relied on religious interpretations that assigned Whites responsibility for the care and instruction of inferior races. Slavery was justified in biblical terms: Africans were seen as the descendants of Ham cursed by Noah to serve his brothers (Goldenberg 2003). Religious narratives were thus used to explain gross inequalities resulting from conquest and the subordination of vulnerable peoples.

There was, however, an unexpected consequence of the teachings of slave masters: the very act of evangelization entailed a conviction that Africans had souls worth saving. This gave people in bondage a form of parity to Whites in the eyes of God. Although the world was fraught with sin, temporal inequalities would be erased in Heaven, where both Blacks and Whites, freed from their earthly fetters, would confront their maker in conditions of equality.

As African Americans contended with their subordinate position, the idea of spiritual equivalence with Whites became a major tool for resistance and struggle (Morris 1984). Quakers in particular, but also members of other denominations, wielded opposition to slavery in the name of religious principles and by resorting to interpretations that differed from those that had justified slavery in the first place. Against the power of masters justifying domination in biblical terms, subordinate Blacks held the power of the crucified Jesus as a constant reminder of their humanity and membership in society (Cone 2013).

After the Civil War too, emancipated Blacks resorted to religious explanations to make sense of lynching. By identifying the cross where Jesus had been immolated with the lynching tree where nearly five thousand Blacks were killed, African Americans could see themselves as more than a persecuted people—their sacrifice was ennobled in ways similar to the way God's own sacrifice had redeemed humanity. Out of the anguish of Blacks facing symbolic as well as actual lynching emerged a new aesthetic that included, among other things, spirituals and the blues (Cone 2013).

W.E.B. DuBois was among the first to attempt a systematic study of Black religion in modern times. In *The Negro Church* (1903/2011), he assigned significance to the ways in which religious affiliation and practices were used by Black migrants from the South to deal with prejudice and hostility. Religion, argued DuBois, gave Blacks places and stories with which to bond together in the spirit of community. As menial workers with little more than nominal citizenship, Blacks confronted low wages and prejudice during weekdays but could show off their best clothes on Sundays, when church became the center of sociability and group identity. Evidence of that still lingers in most American inner cities. Although younger generations vie for more secular identities, their elders cling to traditions and beliefs that have strengthened the African American community for more than four centuries.

Like Emile Durkheim before him, DuBois emphasized the social significance of religious practice and noted the ways in which churches offered shelter and dignity to working-class and impoverished Blacks. Years later, E. Franklin Frazier (1963) developed the same ideas, noting that African American religion has functioned over time as a "refuge in a hostile white world." His work prefigures that of Charles Hirschman (2004) who identified religion's three distinctive "R's"—refuge, resources, and respect—as vital to the experience of immigrants in the United States. Among African Americans, those functions are magnified; religion emerges among them as a distinct form of cultural identity and resistance to a White-dominated society.

African American religion diversified in the early twentieth century as an increasing number of Blacks began to migrate from the rural South to midwestern and northeastern cities (Best 2007; Murphy, Melton, and Ward 1993; Yokley, Nelsen, and Nelsen 1971). Two National Baptist associations and three Black Methodist denominations became mainstream churches in Black urban communities. Congregations affiliated with those denominations often cut across class lines. Similarly, Black congregations affiliated with White-controlled Episcopalian, Presbyterian, and Congregational churches catered primarily to elite African Americans. Although most Blacks joined Baptist churches, smaller numbers of upwardly mobile Blacks joined other denominations partly as an expression of their higher social position.

In his study of African American religion in Chicago after the Great Black Migration, Wallace Best (2007) analyzes various ways in which spatial relocation altered religious beliefs. He shows how migration fueled a new sacred order among urbanized Blacks that reflected aspects of both southern Black religion and modern city life. This new sacred order was also largely female, as African American women constituted more than 70 percent of the membership in most Black Protestant churches. Best thus shows how Black southerners imparted a folk religious sensibility to Chicago's Black churches. In doing so, they ironically recast conceptions of modern and urbanized African American religion in terms that signified the rural past. In the same way that working-class cultural idioms such as jazz and the blues emerged in the secular arena as a means to represent Black modernity, African American religion, with its negotiation between the past and the present, rural and urban, revealed African American religion in a modern form (see also Patillo-McCoy 1998).

Throughout the first half of the twentieth century, the Great Black Migration further contributed to the formation of communities of faith that played a major role in the constitution of the 1960s civil rights movement. It is impossible to understand the work of prophets like Martin Luther King Jr. and his emphasis on nonviolent resistance without reference to a long-standing tradition of religious involvement among African Americans both in Southern and Northern U.S. locations. Religion was the common ground upon which activists, Black as well as White, joined hands and hearts to overcome the egregious forces of segregation in their struggle for racial justice (Marsh 2006).

In other words, the African American experience cannot be understood without giving attention to specific forms of religiosity seen as responses to exceptional forms of violence and oppression. Relocation from the rural South to midwestern and northeastern cities was part of an experience that many African Americans understood as a religious journey.

Nicholas Lemann (1992) vividly describes how Black migrants from the Mississippi delta regularly fell on their knees and kissed the ground when arriving in Chicago, where they expected to find the Promised Land. With their gestures, they were appropriating the imagined memory of the Israelites after wandering for forty years in the desert. By equating their experience with that of the Hebrews following Moses, Black migrants uplifted their search for membership in American society.

For many Blacks, life in the city did not bring about the anticipated results. Multitudes were eventually trapped in ghettos marked by the absence of resources and the abundance of government agencies whose unintended effects have been to diminish personal autonomy, curtail agency, and restrict integration into the larger society. In such environments, Durkheim's differentiation between the sacred and the profane and his emphasis on rituals as practices that make real that distinction are especially meaningful. Impoverished Blacks lack institutional connections and regular contact with mainstream institutions. Very poor people are less likely to have a best friend, less likely to have a partner, and less likely to know most of their neighbors, belong to a voluntary organization, or attend church services (Wacquant 2009a; Crawford Sullivan 2012). Under such circumstances, the tendency is toward the development of personal forms of religiosity that draw upon childhood teachings to construct rituals and separate moments in time for the affirmation of transcendent realities.

That was true for Norma Bench, a twenty-seven-year-old Baltimore mother of two who held her Bible as a treasured possession and began the day with devotions. Reading passages from the Old and New Testaments was part of her observance. She had developed a series of deliberate actions meant to impress a sacred meaning on portions of her time:

> First thing I do when I wake up is to open my Bible with my eyes closed. That way I don't know what page will open. I leave it to God to instruct me, and then the first passage I see leads me to the day's teaching. I read and I learn, and I try to use the words to guide me through the day.

After prayer every morning, Norma took her children to school and then addressed routine concerns. In 1996 she was temporarily working as a teacher's aide. Although her wages were paltry, she was proud to have a real job, at least for a few months. In the afternoons, after her children returned home from school, she sat down with them and repeated the morning's ritual:

> My kids, I love 'em, and now they older, like, Brenda is seven and Jamal nine, and they can understand and so I want them to know about God and God's love, especially [God's love] for children. They still kids, but they love the stories of the Bible. . . . Reading to my kids is my favorite thing; it makes my time with them special.

At night, after putting the two youngsters to bed, Norma returned to prayer before dozing off herself. It was the repetition of that daily cycle that gave her life structure and stability.

Norma admitted that most people did not know about her intimate religious practices: "They all my own," she said. "It's all private because my love for God is private." Furthermore, she felt that boasting about her religiosity would give people the wrong impression: "I'm just an unwed mother of two, living alone in a bad neighborhood. People would laugh if they knew I'm all prayerful and that!"

In other words, the woman thought that truly religious people, people deserving of respect, had lives different from her own and could thus present themselves in churches without fear of being judged. By keeping her religiosity private, she resolved the contradiction between her lowly status and her search for dignity. In addition, she saw her intimate rituals as acts that lifted her social position, separating her from those who avoided religion. Although she didn't have many witnesses, Norma could see herself as a decent woman, in contrast to those who ambled rudderless in a world without God.

Finally, her religious rituals allowed Norma to divide her time in ways filled with meaning; during those moments she was not just a poor woman but a mother instructing her children in the ways of the Almighty.

Like Norma Bench, many of the women I knew in West Baltimore saw religion as an important part of their lives but also as a private matter. There were some, however, who viewed their capacity to join congregations as the preeminent mark of decency. Such was the case of Lydia Forrest whose conversion to the faith of Jehovah's Witnesses had enabled her to move beyond the boundaries of family to join a larger community in its fight for redemption.

The same was true of Alina Cummings. In her late thirties, she was living with Trevor Marsh, her common-law husband, and four children in a rented floor at a home situated on Mosher Street. Like nearly everyone else in the neighborhood, Alina and her family struggled on many fronts. Trevor was a high school graduate who had held a string of menial jobs and was, at that time, laid off. Alina worked as a custodian at a government-funded nursing home. Their children, ranging in age from three to fourteen, were faring well in school, but the parents worried about their future. That made the family's religious involvement all the more essential. They regularly attended the Church of the Divine Shepherd, one of three Pentecostal centers in the area. Alina saw her religious participation as a source of comfort and affirmation but also of social capital. "I love my church," she said.

> It's only two hundred people in the congregation, but we do lots of stuff for a small church—like we bring food to the soup kitchen and manage day care for some of the children. . . . Before I became part of

Divine Shepherd, I didn't have many friends. Now it's different 'cause I know most of the people who go there, and some of those people are trying to get Trevor a new job. I feel like part of the world when I'm worshiping there.

Alina's religious practices thus enabled her to attain a sense of respectability while at the same time strengthening bonds of trust and reciprocity with other members of her congregation. She regularly met with some of them to share information and plan volunteer activities. In addition, Alina thought of the church as a safe environment where her children benefited from participation in Sunday school but also by becoming members of its gospel choir. Self-expression was important to Alina and her children. "The music is beautiful," she said, "inspiring, and when you surrounded by beauty and uplifting messages, you can't go bad."

Churches abound in destitute residential areas partly because they enable people with very little wealth to share material as well as social assets. Even storefront churches offer spaces for members to find solace from the grinding pressures they confront in the outer world; they provide opportunities to raise personal standing. Because impoverished families face numerous, and sometimes unexpected needs, membership in a church can become a critical means for assistance and survival.

When Mary Spencer, a member of the Baptist Good News Church, lost her baby to a bout of meningitis, it was her fellow congregants who banded together to make sure she had food and company during the days that followed the heartbreaking event. They prayed for her and visited her home regularly to give her a sense of belonging. "I wouldn't have survived without them," said Mary. She was twenty-seven and living alone. Still in pain over the death of her infant daughter, she maintained hope, thanks largely to the support extended by her fellow church members.

MUSLIMS IN THE INNER CITY

Although most religious residents in West Baltimore adhere to Christian denominations, a small but visible minority espouse Islam. Their numbers may be small, but Muslim converts stand out because of their clearly defined motivations (Gomez 2005). Suhira Omar was twenty-nine when she decided to become a member of the Nation of Islam, an organization founded by the controversial Minister Louis Farrakhan. Although there was not a distinct mosque in West Baltimore, Muslims like Suhira gathered at the headquarters of the Nation of Islam in accordance with the noncongregational and nonhierarchical structure of that religious faith. The focus on family, structure and order, and respectability were all factors that Suhira found compelling:

> I've made mistakes in my life . . . but that was before I understood there is a true path. My reading of the Holy Koran gave me a way to change; it gave me strength. I go to the Center to pray with other people who believe like I do, and I wear the veil all the time so that people know I'm a decent woman, a woman who believes in Allah.

Islam is one of the fastest-growing religious movements in American prisons and the reasons are not very different from those submitted by Suhira for her conversion. In the outer world, Muslim beliefs and practices can be a powerful means for self-distinction and the construction of a moral self. In prisons, where personal liberties are nonexistent and dangers abound, conversion to Islam is a way to realize a form of resurrection.

Mohammed Abdullah, whose original name had been Curtis Johnston, was a friend of Beamy Forrest, Lydia's incarcerated son. Mohammed, who was nearly forty years old and had lived behind bars for nearly two decades, took an interest in Beamy soon after the youngster arrived after being convicted as an accessory to the murder of a cab driver. Although Mohammed had not succeeded in his efforts to convert Beamy to Islam, he still saw his role in the younger man's life as decisive to his own identity:

> Thing about being in the glory of Allah is that you have to look out for the well-being of others. God can't do nothing without us, people in the world, so I look out for Beamy and others like him to glorify God and make his presence known in the world.

Although he had spent nearly half of his life in prison and saw little chance that his application for parole would be approved, Mohammed did not yield to despair—his time was filled with ideas and actions aimed at helping other prisoners. He saw himself in partnership with a

divine force whose intents could not be realized without human cooperation. He assiduously read passages from the Koran and never shied
away from preaching his convictions. With other fellow Muslims, he
prayed five times a day with his face turned to Mecca, in his mind thus
joining millions of other devout Muslims in the Ummah, God's community of believers. And, because imprisonment presents the horrific
perspective of endless time spent in waste, the embracement of a religious faith like Islam offers empowerment. Said Mohammed:

> To be in prison is more than a living hell if you don't have your eyes
> set on God—you's less than dirt because at least dirt can't feel noth-
> ing, but you can and you's in pain all the time. But if you turn your
> eyes to God and you pray with others and you read the Holy Book,
> then you human—you don't have as much pain 'cause you time ain't
> wasted.

In that interpretation, religion is a mark of true humanity, and
human agency is directed at creating spatial and temporal differentia-
tions between the transcendent and the banal. Such ideas were in evidence during Ramadan, the one-month period dedicated by Muslims
to fasting, praying, and the exaltation of Allah. According to Mohammed Abdullah:

> Tha's when all of us Muslims here in prison are in control of our
> time. By law, we have the right to observe Ramadan in proper form.
> Security guards, administrators, can't do nuthin' to prevent us from
> praying and breaking the fast in the evening, and sometimes that
> gets long and we's in charge of our time. It only happens once a year.

In other words, prisoners best illustrate the instrumental value of
religion in destitute settings. By anchoring their identity in religious
faith, individuals are able to secure small amounts of power which, in
places like prison, are enough to elevate personal and collective identity.

THE FLIP SIDE OF EMPOWERMENT

The preceding sections dwell on the ways in which religion serves as a
vital means for impoverished people, men as well as women, to redefine their position in the world, attain respectability, expand their social

networks, and secure a measure of agency in environments they cannot control. Nevertheless, religion can also exacerbate high levels of isolation. In the case of millenarian cults, the result can be a withdrawal from the society and a negation of the elements that buttress citizenship. Lydia Forrest's case is an apt illustration. Her conversion to the faith of Jehovah's Witnesses affirmed her sense of self but also led her to decisions that further separated her from mainstream society. Below, I look at how Jehovah's Witnesses illuminate the ways in which religion can both empower and marginalize impoverished people.

In 1997 there were approximately 43,000 residents living in Sandtown-Winchester and Lower Park Heights, the two West Baltimore neighborhoods where I conducted my research. That figure remained unchanged in 2011. Ninety-seven percent of residents in the two neighborhoods are Black and 37 percent are twenty-four years of age or younger. More than half of households in the area have incomes under $25,000. Almost 20 percent of working-age residents are unemployed, compared with 11 percent in the city at large. The family poverty rate is nearly 30 percent, and the percentage of single-parent households exceeds 35 percent (Baltimore City Health Department 2011).

Although there are no official surveys, an estimated 30 percent of those living in the two residential areas attend religious services regularly, and most are Christian. Baptists are in the majority. Pentecostals and Seventh-Day Adventists are large minorities—at least four churches representing those religions exist in West Baltimore. In 1997, fewer than three hundred residents identified as Jehovah's Witnesses. By 2011, that number had more than trebled. This is in agreement with national trends. Jehovah's Witnesses represent the fastest-growing faith in America's inner cities.

The same tendency is visible at the international level. As of August 2011, Jehovah's Witnesses reported an average of 7.39 million *publishers*—the term they use for members actively involved in preaching—distributed in more than 169,000 congregations worldwide (Holden 2002). Since the mid-1990s, the number of publishers has increased from 4.5 million to 7.65 million. Jehovah's Witnesses estimate their current worldwide growth rate to be 2.4 percent per year (Chryssides 2008). Although they have a low retention rate—only about 37 percent of children raised in that religion hold on to the same religious identity as adults—the National Council of Churches has concluded that Jehovah's Witnesses have "the largest growth of any single denomi- nation" in the United States with a 4.7 percent increase in 2008 (Pew Forum on Religion and Public Life 2008).

In other words, since their origination in late-nineteenth-century America, Jehovah's Witnesses have evolved into a global organization. The Watch Tower Bible and Tract Society—the movement's legally incorporated name—takes special pride in its international and mul- tiethnic membership, noting that a "Christian brotherhood unmarred by racial distinctions is a reality among Jehovah's Witnesses" (Watch Tower Bible and Tract Society of Pennsylvania 1993: 5). Followers worldwide routinely gather together in their circuit and district con- ventions to "rejoice in the sameness" that transcends national, ethnic, and cultural differences.

The inclusive character of the Jehovah's Witnesses narrative has been a source of consolation among African-American converts in places like West Baltimore where the signs of abandonment are ever present. That was true for Leona Mitchell, a woman in her forties who converted to that faith in 1998: "When I was younger," she said:

> I had this sense that my life needed something new, something dif- ferent. My mom, she was a Baptist, but we didn't go to church much. Then, after I had my first kid, I started thinking about God and church, . . . so I went to all kinds of churches but I found no com- fort. It was only in Kingdom Hall that I found the truth, and mostly because [Jehovah's Witnesses] don't look down on you 'cause you Black or poor or a woman. So I said, yes, this the place I wanna be cause here I stand like a person.

Lydia Forrest agreed. She too had searched for ways to organize her life and make sense of her surroundings, and Jehovah's Witnesses had provided that opportunity:

> For a while, I went to a Catholic church, but I didn't feel that I was a real member of the congregation on account that I was poor and people saw I was of a dark complexion, but the Jehovah's Witnesses who first knocked on my door, they was White and just as kind as can be! I felt then that all those other [superficial] things din't matter

cause we just talked about good stuff and how God don't care about people's looks, just what's in their heart.

Although official statistics do not break membership figures down by ethnicity or color, Americans of African descent appear to be significantly overrepresented among Jehovah's Witnesses; estimates in the 1960s placed African-American membership at 20 to 30 percent of their constituency in the United States. This is in contrast with the representation of Blacks in positions of authority within the Watch Tower Society—historically, few have attained positions of prominence (Carr 2002). Yet that is of little consequence to people like Lydia Forrest or Leona Mitchell whose main focus is on the message of the faith, not the religion's hierarchical structure.

In addition to a democratic outlook that minimizes racial and ethnic differences, a second benefit derived from adherence to the faith of Jehovah's Witnesses is a sense of security derived from its authoritarian chain of command. James A. Beckford (1975) has drawn attention to the totalizing outlook of Jehovah's Witnesses, which includes an assertive leadership, specific and narrow objectives, control over competing demands on members' time and energy, and high levels of scrutiny over the quality of new members.

While most religious people in the United States adhere to Protestant denominations, which emphasize individual freedom and a personal connection with God, Witnesses discourage independent thinking, cautioning followers against studying the Bible on their own and demanding that they rely on approved publications to interpret the Gospels. Followers are expected to demonstrate absolute confidence in their leaders and avoid skepticism over Watch Tower teachings. That was one of the reasons why Witnesses like Eva Martin, a forty-five-year-old mother of three, converted. According to her:

> [Other religions], they say different things; believe different things, ask you to do different things. There's a lot of confusion about the word of God and what God wants from you, so you need to have trust that you being taught the truth. I have that trust that Witnesses are the true followers of the only true God, Jehovah.

A Watch Tower publication from 1979 is unabashedly titled *Avoid Independent Thinking*. Filled with colorful illustrations of a multiethnic society, it states that "In a world where people are tossed about by confusing winds of religious doctrine, Jehovah's people need to be stable, full-grown Christians. Their position must be steadfast, not shifting quickly because of independent thinking or emotional pressures." To support that exhortation, the booklet cites Ephesians 4:13: "*Until we all reach unity in the faith and in the knowledge of the Son of God and become mature, attaining to the whole measure of the fullness of Christ.*" Biblical scholars may debate the meaning of that text, but Witnesses allow for only one interpretation, one affirming their own superior morality.

In other words, by restricting individual autonomy, Witnesses diminish the anxieties associated with diverse and sometimes opposing readings of religious narratives. This is of paramount significance in environments characterized by a paucity of resources and high levels of social disorganization. In poor neighborhoods, where services are scarce, danger is ever present, and the hand of the state reaches into the most intimate corners of people's lives, an unambiguous understanding of God's word offers comfort and shelter from bureaucratic intrusion. Kingdom Hall provides not only respite but also a place where congregants can find peace through the shared repetition of known readings without the responsibility for analysis.

A third benefit accruing from membership in a Jehovah's Witnesses congregation has to do with the character of the religious narrative itself. Jehovah's Witnesses' moral views reflect conservative Christian values. All sexual relations outside of marriage are grounds for expulsion, and expulsions entail high levels of public humiliation. Homosexuality is considered a serious sin, and marriage between individuals of the same sex is forbidden. Abortion is considered murder. Modesty in dress and grooming is emphasized. Gambling, drunkenness, illegal drugs, and tobacco use are forbidden, although the ingestion of alcoholic beverages is allowed in moderation.

That long list of provisos leaves little to individual discretion while presenting a clear blueprint for evaluation and action. It was the Jehovah's Witnesses' emphasis on patriarchal norms and matrimony that gave Lydia Forrest the courage to press the father of her children into marriage. She expected her union to be long lasting because Witnesses discourage divorce and most remarriages are considered adultery.

Finally, adherence to the faith of Jehovah's Witnesses enables believers to shun worldly interests, including those derived from political action. Jehovah's Witnesses believe their highest allegiance is to God's kingdom, which is viewed as an actual government in heaven, with Christ as supreme monarch. Thus, they remain politically neutral, do not seek public office, and are discouraged from voting. They abstain from celebrating religious holidays and birthdays and reject customs they believe have pagan origins. They do not work in industries associated with the military or serve in the armed services.

Historically, Witnesses' refusal to endorse nation-bound actions has resulted in their arrest and imprisonment; they were top targets in Nazi Germany. Witnesses do not salute or pledge allegiance to flags or sing national anthems or patriotic hymns. They see themselves as a worldwide fellowship that transcends borders. Most dramatic in the long list of norms separating Jehovah's Witnesses from the secular world is their refusal to follow conventional medical practices, especially those involving blood transfusions. Any interference with natural processes is considered a defiance of God's will (Beckford 1975).

All religions mark a clear delineation between the temporal world and the world of lasting truths through the observance of norms. In the case of Jehovah's Witnesses, the list of regulations is longer, more deeply inflected, and, for that reason, more meaningful for true believers. Along with Muslims, most of whom also are converts, Jehovah's Witnesses emphasize their contempt for the secular world and their trust in eternal realities.

Both Jehovah's Witnesses and Muslims are in tension with the world and affirm individuals' sense of moral superiority through the rejection of conventional beliefs and behaviors (Bakalian and Bozorgmehr 2009). In both cases, the effect can be further isolation from existing political and social structures. Jehovah's Witnesses and Muslim converts in West Baltimore represent religious minorities. Nevertheless, the reasons that motivate members to adhere to their stringent demands illustrate a broader point about religion and poverty—that is, the use of religiosity among very vulnerable populations to affirm their respectability and moral worth by spurning worldly advantages.

Lydia Forrest had struggled mightily to provide her children with the elements of a middle-class life, American style. Unable to do so, she felt the unbearable sting of impotence, especially on their birthdays and at Christmas when she did not have the money to buy the presents they craved. It was life-changing to learn, from Jehovah's Witnesses, that such things did not matter in the eyes of God. By turning away from market expectations and hopes of upward mobility, she found a form of respite. As far as she was concerned, isolation was not a high price to pay in exchange for moral integrity. After all, she had always felt abandoned by others.

Lydia's actions speak eloquently as a reflection of cultural practices that are deployed by impoverished people residing in poor neighborhoods to resist and respond to the forces that threaten to erase their humanity. Those practices are an adaptation to their residential insularity and the absence of mainstream channels to connect them with the wider society, but they also represent a search for instruments to enact a normal existence. Lydia had tried hard to build a good reputation but often found herself at the mercy of liminal government agencies that questioned her aptitude as a parent and her honesty as an individual. It was her religious identity that kept her afloat.

Like Lydia Forrest, a multitude of African Americans living in poverty resort to the legacy of generations and deploy religious convictions to affirm their humanity even while living in the shadow of the state.

15 MANNY MAN

ACCORDING TO THE TESTIMONIES OF HIS MOTHER, SHARON, AND his aunt, Toya, the boy known in the streets of West Baltimore as Manny Man came into the world wailing and thrashing on August 13, 1978, close to the crack of dawn. The two women were not surprised. Pangs and jolts had punctuated Sharon's pregnancy. Two years earlier, her daughter, Shennelle, had grown almost undetected inside her womb, and had arrived, conveniently, in the late morning.

This time around, the certainty of delivery had awakened Sharon three hours after midnight—too early to face the new day and too late a moment to be considered part of the previous night. Rushed to Union Memorial Hospital, she had experienced acute pain. Against the baby's will, gasping and drenched in blood, she pushed him out of her body. Then she had a premonition. Her travails, she thought, were a harbinger of things to come. She shuddered in fear but loved the boy anyhow. His name was Emmanuel Travis Williams, the son of Marcus Williams III.

On the fateful day of his son's birth, Marcus Williams III, was miles away operating a limousine. For the last five years, he had been working mostly as a driver, but his sights were fixed higher. He had a college degree. A diploma from Morgan State University hung proudly in the living room at 37 West Lafayette Street, the home of his boyhood. No one in his family had reached that far before. And, in contrast to many of his peers, he had genuinely enjoyed being a student. His senior adviser, Dr. Angus Miller, thought Marcus was bound for success. The young man hoped the professor was right because he meant to be a businessman, an entrepreneur, someone worth something. Several years after his graduation, that goal remained elusive. Guilt filled his chest as he sped south on the Pulaski Highway, driving a car for rent. He was about to miss his son's birth, and there was nothing he could do about it: he needed the money.

Long before dawn, he had taken Sharon and her sister, Toya, to the maternity ward with the promise to return as soon as possible. By seven o'clock, after changing into a suit and grabbing a bite, he had arrived at the Starlight Limousine Company, there to confirm an assignment and exchange his battered Chevy for a Lincoln Town Car. Then he was off to suburban Cockeysville, where he was supposed to pick up a bride at nine.

Sharon, he recalled, had not had a proper wedding. When she became pregnant for the first time, she had been in a hurry to make things legal because she didn't want the baby to be born out of wedlock. Marcus was then twenty-three and she was twenty-two, old enough, she pleaded, to assume responsibility for a family. She wanted her own home, tired as she was of living with her grandmother, fading away, waiting on tables in the daytime and trying to get her high school diploma by night. Led by impulse, Marcus had agreed to marry Sharon, although he knew his parents would be disappointed. He could almost hear them say, "What? A girl darker than us and without a proper education?" Their origins were humble, but their hopes for him were high.

The Williams family had lived in Danville, Virginia, for at least four generations, as far back as the eldest of the clan could remember. Several relatives were still there, and in towns with names like Farmville, Suffolk, and Emporia. Others had been swept up by the northbound winds. Nellie and Marcus Williams II had moved to Baltimore in 1956 when their eldest son, Marcus III, was only four years old. Realizing there was no future in the countryside, they had sold off a patch of land, packed up a few belongings, and driven with their three children to Baltimore in a borrowed truck. For almost a year after their arrival, they had lived with Marcus's sister, Amelia. Then, after Marcus found a permanent job as a janitor, the couple set up housekeeping on their own. Their new situation may not have seemed like much to others, but from their point of view it was a major step in the right direction.

They were honorable folk, thrifty and hardworking. Eventually Marcus II became a watchman at the Baltimore Gas and Electric Company, and he worked there for twenty-five years. Nellie never failed to take care of their home, and she cleaned other people's houses to supplement her husband's income. It had taken the Williamses almost a decade to save enough money for the down payment on the house at West Lafayette Street, but they expected to own it before they were too old to enjoy it. It was a two-storied structure with an ochre exterior, iron banisters along the sides of the marble front steps, and a little awning framing the entrance, a typical Baltimore row house. Although the house wasn't large—two bedrooms, one bathroom, a kitchen, a dining room, and a living room—it was their property, something they could hold on to.

When the Williamses first arrived in Baltimore in the late 1950s, the city was experiencing re-segregation. Whites were decamping to the suburbs at a brisk pace. In little over a decade, neighborhoods populated exclusively by the descendants of European immigrants had become nearly all Black. Businesses owned by African Americans multiplied to replace the resources that had vacated the area.[1] Most were small, but they lent necessary services to what was, for all practical purposes, a captive clientele. The neighborhood had seemed poised to prosper.

Then, in the 1960s, two things happened. The civil rights movement filled hearts and minds throughout the nation with new ideas about the meaning of citizenship, raising the hopes of families like the Williamses. This occurred even as an increasing number of Blacks were arriving from the rural South, indelibly altering Baltimore's demographic profile. Then, starting in 1968, the civil disturbances that followed the Reverend Martin Luther King's assassination led even more residents to desert the city. The few remaining White-owned shops ended up in the hands of Chinese and, especially, Korean entrepreneurs. With that exception, productive business activity virtually disappeared from West Baltimore. The area began to experience rapid decay. For years, the Williamses worried about the value of their home. It hadn't appreciated much since they had first acquired it. They didn't intend to sell it but even if they had, it was unlikely they would have found buyers.

Marcus and Nellie Williams brought up their children to worship God and make a future for themselves. They were willing to endure and persist in the hope that the new generation would do better than they had done and worse than their grandchildren would do. In the spring of 1994, when I first had a conversation with Mr. Williams, he still held the same principles that had guided him and his family through life:

You gotta understand we was country folk an' hardly knew the ways of the city, but we was working people and willing to sacrifice. We wanted the young'uns to have it better. That was true with most families. Some of the childrun did good, others din't, but we always kept our hopes alive.

Nellie and Marcus Williams were especially proud of their son, who had been a gentle child, full of curiosity and easy to teach. Because he did well in school, his parents learned to take his achievements for granted and expect even more. When Marcus III received a scholarship to attend college, the family was overjoyed and had a celebration. Nellie's sister took a train up from Virginia to congratulate her nephew in person. Romulus, the Williamses' second boy, hadn't fared badly either. He had completed high school on time and gone on to work for the post office. It was Minerva, Romulus's twin sister, who had worried her parents. She had seen difficult times as a teenager, but in the end, she too had completed high school and found a job as a filing clerk. In her late twenties, Minerva, nicknamed Minnie, married Marvin Lewis, an accountant. On the whole, the Williamses were proud of their brood. They had accomplished much of what they had set out to do.

In Mr. Williams's mind, even more important than success was decorum. His children had held their heads high, sparing the family embarrassment. He had seen many in his own generation brought down by youngsters who went wild in the city:

We was a Negro family, and the White folk looked down on Blacks like us. They was polite, but we knows they was prejudiced. We had to try harder to lift ourselves up in their eyes and in our mind. Sometimes you had a good family from the South, jus' like us, comin' to the city, and the ma and the pa they work hard, like slaves to make the childrun's lives better. An' then, the son turns out to be a bum who don't care and disgraces his people. . . . So we's grateful to God that it din't happen to us.

Life in the Williams household was divided between work, church, and the rituals of sociability. They visited regularly with friends and went back to Danville every other year for family reunions. After Marcus III graduated from college, his parents were hoping he would find a good wife. If their boy was to succeed in business, as he kept saying, he would need an ally and companion. They were not convinced that Sharon Belay, the young woman their son had been seeing on and off for two years, fit that description. Yet upon learning about the young couple's intention to marry, the Williamses had not been upset. This would be the first wedding in their immediate family, and they were eager to have grandchildren. On April 10, 1976, a frigid but luminous morning, Marcus Williams III and Sharon Belay were married at the First Baptist Church on Lafayette Square. Only members of the immediate family attended the ceremony. The event was brief and no reception followed. Wedding preparations had been cut short by the condition of the bride. She was expecting her first child.

The newlyweds lived with Mr. and Mrs. Williams for nearly two years. Always the appeaser, Nellie checked her misgivings about her daughter-in-law and welcomed Sharon into her home while the young couple looked for new quarters. Marcus wanted to leave the neighborhood. It had changed so much since he was a child that he couldn't recognize it sometimes. Lafayette Square, where he once strolled with his parents on Sundays at dusk, was now an open drug market. Sometimes, in the pit of night, you could hear the sound of guns blasting in the distance.

On the other hand, Marcus thought, this is where I grew up and where my parents have lived for most of their lives. They weren't getting any younger, and he wanted to stay close to them. Not having much of a family of her own, Sharon would need assistance during her first year as a mother, especially if she was to continue her education. In the end, Marcus found a house for rent in Edmonson Village, a home built in the Keelty Daylight style. The house dated back to the 1920s, when it was erected as part of large residential complex by the builder, James Keelty, before earlier residents, mostly Jewish families, had decamped to the expanding suburban fringes.[2] Formerly the destination of upwardly mobile groups, Edmonson Village had become an elongation of the Black ghetto, but to Marcus it seemed a step up, neither too far nor too close to his old neighborhood.

Five months after her wedding, while still living with her in-laws, Sharon delivered her first child, a girl whom she called Shennelle. The name was her invention, combining letters from her own name and those of her closest friends. "A child's name is like a prayer." Sharon said, "When you name your child after the people you love, you pay them honor, and they become like guardian angels to your baby." Shennelle had big eyes, a tiny nose, and a joyful disposition. Her granddaddy swore that she smiled at him the very first day he visited the hospital, shortly after her birth.

Two years later, the Williamses were looking forward to the arrival of Sharon's second child. This time they hoped it was a boy. He would be their first grandson and the keeper of the family name. In anticipation, Nellie began knitting the tiny layette that would be the child's first possession. She was proud of the skills she had learned back at the farm and saw with displeasure that the young women in her neighborhood were no longer interested in the kind of knowledge that made women different from men. They found no sense of accomplishment in tasks that required patience. She recalled:

> Back [in the South] a mutha started teaching the girls when they was three or four, how to crochet and knit, how to cook and keep a house. We didn't have much, so we had to be resourceful. And it was what you knows as a woman that found you a good husband. Now, in the city it's different. Women don't have time to take care of they own 'cause they gotta work for money to help the man, so many of the things we used to know are lost.

Nellie Williams was determined to honor traditions which, she was convinced, would preserve her family's integrity.

By the time Baby Shennelle turned two, young Marcus and his wife had moved out of the Williams home. The transition had required new adjustments. Keeping house and taking care of a toddler while expecting a second child demanded that Sharon postpone plans to advance her education. She spent most of her days at home, cleaning and cooking. Because her husband worked long hours, there was little time for outings. Sharon shared his desire to prosper, but she was lonely for him. Marcus, she complained, didn't know what it was like to spend long days all alone with no adult company; without a car and no way to move outward or upward. She couldn't rely on her neighbors; many, she thought, were lowlifes. She was therefore pleased when her sister, Toya, who lived in Prince Georges County, offered to come down and be with her for the birth of her second baby.

On the day the child was born, Marcus Williams III had completed a full shift before finally returning to the hospital in search of news. His gloom was dispelled after learning that a boy had indeed arrived, as it had been the hope of his parents. He saw his son sleeping serenely, wrapped in a white blanket, and his determination to succeed was set ablaze: "My boy," he thought "is gonna have something worth having. I'll find a way to give him a name and inheritance." He had yet to become an entrepreneur as he had planned during his college years.

The problem was that he and his family didn't have much by way of capital, and he needed collateral before going to a bank to ask for a loan. His parents' home was not fully owned, and in the eyes of financial institutions, its location in a declining neighborhood made it an unlikely guarantee of future gain. True, his social circle was wide, but the extent to which friends and acquaintances could help was limited. Several of the young men he knew were broke, and those who weren't lived precariously from paycheck to paycheck. They were social workers, mail carriers, teachers, clerks, and bus drivers—not exactly poor but not rich enough to make loans. Then again, he was willing to work for someone else, at least for a while, but he hadn't found the right job. In this he held fast to principle. Not for him a menial occupation. His father had been a custodian for most of his adult life. Jobs like that were not up to the son's standards. On the other hand, he didn't have the qualifications to be a manager or an accountant, and he couldn't afford to go back to school, especially after marrying Sharon. So he had settled for driving the limo, all along defining the job as a way to set aside money for a business. The truth was he hadn't been able to save much.

Four years elapsed between Emmanuel Travis's birth and that of his little sister, Tamika. During that time Marcus III kept his ambition alive. Although red tape frustrated him, he applied for a loan through the Small Business Administration. In the wake of the protests ignited by the death of the Reverend Martin Luther King, the government had created programs to assuage ghetto malaise. Most of them had dissipated as the memory of the civil disturbances faded, but others, intended to promote self-employment, were still in operation. Marcus thought he stood a good chance of obtaining the financial assistance he needed.

It took him nearly two months to assemble the information required by the SBA and almost an equal period to fill out the unwieldy forms.

It bothered him not to have more time for the application process. He was still giving upward of twelve hours a day to the limousine company. On weekends, he drove a rented cab. There was little time for anything else but work.

In the spring of 1980, Marcus's hopes were high that he would soon be able to open a small hauling firm. Construction companies were always looking for good contractors. Sharon, who, by then, was attending a local community college, had agreed to help him. She was willing to take customer orders and keep the company books. She was good with numbers, and Marcus thought they could get along without extra help, at least in the beginning. The couple had even agreed on a name for the company, "Marcus Williams and Son Hauling, Inc." All he was asking for was a $10,000 start-up fund from the SBA, mostly to put a payment down on a trailer truck, engage in some promotional marketing, and purchase office equipment.

Another four months elapsed before Marcus Williams received the demolishing news that his application had been rejected. He didn't have the necessary experience. The agency was short on technical personnel and couldn't offer training assistance. Regretfully, it said, his request could not be approved.

Still Marcus didn't give up. This time he put aside scruples and asked his parents for help. They were willing to take a second mortgage on their house, but that too proved difficult to obtain. In their case no application was necessary; during their first visit to the Maryland National Bank, the financial officer in charge explained that the odds were not good that their application would be approved. Marcus II and Nellie then tapped their savings. They were able to put together about half of the sum their son needed to carry out his project. Nellie's brother, Raymond, who had never married and worked for the Board of Education, contributed the other half. It wasn't quite the amount that Marcus had requested from the SBA, but it was enough to start payments on a used truck and finance licensing fees. He advertised by word of mouth, dropping off flyers in strategic locations and scheduling appointments at a few companies. After securing three small contracts, Marcus quit his driving job and gave his full attention to his nascent firm.

With some difficulty, the company survived the onset of "stagflation" in the early years of the Reagan administration and by the mid-1980s, it began to flourish. Marcus developed a roster of clients. In 1987, he bought a second truck. By the beginning of the new decade, he secured a new loan, this time from a legitimate institution. He repaid his parents and Uncle Raymond, and set out to expand his company. Emboldened by his achievements, Marcus now saw himself in league with other capitalists. He explained:

> I had to spend big if I was going to make it big. So I began investing in advertising. I even had a little commercial on the local TV station. Then I rented space on Liberty Avenue, got letterhead stationary, office supplies and a work station with a computer, a printer and a telephone with two lines—call waiting and forwarding service—all that. I even got a fax machine. But those were small bites compared to the regular truck repair expenses. I had two drivers, one of them full-time, and a full-time mechanic. The company was doing real good, but the expenses, they was killing me.

Throughout the period of the firm's expansion, the family remained in Edmonson Village, but Marcus and Sharon hoped to realize a profit large enough to buy a home in a different neighborhood. On and off, they worried about the schools that Shennelle and Emmanuel were attending, but the children were still young and attached to their parents. Tamika was still a baby. There was plenty of time before a good middle school and high school became pressing needs.

Memory has a way of imposing retrospective meaning upon events that initially give no hint about the future. The day Emmanuel Travis was born, Toya sat by Sharon's bedside sharing impressions. Years later, she said, "From the beginning, that boy was rowdy; you just knew he wasn't gonna be easy." His mother had a different recollection. Her son's early childhood did not bear out Toya's judgment. Emmanuel Travis was a lively and inquisitive child, no more pugnacious than other little boys. He could be sweet and affectionate, and in kindergarten he demonstrated high intelligence. As a first- and second-grade pupil, he became interested in books. Agatha Randall, a third-grade teacher at Emmanuel's school, remembered him as "a boy who could read like no one else and who wanted to become a school principal." That struck her as odd because most children of his age were in awe of athletes and rap singers. When he was fifteen, Emmanuel explained his early ambitions as follows:

Yeah, I remember. That was stupid but I was just a kid then. I wanted to be a principal cause I thought I could help . . . children, you know, like a school principal is the same as a boss; he got authority, tells you what to do and what not [to do]. If you get sent to the principal's office you's in trouble. But if he good to you, like a mentor, he can make a big positive difference in your life. It didn't take me long to find out I had it all wrong. School principals don't have no power. But I din't know that then.

Emmanuel spent long hours reading about heroes and their adventures. He reveled in the feats of Captain Mars, who was always rescuing fellow humans from dangerous predicaments. The boy saw himself as capable of such feats. A ferment of conscience set off his strong temperament. In response to what he thought was an unfair reprimand, Emmanuel would stand in defiance stiffening his body, with his lips pursed in silence, eyes glaring, hands stuck stubbornly inside his pants' pockets. On those occasions, neither teacher nor parent could extract an apology. Sharon, his mother, secretly liked the way Emmanuel Travis held himself, just like a little man, but she didn't know whom the boy had taken after. Marcus was an affable dreamer, and she saw herself as quiet and unimposing. Surely, Emmanuel Travis had a soul all his own.

When he was eleven years old, in fifth grade, dark clouds began to loom on the boy's horizon. Because he was bright and spirited, the school routine bored him. His class was large, and teachers spent much of their time trying to discipline students or capture their attention. Looking to amuse himself and others filled Emmanuel's day. One day, he used chewing gum to glue together the pages of Lachonda Merrill's math notebook. The girl threw a fit, and the whole class was in stitches as she complained to the teacher. The teacher, in turn, asked for an urgent conference with Emmanuel's mother. It wasn't the first time that the boy had disrupted her class. Sharon saw the meeting as a turning point in her son's life:

They couldn't figure out what was goin' on because the boy, he had always been quiet and paid attention, and then he starts actin' up so they told me he had ADD [attention deficit disorder], you know, and he had to take medication so that he didn't disturb the other children. What could I do? They was the teachers and the doctor; they were supposed to know what they was doing.

Being forced to take Ritalin every day did not improve Emmanuel's disposition. He said:

It got me pissin' mad. They was treatin' me like I was some kind of freak. I was no freak. I was bored to death, and they din't have the brains to know it. I lost respect for the teachers and my mama—she was weak for takin' them teachers serious!

As recompense for his teachers' misrecognition, Emmanuel tried to fulfill their worst expectations: "They thought I was off the rim? I prove 'em right; I give them crazy for real!" Increasingly, the boy found himself on the wrong side of adult approval.

Then, one day after school, he and his friend, Reggie, went to the store located at the corner of Edmonson and Normandy to buy a Coke and sandwich bread for his mother. He liked the store for its variety of candy and baked goods. The store owner, whose name he didn't know, was a combative old man who had survived every change in the neighborhood. On the day in question, Emmanuel bought the sandwich bread that his mother had asked for, and Reggie paid for two Cokes. No words were exchanged between the boys and the store owner. As he walked out, Emmanuel noticed a pile of cookies on the counter—chocolate chip, his favorite. The owner was momentarily out of view. Impulsively, he grabbed the cookies and ran.

Less than one hour later, a police officer and a social worker were at the Williamses' doorsteps. They needed a parent's signature to refer the boy to Dell House, a state-funded juvenile facility, whose purpose was to identify potential delinquents before they became involved in serious offenses. Emmanuel was under observation at Dell House for less than two weeks, but nothing was the same after that. He now harbored genuine resentment:

The fuckin' cop, man! He thought I was a regular booster, shoplifter and dat. It was jus' a mistake. I was just a kid and it was jus' some cookies. They be puttin' too much on it. That got me thinkin' that people's no good and I gotta find ways to protect myself.

The kids he hung out with in school were impressed by Emmanuel's latest feat. In their eyes, he had confronted danger and survived. It was like being behind bars just as some of the tough men they knew were. Understanding their awe, Emmanuel amplified the details of his experience. In time, he started believing his own exaggerations.

His teachers saw no change in his level of motivation, but now he reveled in confrontation. In a class of thirty-six, he was likely to be the first to complete an assignment, and he was good about homework, but his conduct gave reason for pause. Fearless before peers and adults he reacted at the slightest provocation, meeting perceived injustice with outrage. When his social studies teacher mistakenly gave him a low grade, he tore up his notebook and marched out of the classroom in fury. More than once, he was suspended for fighting with youngsters who didn't show respect. The inside of the principal's office became familiar to him but, contrary to his early fantasies, he found no respite within its walls. Mr. Double, the principal, mostly pushed paper.

Tall and muscular for his age, Emmanuel Travis became a commanding presence in the playground. His classmates looked up to him. They called him "Man." In time, the sobriquet took an expanded form sung as an expression of loyalty and admiration: "Manny Man, yo's the man, yo! Man." Boys approached him deferentially and girls competed for his attention. In character as well as deportment, Emanuel Travis exhibited the promise of a true leader.

His father saw Manny's evolution with mixed feelings. On the one hand, Marcus was impressed by the boy's self-reliance and he understood that his trespasses were venial. On the other hand, now more than ever, he shared his wife's anxieties about the noxious effect of the neighborhood on his son's development. He wanted the boy to attend a better school. Plans to move out of Edmonson Village, however, were repeatedly stalled because of Marcus's demanding schedule. When Emmanuel Travis was almost twelve and his father thirty-eight, Marcus was still working upward of sixty hours a week and not making a significant profit. His costs continued to outstrip his revenues. That was largely because of the debts incurred to expand the business. Almost inadvertently, at every stage of his entrepreneurial career, Marcus had relied on standards that applied to firms larger than his own. It took every ounce of energy to keep the company going.

Sharon, on the other hand, was tiring of the long journey. Working as a business partner, minding the house and children, and trying to improve her education had taken a toll. She had obtained a high school diploma, but her commitment to further advancement went by the wayside to the chagrin of her husband who thought she was getting lazy. She, in turn, grew resentful of the way Marcus appropriated her services without pay. They began to argue bitterly. She was still young and attractive, she said, and she was squandering her best years. What was the use of the damn business if they couldn't do the things couples were supposed to? The hell if she was going to give up her youth for some crazy dream! Her mother had died when she was ten. She had dropped out of school at sixteen. She had expected Marcus, with his polite ways and college degree, to improve her life. Instead, he wanted her to behave as if she had just arrived from the farm: "He thought because I was a woman I should be at his beck 'n' call. No way! I wasn't goin' to be no slave to no man, no matter how big he was." Her desire was no longer in harmony with her husband's vision.

In the autumn of 1993, twelve years after its founding, the small hauling company that had constituted Marcus's greatest ambition had to be closed down under the irreparable burden of long-term debt. Two of the three trucks Marcus owned were repossessed, and after years of hard work he found himself at the brink of bankruptcy. With his credit destroyed and customers scattered, he was unable to resurrect the firm.

Sharon was short on compassion. Over the years, she had grown weary of her husband's lack of realism and his blind persistence. As he knocked around, looking for his old job as a limo driver, the quarrels became louder and more desperate. Early in 1994, when Emmanuel Travis was sixteen, the couple separated. Marcus Williams III returned to his parents' house.

It is difficult to ascertain whether it was the crescendo of his discontent or the turmoil around him that eventually sealed Manny Man's fate. As their marriage unraveled, Marcus and Sharon had little time to notice that their son had long ago left them behind. His world was more and more in the streets where he was appreciated and valued. It was there that he looked for ways to boost his public image. Imposing in height, with his mother's dark complexion, he appropriated a disdainful, intimidating demeanor. Shrouded beneath the hood of a sweatshirt, a bandana, or a do-rag, he assumed the asymmetrical gait of masculinity, the gangsta limp that sent the old heads looking for cover, especially when bopping down the street with his homies.[3]

His boys, those with whom he hung out, showed contempt or, worse, indifference toward the manner and dress of older people. They knew the meaning of cool and, believe you me, silk ties and vested suits were not cool. The country folk had wasted their lives in jobs that were hard and paid little. They had been the nannies and the servants, the factory hands and common laborers, the janitors and petty clerks; they had played by the rules and stayed poor. Where the hell had their efforts led them?

To survive nowadays you had to show a little attitude, let everyone know you're tougher than the blows life deals you. "Yeah, man! Let them muthafuckas know you the Man, you the Nigga!" Manny and his peers walked about the West Baltimore streets, every inch of their bodies announcing condescension for the old proletarian ways, inverting the meaning of garments once worn as signs of class identity. Cap brims intended to shield the face now turned around to expose belligerent expressions. The straps of overalls meant to protect the body intentionally let loose, shoe laces left untied, elephant pants, blue jeans several sizes too large and worn below the waist to expose the patterned design of boxer shorts—those were the proud badges of stylistic insurrection.[4]

Demeanor was matched by speech patterns. Manny Man was articulate in dialogue with his boys, whose loyalty he needed and whose misadventures filled his own tumultuous hours. With them he spoke a coded language. Toward women, as toward all outsiders, he mostly communicated through monosyllabic terms, trying not to show his true feelings. M-O-B (Money Over Bitches) became his crew's motto, affirming allegiance to one another over love for women. Toward strangers, Manny Man was distant; with his homeboys he indulged in loud banter. Although Manny Man had not grown up in the projects, many of his friends had. In solidarity, he adopted their ways. His parents had striven to speak with polish; he devolved to ghetto parlance. Notwithstanding his father's desire, the 'hood had won Manny Man's heart.

He no longer pretended to go to school. That shit was finished. His father had a college degree and what good had come from that? He was in a hurry to make a mark in the world, "be a playa, ballaholic an' all that. . . . Better to have a short life than a forgettable life." There was money to be made on the streets. His posse grew large and more audacious. It dominated a sizable triangle of urban space between Edmonson Avenue and George and Saratoga Streets. Manny Man saw his posse as a tool to fulfill larger goals:

> We was no five-percenters or nothin' like dat. At first we was peace-lovin' niggas, but we meant to protect the streets. Everybody knows you have a territory and no one gets in you face, not even the po-lice. Then I got to know Calvin Cooper. . . . They call him Blackjack.

Cooper had connections with the Jamaican drug cartel that made inroads in West Baltimore throughout the 1990s. He was looking for smart partners, people with guts and heart. Manny Man saw an opportunity opening:

> Until then we was just doin' small stuff, you know. If we needed skrilla[5] we throw a brick, like coppin' stores or biddies, li'l stuff like that.[6] One time, we went uptown 'n' scared the beejubies out of a bunch of lacrosse players, stole their twinkies,[7] that kinda thing. With Blackjack 'twas different. He was into serious stuff.

It was through Blackjack that Manny Man had acquired his first Glock at the age of fifteen, old by the standards of his homies. And it had been Blackjack, only a year earlier, who had insisted he smoke weed for the first time, also at an older age than most of the people he knew. But, in contrast to others, Manny Man didn't become addicted to either "gage" or "candy cane." Only once did he get stoned, and that had been enough: "I was toed up from the flo' up," he admitted, "so I give it up." He didn't like being out of control. His aim was to be successful, not to become a captive to dope.

A quick study in his own right, Manny Man soon became an able street entrepreneur. He learned to cut crack cocaine and mix it with talcum powder to increase the number of sales. It was important that the powder was fragrance-free; otherwise customers caught on and didn't buy. When he got a new allotment, he and his associates would lock themselves in Manny's crib—the basement of his mother's house—to prepare the merchandise in ways it could draw profits. After trimming the drugs and packaging them, Manny and his partners distributed plastic baggies filled with a variety of illicit substances in the "balloon rooms" dotting West Baltimore. Permanently separated from her husband, Sharon was now working full-time and unaware of her son's comings and goings during the day.

But Manny went farther, beyond relatively protected interior spaces. He divided his gang into categories, each with specific responsibilities. Older boys like Monsta Willis held down street corners and hung out waiting for potential customers. They never carried dope on them— that was left to boys as young as seven or eight, who couldn't be put in jail for any length of time when caught by the police. Little boys also worked as lookouts. For a few hours every day, Manny Man stood cool but alert at the intersection of Mosher and Saratoga ready to sell. Little Gator, his nine-year-old partner, sat at the stoop across the street. Said Manny:

> Bidness is always good. You see a car comin' and wait for the driver to slow down an' ask, "Are you anywhere, man?" Meaning, "Do you have drugs?" You ask what kind and give the nod. He passes the money and you point to the kid. The kid walks over and drops the bag. It takes only seconds. You done and waitin' for the next sale. It was a good deal. . . . After a few months, we blew up.

Swollen with cash, Manny Man aimed at strengthening his reputation through largesse. He bought a gold ring for his granddaddy and a string of genuine pearls for his grandmother, Nellie. Sharon, his mother, thought her son's leave from school was temporary. She had been encouraged when he told her that he was working at Wendy's. To her delight, he bought an expensive stereo system with his own money. She mistakenly concluded that her son was good at saving. "I was in there like swimwear!" Manny said, rejoicing in his early accomplishments.

As generous as he was toward his family, he was even more magnanimous with friends and associates. Toward them he became a patron and protector. When Monsta Willis was stabbed by a disgruntled dope head—one of his regulars who went crazy on him—it had been Manny Man who had done him a solid, taking Monsta to a private clinic and paying his medical bills. When the family of Bungie Brooks was evicted, Manny Man found them a new place and gave them two bulky rolls of "president-heads"[8] to ease their transition. And, as he grew in fame and reputation, he felt the need to improve his appearance. For his seventeenth birthday, he got himself a gold cap on his front tooth. It cost him over a thousand dollars, but he thought the expense was justified. The tooth shone every time he smiled, giving testimony to his newly acquired status and prosperity.

It was shortly afterward that he was detained carrying six glassine bags; five contained fine-grade marijuana and one was filled with one ounce of crack cocaine. Throughout his rapid immersion in street transactions, Manny Man had always paid attention to detail. He had never been caught. It was only because he was in a rush, looking out for Little Gator to finish a big sale, that he had missed a step. In the mid-1990s, "possession with the intention to sell" carried mandatory sentences of up to five years in prison. The police officer that arrested him knew his parents, and because this was his first offense, Manny Man was able to escape comparatively unscathed. He was charged with a lesser drug violation but still had to spend six months in the Baltimore City Jail. That had been a time of reckoning: "When you's iced, you have time to think," he said. "I knows then dat I got to go into bigger things." Manny Man was ready to follow his ambition and explore other avenues for achievement.

He came out of jail in cornrows, but soon afterward, he let his hair out, made it shiny with axle grease, and took to wearing a pick. He had seen men in prison use the four-pronged combs as weapons. In his eyes, a pick in the back of the head conveyed a fierce warning, proclaiming: "Don't fuck with me. I been in the system and knows my way around." He tried to hook up again with Blackjack but Blackjack was reluctant to renew their friendship; he thought the boy had acted the fool by getting arrested like a common "busta." His ears perked up, however, when Manny described what he had in mind.

It was a question of turf, Manny explained. If his group took over the eastern side of Edmonson Avenue, then under the control of Big Bolly Mossy, they could expand business by twentyfold. Blackjack, who was more experienced than Manny Man and almost seven years his senior, thought the idea was tempting but overly dangerous. Big Bolly

Mossy was known to carry an AK-47, and his twelve associates peddled "ninas"[9] in addition to drugs. They maintained a veritable arsenal in Mossy's basement.

Manny Man knew that to be true because not long ago he had been tight with Mossy. They had grown apart over the affections of the same girlfriend after they began forming their respective gangs. Manny thought Big Bolly Mossy had wronged him. In jail, he had figured out a way to take revenge; it was snitching he had in mind. He would let the cops do the heavy lifting, stay low for a while, spying and waiting for Mossy and his band to disappear.

You could tell when Manny Man called the cops on Big Bolly Mossy because almost immediately a full raid took place, put into operation by a SWAT team, screeching police cars, and even two "ghetto birds"[10] circling above the street where Big Bolly lived. The police had confiscated enough illegal items from his crib to keep the twenty-five-year-old felon behind bars for a long time. Emboldened by the success of his latest gambit, Manny Man deployed his troops in strategic locations that formerly had been under the control of the rival gang. Cash flowed into his hands like water released from a dam.

He wasn't old enough to get a permanent driver's license, but with Blackjack's help he purchased a white Acura and paid for a permit. He also bought expensive "bebop" glasses; a new wardrobe, including several pairs of three-hundred-dollar sneakers; and jewelry, including a dookie rope chain encrusted with diamonds and a crucifix also dotted in "ice." He was thinking that he should put some money in the bank and let the dividends grow. That was the smart thing to do, now that he was "phat with cash." But he had also acquired obligations; his people expected him to be generous, and his public image required constant enhancement. He told me:

> Things are copacetic, but I have some problems. In the 'hood you's always being seen 'n' compared. If you want to keep respect you have to pay mind to yo' community. So it's not that easy to save or get away. You's always in debt with your posse.[11]

Shortly before his eighteenth birthday, Manny Man heard that Damon Smith, an associate of Big Bolly Mossy, was back in the neighborhood. Smith had been released from prison and was going around flapping his tongue, assuring everyone who cared to listen that he meant to put a cap in Manny's ass. Manny Man was unperturbed. Everybody knew that Smith was all talk and no action. He went about his business as usual, with high hopes of retiring before his twenty-fifth birthday. By then, he figured, the way things were going, he would have enough money to build himself a palace in the 'hood.

On a warm summer evening in 1996, at his grandparents' house, Manny Man reviewed the events of his young life: "When I was jus a little boy," he said, "I wanted to be like my father."

Straight and hard workin', but you never know—it turn out different sometimes. Sooner than you think, you's in a different place. You know how parents tell you dat you can be anythin' you wanna be? When you're a kid you believe it, but then you grow up and it ain't true. You gotta hustle to survive. Fate jus' takes over and you's there list'nin' to the beat go on and on and on. Do you understand me?

Less than two months later, Manny Man Williams, who had walked the Baltimore streets with frightful determination and a generous heart, was found sprawled on the steps of his mother's house with two bullets deep in his cranium. Brain matter splattered the front door, and blotches of red covered the stoop like a decorative mat. In the glow of dawn he reposed, wearing new Timberland boots, a blind stare, and lips slightly parted—the gold in his mouth shining through. Ten-year-old Tammina Mitchell, a neighbor, said it had been a drive-by shooting. Rumor got around that Damon Smith had made good on his word.

Toya, Manny's aunt swore that, upon discovering her son's body, Sharon's howls could be heard blocks away. The boy's grandmother, Nellie, on the other hand, received the news in tearful but quiet resignation. She took out her old Bible, the same book she had carried forty years earlier, as a young mother travelling from Danville to Baltimore, and she read from Genesis 28: *Know that I am with you and will keep you wherever you go.*

In Nellie's mind, that meant God never allows a life to end unless its purpose is fulfilled. She found comfort in that assurance.

16 DIVIDED ENTREPRENEURSHIP AND NEIGHBORHOOD EFFECTS

THE TRAJECTORIES OF MANNY MAN WILLIAMS AND HIS FATHER, Marcus Williams III, illustrate two types of business involvement and entrepreneurship; one that tenders limited results because of multiple deficits—experiential, informational and financial—and one that succeeds, tragically, through the operations of predatory capital.

For many young men living in America's inner cities, opportunities for legitimate employment and business formation are thin, even in neighborhoods like Edmonson Village in West Baltimore, which have a rich historical past; it was there that the Williams family resided, and it was there that Marcus Williams sought to become a businessman.

His son, Manny Man, faced a different set of choices. In the wake of capital divestment, residential segregation, and the absence of developmental action on the part of the American State, young people growing up in poor urban areas have few options for generating revenue other than participation in a flourishing trade of illegal substances. Although African Americans represent 28 percent of the population in the state of Maryland, 68 percent of individuals arrested for drug abuse violations and 90 percent of those incarcerated for drug offenses are African American (Schiraldi and Ziedenberg 2003). The majority are youngsters like Manny Man.

In tandem with predatory commerce, the proliferation of firearms throughout the nation, especially in poor urban areas, virtually guarantees that violent confrontation will be an integral part of economic exchanges. Add socialization processes that lead boys and young men to enact dangerous versions of dominant masculinity and the picture is nearly complete. The last strokes are put in place by hypervigilance on the part of a justice system that targets children in inner-city neighborhoods, especially boys, as potential felons in need of surveillance and punishment—clear evidence of *distorted engagement,* as discussed in chapter 6 of this book. Manny Man's life aptly reflects the forces operating in American inner cities—capital retrogression, predatory commerce, and government omnipresence.

Here, I take the experience of Marcus Williams III and his son, Manny Man, as points of departure to investigate the relationship between entrepreneurship, neighborhood effects, and government action. First, I summarize lessons derived from the two lives sketched in the previous chapter. I follow with a discussion of neighborhood effects, reiterating a point adumbrated earlier: location matters. Concrete urban spaces critically shape the limits and possibilities of social and economic action.

I then discuss business formation among African Americans, especially in relation to the Small Business Administration, a government agency directed to spur the yearnings of would-be entrepreneurs like Marcus Williams III. Finally, I return to predatory capital from the point of view of liminal government institutions and their impact on young Black men.

TWO MEN, TWO FORMS OF ENTREPRENEURSHIP

Research shows that a major barrier for the involvement of African Americans in business formation is the paucity of financial resources to sustain firms, especially in their early stages of development (Fairlie and Robb 2008). Marcus Williams was typical in that respect; he faced daunting obstacles when seeking start-up funds for a hauling firm through the backing of the Small Business Administration. His application was declined for reasons that remained opaque but pivoted around his lack of business experience and reduced collateral. From the point of view of lending institutions, Marcus was not a good bet or guarantor of future profit.

In lieu of institutional support, Marcus fell back on loans from members of his kin network but, from the outset, those funds were insufficient to sustain his efforts. Wealth holdings among African Americans are a fraction of those accumulated across generations within other social sectors (Oliver and Shapiro 1995/2006). As a result, assets needed to fuel businesses are extremely limited among African Americans, whose perennial lack of financial wherewithal becomes a major impediment to formal self-employment.

As the life of Marcus Williams III also shows, money shortages are magnified by the absence of external connections.[1] Marcus Williams did not have "weak ties" joining him to outside sources of information and capital. To keep his business going, he was forced to rely on the "strong ties" available in his proximate sphere of interaction (see Granovetter 1973). In environments characterized by accumulated business experience and material assets—Jewish and Indian entrepreneurs come to mind—the risks derived from insularity can be overcome, but in urban spaces marked by historical neglect and dispossession, separation from the larger society presents nearly insurmountable obstacles.

Trapped in urban areas bereft of capital and meaningful outside links, men like Marcus Williams face a reduced potential for effective self-employment and entrepreneurship. That is one of multiple neighborhood effects suggested by relevant studies conducted recently (Brooks-Gunn, Duncan, and Aber 2000; Brooks-Gunn et al. 1993; Sampson 2013).

A third factor limiting African American entrepreneurship concerns embodied knowledge. Entrepreneurial savvy has not been part of the African-American habitus for historical reasons.[2] Blacks did participate in small-business formation and vital commerce since the time of slavery and beyond (Walker 2009; Wagner 2008) but many of the skills mustered through such practices were not transferrable to large-scale business participation in modern times. A legacy of marginalization, residential segregation, and a paucity of sustained interactions with other segments of the society have had an impact upon the capacity of African Americans to build viable business networks.

A fourth, related factor concerns generational outlooks affecting the relationship between realities and expectations. Marcus Williams entertained big, mainstream ideals. His sense of entrepreneurship significantly focused on the sumptuary elements of business—office facilities, sophisticated telephone and computer systems, and several paid workers—whose costs outstripped revenues. Without direct business knowledge, he kept on believing those expenses were necessary long after they had become a problem.

Lost in the dreams of men like Marcus Williams is a lived understanding of day-to-day management details that determine efficacy or disaster. By incurring costs that realized entrepreneurial *appearances* more than *substance,* Marcus saddled his small hauling firm with a debt that grew over time and, eventually, led to bankruptcy. This dramatically affected his life and that of his son, Manny, for whom his father's failure became an incentive for rebellion and innovation.

In other words, throughout his entrepreneurial career, Marcus Williams experienced cognitive dissonance between his socioeconomic reality and the measure of his aspirations. As the first member of his family to obtain a college degree, he had good reasons to be motivated, but he lacked forms of knowledge that are acquired through personal experience, not just formal instruction. Bereft of expertise, social contacts, and adequate support on the part of the public and the private sectors, he could not withstand the leveling pressures that eventuated in the collapse of his small firm. His story is another example of the extent to which normative institutions and developmental action on the part of the American State have been insufficiently present in the lives of striving Blacks, including those with comparatively high levels of education and drive.

By contrast, Marcus Williams's son, Emmanuel, illustrates a profitable if deadly form of illicit entrepreneurship. Literary and journalistic narratives are filled with descriptions of criminal business acumen, but sociological writings seldom examine illegal activities from a business point of view. Crime is typically portrayed as a social problem in search of a solution while legitimate business is viewed as an expression of the capacity for coordination, competitive ability, and self-reliance. Such qualities, however, are abundantly present among drug purveyors, as shown by Manny Man's tactical calculations and organizational decision making (see also DiMaggio 2001; Cross and Peña 2006). We may question the boy's ethical judgment but not his entrepreneurial ability. Like Manny, those involved in illicit trade accurately perceive the potential advantages of competition in marginal but dynamic markets (Goffman 2009).

Manny Man's biography also reveals some of the effects of government intrusiveness on the choices boys make while growing up in poor neighborhoods. Manny's life illustrates a decision-making chain forged in direct interchange with agents of the state. Bright and lively, he was first tagged by teachers and counselors for special care after being diagnosed with attention deficit disorder, but like multitudes of youngsters undergoing similar treatment, Manny may have been simply uninterested and made restless by an inadequate educational curriculum. His behavior may have been a normal response to anomalous conditions; he may have been a casualty of the *medicalization* of poverty (Horowitz 2003). In any event, Manny interpreted his treatment as a form of misrecognition (see chapter 6)—an attempt to erase his individuality and belittle what he felt was legitimate outrage.

Also, as a young boy, after stealing cookies from a corner store, Manny was identified as a potential risk and confined for a time to a therapeutic facility managed by the Department of Juvenile Services. His was a venial transgression that would have scarcely attracted attention in richer neighborhoods. In this case, however, the theft was enough to put Manny in further contact with the punitive arm of the state. The mission of the agency in charge of Manny's case was to provide assistance to troubled youths, but behind its overt magnanimity stood the threat of real punishment. Outsiders cannot easily fathom the extent to which children in poor neighborhoods undergo such experiences (Nolan 2011; Schlossman 2013). Regular contact with the court system, police officers, social workers, and other public servants has a profound impact upon their sense of self. At an early age, Manny understood that he was in contention with an unforgiving world.

The attempt of boys to normalize disconcerting events can lead to unexpected outcomes. Like other boys, Manny saw his confinement in the therapeutic facility as a rite of passage that ushered in a premature sense of manhood. That shift, in turn, brought about a constellation of assumed responsibilities that further pushed him into the streets in search of vindication and a sense of agency. Under such conditions, it is easy to gravitate toward illicit commerce.

In other words, it is not possible to understand the involvement of young Black men in criminal forms of trade without also appreciating their specific relation to liminal government institutions and the effect those institutions have on personal identity, especially in the transition to adulthood. In systematic interchange with public functionaries, as a byproduct of government's supervisory function, young men develop an explicit logic well illustrated by Manny Man's way of thinking—he saw himself as a warrior involved in survival but also responsible toward his family, business associates, and friends. He evinced a coherent way of thinking flowing from membership in social networks without viable connections with the larger society and whose members' lives are partly molded by the actions of punitive government institutions.

Marcus Williams III represents the strivings of recently arrived Black migrants in urban areas, people bent on success and integration into the American middle class. Manny Man, his son, exemplifies processes of downward mobility (Portes 1981) as they are occurring among the members of younger generations with limited educational and employment opportunities, whose choices are circumscribed by features embedded in deprived neighborhoods.

Despite generational differences, both Marcus, the father, and Manny, the son, shared one characteristic in common: their aspirations were high as is to be expected from Americans whose ancestors have resided in the United States for nearly four centuries. In the case of people living in resource-depleted areas, however, great expectations often collide with the reality of insufficient means to achieve them (Merton 1938). Statistically, that is reflected in low rates of formal entrepreneurship and intense participation in economic activities fueled by predatory capital.

UNDERSTANDING NEIGHBORHOOD EFFECTS

Neighborhoods have not been conceptualized, until recently, as independent forces shaping individual and collective action despite a long tradition of research in urban settings, starting with the Chicago school of sociology (Thomas and Znaniecki 1918/1996) and continuing in the following decades (Harvey 1998/2009; Jacobs 1961/1992; Logan and Molotch 1987/2007; Massey and Denton 1993; Massey 1994; Park and Burgess 1967; Sassen 2001). It was only in the 1980s that a few scholars—Susan Mayer and Christopher Jencks (1989), in particular—began to probe the experiences of youngsters residing in inner-city tracts. Their objective was to understand whether the very character of physical space had an autonomous impact upon individual choices and conduct. Their ideas were transformative. By drawing attention to resources embedded in concrete localities, such authors were framing a new way of looking at poverty and its associated afflictions. If there is such a thing as *neighborhood effects*, the logical inference is that those effects will endure over time as long as the residential areas in question remain unchanged.

In subsequent years, studies of neighborhood effects proliferated. Between 1995 and 2000, approximately one hundred papers on that topic were published (Sampson, Morenoff, and Gannon-Rowley 2002). Such articles increasingly focused on social processes that explain how neighborhoods relate to phenomena such as school abandonment, premature motherhood, and delinquency.[3]

Among those conducting research on neighborhood effects are also economists and quantitative sociologists mining large samples from national data sets. Such works may be seen as a response to writings in the 1980s that described the emergence of a permanently marginalized population, as described most effectively by William J. Wilson (1987). Since then, a large literature has examined neighborhood effects on child development, educational outcomes, crime, health, employment, and earnings (Jencks and Mayer 1990; Ellen and Turner 1997; Shonkoff and Phillips 2000). Almost absent, however, are systematic investigations of the relationship between neighborhood effects and self-employment and business formation.

Relevant to that subject, however, have been several projects describing the effects of neighborhood living on renters and property owners who tend to have different levels of interaction within and outside the places where they either live or lease out homes, apartments, and places of business. Atkinson and Kintrea (2000, 2001), for example, found that renters conduct most of their daily activities within the boundaries of their neighborhoods and have little or no regular contact with people in other parts of the city. Owners, on the other hand, tend not to live in the areas where their properties are located and have almost no interaction with residents in those neighborhoods. In each case, factors related to capital flows, the supply and demand of real estate, and local and federal laws and ordinances are implicated. Such variables are of inherent interest to the study of business formation in specific urban spaces.

Beyond their substantive value, studies of neighborhood effects have been notable for their degree of methodological innovation. In the 1990s, despite the intensification of research, it was not possible to reach reliable conclusions about neighborhood effects because the tools needed to identify and measure mechanisms that reproduce disadvantage at the ground level had not been developed. Today, many of those limitations have been overcome through a multiplicity of new approaches. Robert Sampson (2013), in particular, took the study of neighborhood effects to unprecedented levels through his application of sophisticated technology and research methodologies.

Community-based surveys, as well, have yielded reliable measures of social and institutional processes in microenvironments. Raudenbush and Sampson (1999) designed and refined new instruments to investigate urban spaces through what they call *ecometrics* by "developing systematic procedures for directly measuring neighborhood mechanisms, and by integrating and adapting tools from psychometrics to improve the quality of neighborhood-level measures" (Sampson, Morenoff, and Gannon-Rowley 2002: 449). Sampson and his colleagues have also used video recordings and detailed descriptions of spatial characteristics. Most significant is their emphasis on systematic observation, an approach eminently suited to and consistent with ethnographic research.[4]

On the basis of such methodologies, Sampson and his colleagues have identified four mechanisms that lead to distinctive life experiences in deprived neighborhoods:

(1) *Social ties and interactions*, including the quality and quantity of social capital available and the frequency and character of social exchanges among neighbors (Bellair 1997; Warner and Roundtree 1997);

(2) *Norms and collective efficacy* predicated on mutual trust and shared expectations among residents, as well as the ability to impose informal social control—what James Coleman (1988) labeled "closure"—especially toward youngsters;

(3) *Institutional resources*, especially the number and nature of community institutions available to address the needs of residents, particularly young people; and

(4) *Routine activities* that are often overlooked but are decisive in shaping neighborhoods. They include the location of schools, the mix of residential and commercial land use, nodes of public transportation and flows of nighttime visitors (Sampson, Morenoff, and Gannon-Rowley 2002: 458).

The list above suggests multiple new avenues for research, and it raises new questions about urban living. Were it applied to affluent neighborhoods—an endeavor yet to be undertaken—that classification would likely yield surprising results to which the exclusive focus on poor residential areas has blinded us. For example, there is no evidence that interactions among residents in prosperous neighborhoods are more frequent or intense than in poor urban areas. Richer neighborhoods do not typically boast community organizations or government programs meant to enhance children's learning capacities or control young people's behavior. The opposite is true: middle- and upper-class neighborhoods are almost bereft of entities charged with government surveillance; the mark of affluent living is reduced interaction with agents of the state.

On the other hand, like poor urban districts, the features embedded in rich neighborhoods produce specific effects. Because they are protected by an abundance of economic and political assets and have organic connections to mainstream institutions, residents in such areas tend to thrive—none of the afflictions present in poor, racially distinct urban spaces are manifest in physical locations where financial, educational, and social resources are clustered. Jeanne Brooks-Gunn and her associates (2000) has been among a few social scientists making that point: it is the strengthening effect of concentrated resources in particular urban spaces that has the greatest influence upon the options faced by children, adolescents, and adults.[5] Changes in the physical environment can constructively alter people's behavior and outlooks. Recent studies involving the integration of impoverished families into better living environments confirm that claim (Massey et al. 2013), pointing to the significance of ecological features.

Although little attention has been given to the relationship between neighborhood characteristics and self-employment, it is possible to take the classification proposed by Sampson and his associates itemized above as a platform to suggest four additional mechanisms that join physical location to business and entrepreneurship:

(1) *Capital flow formations.* By this I refer to specific types of investment that facilitate or prevent business activity and the functioning of regular markets. The absence of financial institutions in poor neighborhoods to counter the impact of redlining and other forms of financial discrimination represents a major obstacle for legitimate self-employment. Because people in those urban areas cannot easily cross physical or social boundaries in search of the resources necessary to make businesses work, they tend to fall back upon indigenous assets that are typically insufficient to develop firms.

(2) *Demand distortions.* Black businesses tend to be small and undercapitalized, but the historical literature shows that a plurality of small firms relying on the demand of co-ethnics can usher in not solely survival but upward mobility (Portes and Rumbaut 2006). There is, however, little demand for the goods and services provided by small firms in poor Black neighborhoods, partly because of the economic fragility of residents but also because small shops do not benefit from economies of scale. Because they purchase merchandise in small quantities, their costs and prices tend to be high in comparison with those found in large, well-capitalized conglomerates and franchises. Consumers respond negatively to the higher prices of products in small shops owned by local entrepreneurs.

(3) *State palliation and liminality versus development.* The absence of legislative action fomenting genuine economic advancement is a critical mechanism perpetuating economic stagnation in racially segregated inner-city tracts (see chapter 6). Bates (1998), for example, was among the first to study the unanticipated effects of government programs on minority wholesaling. He found that undercapitalized government initiatives reduced loan availability for viable firms in inner-city neighborhoods and increased the overall incidence of default on loans to Black borrowers. Other research shows that developmental state action in poor urban areas has been

fragmentary and politically compromised, presenting a stark contrast to government initiatives that have promoted economic development and prosperity in other sectors of American society.[6]

In addition, the presence of liminal government agencies—and their affiliates and subcontractors—in poor neighborhoods are major mechanisms fostering anomalous conditions.[7] The criminalization of poverty has yielded bountiful profits for a large social segment formed by professionals, including program designers, policy makers, and developers and builders of correctional institutions, subsidized-housing complexes, and other similar facilities. Such populations, however, tend not to live in poor neighborhoods. They represent a form of highly lucrative entrepreneurship that depends on the existence of poverty but whose implementers reside in more prosperous milieus.

The proliferation of liminal government institutions—and their affiliates charged with surveillance and discipline—discourages the development of dynamic markets and business formation. Similarly, the presence of community organizations and ameliorative programs attempting to make up for deficits created by capital retrogression interferes with business creation (Porter 1995). Many enterprising residents in poor neighborhoods end up as underpaid staff in not-for-profit organizations subcontracting services to government. They become part of the thick network of organizations maintaining irregular conditions in dispossessed urban spaces.

(4) *Locational factors.* The previous three mechanisms have an impact on the character of urban space. Poor neighborhoods are therefore bereft of facilities for conducting regular business. Rents tend to be comparatively high in such areas, and the elements of infrastructure necessary to open firms are generally absent. Under such circumstances, business activity in poor neighborhoods tends to be in the hands of absentee landlords and shop owners who reside outside those subdivisions. Lacking competition, they have few incentives to improve business practices. Large food markets, for example,

have no incentive to serve inner-city residents. In tandem with limited demand, ineffectual market competitiveness, and government omnipresence, locational deficiencies reduce the probability of business involvement in poor neighborhoods.

The classification outlined above may be taken as a program for further research. There are few, if any, studies examining the joint operations of the four mechanisms listed. In particular, there is no serious investigation about the role of liminal institutions and government's palliative action on local market interactions. It stands to reason, however, that the character of government institutions embedded in poor urban areas significantly influences the presence or absence of independent business creation.

EFFECTS OF RACE AND ETHNICITY ON BUSINESS FORMATION

There is a voluminous literature on the relationship between race, ethnicity, and entrepreneurship. Many writings contrast rates of self-employment and business creation among diverse immigrant populations and their descendants. A main question centers on the uneven distribution of business capacity among groups of different nationalities. Two focal points anchor those discussions. One examines the role of cultural and structural variables in business involvement (Sowell 1981); another one investigates the functions of entrepreneurship, whether as a vehicle for survival or a true path for development and prosperity (Light and Bonacich 1981). The most reliable data support the idea of self-employment and business development as effective paths toward social integration.

When successful, entrepreneurship provides immigrants and racial and ethnic minorities with shelter from the risks associated with wage employment in exploitative economic sectors. Businesses, even when small, can also protect distinct groups from discrimination. Immigrant entrepreneurs—ranging from Eastern European Jews to Chinese to Cubans—have translated their economic gains into educational and occupational advantages for their children (Goldscheider 1986; Huynh and Yiu 2012; Kim 1981; Kim 2006; Petersen 1971; Portes and Bach 1985; Rischin 1962; Zhou and Bankston 1998).

While there are sufficient data to show that self-employment can lead to desirable social and economic outcomes, the causes behind the uneven distribution of entrepreneurial ability across various groupings calls for further explanation. In 2010, for example, the self-employment rate among White male workers aged twenty-six to fifty-five was 13.5 percent, more than double the figure for African Americans, assessed at 6.2 percent. Equivalent rates among other immigrant populations ranged from 34 percent for Israelis, 29 percent for Iranians, and 27 percent for Koreans to just 10 percent for Mexicans and 9 percent for Dominicans (U.S. Census Bureau 2011; Portes and Yiu 2013). What explains such large variations?

Despite their prima facie appeal, cultural explanations of differential business involvement tend to be unsatisfactory because they operate on a post factum basis; once a group attains entrepreneurial success, it is easy to impute that achievement to norms and values shared by the members of the group in question, a logic that leans toward the tautological. Furthermore, worthy ethical principles are broadly distributed among groups with limited and abundant success in business (Light and Rosenstein 1995; Portes and Yiu 2013).[8]

The shortcomings of cultural explanations become all the more obvious when observing the multiplicity of national, cultural, and religious backgrounds among groups that have achieved entrepreneurial efficacy. Minorities with high rates of business ownership include Jews and Arabs, southern and northern Europeans, Asians, Middle Easterners, and some Caribbean and Latin American peoples whose cultural characteristics are manifold and sometimes opposed to one another; they are Protestant, Catholic, Greek Orthodox, Buddhist, and Muslim, giving testimony to highly diverse religious nomenclatures.

Finally, both success and failure in business are found among people with similar cultural traditions. Chinese Buddhists are highly prone to entrepreneurship, but Cambodian Buddhists are not. Cubans, a preponderantly Catholic population, have among the highest rates of successful entrepreneurship in the United States while Catholic Mexicans have one of the lowest. Even a cursory review of the facts debunks cultural explanations of entrepreneurial success or failure.

This is especially true in the case of African Americans. Juliet Walker (2009), for example, shows that shortly after their arrival in the American colonies, slaves applied traditional knowledge acquired in their places of birth to participate in informal commerce and the provision of services. After emancipation and throughout the latter part of the nineteenth century, a multiplicity of Black-owned businesses spread throughout the American South and in northern locations. Although they tended to be tiny and undercapitalized, those businesses attested to the vitality of would-be Black entrepreneurs (Wagner 2008).

Butler (1991) further shows that African American involvement in business activity was intense during the times of formal segregation—in the absence of alternative places to shop for services and commodities under Jim Crow laws, Blacks fell back upon their own resources, creating extensive business networks that included everything from taxicab companies to insurance companies, garment factories, millineries, grocery stores, dress shops, barbershops, gas stations, and multiple places of entertainment (Krueger 1963; Immergluck and Mullen 1998). Commerce and self-employment grew in segregated neighborhoods whose residents were unable to assimilate into the larger society.

The 1960s and subsequent decades brought about a paradox: desegregation, forced by the passage of federal legislation, resulted in greater political inclusion for African Americans, but it had a negative impact on their capacity to sustain businesses. As more and more Blacks gravitated to shopping malls in search of cheap products, but also of feelings of membership in the larger society, small and medium-sized enterprises in segregated neighborhoods lost patrons and, eventually, were closed down or sold to a new class of mostly Jewish entrepreneurs (Wagner 2008).

Business activity in Black neighborhoods was dealt another blow in the aftermath of violent protests that followed the assassination of Martin Luther King Jr. in 1968. Shops not vandalized or burned to the ground were soon shut down or sold to a new class of immigrant merchants, mostly Chinese and Koreans. In Baltimore districts like Sandtown-Winchester, Upton, and Lower Park Heights, it was those middlemen minorities who accounted for much of the legitimate commerce during the 1990s.

In other words, political inclusion, fueled by the civil rights movement and new government legislation implemented during the 1960s, did not translate into a major expansion of economic opportunities for

African Americans in the latter part of the twentieth century. Limited participation in business formation was part of that evolution.

Contextual factors represent better explanations than culture in self-employment. As Portes and Yiu (2013) put it, entrepreneurial dynamics and business niches will emerge in situations that meet two conditions: (a) the presence of a population with significant numbers of individuals adept in what E. Franklin Frazier (1949) called "the art of buying and selling" and (b) a favorable, or at least neutral, economic, political, and social context where those skills can be deployed (see also Raijman 2001). By contrast, when ethnic or racial groups encompass mostly low-skilled workers, and when those workers face high levels of hostility, only a small number of businesses catering mainly to other members of the same group can emerge (Rischin 1962; Portes and Stepick 1994; Zhou and Bankston 1998; Min and Bozorgmehr 2000; Huynh and Yiu 2012).

Entrepreneurial efficacy is thus best explained through attention to the interaction between preexisting experience and features embedded in physical and institutional environments. Such theories also clarify why some immigrant minorities—Cambodians, Laotians, Haitians, and Mexicans—have not shown a strong business presence (Zhou et al. 2008; Stepick et al. 2001; Telles and Ortiz 2008). Those are highly vulnerable populations formed by laborers, without entrepreneurial experience in their places of origin, who have also endured high levels of discrimination in the United States. Without resources, either human or financial, to constitute businesses, they have become permanent providers of cheap labor. Their experience bears some resemblance to that of African Americans.

In stark contrast, Cubans, Koreans and Chinese are among the most likely to be involved in self-employment and business creation in the United States. If firm size is considered, Indian firms emerge as the largest entrepreneurial group, followed by Korean-Americans. Whether judged by level of self-employment or firm size, Mexicans, and African Americans rank low in their propensity to start and maintain businesses.

African Americans, in fact, have the lowest rates of participation in formal business, even below those of Mexicans. There are numerous Black- and Hispanic-owned firms in the United States—more than four million, according the 2007 U.S. Census, which provides the latest available data—but as a proportion of their respective ethno-racial groups, Blacks and Mexicans rank at the bottom of the entrepreneurial scale (Portes and Yiu 2013). One in ten White Americans, but only one in eighteen Mexicans and one in twenty African Americans, own businesses (U.S. Census Bureau 2007).

That Mexicans rank low as business owners is unsurprising. Although they represent the longest continuous immigrant flow to the United States, most Mexicans have comparatively low levels of formal education, and the majority have entered the country as providers of low-cost labor. Many are undocumented immigrants whose vulnerability turns them into easy prey for abuses. As a whole, they represent a durable working class that fuels economic activity in labor-intensive sectors, including agriculture and services. African Americans, on the other hand, entered U.S. territory long before the country officially came into existence. They have an even lengthier history of struggle for actual citizenship than Mexicans. In the aftermath of the civil rights movement, expectations were high for their incorporation into the larger society, including prospects for higher levels of self-employment and business formation. Why haven't those hopes materialized?

A possible answer to that question is suggested by research conducted by Fairlie and Robb (2008). On the basis of U.S. census data, they investigated factors associated with human and financial capital and family business background in relation to successful business ownership among Whites, Asians, and African Americans. They found that the availability of start-up capital is the most important factor contributing to the success of Asian-owned businesses, and its lack for the reduced efficacy of Black firms. Because nearly half of Black families have less than $6,000 in total wealth, they are not in a good position to support viable businesses. Higher education levels among Asian proprietors also explain much of their effectiveness in comparison with Whites and African Americans. Finally, Fairlie and Robb found that Blacks have fewer opportunities than Whites to acquire prior experience by working in family businesses.

As a result, businesses owned by African Americans tend to have lower sales, fewer employees, smaller payrolls, lower profits, and higher closure rates than businesses owned by Asian Americans. By contrast,

Asian-owned firms tend to be highly lucrative. Although they represent 4.8 percent of the U.S. population, Asian immigrants own more than 1.5 million businesses, while African Americans, who encompass nearly 13 percent of the country's population, hold fewer than 2 million firms. Asian American firms also tend to be larger in terms of employees, receipts, and profits. That comparison shows that the causes behind diverse outcomes in self-employment among ethnic and racial minorities relate to a complex landscape in which different paths to entrepreneurship are determined by concrete historical trajectories, the amount and quality of resources available to specific groups, and the characteristics of the context in which various populations operate (Portes and Yiu 2013).

ZOOMING IN: BLACK ENTREPRENEURSHIP AND STATE ACTION

According to the 2007 Survey of Business Owners—the most recent data available—there are 22,689,491 firms in the hands of White entrepreneurs in the United States, representing 86 percent of all formal companies in the nation. The equivalent figure for Blacks is 1,922,806 and for Hispanics, 2,261,706. Together, the two minority groups account for less than one-sixth of all business proprietors in the country.[9]

Table 2 further shows estimated receipts, number of employees, and annual payroll figures for White, Black, Asian and Hispanic firms.

TABLE 2

Estimated Receipts, Number of Employees, and Annual Payroll for White, Black, Asian, and Hispanic Firms

Race	Firms	Receipts ($000)	No. of Employees	Annual Payroll ($000)
All classifiable forms	26,392,237	10,947,539,589	59,316, 163	1,940,804,078
White (85.9%)	22,689,491	10,240,333,845	54,964,724	1,824,533,907
Black (7.2%)	1,922,806	135,615,500	958,322	23,357,498
Asian	1,544,624	505,063,966	2,974,201	79,046,001
Hispanic (8.5%)	2,261,706	350,763,923	2,026,406	54,367,702

As may be seen, across the three categories, White-owned firms vastly overpower those owned by minority entrepreneurs. Most remarkable, however, is the comparative weakness of Black enterprises; they represent less than 2 percent of total receipts, number of employees, and annual payroll expenditures. That is less than half of the equivalent figures for Hispanic firms.

Even more revealing is that the numbers on Black entrepreneurship actually represent historical improvements. Between 2002 and 2007, the number of firms owned by African Americans increased by 60.5 percent, more than triple the national rate of 18 percent. Black businesses also constituted one of the fastest-growing segments of the U.S. economy, both in terms of number of companies and total sales. On the other hand, those businesses tend to be diminutive; 87 percent had sales below $50,000, as compared with 65 percent of all firms, and most Black-owned firms have fewer than five employees.

GOVERNMENT ACTION AND BLACK ENTREPRENEURSHIP

A major factor dooming entrepreneurship among African Americans has been the absence of developmental government action, represented in this case by the Small Business Administration, the agency to which Marcus Williams III, the protagonist of the previous chapter, applied for seed money to create his firm.

Formed in 1953 under the Dwight D. Eisenhower administration, the SBA was created to "aid, counsel, assist and protect, insofar as is possible, the interests of small business concerns," and also to ensure small businesses receive a "fair proportion" of government contracts (U.S. Small Business Administration 2013). From the outset, the SBA focused on the provision of capital, contracts, and counseling. Although it has been an invaluable source of funding for striving people, that agency has relied on a tiny fragment of the federal budget—less than one billion dollars in 2012—and its resources have been repeatedly slashed throughout its sixty-year history. Especially under the Reagan and Bush Administrations, the SBA was seen by Libertarians and Conservatives as an example of governmental intrusion on the workings of the free market (Nopper 2011). Although the budget of the SBA has been somewhat expanded under the Obama administration, it remains an insufficient source of funds for would-be entrepreneurs in deprived urban areas.

In other words, the Small Business Administration and other government agencies aiming at promoting entrepreneurship have themselves met with limited success for lack of adequate investments. Their financial and political backing pales in comparison with those that made possible broad legislative actions—the 1944 GI Bill comes to mind—promoting sizable economic and educational advancement among mainstream populations, especially the descendants of European immigrants.[10] Although the objectives of the SBA are consistent with the developmental outlook of the American State, its material and political support has been weak. That situation has had an especially negative impact upon African Americans.

Other government programs and agencies created to ignite Black self-employment in the 1960s—community corporations, credit unions, government-supported banking and insurance institutions—rapidly declined in the 1980s for similar reasons: lack of adequate political and financial backing. Neoliberal policies favored in the Reagan and Bush years further diminished their potential. Finally, onerous bureaucratic requirements surrounding the application for funds have also delayed the entrepreneurial involvement of African Americans, who tend to have comparatively low levels of formal education and direct experience in business.

Despite its limited funds, the SBA has been a major resource for young firms started by ethnic minorities and immigrants, especially under its 7(a) and 504 programs, which provide loan guarantees and monies for firm owners to purchase fixed assets. For example, in Florida, Cuban exiles received more than half of the grants awarded by the SBA between 1959 and 1973. In tandem with the hard work of exiles and refugees fleeing the island country after Fidel Castro's revolution, the financial and technical assistance provided by the SBA enabled Cubans to transform South Florida into a business center that still sustains much of the prosperity in that region more than fifty years later (Portes and Stepick 1994).

By contrast, SBA support for small businesses owned by African Americans has been puny. During the same period that Cubans obtained significant outlays to build an impressive business enclave, African Americans in Florida received less than 6 percent of all grants awarded by the SBA. Cubans were at an advantage because of their higher levels of education and prior business experience and also because their integration into American society was seen as a high priority during the Cold War years.

Uneven government action through agencies like the Small Business Administration relates to the persistence of negative neighborhood effects. For example, Immergluck and Mullen (1998) examined the distribution of business loans made by the Small Business Administration's 504 development company program in the Chicago metropolitan area over a five-year period. They found that, after controlling for firm density, firm size, and industrial mix, higher-income and suburban areas received more loans than lower-income and inner-city neighborhoods. This has had a profound impact on the creation of successful businesses and the differential development of cities and their fringes.

Even more recently, the tendency has been for the SBA to apply "color-blind" criteria for the allocation of its grants. By some estimates, such policies have benefited mostly immigrants from Asia, Latin America, and the Caribbean, especially those with prior business experience and higher levels of formal instruction. On the basis of interviews with SBA employees in Los Angeles and New York, Nopper (2011) found that color-blind approaches focusing on race and minority status tend to benefit non-Black minorities but not African Americans.[11]

In Baltimore, a predominantly Black city, less than 10 percent of funds were awarded to African-American entrepreneurs during the 1990s, the same period during which Marcus Williams made his entry into business. Nearly two decades later, the situation has not improved. The number of SBA-backed loans to firms owned by African Americans in the Baltimore metropolitan area decreased by 85 percent between 2007 and 2010 (U.S. Small Business Administration 2011). In 2007, at the outset of a major recession, the SBA guaranteed 249 loans to Black-owned businesses under its key 7(a) program, totaling $27.8 million. In 2010 that figure was cut to thirty-eight loans, worth a total of $4.3 million.[12]

At the national level, the landscape is not very different. Between 2009 and 2013, loans to Black-owned businesses declined by 47 percent, while loans to businesses owned by Asian Americans increased by 21 percent. To make up for bank cutbacks in small business lending

TABLE 3

Number of 7(a) Loan Guarantees Approved by the SBA[a]

	2001	2006	2007	2009	2010	2011	2012	2013
All firms	42,958	97,291	99,606	30,513	38,464	38,145	36,645	37,285
Black-owned[b] (%)	5.1	10.0	11.5	8.9	4.2	3.7	2.4	2.3
Asian-owned (%)	11.8	12.8	13.4	14.5	13.7	14.0	11.7	12.9

Source: U.S. Small Business Administration
[a] Loans to existing businesses only, nationwide approvals.
[b] Percentage of all 7(a) loans approved by the SBA given to firms owned by African Americans.

during that period, the SBA increased its outlays to small firms through its 7(a) program, which provides banks with guarantees against loan default. As a result, SBA infusions to small firms increased significantly in 2010. Loan approvals rose from 30,513 to 38,464 nationwide, and loans to Asian-owned firms increased from 4,439 to 5,261.

By contrast, the number of loans approved to Black-owned small firms fell from 2,711 in 2009 to 1,601 in 2010 and to 1,410 in 2011. The 47 percent decrease in the number of loans caused the share of Black business SBA 7(a) loan approvals to decline from 8.9 percent in 2009 to 3.7 percent in 2011. Such figures are all the more striking when considering that the number of African Americans living in the United States by far exceeds that of Asian Americans.[13]

Among the reasons behind such figures is the insufficient support provided by banks working with the SBA. Lenders afforded borrowers 20 to 80 percent less funding than they requested in their business plans, making it less likely that entrepreneurs could sustain firms without seeking alternative funding, which was often unavailable from other sources. Although the SBA was originally constituted to provide public backing for striving entrepreneurs, it has adapted over time to meet the market demands of regular lenders, thereby marginalizing in many cases the applicants who most need government assistance.

Thus, a review of the evolution and practices of the Small Business Administration suggests that with respect to depressed urban areas and impoverished African Americans, the government has taken approaches that vastly differ from those taken to stimulate purchasing demand among the members of other groups. The Small Business Administration represents an important case because although its mission is in alignment with tried and proven methods of economic development, its actions often contribute to the expansion of inequalities among various racial and ethnic sectors.

Finally, persistent patterns of racial discrimination must also be considered. Ivan Light (1980) first gave attention to what he called the "interaction hypothesis," by which he meant the ways in which supply and demand relate in the presence of racial variables. When prejudiced purchasers discriminate, they demand suppliers of a particular ethno-racial type, not solely qualified suppliers. That has an effect on the potential of firms owned by members of groups shunned by the broader society (Light and Rosenstein 1995: 83–85). Borjas and Bronars (1989: 581, 592) further note that consumer racism reduces the self-employment of African Americans thus limiting their chances for successful entrepreneurship.[14]

Cavalluzzo and Wolken (2005), among other authors, show that Black-owned businesses get turned down more often than White-owned companies with similar profiles and face rejection more often than Hispanic and Asian entrepreneurs when applying for loans from financial institutions. Whether such outcomes are directly caused by racial discrimination is not obvious, however, because decisions to reject loan applications are based on an applicant's experience, collateral, credit rating, and personal worth. Because African Americans tend to be more vulnerable along those indicators, they pose a higher financial risk than members of other demographic sectors. In the case of business formation, individual applicants face not just immediate barriers but the legacy of historical exclusion that weakens their competitiveness in present-day America.

NEIGHBORHOOD EFFECTS AND PREDATORY COMMERCE

In 1996, the year that Emmanuel Travis Williams met his untimely end at the age of eighteen, another enterprising young man was shot outside a casino in Las Vegas, Nevada, that time by members of the Southeast

Crips Gang. The victim had been born in East Harlem, New York, to parents who had been active participants in the Black Panther Party during the 1960s and 1970s. His family had relocated to Baltimore in 1986, and it was there that the talented boy had studied poetry, jazz, and ballet at one of the city's most prestigious institutions, the Baltimore School for the Arts. In time, he became an international celebrity who, by 2010, had sold more than seventy-five million records throughout the world. That was fourteen years after he was gunned down in Las Vegas. He was only twenty-five at the time of his death—his name was Tupac Shakur.

In a smaller scale, Manny Man's life mirrors that of the iconic rapper. Like Tupac Shakur, Manny had large dreams and a conscience. Both men had an early contact with oppressive institutions that infused their minds with a sense of violated justice. One responded through artistic expression; the other by becoming directly involved in illicit commerce. Both had dealings with street gangs and saw themselves as rooted in and responsible towards communities formed by vulnerable people. The two were generous benefactors to friends and family. Both suffered violent deaths spurred by masculine aspirations and a context marked by the easy availability of firearms.

In 1996 as well, the year that the two men died, there were 1,542 non-fatal shootings and 331 homicides in the city of Baltimore (Hermann 2009). Most of the shootings were inflicted by Black men upon other Black men, and most of the incidents were related to the drug trade. Those implicated tended to be individuals with a history of repeated arrests. Like Manny Man, they had experienced early incursions into marginal activities and had a history of repeated contacts with agents of the state, starting in childhood.

More than a decade later, in 2008, the Baltimore landscape had not changed by much. The 107 people charged with murder that year had accumulated more than one thousand prior arrests, 380 were related to guns and ninety-nine to drugs. Victims did not differ much from perpetrators: the 234 individuals killed that year had a combined 2,404 prior arrests, 162 related to guns and 898 related to drugs, with an average of ten arrests per suspect and ten arrests per victim. The figures were nearly identical the following year, 2009, and those numbers were virtually the same as those from a decade before (Hermann 2009).

In 2011, the violent crime rate in Baltimore was 795.9 per 100,000, compared with 213.6 nationwide; and that was significantly down from

2000 when the rate was 1,346 per 100,000, compared with the national figure of 278 per 100,000. Throughout the nation, including Baltimore, crime rates have declined, but in poor neighborhoods they remain an entrenched reality. Relevant data are not time sensitive—despite ebbs and flows, crime resists change and remains high in poor subdivisions (U.S. Census Bureau 2012).

Given such facts, it does not surprise that in 2013, among cities with 500,000 residents or more, Baltimore ranked second in the nation in terms of violent crime, below only Detroit, a city that declared bankruptcy the same year not solely as a result of political corruption and administrative malpractice but also as a consequence of long-term industrial decline and ingrained poverty. In both cities, a large proportion of deadly deeds are related to drug commerce. Eighty-three percent of violent deaths in Detroit are of African Americans; 84 percent of those in Baltimore belong to the same racial group. It is hard not to detect a pattern connecting race, gender, economic decline, and the workings of illegal trade.

How did West Baltimore and similar inner-city areas arrive at their present situation? To answer that question, it is first necessary to consider the combined effect of capital retrogression and residential segregation during the first part of the twentieth century, which transformed working-class neighborhoods into Black ghettos characterized by persistent indigence and disconnection from the larger society (Massey and Denton 1993; Philpott 1991). Second, the spaces left empty by the departure of productive investments were then occupied by two social actors whose joint effects critically altered the lives of residents: one was predatory commerce and the other consisted of multiple government agencies and programs exercising what I call *distorted engagement* between the American State and the urban poor. The focus of such agencies has been on palliation, surveillance, and punishment.[15]

In other words, with respect to destitute populations in urban areas, the American State has consistently deviated from its developmental stance, opting for practices that contribute to the perpetuation of irregular conditions among impoverished people. In the absence of genuine investments in education, business formation, and full citizenship—the three mechanisms that best explain the success of U.S. government vis-à-vis mainstream constituencies—the urban poor face increasing isolation, separation from remunerative employment, and weakened citizenship.

The disturbing facts related to the drug trade in deprived urban areas reflect two kinds of violence. One is promoted by the involvement of young people, especially boys and men, in dynamic but illegal markets that pivot around dangerous narcotics but also guns. Although firearms represent a widespread problem in the society at large, their use as part of illegal business activity has had especially lethal consequences, as shown by the figures reviewed earlier in this section and as multiple authors have noted (Alexander 2010). The astonishing levels of incarceration of Black men in the United States are partially the result of their involvement in the only kind of business that thrives in deprived urban spaces (Pager 2009; Wacquant 2009b; Western 2007).

The second form of violence emanates from government institutions. While normative institutions have promoted success through incentives in education and property accumulation, liminal agencies, like those in poor neighborhoods, function to repress and contain marginal groups. In the inner city, normative institutions are scarce, but liminal institutions proliferate as part of a landscape of actual and symbolic violence.

The role of government bureaucracies must therefore be considered in any explanation about the exceptional character of poverty in America's inner cities. Max Weber (1919) first offered a cogent explanation of bureaucracies, which he saw as iron cages trapping individuals in systems based on teleological efficiency, rational calculation, and control. Beyond explicit objectives, the first principle of bureaucratic survival is self-perpetuation. Those whom Michael Lipsky (1980) called "street-level bureaucrats"—from police officers to the staff in various court systems, parole officers, social workers, and therapists—actively seek to justify and expand their mandates. Bureaucratic intrusion is thus directly related to the quantity of personnel involved in government undertakings. The large-scale presence of agents of the state in poor neighborhoods often begets the problems they are charged to address.

A recent example encompasses the growth in the number of "school resource officers," police officers whose mandate is to patrol the grounds of schools throughout the nation. Their actions have resulted in the expansion of detainments and arrests for comparatively small offenses that used to be left in the hands of principals, teachers, and counselors (Beger 2002; Myrstol 2011). This has resulted in over three million cases of expulsions. African American youngsters are overrepresented in that population (Brewer and Heitzeg 2008).

Such circumstances prompt actions on the part of young people that may be construed as deviant and even criminal. As shown by the experience of Manny Man Williams in the preceding chapter, small transgressions are easily criminalized under the gaze of hypervigilant functionaries attached to liminal government agencies. The tendency to severely penalize even small misbehaviors raises concerns about what some call the "school-to-prison pipeline" (Brewer and Heitzeg 2008; Heitzeg 2012).

Black boys, from age ten to seventeen, face a five times greater likelihood of arrest and detention for violent crimes than White boys in the same age cohort. Two-thirds of Black children detained by the authorities, however, have committed nonviolent acts. Black and Hispanic children are among the most likely to be waived into the adult justice system once detained. No matter the reasons, once youngsters are handled by liminal government agencies, the probability that they will interact repeatedly with public officials is high. The probability also increases that they will develop styles of interaction based on defiance, thus strengthening a vicious cycle. It is not possible to conduct a proper analysis of the link between state action and young populations in poor neighborhoods without giving attention to processes of criminalization and violence inflicted on impoverished children.

Systematic violence against indigent youngsters partly explains high rates of incarceration. The greatest number of people living behind bars in the world is in the United States; while America has 5 percent of the world's population, it harbors 25 percent of the world's prison population (Alexander 2010). That amounts to nearly 2.5 million people, at least 60 percent of whom are Black and male. Such a disproportionate representation may be seen as the effect of distorted engagement between government officials and impoverished, racially distinct groups.

Given the patterned character of those interactions, Loïc Wacquant (2009) speaks about the prison industry as the "third peculiar institution," similar in character to slavery and the urban ghetto, and representative of historical trends that began nearly four centuries ago and continue today. Michelle Alexander (2010) develops a similar argument by referring to prisons as a new Jim Crow system. In their analyses, both authors highlight the unique character of government interaction with the urban poor.

Neighborhood effects are thus not an abstraction; they are concrete outcomes made possible by the characteristics of the physical environments in which people live. Formal entrepreneurship, of the kind that Marcus Williams III yearned for, is difficult to undertake in inner-city environments for multiple reasons, including the absence of productive investments and a genuine developmental involvement on the part of the American State. On the other hand, illegal entrepreneurship of the sort practiced by Marcus's son, Manny Mann, thrives as part of the dynamic markets operating in the vacuums created by the retrogression of productive capital.

Finally, it is necessary to consider a third form of entrepreneurship that also booms in inner cities: a business network made possible by distorted engagement and its liminal institutions and affiliates (see also Ehrenreich 2012). Investments in the promotion of legitimate entrepreneurship in poor neighborhoods have been negligible, as illustrated by the development and allocations of the Small Business Administration reviewed earlier. In contrast, investments in palliative and punitive programs on the part of government agencies and not-for-profit organizations charged with surveillance and control have been much larger. For example, in 2011, the total budget of the Small Business Administration was $985 million, a 45 percent decrease from 2010. That year, $39 *billion* were allocated to cover the costs of prisons throughout the nation. While only a fragment of SBA allocations benefits low-income African American entrepreneurs, most of those living in prisons are impoverished African American men.

That disparity alone stands as an emblem of the differential treatment that the American State has leveled against one of the most vulnerable segments of the society.

CONCLUSION: DISTORTED ENGAGEMENT AND THE GREAT IDEOLOGICAL DIVIDE

SEVERAL OBJECTIVES ANIMATED THE WRITING OF THIS BOOK. ONE was to salvage biography in the study of impoverished persons. In the age of sophisticated technology and social media, biography is a much-pursued means of self-expression, but most biographies are of people with at least some power and influence. By contrast, the actual experience of impoverished individuals remains concealed behind narratives pivoting around "social problems." An unintended and brutal effect of class and racial inequality is the eviction of existential logics informing the decisions and thinking of vulnerable people, including children.

In that context, it becomes a political necessity and scientific imperative to reclaim biographical dimensions as part of an effort to achieve a more precise interpretation of the realities behind statistical facts. It is then that ethnography can become an integral component of the scientific mission and a tool to reveal its moral ramifications. Individuals recognized in this volume were not selected capriciously but as exponents of typical and generalized experiences. Each biography included here may be seen as a record of a unique person but also as a lens to discern broader structural factors shaping the social sectors to which that person belongs. By arranging the content of this book around seven biographical narratives complemented by analytical chapters, I hope to open new avenues to reconcile ethnographic procedures with broader investigations of macro-level forces underpinning personal experience.

There is now a voluminous literature about the urban poor, both in the form of memorable ethnographic studies and theoretical tracts specifying the relationship between globalization and new collectivities made redundant by economic change. Those studies represent a treasure trove of information to back new comprehensive initiatives tackling urban poverty through structural reform. Yet, as the new millennium advances, most Americans are content to regard impoverished people as victims of their own misdeeds. The time is ripe for new undertakings to give voice to groups that remain invisible and to use their experience in the production of new and more reliable knowledge. In the fullness of time, such efforts may justify the implementation of legislative initiatives centered on the valorization, not the containment, of people enduring destitution, many of whom are young.

A second, equally important aim of this book is to *bring the state back into* the assessment of urban poverty in America. Both in the society at large and in specialized circles, poverty continues to be seen as a problem solvable through the application of piecemeal policies. A vast industry formed by consultants, public officials, academics, and researchers has grown around penury viewed as the inevitable result of historical sins of commission and omission, no longer susceptible of change. In that fatalistic outlook, the only course of action is the multiplication of ad hoc assistance programs to address poverty's multiple afflictions. For the most part, those efforts have failed. Missing in them, and in the theoretical frameworks that inform their design, is a candid reexamination of government's role in the perpetuation of dispossession.

When discussing the subjects that concern this book, colleagues and friends query me about alternatives to existing measures addressing destitution and urban decline. Other than whining, they imply with various degrees of exasperation, what do *you* propose to end the cycle of violence, drug addiction, persistent unemployment, premature motherhood, and school abandonment? The answer to that question has little to do with me; it is lucidly revealed by the success of the American State, which stands at the center of this book's argument. Huge investments in education, the expansion of property rights, material accumulation, and political participation have conferred on several generations of working-class people access to prosperity and the benefits of democracy. There lies the true meaning of the American Dream. Visionary items of progressive legislation, including the 1944 Veterans

Readjustment Act—the GI Bill—gave ordinary citizens a stake in the society and a sense of belonging that, despite economic downturns, persists to this day. Similar investments have never been made to buttress the aspirations of impoverished, racially distinct populations whose descendants now live in depressed urban areas. It is not that we have no solutions to urban poverty but that we, as a nation, have never made the necessary commitment to afford excluded populations a true sense of economic and political citizenship.

In lieu of capital infusions and legislative muscle, we have opted for a punitive behemoth to control the outcomes of neglect, the very problems we collectively created for lack of political will and moral conviction. The question therefore is not whether there are better alternatives to address urban poverty—there are—but whether we are willing to look hard into our own history to tap the proven solutions that gave mainstream populations, the sons and daughters of exploited immigrants, the tools to succeed economically, socially, and politically. To extract from that history more-effective policies to support people living in squalor would be consistent with America's trajectory of faith in the capacity of humans to improve their circumstances.

While progressive approaches to urban poverty await implementation, blaming the poor for their fate is as popular as it has ever been. Conservatives cast the poor as parasites and burdens on the society, while liberal outlooks tend toward the infantilization of impoverished people who are seen as broken vessels in need of repair. Most programs to address poverty and its hardships are inspired by principles of self-improvement, not structural reform. Illustrations range from policies to encourage marriage and learn effective life skills to initiatives on good parenting, impulse control, developing a work ethic, and dressing for success. Most of us can benefit from such worthy instruction, but it is folly to believe that it alone can counter the effect of historical abandonment, racial discrimination, and disinvestment. The most durable consequence of such programs has been to support multitudes of altruistic mentors, program designers, public servants, and personnel in not-for-profit organizations. Palliative programs have constructive functions—multiple lives have been improved by caring individuals and organizations—but they cannot substitute for authentic stakes in the well-being of impoverished urban populations.

The systemic character of factors perpetuating destitution and inequality remain hidden partly because it is easy for both liberals and conservatives to see their power, wealth, and influence as a result of their own virtue and poverty as the consequence of other people's moral failings. Despite self-serving judgments and given the colossal amounts of wealth amassed in the United States—a $16.6 trillion economy in 2013—it would be reasonable to expect high levels of prosperity and a more equitable distribution of income. That, in fact, was the tendency throughout the first half of the twentieth century for most working-class Americans. The application of neoliberal reforms beginning in the 1980s arrested that trend and brought about rising disparities. White working-class Americans have borne the brunt of such shifts, but African Americans were excluded from the paths that brought about prosperity long before globalization took its toll.

Between 2000 and 2011, poverty rates in the United States rose from 11.3 percent to 15 percent, and poverty among children 18 years old or younger increased from 16. 2 percent to 21.9 percent. Perhaps more revealing, overall poverty rates remained fairly stable at 15 percent between the mid-1990s—when I was conducting research in West Baltimore—and 2011. Among Whites, those rates went up from 8.5 to 9.8 during the same years. Although poverty rates among African Americans dropped somewhat, from 33.4 percent to 27.5 percent over the same stretch, they are still three times as high as they are among Whites (U.S. Census Bureau 2011). Altogether, 46 million Americans currently live in poverty, and a disproportionate number of them are African Americans dwelling in cities.

The scandal of persistent poverty in the world's wealthiest nation has been compounded by growing income inequality: at present, the top 1 percent of Americans control 43 percent of financial wealth while the bottom 80 percent owns 7 percent. To put it another way, the top 20 percent of the American population holds 93 percent of all financial assets in the country (Wolff 2010). Such disparities are uncommon in the advanced world and close to those that prevail in less developed countries.

The unusual character of American poverty is all the more obvious from a comparative vantage point. In less developed nations, want and injustice can be partly explained as functions of a past marked by colonialism and economic dependency. Most Latin American cities emerged as administrative hubs for the transfer of agricultural and artisanal wealth from colonial territories to Europe. In the service of political powers across the Atlantic, such cities dotted a vast countryside that was at the same time underutilized and harshly depleted. The irregular growth of Latin American cities, their swarms of rural-urban migrants in search of opportunity, their squatter settlements and petty vendors all attest to the legacy of economic and political subordination. Even today, poverty in Latin America reflects above all that continent's subservient position in the international system of production.

None of that is true about the United States. Sparsely populated, early American cities did not exhibit the large inequalities found in Latin America, nor did they experience that continent's degree of colonial oppression. Independence brought about the framing of a philosophical agenda that privileged equality before the law and individual rights in a context in which those goals were not doomed to failure from the outset. The nineteenth century witnessed accelerated industrialization. Exploitation was rampant, but so was popular mobilization, which fueled government policies to give ordinary people a stake in the society. In tandem with military and political expansion to overseas locations, that design soon produced unprecedented prosperity the effects of which are still being felt in the early decades of the twenty-first century. In other words, in the United States, urban poverty is not a byproduct of the country's lowly position in a larger structure of international inequality. Rather, it is an aberration maintained for reasons particular to America's racial obsessions.

In the 1960s, under the Lyndon B. Johnson administration, efforts to eradicate penury and destitution took concrete shape in the form of federal expenditures backing a so-called War on Poverty. Fifty years later, poverty has not disappeared among White Americans, and it has become a permanent feature of life among Blacks. In the aftermath of the Great Recession that began in 2008, economic inequalities between the two populations have widened, even as Whites lose ground in employment.[1]

Several factors explain such developments, including the expansion of an aged population, growing automation, and technological innovations in multiple sectors of the U.S. economy. Globalization, especially the relocation of manufacturing jobs to overseas locations, has also played a part. Nevertheless, social and economic inequalities cannot be fully explained without interrogating the part played by the American State. With respect to impoverished African Americans, the government has consistently taken an approach that markedly differs from the one it took toward mainstream populations.

In this book, I have argued that the state's treatment of impoverished urban populations is not a historical accident but the systematic effect of *distorted engagement* realized through *liminal government institutions*. Conventional agencies address members of the society as consumers and citizens. By contrast, liminal institutions operate on the fringes of standard deportment and practice. They disfigure and transform conventional interactions through a mixture of benevolence and aggression. In the first case, individuals who observe laws and regulations are granted the rights and privileges accruing to full members of the society. In the second case, children and adults living in poverty soon learn to see themselves as burdens and victims in permanent contention with government bureaucrats. In the 1960s, government waged a war against poverty; in the second decade of the twenty-first century, it continues to wage a war against the poor, as Herbert Gans (1995) first noticed.

To be poor in the United States is not solely about material deprivation but also about being subjected to perennial supervision and intrusiveness on the part of agents of the state. Deep privation exists throughout the world, but in most countries, the state does not have the financial and human resources necessary to invade the lives of vulnerable citizens on a routine basis. The opposite is true about the United States, where a large bureaucratic engine has taken shape over time to interfere with the lives of vulnerable citizens. It is the unique part played by the American State—what I call distorted engagement—in combination with capital retrogression and the operations of predatory commerce that best explains American destitution.

By drawing attention to the role of the American government in the reproduction of conditions that perpetuate dispossession, my aim is to invigorate an intellectual dialogue about the liberal state in the age of economic globalization. For too long, studies of poverty have either condemned the government or understood it as the instrument of remediation. It is time to reconsider the public institutions that contribute to the maintenance of irregular conditions in American cities. That, I contend, must be part of a future progressive agenda.

Since the 1960s, neoconservative intellectuals have been assailing without respite the unintended effects of social legislation aimed at ameliorating poverty in American cities. Although there is no dearth of names among those who see the government as a problem rather than a solution—starting with President Ronald Reagan—the political scientist Charles Murray stands alone in his capacity not only to summarize conservative grievances but also to make them work. Murray is the author of two major works that have influenced the nation's political thinking. One, *The Bell Curve* (1994, with Richard J. Herrnstein), explored the differential distribution of intelligence across racial and class lines. It became a best-seller and continues to be reprinted, giving testimony to its resonance in wide circles.

Even more important was Murray's earlier publication *Losing Ground: American Social Policy, 1950–1980* (1984), a book that indicted welfare policies for creating the wrong market incentives, for example, leading young women to have children to qualify for government support. In Murray's imagination, girls like Towanda Forrest, whose story is told in this book, deliberately engage in premature sex and sustain pregnancies as a function of government's misplaced incentives. The condition of pregnancy—nine months of physical discomfort followed by years of demands on behalf of wanted or unwanted children—is envisioned by Murray and like-minded thinkers as a price well worth paying to receive welfare benefits. Yet in 1994, the year that Towanda delivered her first child at the age of fourteen, the average welfare payment was less than three hundred dollars per month for a mother and two children: an amount hardly worth the need for deception or the complications of motherhood. Other factors more plausibly explain the behavior of girls like Towanda: social isolation, a paucity of material resources, and, significantly, a desire to attain adult status in deprived environments where few alternatives exist.

Notwithstanding its gross overstatements, ideological bias, and plain disregard for facts, *Losing Ground* was a decisive force contributing to welfare reform under the Clinton administration. It was not scientific rigor that consecrated Murray's work but its capacity to capture public resentment against poor, mostly Black, people.

Ostensibly, Murray's books were about the social distribution of intelligence in the case of *The Bell Curve* and about welfare dependency in the case of *Losing Ground*, but those two themes were secondary to a larger ax to grind, the author's libertarian belief that government interference with the normal functioning of markets leads to unanticipated, deleterious consequences that wreak havoc and induce moral corrosiveness. In that sense, Murray may be seen as an intellectual heir of Herbert Spencer, who equated the workings of society to those of nature and likened the poor to unfit animals best left to fend for themselves, and die, to preserve the purity of civilization.[2]

The musings of neoconservatives like Charles Murray are in correspondence with Spencer's harsh ideology; they envision poverty not as the effect of collective neglect and state inaction but as evidence of the lack of qualities that enable the fit to survive. *The Bell Curve*'s ultimate target was not the distribution of intelligence per se but affirmative action programs that were said to promote educational and economic advancement among categories of undeserving people with little intellectual capacity. *Losing Ground* was, in the end, a plea for the government to reduce wasteful spending on social programs that encourage the poor to reproduce.

Such ideas are ingrained in large segments of American society. For that reason, opportunistic politicians use them in their attempts to galvanize constituencies. Evidence of that was provided in 2010 by South Carolina's lieutenant governor Andre Bauer when he compared poor people on welfare to stray animals. Providing hungry people with an "ample food supply," said Bauer only encourages them to breed more poor wretches whom the state is forced to feed. Such statements were uttered even as South Carolina reached a nearly 13 percent unemployment rate, partly as a result of the largest economic downturn the nation had experienced since the Great Depression of the 1930s.

Similar in tone were Mitt Romney's remarks, during the 2012 presidential campaign, about 47 percent of Americans who, in his words, "are dependent upon government, who believe that they are victims; who believe that government has a responsibility to care for them; who believe that they are entitled to health care, to food, to housing, to you name it." By defining people with incomes too small to pay federal taxes as takers and moochers, Romney was tapping widespread veins of public resentment against the poor. The racial overtones in such comments were latent.

While conservatives and libertarians denounce the shortcomings of the government and devalue its constructive, developmental role, liberals see the state as part of the solution to social inequities. Having inherited the views of nineteenth-century utilitarians like John Stuart Mill (1825/1984) and Jeremy Bentham (1781/2007), liberals tend to agree that the government *can* improve social well-being by conferring access to vital economic, social, and political resources.

Outlooks first made cogent by Mill and Bentham also echo in the works of contemporary sociologists and policy makers who support government actions to uplift the poor and marginalized. Authors like William Julius Wilson, a major contributor to our understanding of the factors that perpetuate poverty in America's inner cities, or Douglas Massey, the most courageous voice denouncing residential segregation, see the government as part of the solution to socioeconomic disparities. Their ideas should have long ago informed comprehensive and proactive policies toward urban poverty.

Noting the success of the American developmental state, as I do in this book, should not preclude a critique of the government's distorted engagement with the poor or the feeble effectiveness of palliative programs in existence today. Social engineering and the criminalization of poverty have proved to be less effective than universalistic programs fostering social inclusion and material accumulation. Conservatives and libertarians may lack compassion, but liberals and progressives have often yielded to the ambivalent character of benevolence; admirable intentions have been thwarted by the conditional, punitive character of government largesse.

The unintended effects of ambivalent benevolence are mostly felt in America's inner cities, where millions of impoverished, racially distinct families struggle for survival. It is in their behalf that ameliorative social legislation has been introduced over the years, the failings of which are seldom if ever acknowledged or investigated by liberal thinkers. Constructive understanding and action cannot be advanced until a reappraisal of existing legislation on behalf of the poor is undertaken. That includes more precise research into the unanticipated effects of agencies like Child Protective Services which tend to combine both failure in addressing egregious abuses and hypervigilance in relation to less serious transgressions. A thread running through the chapters in this book is how such government actions have further fractured the weakened authority that adults hold vis-à-vis children in poor neighborhoods.

In other words, an honest reappraisal of the forces that delay and diminish the full incorporation of impoverished inner-city populations into society must entail a frontal encounter with liberal policies that have eroded the agency of people already living in squalor, poverty, and despair. To do so is not to countenance the cruelties woven into much conservative thinking but to open up the black box of ideological persuasion to contemplate dispassionately the ways in which the developmental state has failed the urban poor.

Influential accounts of poverty tend to be oblique or unabashedly partial with respect to the state. Inattention to the workings of bureaucracies is evident even in the writings of liberal-minded authors who endorse the government's ameliorative functions. Such approaches neglect the effects of distorted engagement.[3] The state is thus signified but not explained. Remaining invisible are the dynamics and consequences of repeated contact between government agents and their clients.

My analysis thus deviates from both liberal and conservative ideologies. I see no compelling evidence of the state either as forthright reformer or as farcical entity in opposition to the market. The two are figments in the imagination of politicians and pundits operating in a context marked by the narrowest of political spectrums. More precise is a conceptualization of the state as a dynamic but fragmented apparatus of governance, a platform where interests at odds in the larger society battle and seek resolution. Antagonism but also collaboration marks the historical relationship between bureaucracies and civil society.

The limitations of public policy are real, but not for the reasons adduced by ideologues. For example, the false assumptions behind programs promoting economic betterment through behavioral modification—the mainstay of palliation—are exposed by mounting research on the working poor, who tend to lead conventional lives adhering for the most part to normative values. Contradicting charges of idleness, they hold jobs that indeed represent rapidly growing portions of the American economy. Yet their wages cannot lift them out of poverty. More relevant to their lives than behavioral deficits are the absence of standard markets and, more precisely, the anomalous interaction of supply and demand for reasons external to economic logic. Capital defection, redlining, residential segregation, and White flight are all forces that work against the capacity of individuals to rise above destitution.

Seen through that lens, the conservative critique of the state seems backward. It was the exodus of investment of the kind that led to prosperity among European immigrants and their descendants that first created vacuums in inner cities that were later occupied by the public sector. From training programs to urban renewal, from public works to empowerment zones, all have been attempts at filling the spaces left empty by capital disinvestment. The deviance and listlessness blamed on the misadventures of the welfare state may be better understood as adaptations to environments surviving on the margins of capitalism. Overwhelming bureaucratic interference and its unforeseen consequences are thus secondary effects of capitalist devolvement.

Since I first began compiling data for this project in the 1990s, many changes have eventuated in the city of Baltimore but few have affected the entrenched character of poverty in its western neighborhoods. A report by the Brookings Institution released in 2012 calls on policy makers and public intellectuals to rethink economic development in the region by pointing to a disturbing trend: a mounting share of low-wage jobs shutting more and more residents out of the middle class. The number of jobs in largely low-paying industries such as retail and food service grew in the Baltimore region more than 60 percent between 1980 and 2007, while jobs increased 36 percent in middle-wage fields and less than 10 percent in high-wage fields.[4] Economic changes that have dramatically improved the odds for professionals have also brought about the expansion of low-paying jobs that are increasingly temporary and bereft of the benefits once attached to membership in labor unions. Employment in low-wage industries accounted for 31 percent of the Baltimore region's employment in 2007, up from 26 percent a generation earlier (Vey 2012). Such shifts have occurred gradually, and they preceded the Great Recession of 2008.

In that respect, Baltimore reflects broader trends in the larger society—the evolution of two nations, one benefiting from technological changes, higher levels of formal instruction, and growing capital accumulation whose members live in comparatively safe spaces; another nation rendered superfluous and clustered in depleted, segregated neighborhoods out of view to those with power. That bifurcation transcends national boundaries. It has been a major effect of globalization and neoliberal economic policies applied throughout large swatches of the planet since the 1980s. Across international borders, professionals in what Saskia Sassen (2001) calls "global cities" have never done better. The landscape also looks good for service providers whose labor cannot be exported to export-processing zones in the less developed world. In advanced countries, such workers are often immigrants working in a plurality of sectors ranging from the hospitality industry to landscaping, construction, and agriculture.

At the bottom of this new world are people like those found in West Baltimore, domestic minorities made increasingly redundant by global economic integration. Their ancestors have resided in the United States for several centuries, and as a result, their aspirations are those of mainstream Americans, but their circumstances give them little access to the benefits of employment and political participation. Many are no longer employable not just as a result of persisting discrimination but also because they do not have the skills or deportment required by either high-paying or low-paying occupations. Mired in scarcity and living in dejected urban areas, they are nominal citizens for whom the benefits of true inclusion are rarely available.

Nearly twenty years have elapsed since I first started gathering information about the lives acknowledged in this book. During that period, only minor scattered improvements have taken place with respect to violent deaths, levels of incarceration, drug commerce, early motherhood, school abandonment, and the proportion of female-headed households in West Baltimore. The persistence of impoverishment over time is a blotch in the otherwise luminous trajectory of the nation.

Most of the individuals and families whose experience I memorialize in these pages still reside in the same places where I first met them or in their proximity. Those who were little boys and girls in the 1990s now have children of their own and face as parents the same challenges that their mothers and fathers faced when I first knew them. For the most part, they are repeating the cycle of misery and hopelessness that for generations have been the mark of urban poverty in the United States. Some are now dead or serving lengthy prison sentences. Miraculously, many continue to communicate with me through letters and visits but also by way of electronic mail and social media. They often lack resources to buy necessities, including food, but they pool accounts in Facebook to stay in touch with family, friends, and acquaintances—a small but informative detail revealing their yearning to connect with the larger society.

At the beginning of this book, as an epigraph, I included words tendered by Joseph Campbell, the most accomplished mythologist of the twentieth century. In *The Hero with a Thousand Faces* (1949), he wrote that "by following the thread of the hero path, we shall come to the standard of our own existence." My long-term incursions in West Baltimore, one of the most dejected ghettos in the nation, thrust me into dialogue with hundreds of imperfect but heroic people whose lives had been irreparably shaped by neglect, disrespect, and constant danger stemming from others around them but also from the very institutions designed to address their needs.

Despite impossible odds and monumental barriers, they kept trying to overcome—those single mothers on welfare with the bad attitude; those unemployed men hustling in the streets; those youngsters riffing and bantering, lost in perennial drama, seeking to be valued while being targeted as pollutants by agents of the state. They kept struggling, those people, those families, those children, often with humor, determination, and faith. They fought despite the leveling forces of bureaucratic intrusion, predatory commerce, and disinvestment. Knowing them brought me closer to an appreciation of our common humanity.

As I complete this book, I wonder whether America too, the country that generously embraced my ambitions, will come to the standard of its own existence by redressing the historical omissions that resulted in the marginalization of poor, racially distinct people. They were all children once and open to possibility; countless are beginning their years in circumstances that belie the nation's promise of fair play and inclusiveness. Many who are only now starting their lives have had their biographies written long before they were born.

Here too, the words of Joseph Campbell are pertinent because by thinking of impoverished urban residents as not fully American, by casting them as different and alien, by tagging them as an *abomination*, we have failed to notice how much they are like us and how their full inclusion in the society is a precondition for our own collective affirmation. I thought I was traveling outward when deepening my acquaintance with people living in Baltimore's western tracts without realizing that I was moving toward the very core of my being. The same could be true about America, the America that still waits.

APPENDIX: SAMPLE OF HOUSEHOLDS IN WEST BALTIMORE (1997)

MAIN PROVIDERS/HEADS OF HOUSEHOLD ARE LISTED FIRST IN BOLD type. Irregular/itinerant household members are included in parentheses. Ages are given in parentheses after each name. Names of children *not* in household appear in brackets. Permanently employed men 16–55 years of age are marked with an asterisk (*). Total number of household members = 263.

1. **Donald B. Wilson*** (55)
   Beverly Wilson (50)
   [Robert] (25)
   [Teresa] (23)
   Donald (18)

2. **Benita Wallace** (33)
   (Herbert Mudd) (25)
   Jamal (2)

3. **Illiad Harwick** (25)
   (Floyd Twigg Sr.) (34)
   Shatirya (4)
   Persia (2)
   [Melinda] (17)
   [Floyd Jr.] (14)

4. **Rita Twigg** (38)
   (Ernie Twigg, father) (50)
   Enoch (19)
   Lewis (15)
   Jabar (12)
   Lawrence (7)

5. **Lucy Twigg** (30)
   (Anthony Moore) (33)
   Davon (10)
   Karla (8)

6. **Missie Forrest** (60)
   Deborah Forrest, her sister (56)

7. **Lydia Forrest** (46)
   (Reuben Chapman, deceased)   James Culver* (42)
   [Reuben] (28)   Felicia (19)
   [Lorenzo*] (26)   Tawanda (17)
                                  James (15)
                                  Clarise, her great-niece (16)

8. **Lucinda Wilkins** (35)
   Frank Wilkins* (33)
   Jared (17)
   Aaron (14)
   Rufus (11)
   Abel (11)

9. **Tamika Lawson** (21)
   (Frank Wilkins) (33)
   Alonso (4)

10. **Jacquanda Booker** (25)
   (Anton Freeman*) (29)
   Camilla (6)
   Livia (3)

11. **Alita Rogers** (26)
   (Damon Artis) (30)
   Damon (9)
   Amyra (5)

12. **Margaret Lawson** (27)
(Henry Brown*) (29)　Peter Lawson (29)
　　Demetrius (10)　Beth (7)
　　　　Flora (5)
　　　　Mary (5)

13. **Adele Samuels** (37)
　Darnell (12)
　　Philip (9)
　　Erma (5)

14. **Susan Daniels** (32)　David Smith* (35)
(Thomas Cameron) (31)　Anna (10)
　Tyrell (15)　Lily (7)

15. **Wanda Foreman** (19)
(Cato Young) (27)
　Marquis (3)

16. **Amelia Thomas** (39)
(Oliver Mason*) (40)
　Adrianne (20)
　Elisa (17)
　Corale (13)
　Nigel (Elisa's son) (1)

17. **Kiyah Mason** (25)
(Raymon Franks) (25)
　Tarah (7)
　Farrid (5)

18. **Davnia Fitzpatrick** (22)
(Cyrus Ferguson) (26)　Michael Carson* (25)
　Amanda (7)　Otis (4)
　　　Leon (2)

19. **Alfonso Davis*** (30)
(Alina Thomas) (25)
　Carmen Davis (his mother) (47)
　Emma (9)
　Elizabeth (7)
　Emile (4)

20. **Mary Washington** (30)
(Calvin Porter*) (32)　Alfred Morris (31)
　Sammy (14)　Eliza (10)
　　　Titus (6)
　　　Eddie (3)

21. **Marsha Cummings** (34)
　Rhonda (14)

22. **Karen Miller** (37)
　Latricia (15)
　Kimberley (13)
　Cameron (10)

23. **Moira Simpson** (31)
　Taresha (13)
　Tyron (10)

24. **Helen Moore** (29)
(Tobby Ellis) (28)
　Chantal (14)

25. **Anna Issacs** (32)
(Tony Love) (34)　August Martin
　Arnie (16)　Joyce (14)

26. **Elsa Rowe** (27)
　Ruddy (8)

27. **Marsha Garrett** (22)
Deiondre Garrett (16), her brother
　Alain (6)
　Brenda (4)

28. **Loretta Gladstone** (55)
Oscar Miner (14), her grandson

29. **Regina Brown** (33)
　Reggie (16)
　Dalia (14)

30. **Allysia Burrows** (24)
(Tarrell Chambliss) (26)
　Allison (6)

31 **Aletta Rodgers** (29)
　Dante Washington (11)
　Venus Morgan (7)

32. **Tracy Bartlett** (37)
　Latanya (20)
　Laurent (16)
　Nikki (10)
　Tasha (8)
　Evanda (Latanya's daughter) (2)

33. **Corinna Barrett** (35)
(Tim Marvin*) (38)
　Latisha (18)
　Jayden (16)

34. **Laila Armstrong** (40)
(Christian Jones*) (38)
　Lisa (16)
　Tercell (8)

35. **Moriah Hunter** (36)
Christopher Lewis (36)
　Makayla (16)
　Tiana (12)
　Elijah (8)

36. **Amanda Owens** (22)
(Carlos Brand) (25)
　Diamond (4)
　Caleb (1)

37. **Katrina Spencer** (23)
　Brandon (3)
　Nevaeh (1)

38. **Maggie Laughton** (44)
(William Ambler) (40?)
　Joshua (15)
　Carmina (10)
　Darcy (9)

39. **LaShawn Carson** 24
(Alvin Asher*) (26)
　Mercedes (8)
　Jasmine (6)
　Justin Carson (15, her brother)

40. **Norma Bench** (27)
Gabriel Bench* (30)
　Jamal (9)
　Brenda (7)

41. **Amanda Owens** (22)
   Malik (4)
   Jada (2)

42. **Katherine Spencer** (23)
   (Terrence Fowler) (24)   (David Richards) (27)
   Terrence (8)   Kiara (5)
              Hailey (3)

43. **Alina Cummings** (37)
   (Trevor Marsh) (38)
   Trevor (14)
   Xavier (12)

44. **Mary Spencer** (27)
   Lotta (2)

45. **Sulima Omar** (29)
   Mohamed (9)
   Imani (6)
   Aliyah (4)

46. **Leona Mitchell** (45)
   Jeremiah Mitchell* (47)
   Angela (20)
   Chloe (17)
   Gabrielle (14)
   Tommy (10)

47. **Angelina Johnson** (36)
   Gary Johnson* (38)
   Glenn (18)
   Brianna (15)
   Alexis (13)

48. **Nellie Williams** (59)
   Marcus Williams II* (60)
   Marcus (40)
   [Romulus] (32)
   [Minerva] (30)

49. **Sharon Belay** (39)
   (Marcus Williams III*) (40)
   Shennelle (20)
   Emmanuel (18)
   Tamika (15)

50. **Cecilia Worden** (21)
   Destiny (3)
   Andrew (1)

51. **Isabel Andrews** (35)
   (Joseph Handler)(39)   (Jacob Jackson) (37)
   Hector (15)   Jackie (10)
              Sabastian (8)

52. **Audrey Morrison** (30)
   (Walter Akers) (32)
   Sara (13)
   Pamela (10)
   Camilla (8)

53. **Tory Campbell** (23)
   Candice (4)
   Desiree (1)

54. **Rebecca Graves** (27)
   Lucy (8)
   Maurice (5)

55. **Nancy Keeler** (33)
   Brettellen (17)
   Victoria (10)
   Martin (7)
   Jonathan (5)

56. **Donna Gibson** (24)
   (Alfred Gomes) (25)
   Alford (7)
   Amber (5)
   Daphnee (2)

57. **Sarah Wilson** (23)
   (Jerome Tate) (24)
   Anastasia (5)
   Dionne(3)

58. **Diana Metcalfe** (30)
   Terrie (13)
   Kirsten (10)
   Dennisse (8)

59. **Kate Peters** (35)
   (Warren McGee) (35)   Austin Madison (36)
   Antonio (15)   Bryan (10)
   Trisha (13)   Olivia (7)
              Andrea (5)

60. **Suzanna Fellows** (24)
   Leena (5)
   Fiona (3)
   Caesar ()

NOTES

INTRODUCTION

1. Over the last fifty years, increased urbanization, rapid transportation, and dazzling technological advances have resulted in the compression of time and the acceleration of human activity. This, in turn, has had a profound impact on research as a knowledge-producing enterprise. Most of us cannot engage in deep immersion within communities studied over a period of years. Ethnographic accounts, like those that made anthropology into a royal enterprise in the early decades of the twentieth century, are now rare. Instead, we gather quotations from interviews with people in small samples to illustrate preexisting arguments. I was fortunate to enjoy the luxury of time spent in the pursuit of familiarity and systematic observation in West Baltimore for nearly ten years. The result was a longitudinal view of the chain of events that articulate social action among impoverished families and individuals.

2. In addition to works focusing on the state's relationship to the urban poor, there is a profuse literature about the challenges faced by impoverished people living in cities. Robert K. Merton, a towering figure in sociology, foreshadowed subsequent efforts in his article "Social Structure and Anomie" (1938), where he distinguished between social means and ends, observing that the condition of poverty entails the internationalization of mainstream norms, values, and aspirations but not the possession of material and social resources to realize them. The stories told in this book are recent illustrations of Merton's lasting insight.

Similarly, writings about the role of race in urban settings abound in sociology, providing a rich reserve of knowledge. They span more than a century and include W.E.B. DuBois's *The Philadelphia Negro* (1899/2012); William Foote Whyte's *Street Corner Society* (1943/1993); St. Clair Drake and Horace Cayton's *Black Metropolis* (1945/1993); Jay MacLeod's *Ain't No Makin' It* (1987/1995); Philippe Bourgois's *In Search of Respect* (1996); Michèle Lamont's *The Dignity of Working Men* (2002); Mary Patillo-McCoy's *Black Picket Fences* (2000); Steven Gregory's *Black Corona* (1999); and Elijah Anderson's *Streetwise* (1999); *Code of the Street* (2000); and *A Place in the Corner* (2003).

Publications on poverty and inequality range from durable ethnographic accounts like those by Elliot Liebow (1967) and Carol Stack (1971/1997) to more recent efforts by Katherine Newman (2000; 2008); Barbara Ehrenreich (2011); Kathryn Edin and Laura Lein(1997), Kathryn Edin and Maria Kefalas (2007); Kathryn Edin and Timothy J.

Nelson (2013); Mitchell Duneier (1994); Duneier, Hasan, and Carter (2000); Sudhir Alladi Venkatesh (2002, 2008, 2009), Mario Small (2004; 2010); Martín Sanchez-Jankowski (1991); Philippe Bourgois (1996); and Bourgois and Schonberg (2009), among others. Such works represent a long and honorable tradition expanding knowledge about social and racial inequality but also humanizing the dispossessed and marginalized. All have had justifiable influence and constitute the remarkable tapestry of scholarly accomplishment against which this book offers its contribution.

3. See Leiter 1980; Geertz 1988; Miles and Huberman 1984; McCracken 1988; Van Maanen, 1983, 2011; Denzin 1989; Gladwin 1989; Marshall and Rossman 1989.

4. To paraphrase Michael H. Agar, quantitative strategies can be used to discern the extent to which a phenomenon occurs in a larger universe; qualitative research is most appropriate to elucidate what the phenomenon means or, in fact, whether it exists at all (Agar 1985).

5. Community mapping involves the identification of key informants whose position in a particular social network makes them superior sources of information about specific locations. Traversing a street, a neighborhood, or a district in the company of such persons while they describe lived experiences is an ideal way to understand the spatial distribution of resources whether material or virtual.

6. With Max Weber (2004) and Clifford Geertz (1977), I believe that the ethnographer's goal is to re-present social processes with precision and to assume responsibility for interpretation. My hope is that years of experience and a disciplined eye have turned empathy into a source of clarification and knowledge, not partiality. To enhance the production of organized knowledge is, in fact, the whole point of ethnographic research.

CHAPTER 1. D. B. WILSON

1. See Best 2007 and Lemann 1992.

2. In his body of work, Elijah Anderson provides a compelling analysis of "old heads" and their relationship to new generations of young Black men in tough urban neighborhoods.

3. Latrobe 1941: 47.

4. Latrobe 1941: 58.

5. Latrobe 1941: 25.

6. Latrobe 1941: 27.

7. Latrobe 1941: 56.

8. Latrobe 1941: 54.

9. In its heyday, Koppers was more than a factory. Creative talent and innovation flourished within its walls. Four renowned metallurgical engineers originally from South Dakota—Paul Anderson, Tracy Jarrett, Erle Hubbard and Arthur Schuck—were credited with major improvements in the strength and durability of aircraft parts. At Koppers they produced an alloyed cast-iron piston ring that enabled pre-jet U.S. bombers and fighter planes to extend their operating ranges. Their efforts made possible nonstop ocean crossings and longer flights over Europe. In recognition to their contributions, the four men were awarded the Navy Silver Star (Latrobe 1941).

10. Such feelings are identical to those discussed by Jane Jacobs in her influential book, *The Death and Life of Great American Cities* (1961).

CHAPTER 2. BALTIMORE: FROM FACTORY TOWN TO CITY IN DECLINE

1. Globalization connected mostly regions in Asia, Europe, Latin America, the Caribbean, and North America—large geographical swaths were left out of the process (Centeno and Cohen 2010). Nevertheless, its repercussions were deeply felt in the United States.

2. The rising demand for personal services and customized products on the part of new professional classes stimulated the employment of immigrants. As Sassen (2001) has noted, old industrial centers, like New York, rebounded as *global cities* where fast-growing world trade is coordinated and where professionals coexist with low-skilled immigrants and displaced native-born workers, many of them African American.

3. A Roman Catholic, he governed in the spirit of religious inclusiveness, instigating the passage of the Toleration Act of 1649, one of the first laws requiring religious forbearance in British possessions. As a result, and in subsequent years, Protestants but also Catholics and Quakers moved in large numbers to Maryland and, later on, to Baltimore, a newly minted city whose evolution was marked from the outset by immigration. That trend has continued to the present.

4. Congress met in one of the city's landmark buildings, the Henry Fite House, from December 1776 to February 1777, effectively turning Baltimore into the capital of the United States during that period. Later, during the Battle of Baltimore—waged as part of the War of 1812—Francis Scott Key, a Maryland lawyer, wrote the poem that would, in 1931, become the national anthem.

5. It was also one of the largest shipbuilding companies in the world and a powerful symbol of American leadership in industrial manufacturing. During World War II, the Sparrows Point Shipyard became a main location for the U.S. government's Emergency Shipbuilding Program to help restore the British Merchant Navy. Liberty ships were its specialty—many of them built at the Koppers Company, where Donald B. Wilson (chapter 1) worked for nineteen years.

6. Some African Americans rose to prominence in business and the arts. By the outbreak of World War I, a small Black middle class had moved into houses along Eutaw Place, Druid Hill Avenue, Madison Avenue, and Mosher Street, formerly occupied by German Jews who, at that time, were moving to suburban developments (Chapelle 2000: 168).

7. In the eyes of the world, and thanks to the efforts of politicians and marketers, Baltimore is "Charm City," a moniker meant to invite, not repel. Yet the new service economy has not met employment demand among the most vulnerable urban dwellers—youngsters and low-skilled workers. Long gone are the days when Baltimore was seen primarily as a gritty factory town.

8. The civil disturbances of the late 1960s also resulted in a massive exodus of Jewish-owned businesses. Jewish-owned jewelry stores and pawn shops, Laundromats and cleaners, grocery stores, and dress shops were sold to a fresh wave of mostly Korean entrepreneurs. As in other similar neighborhoods throughout the United States, there is resentment against the new shopkeepers in West Baltimore, who tend to live away from the inner city and whose merchandise is sold at comparatively high prices. Other than a limited number of jobs afforded by small businesses, there are virtually no employment opportunities in the area.

CHAPTER 3. BIG FLOYD

1. At the time, strict regulations barred women receiving public assistance from living with men or receiving money from them or other sources.

2. For a superb rendition of America's romance with illegal drugs and the way they affected impoverished neighborhoods, see Jonnes 1996.

3. CNN All Politics 1998.

4. See Lincoln 1994; *New York Times* 1994.

CHAPTER 4. INTERSECTIONS OF POVERTY, RACE, AND GENDER IN THE AMERICAN GHETTO

1. Such calculations do not include women working in the informal economy and therefore underestimate the actual number of women working for pay.

2. Since then, the U.S. prison population has declined somewhat. In 2012, the number of individuals in U.S. jails and prisons stood at 1,571,013 (U.S. Bureau of Justice Statistics 2013).

3. An identical number of White women were welfare recipients that year, but they represented a smaller proportion of total White women than Black women did as a percentage of all African American women in the nation.

4. An example was Donald Wilson's enthusiasm after being promoted to head chauffeur at the Koppers Company—a modest position by the standards of more affluent people but, in his mind, a great achievement for a young man from the rural South.

5. Clustered in inner cities with decaying infrastructures, negligible investment, and ineffectual schools, new generations of Black American men are more likely to be permanently unemployed than their ancestors. They increasingly constitute a nonworking class whose existence challenges previous hopes for assimilation.

6. Modern-day gangs formed by Blacks and Latinos represent the last iteration of an enduring phenomenon. The Neapolitan Camorra and Sicilian Mafia bear witness to similar developments among the poor of previous generations. *West Side Story* (1961), a jewel of American cinematography, features a stylized portrayal of gangs in Manhattan's working-class neighborhoods during the 1950s. Martin Scorsese's *Gangs of New York* (2002) reenacts the confrontation between Irish immigrants and native-born Americans that turned nineteenth-century New York into a cauldron of street warfare. Attachment to gangs has defined masculinity among working-class and impoverished youngsters since the beginning of modern urbanization. African American youths are no exception.

7. I pursue this subject at greater length in chapter 8.

8. I review the life of Emmanuel (Manny Man) Travis Williams in chapter 15).

9. Since the implementation of Temporary Aid for Needy Families (TANF) in 1996, under the Clinton administration, the focus of public assistance has been on families rather than individual women. In the spirit of reform, that program has also supported literacy and job training as well as the provision of child care and health services. Despite such improvements, TANF continues a pattern of tough bureaucratic supervision and harsh penalties for noncompliance, all features inimical to the cultivation of permanent relationships between men and women (Cancian and Danzinger 2009; Danzinger and Haveman 2001).

CHAPTER 5. SHAPING THE INNER CITY: URBAN DEVELOPMENT AND THE AMERICAN STATE

1. Ironically, the effectiveness of the American State has paralleled the dissemination of views maintaining that personal effort and market competition, not government action, are the sole causes of social and economic success. Antigovernment attitudes have grown even as more Americans become the beneficiaries of effective public policy. No image is more revelatory in that respect than that of vociferous protesters opposing health care reform in 2009 and 2010 out of a concern that the new laws might diminish benefits under Medicare, a vintage government program.

2. Historically, Hispanics, especially those of Mexican ancestry, have constituted a solid working class with few avenues for social ascent, but they have not, until recently, faced a danger of entrenched and concentrated poverty. Puerto Ricans represent an exception to that generalization. Over the last two decades, however, Hispanics—second- and third-generation Mexicans and Central Americans, in particular—show signs of what Portes and Zhou (1993) call "downward assimilation."

3. Gunder Frank (1967) revolutionized theories of socioeconomic development by reconceptualizing poverty in Latin America as a product of that region's subordination in the world economy. Capitalist processes of extraction, distorted industrialization, and dependence on the production of agricultural and mining commodities reproduce inequalities and dispossession among large segments of the population in that part of the word.

4. Ironically, homesteading became the epitome, not of cooperation between public and private sectors, but of achievement through rugged individualism. That interpretation, made popular by the TV series *Little House on the Prairie* (1974–83), was first put forth in the books for children penned by Laura Ingalls Wilder (1932; 1994) whose daughter, Rose Wilder Lane, a novelist and political theorist, was—with Ayn Rand and Isabel Peterson—a founder of American libertarianism. Despite such bucolic renditions that emphasized success through personal effort alone, homesteading was also made possible by government action.

5. A large body of research, spearheaded by Alejandro Portes (1981), shows that only a small number of factors determine successful assimilation and upward mobility: social tolerance, economic options, and incentives to education. More than nationality or cultural idiosyncrasies, such features have determined success or failure across generations.

6. I provide an overview of that evolution in chapters 1 and 2 of this book.

CHAPTER 6. DISTORTED ENGAGEMENT AND LIMINAL INSTITUTIONS: RULING AGAINST THE POOR

1. The Social Security Administration, the Department of Veterans Affairs, Medicare offices, motor vehicle administrative centers and even the Internal Revenue Service are among such mainstream institutions.

2. Between 1962 and 1996, Aid for Families with Dependent Children (AFDC), the bulwark of welfare as understood by most Americans, consumed on the average $12 billion per year (including administration, benefits, and emergency assistance). In 1992 AFDC and food stamps cost $24.9 billion. Together, the two programs

constituted 2 percent of a combined federal, state, and local budget of $2,500 billion (Library of Congress 1992). By comparison, the same year, Medicare took $131 billion; Defense, $281 billion; and Social Security, $305 billion.

3. In that famous instance, *Buck vs. Bell*, heard by the U.S. Supreme Court in 1927, the woman, her mother, and her child were White. The Justice writing the decision was none other than Oliver Wendell Jones Jr., whose memorable words encapsulated the fundamental questions in the case: "Three generations of imbeciles is enough," he affirmed, echoing public concerns about the genetic threats presented by impoverished and damaged mothers. Nonetheless, as Stephen Jay Gould (1985) discovered, none of the women around whom the case was built were mentally deficient (see also Lombardo 2008). The connection between poverty and mental impairment was mostly assumed.

4. The focus on the sexual conduct of impoverished people is related to an even deeper concern over fairness. The thinking is that undeserving individuals should not exploit the good intentions of taxpayers. Bureaucratic procedures reflect that anxiety by restricting the right to privacy of indigent individuals and families. A recent example is the requirement that people receiving food stamps undergo drug tests, which was included in bills introduced in 2013 by members of the U.S. House of Representatives. Although most of those laws have not been implemented, they are evidence of the differential treatment toward the poor. Even Michael Bloomberg, New York's progressive mayor, supported such policies. In the words of the political analyst Mark Shields, "it appears corrosive to the nation's character to provide children with food stamps but it does not seem corrosive for corporations to receive huge government subsidies—it's a strange moral standard" (Shields 2013).

5. Such women illustrate feelings and emotions that were artfully portrayed by Ken Kesey in *One Flew Over the Cuckoo's Nest* (1963).

6. Terms like "exploitation," "oppression," or "dispossession" are seldom included in government reports or academic narratives. Exceptions to that generalization are left-of-center analyses, which capture little public attention and are frequently portrayed as the ranting of ideological extremists.

CHAPTER 7. LITTLE FLOYD

1. Outsiders find hard to believe the regularity with which children in poor neighborhoods face the probability of death or injury. Presented with the terrifying facts, they conclude that violence is rooted in culture. "People won't talk about it for fear of criticism," one of my colleagues at the Hopkins Institute for Policy Studies told me once, "but no matter how you cut it, Blacks are more violent and disorganized." Culture is a convenient term to explain away contextual forces. Violent behaviors are facilitated by the shape and content of physical environments (Sampson 2013; Sharkey 2013; Wacquant 1998).

2. See also Kotlowitz (1992) and Venkatesh (2008).

3. In both cases, I was the sponsor.

CHAPTER 8. DOWN THE RABBIT HOLE: CHILDHOOD AGENCY AND THE PROBLEM OF LIMINALITY

1. For a more detailed discussion of liminal institutions and associated concepts refer to chapter 6.

2. Melvin Kohn's extensive research of the relationship between personality and work provides further evidence of the powerful effects of social and physical location on the construction of knowledge deployed to negotiate quotidian challenges (Kohn 1989). Echoes of the same general precept can be found in the literature on immigration, race, and ethnicity. Research on the immigrant enclave, for example, documents the extent to which membership in a group distinguished by national origin, place of destination, and type of economic insertion influences collective outlooks as well as the character of ethnic identity (Portes 1981; Fernández-Kelly and Konczal 2006).

3. All in all, programs aimed at alerting parents and their children about the perils of abuse are short on balance. Sexual and physical maltreatment are discussed at length, but children receive little information about appropriate forms of discipline. Increasingly, abuse becomes an all-encompassing term to designate discomfort.

4. The American Association of Black Social Workers, for instance, has successfully resisted the adoption of African American children by White families, equating that practice to genocide. Their aim has been to protect family integrity and support the reintegration of Black children to their parents, an urgent need in light of the facts—in 2013, there were 556,000 minors in foster care throughout the nation and 40 percent of them were of African ancestry (NABSW 2013).

CHAPTER 9. CLARISE

1. Heyns 1978.
2. Chapelle 2000: 133.
3. Alexander, Entwisle, and Olson 2001.
4. Putnam, Feldstein, and Cohen 2004; Will 1994.
5. As discussed in the next chapter, Jehovah's Witnesses are among the fastest-growing religious communities in America's inner cities. Their millenarian beliefs have found an echo in urban environments overwhelmed by violence, scarcity, and social disarray. For Witnesses, decency represents a pathway toward salvation. The world is a field where Satan and God battle continually; therefore, it must be shunned, together with everything that smacks of idolatry, including saintly images, flags, national holidays, and birthdays. Christmas and the Fourth of July are equally objectionable. The only exceptions allowed are a Passover observance to mark the birth of Jesus and regular attendance at meetings in Kingdom Hall, their stark worship space. While other denominations promote social engagement, Witnesses favor withdrawal. And, because all people must be given an opportunity for deliverance, they see proselytizing as a duty. To mark the Sabbath, they walk about in clusters knocking on doors, bringing to people the good news of the Bible. Residents in prosperous neighborhoods scoff at them, but for those left behind, Witnesses are the purveyors of dignity.

CHAPTER 10. PARADOXES OF SOCIAL CAPITAL: CONSTRUCTING MEANING, RECASTING CULTURE

1. In this analysis, I do not differentiate between normative goals and dominant (mainstream) values. Although there may be conceptual advantages in that differentiation to achieve some analytical purposes, here I assume that values mirror normative goals. My interest is in the relationship between what people *say they believe*

in and their *actual behaviors*. Whether there is correspondence between those two phenomena depends mostly on context, I contend.

2. A possible variant was Manny Man Travis Williams, whose actions were the fruit of both rebellion and innovation.

3. In chapter 8, I give attention to the same point as it relates to the diffusion of information connecting children with liminal government institutions. In both cases, the characteristics of social networks *and* their location in specific spaces determine the way in which information is processed, communicated, and used to shape behavior.

4. Although that concept was adumbrated since the nineteenth century, it was systematically developed in more recent times by writers like Glen Loury (1977), James Coleman (1988), and Pierre Bourdieu (1986).

5. I discuss that subject in greater detail in chapter 6.

6. Jeremy Boissevain (1974) prefigured similar ideas when proposing the term *multiplexity* to designate situations in which a single actor may provide advantages derived simultaneously from strong and weak ties to the same individual—a mother, for example, who is also a business executive can give her child emotional support but also a summer job or internship. Impoverished relatives, by comparison, are not in a position to act as agents of multiplexity.

7. More than fifty thousand copies of that influential book were sold in the three years after its first printing—an extraordinary achievement for an academic author.

8. There is an inextricable relationship between cultural and symbolic capital and I make no effort here to rigorously distinguish between the two. Cultural capital designates generalized behaviors frequently found among the members of a group; symbolic capital denotes more restricted expressions of an aesthetic character.

9. Heyns also found that large amounts of time watching television depress the internalization of formal knowledge among all kinds of children. By contrast, participation in library reading programs was strongly correlated to enhanced learning. Socioeconomic status and race had little impact on reading scores, especially among children who regularly used public libraries throughout the year.

10. While the average kindergarten learning rate was 1.65 test points per month, a standard deviation's advantage in socioeconomic status predicted a relative gain of 0.16 points per month during summer, 0.07 points per month during kindergarten, and 0.05 points per month during the first grade.

11. In his study, Gaddis included temporal factors, racial similarities, levels of trust, social-class differences and intergenerational closure as indicators of social capital.

12. Pairings involving children under high levels of stress at the beginning of their association with a Big Brother or Big Sister were likely to end prematurely, as were relationships involving college students as mentors.

13. Such studies confirm the importance of time spent in a relationship as an important factor explaining effect variations in community-based mentoring programs. Duration, in fact, tends to be associated with close relationships and strong programs.

14. Another way to conceptualize the same issues is this: all children can benefit from exposure to a plurality of individuals in constructive and enduring relationships with them. Very rich children too tend to experience high levels of insularity

because their interactions occur mostly with others like themselves. As a result, they are susceptible to forms of ignorance resulting from social separation, but an abundance of material resources protects them from deleterious effects. This protection is only effective in the absence of political mobilization or insurrection from the bottom up. When impoverished and marginal populations rise violently to fight oppression, multitudes of well-meaning but deeply ignorant people in positions of privilege face dire consequences.

CHAPTER 11. TOWANDA

1. Healthy Teen Network 2010.
2. The Murphy Homes, Baltimore's most notorious subsidized housing project, were leveled in 2002 as part of yet another attempt to scatter poor families around West Baltimore.

CHAPTER 12. CULTURAL CAPITAL AND THE TRANSITION TO ADULTHOOD IN THE URBAN GHETTO

1. Youngsters in Baltimore are more likely to have had sexual intercourse than those in the rest of the nation. One-fourth of young people in that city are out of school, and over 60 percent of them have had four or more sexual partners. Sexually transmitted diseases are three times Maryland's average; and the incidence of HIV/ AIDS is among the highest in the country.
2. In 2007, the Baltimore City teen birth rate was 66.4 births per thousand among girls aged fifteen to nineteen. That figure represented double the Maryland rate of 34.4 births per thousand (Baltimore City Health Department 2008) and was substantially greater than the U.S. rate of 42.5 per thousand females aged fifteen to nineteen (Hamilton, Martin, and Ventura 2011).
3. The alarm over teen pregnancies cannot be automatically attributed to racism. Other factors, including concern for the well-being of young mothers, are considered by legislators, government officials, and the public at large. Nevertheless, ideas about racial and cultural predispositions play a part also. In 1991, I interviewed ten top legislators and government officials in Baltimore. Seven answered in the affirmative when asked, "Do you believe that culture plays a role in the continuation of poverty among African Americans?" Five said yes when asked, "Do you believe that Blacks are more likely to fall into poverty because of their race?" An equal number agreed that teen pregnancies were probably influenced by inherited cultural and biological propensities. The size and nonrandom character of the sample precludes generalizations. However, I made no effort to interview atypical functionaries.
4. June is still the month of brides in the United States as a vestige of an earlier period, extending well into the 1950s, when marriage and babies followed graduation from high school.
5. The widespread consensus is that a family needs at least two adults who both earn adequate incomes to provide proper child care. Daniel Patrick Moynihan anticipated such ideas in *The Negro Family: The Case for National Action* (1965). In that influential report, he painted a dismal portrait in which presumed matriarchal domination and the absence of effective fathers among African Americans caused a

spectrum of social ills. His pessimistic outlook suggested that little could be done to correct the cultural deficits that cause premature births and early motherhood.

6. Tienda and Steir (1991) agree that diverse behavioral patterns are situational and that statistically normative patterns do not necessarily imply a deviation from social and cultural norms.

7. For a more detailed discussion of this point, see chapter 10.

8. Such are the perceptions that underlie the remarks of conservative pundits like Anne Coulter and libertarian writers like Charles Murray, whose latest book, *Coming Apart: The State of White America, 1960–2010* (2013), builds upon the notion that poverty is mostly a reflection of deviant cultural patterns.

9. More on this subject is discussed in chapter 17.

10. Respect is a key concept in the outlook of young people in poor neighborhoods. Germane to this point are Hannerz (1969), Wacquant and Wilson (1989), and Taub (1991).

11. In Taub's words (1991: 20): "In lieu of a material base where to hang the cloak of honor, impoverished blacks must find honor where possible and hold on to it. Since occupational achievement for men is limited, they have sought alternative sources of status, including the capacity to drink heavily, to fight well, and to have sexual prowess. Terms in ghetto language, such as 'pussy' to communicate lack of toughness, and 'dissing,' both point in the honor direction."

CHAPTER 14. FAITH AND CIRCUMSTANCE IN WEST BALTIMORE

1. Stories of downfall and redemption are as old as the Enûma Eliš, the Babylonian creation myth that, according to biblical scholars, inspired Genesis—the first book in the Judeo-Christian Pentateuch. Such narratives are the stuff that classic religious texts are made of, including the Old and New Testaments and the Holy Koran.

2. An exception is Crawford Sullivan 2012.

CHAPTER 15. MANNY MAN

1. For the best analysis yet of entrepreneurship in the times of formal segregation, see Butler 2005.

2. Orser 1997.

3. For complementary descriptions of young men's style and demeanor in inner-city neighborhoods, see Anderson 2000.

4. These are deliberate displays of self distinction. Not enough research has been conducted about body management and attire as reflections of what Portes and Zhou (1993) call "reactive formations" associated to downward social and economic mobility.

5. Vernacular term for "cash."

6. In the vernacular, "to throw a brick" means to commit a petty crime.

7. In the vernacular, a "twinkie" is a twenty-dollar bill.

8. In the vernacular, hundred-dollar bills.

9. In the vernacular, the term "nina" means nine of anything. Here it applies to 9 mm guns.

10. In the vernacular, helicopters.

11. This remark aptly illustrates the negative dimensions of social capital, more amply discussed in chapter 10.

CHAPTER 16. DIVIDED ENTREPRENEURSHIP AND NEIGHBORHOOD EFFECTS

1. The paucity of "bridging social capital" is a factor that influences business creation in ways similar to those affecting the educational prospects of children in poor neighborhoods I give attention to that subject in chapters 9 and 10.

2. For further discussion of this subject, see chapter 5.

3. Research on urban areas has also included community studies, conducted mostly by anthropologists, sociologists, and human geographers (Glennerster, Lupton, et al. 1999), that have taken a targeted approach and generally depend on ethnographic methods. Such studies focus mostly on impoverished populations with few comparative cases contrasting outcomes in affluent and deprived neighborhoods. Examples include work by Anderson (2003), Liebow (1967); Forrest and Kearns (2001); Meegan and Mitchell 2001; and Power and Mumford (1999).

4. As they point out, however, most observational studies of neighborhood effects are cross-sectional and do not account for changes over extended periods of time.

5. Brooks-Gunn's materialist approach is consistent with my research findings. When some of the children whose lives are acknowledged in this book were able to attend a parochial school, away from the dismal places where they lived, their academic scores consistently improved, as did their vocabulary and sense of where they belonged in the larger society. That was the case even for Little Floyd (chapter 7), a boy who had confronted extreme disadvantage from the moment of birth but whose standardized test scores moved up from the 11th percentile to the 50th percentile while enrolled at the parochial school. His older sister, Clarise (chapter 9) displayed more impressive advances; her marks went up from the 18th bottom percentile to the top 68th percentile. When factoring out vocabulary deficits—always the last redoubt of class and racial inequalities—her scores approached the 80th percentile (see also Kerswill 2006). Those were colossal achievements made possible by small changes in social context .

6. For a broader treatment of this subject, see chapter 5.

7. See chapter 6.

8. Ivan Light (1980) was among the first to note that cultural theories of self-employment can be traced back, directly or indirectly, to Max Weber's postulations regarding the elective affinity between capitalist accumulation and the Protestant work ethic. Weber (1912/2002) hypothesized that for markets to function properly, a cultural substratum must be in place whose moral imperatives are in correspondence with economic demands. Entrepreneurship, therefore, should most likely emerge in groups whose outlooks center on self-reliance, frugality, discipline, and other such virtues that promote material accumulation.

9. African Americans make up about 13 percent of the total U.S. population, but they represent only 7.2 percent of all business holders, below Hispanics, who encompass 16 percent of the U.S. population and 8.5 percent of all business holders.

10. I discuss that subject at greater length in chapters 5 and 6.

11. That is because such practices fail to take stratification patterns into consideration.

12. While all small businesses in Baltimore saw a decrease in loans as a result of the Great Recession of 2008, that decrease was greater among Black-owned businesses and the reduction in lending had greater consequences for them, given the historical limitations in capitalization and the lack of alternative sources of financial backing. A drop in the number of small businesses in the area also translated into fewer jobs at a time when the unemployment rate among Blacks was 17.5 percent, almost double the national average of 9.1 percent (Switzky 2012).

13. Other reports paint an equally discouraging picture. For example, on the basis of SBA data obtained through a Freedom of Information Act request, the *Washington Business Journal* (Zwitzky 2012) found that the Black business community suffered a significant reversal of fortune between 2003 and 2008, even before the onset of the Great Recession. During that period, nearly 44 percent of the 2,408 SBA loans disbursed to local Black-owned businesses in the Washington area defaulted, meaning they were either written off as a loss or were in liquidation. The default rate for non-Black borrowers during the same period was 25 percent.

14. If racial and ethnic groups were evenly distributed among all economic sectors, the uneven character of market opportunities would not affect the entrepreneurial hierarchy; each group's participation in each industry would equal its share of the labor force as a whole. But, as discussed above, that is not the case. African Americans experience rates of entrepreneurship so low that racial discrimination cannot be ruled out as a possible factor limiting their capacity to preside over effective businesses.

15. Distorted engagement is the opposite of *embedded autonomy*, the term used by Peter Evans (1995) to designate truly developmental policies that strike a balance of distance and connection between public officials and segments of civil society (see chapter 6). When national states achieve embedded autonomy, their actions benefit diverse social groups without extreme partiality.

CONCLUSION: DISTORTED ENGAGEMENT AND THE GREAT IDEOLOGICAL DIVIDE

1. In 2013, the overall labor force participation rate in the United States stood at 63.5 percent, down from 65.9 percent in 2003. Between 1953 and 2013, the labor force participation rate among White men aged twenty and older plummeted from 88 percent to 73 percent. In 1973, the labor force participation rate for Black men aged 20 and older was 78 percent; by 2013, it had dropped to 66 percent (U.S. Bureau of Labor Statistics 2013c).

2. In the book that first made him famous, *Social Statics: or, The Conditions Essential to Happiness Specified, and the First of Them Developed*, Spencer wrote (1851/2012: 352–354): "Pervading all nature we may see at work a stern discipline, which is a little cruel that it may be very kind. . . . [T]he poverty of the incapable, the distresses that come upon the imprudent, the starvation of the idle . . . are the decrees of a large, far-seeing benevolence. . . . [W]hen regarded not separately, but in connection with the interests of universal humanity, those harsh fatalities are seen to be full of the highest beneficence which brings to early graves the children of diseased parents, and singles out the low-spirited, the intemperate, and the debilitated."

3. This is all the more apparent among those who see poverty not as the result of historical or structural processes but as the consequence of injurious behaviors. Their

focus is on government efforts to sway conduct, not on the unintended consequences of those attempts.

4. Small segments of the Baltimore population are becoming part of the high-powered global economy; they are professionals in technologically advanced fields that include medicine, architecture, computer software development, and other like occupations.

BIBLIOGRAPHY

Agar, Michael H. (1985) *Speaking of Ethnography*. Sage.
Aldridge, Stephen, David Halpern, and Sarah Fitzpatrick. (2002) "Social Capital: A Discussion Paper." Performance and Innovation Unit, London, England.
Alexander, Karl L., Doris R. Entwisle, and Linda S. Olson. (2001) "Schools, Achievement, and Inequality: A Seasonal Perspective." *Educational Evaluation and Policy Analysis* 23, no. 2: 171–191.
———. (2007) "Lasting Consequences of the Summer Learning Gap." *American Sociological Review* 72: 167–180.
Alexander, Michelle. (2010) *The New Jim Crow: Mass Incarceration in the Age of Color Blindness*. New Press.
Allington, Richard L., and Anne McGill-Franzen, eds. (2013) *Summer Reading: Closing the Rich/Poor Reading Achievement Gap*. Teachers College Press.
Anderson, Elijah. (1999) *Streetwise: Race, Class, and Change in an Urban Community*. University of Chicago Press.
———. (2000) *Code of the Street: Decency, Violence, and the Moral Life of the Inner City*. W. W. Norton.
———. (2003) *A Place in the Corner*. University of Chicago Press.
Anheier, Helmut, and Jeremy Kendall. (2002) "Interpersonal Trust and Voluntary Associations." *British Journal of Sociology* 53, no. 3: 343–362.
Annotated Code of Maryland. (2012) https://govt.westlaw.com/mdc/Document/N4038C5D0C57A11E18559D0A08176E282?viewType=FullText&originationContext=documenttoc&transitionType=CategoryPageItem&contextData=(sc.Default).
Appadurai, Arun. (2001) *Globalization*. Duke University Press.
Aries, Philippe. (1965) *Centuries of Childhood: A Social History of Family Life*. Vintage.
Arrighi, Giovanni. (1994) *The Long Twentieth Century*. Verso.
———. (2010) *The Long Twentieth Century: Money, Power, and the Origins of Our Times*. Verso.

Atkinson, Rowland, and Keith Kintrea. (2000) "Owner-Occupation, Social Mix and Neighbourhood Impacts." *Policy and Politics* 28, no. 1: 93–108.

———. (2001) "Disentangling Area Effects: Evidence from Deprived and Non-Deprived Neighbourhoods." *Urban Studies* 38, no. 12: 2277–2298.

Aziz, Fahima. (2009) "Trends in Labor Force Participation Rates by Gender and Race." Working Paper. Economics School of Business, Hamline University, Saint Paul, MN.

Bakalian, Anny, and Medhi Bozorgmehr. (2009) *Backlash 9/11: Middle Eastern and Muslim Americans Respond.* University of California Press.

Baltimore City Department of Social Services. (1973) "Adapting to Serve the Community." Annual Report.

Baltimore City Health Department. (2008) "Baltimore City Health Status Report." http://www.baltimorehealth.org/hsr2008.html.

Baltimore City Health Department. (2011) "2011 Neighborhood Health Profile: Sandtown-Winchester/Harlem Park." http://www.baltimorehealth.org/info/neighborhood2011/47%20Sandtown.pdf.

Baltimore City Department of Welfare. (1953) *Public Welfare in Baltimore.* Nineteenth Annual Report.

———. (1959) *Public Welfare—A Community Responsibility.*

———. (1960) *The Needy under the Shadow of Guilt.*

Baltimore Sun. (2013) "Shifting Prison Populations." http://articles.baltimore sun.com/2013-03-04/news/bs-ed-prisons-blacks-20130304_1_prison -population-incarceration-rates-racial-makeup.

Bane, Mary Jo, and Lawrence Mead. (2003) *Lifting Up the Poor: A Dialogue on Religion, Poverty, and Welfare Reform.* Brookings Institution Press.

Barnette, Curtis H. (1995) "Bethlehem Steel Corporation—American Manufacturing Leadership in a Changing Global Economy." Address delivered at the 1995 Philadelphia Meeting of the Newcomen Society of the United States. Philadelphia.

Bates, Timothy. (1998) *Race, Self-Employment, and Upward Mobility: An Illusive American Dream.* Johns Hopkins University Press.

Becker, Howard S. (1997) *Outsiders: Studies in the Sociology of Deviance.* Free Press.

Beckford, James A. (1975) *The Trumpet of Prophecy: A Sociological Study of Jehovah's Witnesses.* John Wiley and Sons.

Beger, Randall R. (2002) "Expansion of Police Power in Public Schools and the Vanishing Rights of Students." *Social Justice* 29: 119–130.

Bell, Daniel. (1978) "The Return of the Sacred? The Argument on the Future of Religion." *Zygon, Journal of Religion and Science* 13, no. 2: 187–199.

Bellair, Paul. (1997) "Informal Surveillance and Street Crime: Disentangling Reciprocal Effects." Paper presented at the annual meeting of the American Sociological Association, Toronto, August.

Bennett, Michael J. (1996) *When Dreams Came True: The G.I. Bill and the Making of Modern America.* Brassey's.

Bentham, Jeremy. (1781/2007) *An Introduction to the Principles of Morals and Legislation.* Dover.

Berger, Peter L. (1967/1990) *The Sacred Canopy: Elements of a Sociological Theory of Religion.* Anchor.

Berman, Evan M., James S. Bowman, Jonathan P. West, and Montgomery R. Van Wart. (2012) *Human Resource Management in Public Service: Paradoxes, Processes, and Problems.* Sage.

Best, Wallace D. (2007) *Passionately Human, No Less Divine: Religion and Culture in Black Chicago.* Princeton University Press.

Billings, Dwight B., and Kathleen M. Blee. (2000) *The Road to Poverty: The Making of Wealth and Hardship in Appalachia.* Cambridge University Press.

Bluestone, Barry, and Bennett Harrison. (1984) *The Deindustrialization of America.* Basic Books.

———. (1990) *The Great U-Turn: Corporate Restructuring and the Polarizing of America.* Basic Books.

Bogan, Vicki, and William Darity, Jr. (2008) "Culture and Entrepreneurship? African American and Immigrant Self-Employment in the United States." *Journal of Socio-Economics* 37: 1999–2019.

Boissevain, Jeremy. (1974) *Friends of Friends: Networks, Manipulators, and Coalitions.* Blackwell.

Borjas, George J., and Stephen G. Bronars. (1989) "Consumer Discrimination and Self-Employment." *Journal of Political Economy* 97, no. 3: 581–605.

Bourdieu, Pierre. (1979/1984) *Distinction: A Social Critique of the Judgement of Taste.* Harvard University Press.

———. (1986) "The Forms of Capital." In *Handbook of Theory and Research for the Sociology of Education* (John Richardson, ed.): 241–258. Greenwood.

———. (1991) *Language and Symbolic Power.* Harvard University Press.

Bourdieu, Pierre, and Loïc Wacquant. (1992/2002) *An Invitation to Reflexive Sociology.* University of Chicago Press.

Bourgois, Philippe. (1996) *In Search of Respect: Selling Crack in El Barrio.* Cambridge University Press.

Bourgois, Philippe, and Jeffrey Schonberg. (2009) *Righteous Dopefiend.* University of California Press.

Boyd, Robert L. (1990) "Black and Asian Self-Employment in Large Metropolitan Areas: A Comparative Analysis." *Social Problems* 37, no. 2: 258–274.

———. (1991) "A Contextual Analysis of Black Self-Employment in Large Metropolitan Areas, 1970–1980." *Social Forces* 70, no. 2: 409–429.

Buck, Nick. (2001) "Identifying Neighbourhood Effects on Social Exclusion." *Urban Studies* 38, no. 12: 2251–2275.

Butler, John Sibley. (1991) *Entrepreneurship and Self-Help among Black Americans: A Reconsideration of Race and Economics.* State University of New York Press.

Brewer, Rose M., and Nancy A. Heitzeg. (2008) "The Racialization of Crime and Punishment: Criminal Justice, Color-Blind Racism and the Political

Economy of the Prison Industrial Complex." *American Behavioral Scientist* 51, no. 5: 625–644.

Brooks-Gunn, Jeanne, Greg J. Duncan, and J. Lawrence Aber, eds. (2000) *Neighborhood Poverty: Context and Consequences for Children.* Russell Sage Foundation.

Brooks-Gunn, Jeanne, Greg J. Duncan, Pamela Kato Klebanov, and Naomi Sealand. (1993) "Do Neighborhoods Influence Child and Adolescent Development?" *American Journal of Sociology* 99, no. 2: 353–395.

Burawoy, Michael, Alice Burton, Ann Arnet Ferguson, and Kathryn J. Fox. (1992) *Ethnography Unbound: Power and Resistance in the Modern Metropolis.* University of California Press.

Burawoy, Michael, Joseph A. Blum, Sheba George, and Millie Thayer. (2000) *Global Ethnography: Forces, Connections, and Imaginations in a Postmodern World.* University of California Press.

Butler, John S. (2005) *Entrepreneurship and Self-Help among Black Americans: A Reconsideration of Race and Economics.* State University of New York Press.

Calhoun, Craig, and Loïc Wacquant. (2002) "'Everything is social': In Memoriam, Pierre Bourdieu (1930–2002)." *Footnotes* 30, no. 2: 7–10.

Campbell, Joseph. (1949) *The Hero with a Thousand Faces.* Pantheon.

Cancian, Maria, and Sheldon Danziger, eds. (2009) *Changing Poverty, Changing Policies.* Russell Sage Foundation.

Card, David, and Alan B. Krueger. (1997) *Myth and Measurement.* Princeton University Press.

Carneiro, Robert L. (1977) *A Theory of the Origin of the State.* Institute for Human Studies.

Carnoy, Martin. (2001) *School Vouchers: Examining the Evidence.* Economic Policy Institute.

Carr, Firpo W. (2002) *Jehovah's Witnesses: The African American Enigma—A Contemporary Study.* Scholar Technological.

Carroll, Lewis. (1865) *Alice's Adventures in Wonderland.* Macmillan.

Cavalluzzo, Ken S., and John D. Wolken. (2005) "Small Business Loan Turndowns, Personal Wealth, and Discrimination." *Journal of Business* 78, no. 6: 2153–2177.

Ceci, Stephen J., and Richard D. Friedman. (2000) "The Suggestibility of Children: Scientific Research and Legal Implications." *Cornell Law Review* 86, no. 33: 34–107.

Centeno, Miguel A., and Joseph N. Cohen. (2010) *Global Capitalism: A Sociological Perspective.* Polity.

Center for Budget and Policy Priorities. (2010) "Income Gaps between Very Rich and Everyone Else More than Tripled in Last Three Decades, Data Shows." Center for Budget and Policy Priorities.

Centers for Disease Control and Prevention. (2011) "Teen Births." http://www.cdc.gov/nchs/fastats/teenbrth.htm.

Chalmers, Johnson. (1999) "The Developmental State: Odyssey of a Concept." In *The Developmental State* (Meredith Woo Cummings, ed.): 32–59. Cornell University Press.

Chapelle, Suzanne Ellery. (2000) *Baltimore: An Illustrated History.* American Historical Press.

Chryssides, George D. (2008) *Historical Dictionary of Jehovah's Witnesses.* Scarecrow Press.

Clark-Lewis, Elizabeth. (1996) *Living In, Living Out: African American Domestics and the Great Migration.* Kodansha America.

CNN All Politics. (1998) "Clinton Signs Deadbeat Parents Punishment Act" (June 24). http://www.cnn.com/ALLPOLITICS/1998/06/24/deadbeat.parents .bill/.

Coleman, James S. (1986) "Social Theory, Social Research and a Theory of Action." *American Journal of Sociology* 91, no. 6: 1309–1335.

———. (1988) "Social Capital and the Creation of Human Capital." *American Journal of Sociology* 94 (Supplement): 95–120.

Coleman, James S., Ernest Campbell, Carol Hobson, James McPartland, Alexander Mood, Frederic Weinfeld, and Robert York. (1966) *Equality of Educational Opportunity.* U.S. Department of Health, Education and Welfare and Office of Education, National Center for Educational Statistics.

Commissioner of Labor. (1894) *Seventh Special Report of the Commissioner of Labor: The Slums of Baltimore, Chicago, New York, and Philadelphia.* Government Printing Office.

Conan Doyle, Arthur. (1891/2012) *A Scandal in Bohemia.* CreateSpace Independent Publishing Platform.

Cone, James. (2013) *The Cross and the Lynching Tree.* Orbis.

Congressional Quarterly. (1975) Washington, DC.

Conley, Dalton. (1999) *Being Black, Living in the Red: Race, Wealth, and Social Policy in America.* University of California Press.

Coontz, Stephanie. (1993) *The Way We Never Were: American Families and the Nostalgia Trap.* Basic Books.

Cooper, Harris, Barbara Nye, Kelly Charlton, James Lindsay, and Scott Greathouse. (1996) "The Effects of Summer Vacation on Achievement Test Scores: A Narrative and Metaanalytic Review." *Review of Educational Research* 66, no. 3: 227–268.

Corsaro, William A. (2010) *The Sociology of Childhood.* Sage.

Costen, Lela B. (1991) "Unraveling the Mary Ellen Legend: Origins of the 'Cruelty' Movement." *Social Service Review* 65, no. 2: 203–223.

Cowie, Jefferson, Joseph Heathcott, and Barry Bluestone, eds. (2003) *Beyond the Ruins: The Meanings of Deindustrialization.* ILR Press.

Crane, Jonathan. (1991) "The Epidemic Theory of Ghettos and Neighbourhood Effects on Dropping Out and Teenage Childbearing." *American Journal of Sociology* 96, no. 5: 1226–1259.

Crawford Sullivan, Susan. (2012) *Living Faith: Everyday Religion and Mothers in Poverty.* University of Chicago Press.

Cross, John C., and Sergio Peña. (2006) "Risk and Regulation in Informal and Illegal Markets." In *Out of the Shadows: Informal Economy and Political Action in Latin America.* Penn State Press.

Cummings, Bruce. (1999) "Webs with No Spiders; Spiders with No Webs: The Genealogy of the Developmental State." In *The Developmental State* (Meredith Woo Cummings, ed.): 61–92. Cornell University Press.

Currie, Janet M. (2008) *The Invisible Safety Net: Protecting the Nation's Poor Children and Families.* Princeton University Press.

Currie, Stephen. (1997) *We Have Marched Together: The Working Children's Crusade.* Learner Publishing Group.

Danziger, Sheldon H., and Robert H. Haveman. (2001) *Understanding Poverty.* Russell Sage Foundation.

Denzin, Norman K. (1989) *Interpretive Biography.* Sage.

Dickens, Charles. (1843) *A Christmas Carol.* Chapman and Hall.

———. (1859/2012) *A Tale of Two Cities.* Doubleplus Editions.

Dietz, Robert. (2002) "The Estimation of Neighbourhood Effects in the Social Sciences: An Interdisciplinary Approach." *Social Science Research* 31, no. 4: 539–575.

DiMaggio, Paul. (1982) "Cultural Capital and School Success: The Impact of Status Culture Participation on the Grades of U.S. High School Students." *American Sociological Review* 47, no. 2: 189–201.

———. (1997) "Culture and Cognition." *Annual Review of Sociology* 23: 263–287.

———. (2001) "Conclusion: The Futures of Business Organization and Paradoxes of Change." In *The Twentieth Century Firm: Changing Economic Organization in International Perspective* (Paul DiMaggio, ed.): 170–194. Princeton University Press.

DiMaggio, Paul, and Joseph Cohen. (2003) "Information Inequality and Network Externalities: A Comparative Study of the Diffusion of Television and the Internet." Working Paper #31. Center for Arts and Cultural Policy Studies, Woodrow Wilson School, Princeton University.

DiMaggio, Paul, and Patricia Fernández-Kelly. (2010) *Art in the Lives of Immigrant Communities in the United States.* Rutgers University Press.

Dolfsma, Wilfred, and Charlie Dannreuther. (2003) "Subjects and Boundaries: Contesting Social Capital-Based Policies." *Journal of Economic Issues* 37, no. 2: 405–413.

Downey, Douglas B., Paul T. von Hippel, and Beckett A. Broh. (2004) "Are Schools the Great Equalizer? Cognitive Inequality during the Summer Months and the School Year. *American Sociological Review* 69, no. 5: 613–635.

Drake, St. Clair, and Horace R. Cayton. (1945/1993) *Black Metropolis: A Study of Negro Life in a Northern City.* University of Chicago Press.

Duany, Andres, Elizabeth Plater-Zyberk, and Jeff Speck. (2001) *Suburban Nation: The Rise of Sprawl and the Decline of the American Dream.* North Point.

DuBois, David L., and Michael J. Karcher. (2013) *Handbook of Youth Mentoring*. Sage.

DuBois, W.E.B. (1899/2012) *The Philadelphia Negro: A Social Study*. Ullan.

———. (1903/2011) *The Negro Church*. Cascade Books.

Duncan, Greg, Jeanne Brooks-Gunn, and Pamela Klebanov. (1997) *Consequences of Growing Up Poor*. Russell Sage Foundation.

Duneier, Mitchell. (1994) *Slim's Table: Race, Respectability and Masculinity*. University of Chicago Press.

———. (2000) *Sidewalk*. Farrar, Straus and Giroux.

Durkheim, Emile. (1912/2008) *The Elementary Forms of Religious Life*. Oxford University Press.

———. (1893/1997) *The Division of Labor in Society*. Free Press.

Earle, Jonathan H. (2004) *Jacksonian Antislavery and the Politics of Free Soil, 1824–1854*. University of North Carolina Press.

Edin, Kathryn, and Maria Kefalas. (2007) *Promises I Can Keep: Why Poor Women Put Motherhood before Marriage*. University of California Press.

Edin, Kathryn, and Laura Lein. (1997) *Making Ends Meet: How Single Mothers Survive Welfare and Low-Wage Work*. Russell Sage Foundation.

Edin, Kathryn, and Timothy J. Nelson. (2013) *Doing the Best I Can: Fatherhood in the Inner City*. University of California Press.

Ehrenreich, Barbara. (2011) *Nickel and Dimed: On (Not) Getting By in America*. Picador.

———. (2012) "Preying on the Poor: How Government and Corporations Use the Poor as Piggy Banks." *Nation*, May 17.

Ellen, Ingrid G., and Margery A. Turner. (1997) "Does Neighbourhood Matter? Assessing Recent Evidence." *Housing Policy Debate* 8, no. 4: 833–866

Elman, Service R. (1975) *Origins of the State and Civilization: The Process of Cultural Evolution*. W. W. Norton.

Engle, Shaena. (2004) "Degree Attainment Rates at Colleges and Universities." UCLA Higher Education Research Institute. http://www.gseis.ucla.edu/heri/darcu_pr.html.

Entwisle, Doris, Karl Alexander, and Linda Olson. (2000) "Summer Learning and Home Environment." In *A Notion at Risk: Preserving Public Education as an Engine for Social Mobility* (Richard D. Kahlenberg, ed.): 9–30. Century Foundation Press.

Evans, Peter. (1995) *Embedded Autonomy: States and Industrial Transformation*. Princeton University Press.

Evans, Peter, Dietrich Rueschemeyer, and Theda Skocpol, eds. (1985) *Bringing the State Back In*. Cambridge University Press.

Evans, Tony, and John Harris. (2004) "Street-Level Bureaucracy, Social Work and the (Exaggerated) Death of Discretion." *British Journal of Social Work* 34, no. 6: 871–895.

Evans-Pritchard, Edward. (1940/1969) *The Nuer: A Description of the Modes of Livelihood and Political Institutions of a Nilotic People*. Oxford: Clarendon Press.

Fairlie, Robert W., and Alicia M. Robb. (2010) *Race and Entrepreneurial Success: Black, Asian, and White-Owned Businesses in the United States*. MIT Press.

Falco, George, and Maximilian D. Schmeiser. (2006) *No Time to Lose: The Decline in Employment and Earnings of Young Black Men in New York State*. New York State Office of Temporary and Disability Assistance.

Falk, Gene. (2013) "The Temporary Assistance for Needy Families (TANF) Block Grant: Frequently Asked Questions." CRS Report for Congress 7-5700, no. RL32760. Congressional Research Service.

Fairlie, Robert W., and Bruce D. Meyer. (2000) "Trends in Self-Employment among White and Black Men during the Twentieth Century." *Journal of Human Resources* 35, no. 4: 643–669.

Fairlie, Robert, and Alicia Robb. (2008) *Race and Entrepreneurial Success: Black-, Asian-, and White-Owned Businesses in the United States*. MIT Press.

Feagin, Joseph R., and Nikitah Imani. (1994) "Racial Barriers to African American Entrepreneurship: An Exploratory Study." *Social Problems* 41, no. 4: 562–584.

Fernández-Kelly, Patricia. (1984) *For We Are Sold, I and My People: Women and Industry in Mexico's Frontier*. State University of New York Press.

———. (2008) "Gender and Economic Change in the United States and Mexico, 1900–2000." *American Behavioral Scientist* 52, no. 3: 377–404.

———. (2012) "Making Sense of the Other: Ethnographic Methods and Immigration Research." *International Handbook of Migration* (Steven J. Gold and Stephanie J. Nawyn, eds.): 494–505. Routledge.

Fernández-Kelly, Patricia, and Lisa Konczal. (2006) "Murdering the Alphabet": Identity and Entrepreneurship among Second Generation Cubans, West Indians, and Central Americans." *Ethnic and Racial Studies* 28, no. 6: 1153–1181.

Fernández-Kelly, Patricia, and Saskia Sassen. (1991) "A Collaborative Study of Hispanic Women in the Garment and Electronics Industries." Executive summary of a report presented to the Ford, Revson, and Tinker Foundations. New York University, Center for Latin American and Caribbean Studies.

Fernández-Kelly, Patricia, and Jon Shefner. (2007) *NAFTA and Beyond: Alternative Perspectives in the Study of Global Trade and Development*. Annals of the American Academy of Political and Social Science, no. 610. Sage.

Finegold, Kenneth, Stephanie Schardin, and Rebecca Steinbach. (2003) *How Are States Responding to Fiscal Stress?* New Federalism: Issues and Options for States, no. A-58. Urban Institute. http://www.urban.org/url.cfm?ID =310658.

Firth, Raymond. (1925) "The Māori Carver." *Journal of the Polynesian Society* 34: 277–291.

Fiske, Susan. (2000) "Stereotyping, Prejudice, and Discrimination at the Seam between the Centuries: Evolution, Culture, Mind, and Brain." *European Journal of Social Psychology*, 30: 299–322.

———. (2013) *Social Cognition: From Brains to Culture*. Sage.

Foner, Eric. (1988/2002) *Reconstruction: America's Unfinished Revolution, 1863–1877*. Harper Perennial Modern Classics.

Foote Whyte, William. (1943/1993) *Street Corner Society: A Social Study of an Italian Slum*. University of Chicago Press.

Forrest, Ray, and Ade Kearns. (2001) "Social Cohesion, Social Capital and the Neighbourhood." *Urban Studies* 38, no. 12: 2125–2143.

Fortes, Meyer, and E. E. Evans-Pritchard. (1940) *African Political Systems*. International African Institute.

Foucault, Michel. (1969/1982) *The Archaeology of Knowledge*. Vintage.

———. (1995) *Discipline and Punish: The Birth of the Prison*. Vintage.

Frazier E. Franklin. (1949) *The Negro in the United States*. Macmillan.

———. (1963) *The Negro Church in America*. Schocken Books.

Freud, Anna. (1966) *Normality and Pathology in Childhood: Assessments of Development*. International Universities Press.

Freud, Sigmund. (1920) *A General Introduction to Psychoanalysis*. Horace Liveright.

Friedman, Milton. (1962/2002) *Capitalism and Freedom*. University of Chicago Press.

Fromm, Erich. (1941) *Escape from Freedom*. Farrar and Rinehart.

Fullerton, Howard N., and Mitra Toosi. (2001) "Labor Force Projections to 2010: Steady Growth and Changing Composition." *Monthly Labor Review* (November). http://www.bls.gov/opub/mlr/2001/11/art2full.pdf.

Furstenberg, Frank F. (2010) "On a New Schedule: Transitions to Adulthood and Family Change." *Future of Children* 20, no. 1: 67–88.

Furstenberg, Frank F., Jean Brooks-Gunn, and S. Philip Morgan. (1987) *Adolescent Mothers in Later Life*. Cambridge University Press.

Gabe, Thomas. (2011) "Welfare, Work, and Poverty Status of Female-Headed Families with Children." CRS Report for Congress 7-5700, no. R4-1917. Congressional Research Service.

Gaddis, S. Michael. (2012) "What's in a Relationship? An Examination of Social Capital, Race, and Class in Mentoring Relationships." *Social Forces* 90, no. 4: 1137–1249.

Galster, George. (1986) "What Is Neighbourhood? An Externality Space Approach." *International Journal of Urban and Regional Research* 10, no. 10: 243–263.

———. (2001) "On the Nature of Neighbourhood." *Urban Studies* 38, no. 12: 2111–2124.

Gans, Herbert J. (1995) *The War against the Poor: The Underclass and Antipoverty Policy*. Basic Books.

Garfinkel, Harold. (1991) *Studies in Ethnomethodology*. Polity.

Garland, David. (1990) *Punishment and Modern Society: A Study in Social Theory*. University of Chicago Press and Oxford University Press.

———. (2010) *Peculiar Institution: America's Death Penalty in an Age of Abolition*. Harvard University Press.

Geller, William A., and Hans Toch. (1996). *Police Violence: Understanding and Controlling Police Abuse of Force.* Yale University Press.

Geertz, Clifford. (1977) *The Interpretation of Cultures.* Basic Books.

———. (1988) *Works and Lives: The Anthropologist as Author.* Stanford University Press

Gilmore, Perry. (1985) "'Gimme room': School Resistance, Attitude, and Access to Literacy." *Journal of Education* 167, no. 1: 111–128.

Giving USA. (2013) "Giving Statistics." http://www.charitynavigator.org/index .cfm?bay=content.view&cpid=42#.Ug0G7zXD_cu.

Gladwin, Christina H. (1989) *Ethnographic Decision Tree Modeling.* Sage.

Glennerster, Howard, Ruth Lupton, Ruth Lupton, Philip Noden, and Anne Power (1999) "Poverty, Social Exclusion and Neighbourhood: Studying the Area Bases of Social Exclusion." CASEpaper 22, Centre for Analysis of Social Exclusion, London School of Economics.

Goffman, Alice. (2009) "On The Run: Wanted Men in a Philadelphia Ghetto." *American Sociological Review* 74, no. 2: 339–357.

———. (2014) *On the Run: Fugitive Life in an American City.* University of Chicago Press.

Goffman, Erving. (1963/1986) *Stigma: Notes on the Management of Spoiled Identity.* Touchstone Books.

Goldenberg, David M. (2003). *The Curse of Ham: Race and Slavery in Early Judaism, Christianity, and Islam.* Princeton University Press.

Goldscheider, Calvin. (1986), *Jewish Continuity and Change: Emerging Patterns in America.* Indiana University Press.

Gomez, Michael A. (2005) *Black Crescent: The Experience and Legacy of African Muslims in the Americas.* Cambridge University Press.

Gordon, David M. (1996) *Fat and Mean: The Corporate Squeeze of Working Americans and the Myth of Managerial "Downsizing."* Martin Kessler Books/Free Press.

Gordon, Linda. (1994) *Pitied but Not Entitled: Single Mothers and the History of Welfare.* Free Press.

———. (2002) *Heroes of Their Own Lives: The Politics and History of Family Violence, Boston 1880–1960.* University of Illinois Press.

Gorn, Elliott J. (2002) *Mother Jones: The Most Dangerous Woman in America.* Hill and Wang.

Gould, Stephen Jay. (1985) "Carrie Buck's Daughter." *Natural History* 93 (July): 14–18.

Granovetter, Mark. (1973) "The Strength of Weak Ties." *American Journal of Sociology* 78, no. 6: 1360–1380.

———. (1985) "Economic Action and Social Structure: The Problem of Embeddedness." *American Journal of Sociology* 91, no. 3: 481–510.

———. (1995) *Getting a Job: A Study of Contacts and Careers.* University of Chicago Press.

Granovetter, Mark, and Richard Swedberg, eds. (2011) *The Sociology of Economic Life*. Westview.

Gray, James P. (2001) *Why Our Drug Laws Have Failed and What We Can Do about It: A Judicial Indictment of the War on Drugs*. Temple University Press.

Gregory, Steven. (1999) *Black Corona: Race and the Politics of Place in an Urban Community*. Princeton University Press.

Greven, Philip J. (1992) *Spare the Child: The Religious Roots of Punishment and the Psychological Impact of Physical Abuse*. Vintage.

Grossman, Jean B., Christian S. Chan, Sarah E.O. Schwarz, and Jean Rhodes. (2012) "The Test of Time in School-Based Mentoring: The Role of Relationship Duration and Re-Matching on Academic Outcomes." *American Journal of Community Psychology* 49, nos. 1–2: 43–54.

Grossman, Jean B., and Jean E. Rhodes. (2002) "The Test of Time: Predictors and Effects of Duration in Youth Mentoring Relationships." *American Journal of Community Psychology* 30, no. 2: 199–219.

Grusky, David, and Tamar Kricheli-Katz, eds. (2012) *The New Gilded Age*. Stanford University Press.

Gunder Frank, Andre. (1967) *Capitalism and Underdevelopment in Latin America: Historical Studies of Chile and Brazil*. Monthly Review Press.

Gunderson, Craig, and James Ziliak. (2004) "Poverty and Macroeconomic Performance across Space, Race, and Family Structure." *Demography* 41, no. 1: 61–86.

Hamilton, Brady E., Joyce A. Martin, and Stephanie J. Ventura. (2011) "Births: Preliminary Data for 2011." *National Vital Statistics Reports* 61, no. 5: 1–19.

Harding, David J. (2002) "Counterfactual Models of Neighbourhood Effects: The Effect of Neighborhood Poverty on High School Dropout and Teenage Pregnancy." Unpublished paper. Department of Sociology, Harvard University.

Haney, Lynne. (1996) "Homeboys, Babies, Men in Suits: The State and the Reproduction of Male Dominance." *American Sociological Review* 61, no. 5: 759–775.

———. (2010) *Offending Women: Power, Punishment, and the Regulation of Desire*. University of California Press.

Hannan, Michael, and John Freeman. (1987) "The Ecology of Organizational Founding: American Labor Unions, 1836–1985." *American Journal of Sociology* 92, no. 4: 910–943.

Hannerz, Ulf. (1969) *Soulside: Inquiries into Ghetto Culture and Community*. Columbia University Press.

Harrison, Bennett. (1997) *Lean and Mean: Why Large Corporations Will Continue to Dominate the Global Economy*. Guilford.

Harrison, Bennett, and Amy Glasmeier. (1997) "Why Business Alone Won't Redevelop the Inner City." *Economic Development Quarterly* (February): 28–38..

Hartigan, John. (1999) *Racial Situations: Class Predicaments of Whiteness in Detroit.* Princeton University Press.

Harvey, David. (1998/2009) *Social Justice and the City.* Blackwell.

———. (2007) *A Brief History of Neoliberalism.* Oxford University Press.

———. (2011) *The Enigma of Capital and the Crises of Capitalism.* Oxford University Press.

———. (2012) *Rebel Cities: From the Right to the City to the Urban Revolution.* Verso.

Hayghe, Howard V. (1997) "Developments in Women's Labor Force Participation." *Monthly Labor Review* (September): 41–46.

Healthy Teen Network. (2010) "Strategic Plan to Reduce Teen Births in Baltimore City." http://www.baltimorehealth.org/info/teen_preg_report_final .pdf.

Heitzeg, Nancy A. (2012) *The School-to-Prison Pipeline: The Role of Police, Courts, Schools and Parents.* John Jay College Center on Media, Crime and Justice/Tow Foundation.

Hermann, Peter. (2009) "Bullets Fly in Baltimore and No One's Surprised. *Baltimore Sun*, July 28.

Herrera, Carla, Jean B. Grossman, Tina J. Kauh, Amy F. Feldman, and Jennifer McMaken. (2007/2011) *Making a Difference in Schools: The Big Brothers Big Sisters School-Based Mentoring Impact Study.* Public/Private Ventures. https://www.bigsister.org/bigsister/file/Making%20a%20Difference%20 in%20Schools.pdf.

Heyns, Barbara. (1978) *Summer Learning and the Effects of Schooling.* Academic.

———. (1987) "Schooling and Cognitive Development – Is There a Season for Learning?" *Child Development* 58, no. 5: 1151–1160.

Hill Collins, Patricia. (2008) *Black Feminist Thought: Knowledge, Consciousness, and the Politics of Empowerment.* Routledge.

Hindman, Hugh D. (2002) *Child Labor an American History.* M. E. Sharpe.

Hirschman, Albert O. (1984) "Against Parsimony: Three Easy Ways of Complicating Some Categories of Economic Discourse." *American Economics Association Papers and Proceedings* 74, no. 2: 90–96.

Hirschman, Charles. (2004) "The Role of Religion in the Origins and Adaptation of Immigrant Groups in the United States." *International Migration Review* 28, no. 3: 1206–1234.

Hochschild, Jennifer L., and Nathan Scovronick. (2004) *The American Dream and the Public Schools.* Oxford University Press.

Holden, Andrew. (2002). *Jehovah's Witnesses: Portrait of a Contemporary Religious Movement.* Routledge.

Hondagneu-Sotelo, Pierrette. (2007) *God's Heart Has No Borders: How Religious Activists Are Working for Immigrant Rights.* University of California Press.

Horowitz, Allan. (2003) *Creating Mental Illness.* University of Chicago Press.

Huff Post Politics. (2011) "Jon Bruning , Nebraska Senate Candidate, Compares Welfare Recipients to Racoons." *Huffington Post*, August 9. http://

www.huffingtonpost.com/2011/08/09/jon-bruning-nebraska-welfare-raccoons_n_922312.html.

Humes, Edward. (2006). *Over Here: How the G.I. Bill Transformed the American Dream.* Harcourt.

Hunt, Matthew O. (2002) "Religion, Race/Ethnicity, and Beliefs about Poverty." *Social Science Quarterly* 83, no. 3: 810–831.

Husock, Howard. (2003) *America's Trillion Dollar Housing Mistake: The Failure of American Housing Policy.* Ivan R. Dee.

Hutchison, Ray, and Bruce D. Haynes, eds. (2011) *The Ghetto: Contemporary Global Issues and Controversies.* Westview.

Huynh, Jennifer, and Jessica Yiu. (2012) "Breaking Blocked Transnationalism: Intergenerational Change in Homeland Ties." Paper presented at the conference on Immigrant Transnational Organizations and Development. Center for Migration and Development, Princeton University, May.

Hyman, Harold M. (2008). *American Singularity: The 1787 Northwest Ordinance, the 1862 Homestead and Morrill Acts, and the 1944 G.I. Bill.* University of Georgia Press.

Iceland, John. (2012) *Poverty in America.* University of California Press.

Immergluck, Daniel, and Erin Mullen. (1998) "The Intrametropolitan Distribution of Economic Development Financing: An Analysis of SBA 504 Lending Patterns." *Economic Development Quarterly* 12, no. 4: 372–384.

Jacobs, Jane. (1961/1992) *The Death and Life of Great American Cities.* Vintage.

Janvier, Meredith. (1933) *Baltimore in the Eighties and Nineties.* H. G. Roebuck and Son.

Jarret, Robin L. (1995) "Growing Up Poor: The Family Experiences of Socially Mobile Youth in Low-Income African American Neighborhoods." *Journal of Adolescent Research* 10, no. 1: 111–135.

Jarret, Robin L., Stephanie R. Jefferson, and Jennelle N. Kelly. (2010) "Finding Community in Family: Neighborhood Effects and African American Kin Networks." *Journal of Comparative Family Studies* 41, no. 3: 299–317.

Jencks, Christopher. (1993) *Rethinking Social Policy: Race, Poverty, and the Underclass.* Harper Perennial.

Jencks, Christopher, and Susan Mayer. (1990) "The Social Consequences of Growing Up in a Poor Neighborhood." In *Inner-City Poverty in the United States* (Lawrence Lynn Jr. and Michael McGeary, ed.): 111–151. National Academy of Sciences Press.

Jencks, Christopher, and Paul E. Peterson, eds. (1991) *The Urban Underclass.* Brookings Institution Press.

Jonnes, Jill. (1996) *Hep-Cats, Narcs, and Pipe Dreams: A History of America's Romance with Illegal Drugs.* Scribner.

Justice Policy Institute. (2010) "Baltimore behind Bars: How to Reduce the Jail Population, Save Money and Improve Public Safety." http://www.justicepolicy.org/images/upload/10-06_REP_BaltBehindBars_MD-PS-AC-RD.pdf.

Katz, Michael. (1990/2013) *The Undeserving Poor: America's Enduring Confrontation with Poverty*. Oxford.

Kearns, Ade, and Michael Parkinson. (2001) "The Significance of Neighbourhood." *Urban Studies* 38, no. 12: 2103–2110.

Kennedy, David M. (2011) *Don't Shoot: One Man, A Street Fellowship, and the End of Violence in Inner-City America*. Bloomsbury.

Kerswill, Paul. (2006). "Migration and Language." In *Sociolinguistics/Soziolinguistik: An International Handbook of the Science of Language and Society* (Klaus Mattheier Ulrich Ammon and Peter Trudgill, eds.): 1–27. De Gruyter.

Kesey, Ken. (1963) *One Flew over the Cuckoo's Nest*. Signet.

Kilty, Keith M., and Elizabeth A. Segal. (2006) *The Promise of Welfare Reform: Political Rhetoric and the Reality of Poverty in the Twenty-First Century*. Routledge.

Kim, Daeyoung. (2006) "Stepping-Stone to Intergenerational Mobility? The Springboard, Safety Net, or Mobility Trap Functions of Korean Immigrant Entrepreneurship for the Second Generation." *International Migration Review* 40, no. 4: 927–962.

Kim, Ilsoo. (1981) *New Urban Immigrants: The Korean Community in New York*. Princeton University Press.

Knight, Amy, and Robert L. Worden. (1995) *Veterans Benefits Administration: An Organizational History, 1776–1994*. Diane Publishing Co.

Knorr Zetina, Karin. (1982) *Advances in Social Theory and Methodology: Towards an Integration of Micro- and Macro-Sociologies*. Routledge.

Kochman, Thomas, ed. (1973) *Rappin' and Stylin' Out: Communication in Urban Black America*. University of Illinois Press.

Kohn, Melvin. (1989) *Class and Conformity: A Study in Values*. University of Chicago Press.

Kotlowitz, Alex. (1992) *There Are No Children Here: The Story of Two Boys Growing Up in the Other America*. Doubleday.

Krueger, Alan O. (1963) " The Economics of Discrimination." *Journal of Political Economy* 75, no. 5: 481–486.

Lacan, Jacques. (2007a) "The Function and Field of Speech and Language in Psychoanalysis." In *Écrits: The First Complete Edition in English: 197–268*. W. W. Norton.

Lacan, Jacques. (2007b) "The Mirror Stage as Formative of the *I* Function as Revealed in the Psychoanalytic Experience." In *Écrits: The First Complete Edition in English: 75–81*. W. W. Norton.

Lack, A. Lloyd. (1919) "Benjamin Franklin's Opinion of German-Americans: Before the Revolution He Pointed Out the Menace to the Country in the German Language Press and People." *New York Times*, October 12.

Lamont, Michèle. (2002) *The Dignity of Working Men: Morality and the Boundaries of Race, Class, and Immigration*. Harvard University Press.

Lareau, Annette. (2011) *Unequal Childhoods: Class, Race, and Family Life.* University of California Press.

Larsen, Larissa, Sharon L. Harland, Bob Bolin, Edward J. Hackett, Diane Hope, Andrew Kirby, Amy Nelson, Tom R. Rex, and Shaphard Wolf. (2004) "Bonding and Bridging: Understanding the Relationship between Social Capital and Civic Action." *Journal of Planning Education and Research* 24, no. 1: 64–77.

Latrobe, Ferdinand C. (1941) *Iron Men and Their Dogs: A History of Bartlet, Hayward and Company.* Ivan R. Drechsler.

Lazarsfeld, Paul, and Robert K. Merton. (1954) "Friendship as a Social Process: A Substantive and Methodological Analysis." In *Freedom and Control in Modern Society* (Morroe Berger, Theodore Abel, and Charles H. Page, eds.): 18–66. Van Nostrand.

Ledbetter, James. (2008) *Dispatches for the New York Tribune: Selected Journalism of Karl Marx.* Penguin.

Lee, Marlene A., and Mark Mather. (2008) "U.S. Labor Force Trends." *Population Bulletin* 63, no. 2: 3–16.

Leiter, Kenneth. (1980) *A Primer on Ethnomethodology.* Oxford University Press.

Lemann, Nicholas. (1992) *The Promised Land and How It Changed America.* Vintage.

Lenski, Gerhard. (1961) *The Religious Factor.* Doubleday.

Levine, C. (1972) "Black Entrepreneurship in the Ghetto: A Recruitment Strategy." *Land Economics* 48, no. 3: 269–273.

Levey Friedman, Hilary. (2013) *Playing to Win: Raising Children in a Competitive Culture.* University of California Press.

Levine, Linda. (2013) "Economic Growth and the Unemployment Rate." CRS Report for Congress 7-5700, no. R42063. Congressional Research Service.

Lewis, Oscar. (1961/2011) *The Children of Sanchez: Autobiography of a Mexican Family.* Vintage.

Library of Congress, Congressional Research Service. (1992) "Cash and Noncash Benefits for Persons with Limited Income: Eligibility Rules, Recipient and Expenditure Data, FY 1990–92," Report 93-832.

Liebow, Elliot. (1967) *Tally's Corner: A Study of Streetcorner Men.* Little, Brown.

Light, Ivan H. (1980) *Ethnic Entrepreneurship in America.* University of California Press.

Light, Ivan H., and Edna Bonacich. (1981) *Immigrant Entrepreneurs: Koreans in Los Angeles 1965–1982.* University of California Press.

Light, Ivan H., and Carolyn N. Rosenstein. (1995) *Race, Ethnicity and Entrepreneurship in Urban America.* Aldine de Gruyter.

Lincoln, Charles Eric. (1994) *The Black Muslims in America,* Wm. B. Eerdmans.

Lincoln, Charles Eric, and Lawrence H. Mamiya. (1990) *The Black Church in the African-American Experience.* Duke University Press.

Lipsky, Michael. (1980) *Street-Level Bureaucracy: Dilemmas of the Individual in Public Service*. Russell Sage Foundation.

Logan, John R., and Harvey Molotch. (1987/2007) *The Political Economy of Place*. University of California Press.

Lombardo, Paul A. (2008). *Three Generations, No Imbeciles: Eugenics, the Supreme Court, and Buck v. Bell*. Johns Hopkins University Press.

Loury, Glen. (1977) "A Dynamic Theory of Racial Income difference." In *Women, Minorities, and Employment Discrimination* (Phyllis A. Wallace and Annette M. Lamond, eds.): 143–186. Lexington Books.

Ludwig, Jens, and Susan E. Mayer. (2006) "Culture and the Intergenerational Transmission of Poverty: The Prevention Paradox." *Future of Children* 16, no. 2: 175–196.

Luhby, Tami. (2012) "Worsening Wealth Inequality by Race." CNN Money. http://money.cnn.com/2012/06/21/news/economy/wealth-gap-race/index.htm.

Luker, Kristin. (1991) "Dubious Conceptions: The Controversy over Teen Pregnancy." *American Prospect* (Spring): 73–83.

Lupton, Ruth. (2001) *Places Apart? The Initial Report of CASE's Areas Study*. CASEreport 14, Centre for Analysis of Social Exclusion, London School of Economics, Centre for Analysis of Social Exclusion.

Lupton, Ruth (2003a) "'Neighbourhood Effects': Can We Measure Them and Does It Matter?" CASEpaper 73, Centre for Analysis of Social Exclusion, London School of Economics.

———. (2003b) *Poverty Street: The Dynamics of Neighbourhood Decline and Renewal*. Policy.

Lynch, Brian. (2011) "Who Owns What." *Data Driven View Points* (blog), September 15. http://aseyeseesit.blogspot.com/2011/09/who-owns-what.html.

MacAllister, Iain, Ron Johnston, Charles Pattie, Helena Tunstall, and Danny Rossiter. (2001) "Class Dealignment and the Neighbourhood Effect: Miller Revisited." *British Journal of Political Science* 31, no. 1: 41–60.

MacLeod, Jay. (1987/1995) *Ain't No Makin' It: Aspirations and Attainment in a Low-Income Neighborhood*. Westview.

Malinowski, Bronislaw. (1922). *Argonauts of the Western Pacific: An Account of Native Enterprise and Adventure in the Archipelagoes of Melanesian New Guinea*. Studies in Economics and Political Science, no. 65. Routledge and Kegan Paul.

Marsh, Charles. (2006) *The Beloved Community: How Faith Shapes Social Justice from the Civil Rights Movement to Today*. Basic Books.

Marshall, Catherine, and Gretchen B. Rossman. (1989) *Designing Qualitative Research*. Sage.

Marshall, Sue, and David Swinton. (1979) "Federal Government Policy in Black Community Revitalization." *Review of Black Political Economy* 10, no. 1: 11–29.

Massey, Douglas S. (1994) *Space, Place and Gender*. Polity.

———. (2005) *Return of the "L" Word: A Liberal Vision for the New Century*. Princeton University Press.

Massey, Douglas S., Len Albright, Rebecca Casciano, Elizabeth Derickson, and David Kinsey. (2013) *Climbing Mount Laurel: The Struggle for Affordable Housing and Social Mobility in an American Suburb*. Princeton University Press.

Massey, Douglas S., and Nancy Denton. (1993) *American Apartheid: Segregation and the Making of the Underclass*. Harvard University Press.

Mayer, Gerald. (2004) *Union Membership Trends in the United States*. Congressional Research Service, Library of Congress.

Mayer, Susan. (1997) *What Money Can't Buy: Family Income and Children's Life Chances*. Harvard University Press.

Mayer, Susan, and Christopher Jencks. (1989) "Growing Up in Poor Neighborhoods: How Much Does It Matter?" *Science* 243: 1441–1445.

Mayer, Susan, and Paul Peterson, eds. (1999) *Earning and Learning: How Schools Matter*. Brookings Institution Press.

Maynard-Moody, Steven Williams, and Michael Craig Musheno. (2003) *Cops, Teachers, Counselors: Stories from the Front Lines of Public Service*. University of Michigan Press.

McConnell, Campbell R., Stanley S. Brue, and David A. Macpherson. (2010) *Contemporary Labor Economics*. McGraw-Hill/Irwin.

McCracken, Grant (1988) *The Long Interview*. Sage.

McDowell, David J., Mina Kim, Robin O'Neil, and Ross D. Parke. (2002) "Children's Emotional Regulation and Social Competence in Middle Childhood: The Role of Maternal and Paternal Interactive Style." *Marriage and Family Review* 34, nos. 3–4: 345–364.

McGuire, Therese J., and David F. Merriman. (2005) "State Spending on Social Assistance Programs over the Business Cycle." National Poverty Center Working Paper # 05-15. http://www.npc.umich.edu/publications/working paper05/paper15/McGuireMerrimanFinal.pdf.

McLanahan, Sara. (1985) "Family Structure and the Reproduction of Poverty." *American Journal of Sociology* 90, no. 4: 873–890.

McLanahan, Sara, Elisabeth Donahue, and Ron Haskins, eds. (2005) "Marriage and Child Wellbeing." Special issue, *Future of Children* 15, no. 2.

Mead, Margaret. (1928/2001) *Coming of Age in Samoa*. Harper's Perennial Modern Classics.

Media Matters. (2011) "Ann Coulter: 'Welfare' Creates Generations of Utterly Irresponsible Animals." Video: http://mediamatters.org/video/2011/08/15 /ann-coulter-welfare-creates-generations-of-utte/182020.

Meegan, Richard, and Alison Mitchell. (2001) "'It's Not Community Round Here, It's Neighbourhood': Neighbourhood Change and Cohesion in Urban Regeneration Policies." *Urban Studies* 38, no. 12: 2167–2194.

Menjívar, Cecilia. (2000) *Fragmented Ties: Salvadoran Immigrant Networks in America*. University of California Press.

———. (2010) "Immigrant Art as Liminal Expression: The Case of Central Americans." In *Art in the Lives of Immigrant Communities in the United States* (Paul DiMaggio and Patricia Fernández-Kelly, eds.): 176–196. Rutgers University Press.

Menjívar, Cecilia, and Sang H. Kil. (2002) "For Their Own Good: Benevolent Rhetoric and Exclusionary Language in Public Officials' Discourse on Immigrant-Related Issues." *Social Justice* 29, nos. 1–2: 160–176.

Merton, Robert K. (1938) "Social Structure and Anomie." *American Sociological Review* 3, no. 5: 672–691.

———. (1972) "Insiders and Outsiders: A Chapter in the Sociology of Knowledge." *American Journal of Sociology* 78, no. 1: 9–47.

———. (1984) "Socially Expected Durations: A Case Study of Concept Formation in Sociology." In *Conflict and Consensus* (Walter W. Powell and Richard Robbins, eds.): 262–283. Free Press.

———. (1987) "Three Fragments from a Sociologist's Notebooks: Establishing the Phenomenon, Specified Ignorance, and Strategic Research Materials." *Annual Review of Sociology* 13: 1–29.

Miles, Matthew B., and A. Michael Huberman (1984) *Qualitative Data Analysis*. Sage.

Mill, John Stuart. (1825/1984) *The Collected Works of John Stuart Mill*. Vol. 21, *Essays on Equality, Law, and Education* (John M. Robson, ed.). Routledge and Kegan Paul.

Mills, C. Wright. (1959/2000) *The Sociological Imagination*. Oxford University Press.

Min, Pyong Cap, and Mehdi Bozorgmehr. (2000) "Immigrant Entrepreneurship and Business Patterns: A Comparisonof Koreans and Iranians in Los Angeles. *International Migration Review*, 34: 707–738.

Mitchell, Thomas W. (2000) "From Reconstruction to Deconstruction: Undermining Black Landownership, Political Independence, and Community through Partition Sales of Tenancies in Common." LTC Research Paper 132, Land Tenure Center, University of Wisconsin–Madison.

Morgen, Sandra, Joan Acker, and Jill Weigt. (2010) *Stretched Thin: Poor Families, Welfare Work, and Welfare Reform*. Cornell University Press.

Morrill Act. (1862) Public Law 37-108, chap. 130. An Act Donating Public Lands to the Several States and Territories Which May Provide Colleges for the Benefit of Agriculture and Mechanic Arts.

Morris, Aldon. (1984) *The Origins of the Civil Rights Movement: Black Communities Organizing for Change*. Free Press.

Morris, Charles R. (2006) *The Tycoons: How Andrew Carnegie, John D. Rockefeller, Jay Gould, and J. P. Morgan Invented the American Supereconomy*. Holt Paperbacks.

Mortimore, Peter. (1997) "Can Effective Schools Compensate for Society?" In *Education, Culture, Economy and Society* (A. Halsey, H. Lauder, P. Brown, and A. Stuart-Wells, eds.): 496–488. Oxford University Press.

Moynihan, Daniel P. (1965) *The Negro Family: The Case for National Action.* Office of Policy Planning and Research, U.S. Department of Labor

Mufford, Juliet H. (1970) *Child Labor in America.* History Compass.

Murphy, Larry G., J. Gordon Melton, and Gary L. Ward, eds. (1993) *Encyclopedia of African American Religions.* Routledge.

Murray, Charles. (1984) *Losing Ground: American Social Policy, 1950–1980.* Basic Books.

———. (2013) *Coming Apart: The State of White America, 1960–2010.* Crown Forum.

Murray, Charles, and Richard J. Hernstein. (1994) *The Bell Curve: Intelligence and Class Structure in American Life.* Free Press.

Myers, John E. B. (2006) *Child Protection in America: Past, Present and Future.* Oxford University Press.

Myrstol, Brad A. (2011) "Public Perceptions of School Resource Office (SRO) Programs." *Western Criminology Review* 12, no. 3: 20–40.

NABSW (National Association of Black Social Workers). (2013) "Preserving Families of African Ancestry." https://c.ymcdn.com/sites/nabsw.org/resource /resmgr/position_statements_papers/preserving_families_of_afric.pdf.

Narayan, Deepa, ed. (2002) *Empowerment and Poverty Reduction: A Sourcebook.* World Bank.

Nathanson, Constance A. (1991) *Dangerous Passage: The Social Control of Sexuality in Women's Adolescence.* Temple University Press.

National Children's Alliance. (2013) "National Statistics on Child Abuse." http://www.nationalchildrensalliance.org/NCANationalStatistics.

Newman, Katherine S. (2000) *No Shame in My Game: The Working Poor in the Inner City.* Vintage.

———. (2008) *The Missing Class: Portraits of the Near Poor in America.* Beacon.

New York Times. (1994) "As Farrakhan Groups Land Jobs from Government, Debate Grows," March 4.

Nolan, Kathleen. (2011) *Police in the Hallways: Discipline in an Urban High School.* University of Minnesota Press.

Nopper, Tamara. (2011) "Minority Black and Non-Black People of Color: 'New' Color-Blind Racism and the U.S. Small Business Administration's Approach to Minority Business Lending in the Post Civil Rights Era." *Critical Sociology* 37, no. 5: 651–671.

Norton, Michael I., and Dan Ariely. (2011) "Building a Better America—One Wealth Quintile at a Time." *Perspectives on Psychological Science* 6, no. 1: 9–12.

O'Connor, Alice (2001) *Poverty Knowledge: Social Science, Social Policy, and the Poor in Twentieth-Century U.S. History.* Princeton University Press.

Ogbu, John U., and Maria Eugenia Matute-Bianchi. (1986) Understanding Sociocultural Factors: Knowledge, Identity, and School Adjustment." In *Beyond Language: Social and Cultural Factors in Schooling Language Minority Students* (California State University, Evaluation, Dissemination, and Assessment Center, eds.): 73–142. Evaluation, Dissemination and Assessment Center, California State University.

Oliver, Melvin, and Thomas Shapiro. (1995/2006) *Black Wealth/White Wealth: A New Perspective on Racial Inequality.* Routledge.

Olson, Sherry H. (1997) *Baltimore: The Building of an American City.* Johns Hopkins University Press.

Orser, W. Edward. (1997) *Blockbusting in Baltimore: The Edmonson Village Story.* University of Kentucky Press.

Ortner, Sherry B. (2006) *Anthropology and Social Theory: Culture, Power, and the Acting Subject.* Johns Hopkins University Press.

Osborne, Alfred E. (1979) "The Perverse Effects of the Sba Loans to Minority Wholesalers." *Urban Affairs Review* 15, no. 1: 87–97.

Page, Stephen B., and Mary B. Larner. (1997) "Introduction to the AFDC Program." *Welfare to Work* 7, no. 1: 3–27.

Pager, Devah. (2009) *Marked: Race, Crime, and Finding Work in an Age of Mass Incarceration.* University of Chicago Press.

Park, Robert E. (1928) "Human Migration and the Marginal Man." *American Journal of Sociology* 33, no. 6: 881–893.

Park, Robert E., and Ernest W. Burgess. (1967) *The City.* University of Chicago Press.

Pattillo-McCoy, Mary. (1998) "Church Culture as a Strategy of Action in the Black Community." *American Sociological Review* 63, no. 6: 767–784.

———. (2000) *Black Picket Fences: Privilege and Peril among the Black Middle Class. University of Chicago Press.*

Pedroni, Thomas C. (2007) *Market Movements: African American Involvement in School Voucher Reform.* Routledge.

Peters, Guy B. (2009) *American Public Policy: Promise and Performance.* CQ Press.

Petersen, William. (1971) *Japanese Americans: Oppression and Success.* Random House.

Pettit, Becky, and Bruce Western. (2002) "Mass Imprisonment and the Life Course: Race and Class Inequality in U.S. Incarceration." *American Sociological Review* 69 (April): 151–169.

Pew Forum on Religion and Public Life. (2008) *U.S. Religious Landscape Survey.* Pew Research Center.

Philpott, Thomas L. (1991) *The Slum and the Ghetto: Immigrants, Blacks and Reformers in Chicago 1880–1930.* Wadsworth.

Piaget, Jean. (1928) *The Child's Conception of the World.* Routledge and Kegan Paul.

Piaget, Jean, and Barbel Inhelder. (1969) *The Psychology of the Child.* Basic Books.

Pietila, Antero. (2010) *Not in My Neighborhood: How Bigotry Shaped a Great American City.* Ivan R. Dee.

Piore, Michael, and Charles Sabel. (1986) *The Second Industrial Divide: Possibilities for Prosperity.* Basic Books.

Piven, Frances Fox, and Richard Cloward. (1971/1993) *Regulating the Poor: The Functions of Public Welfare.* Vintage.

Porter, Michael E. (1995) "The Competitive Advantage of the Inner City." *Harvard Business Review* (May–June): 55–71.

———. (1998) *The Competitive Advantage of Nations.* Free Press.

Portes, Alejandro. (1981) "Modes of Structural Incorporation and Present Theories of Immigration." In *Global Trends in Migration: Theory and Research on International Population Movements* (Mary Kritz, ed.): 279–297. Jerome S. Ozer.

———. (1993) "Embeddedness and Immigration: Notes on the Social Determinants of Economic Action." *American Journal of Sociology* 98, no. 6: 1320–1350.

———. (1998) "Social Capital: Its Origins and Applications in Modern Sociology." *Annual Review of Sociology* 24: 1–24.

———. (2010) *Economic Sociology: A Systematic Inquiry.* Princeton University Press.

Portes, Alejandro, and Robert L. Bach. (1985), *Latin Journey: Cuban and Mexican Immigrants in the United States.* University of California Press.

Portes, Alejandro, and Rubén Rumbaut. (2014) *Immigrant America: A Portrait.* University of California Press.

Portes, Alejandro, and Alex Stepick. (1994) *City on the Edge: The Transformation of Miami.* University of California Press.

Portes, Alejandro, and John Walton. (1981) *Labor, Class, and the International System.* Academic.

Portes, Alejandro, and Jessica Yiu. (2013) "Entrepreneurship, Transnationalism, and Development." *Migration Studies* 1, no. 1: 75–95.

Portes, Alejandro, and Min Zhou. (1993) "The New Second Generation: Segmented Assimilation and Its Variants." *Annals of the American Academy of Political and Social Science* 530 (November): 74–96.

Portfield, Jason. (2005) *Homestead Act of 1862: A Primary Source History of the Settlement of the American Heartland in the Late 19th Century.* Rosen Publishing Group.

Power, Anne, and Katharine Mumford. (1999) *The Slow Death of Great Cities? Urban Abandonment or Urban Renaissance.* Joseph Rowntree Foundation.

Puma, Mike, Stephen Bell, Ronna Cook, Camilla Heid, Pam Broene, Frank Jenkins, Andrew Mashburn, and Jason Downer. (2012) "Third Grade Follow-Up to the Head Start Impact Study." Final report submitted to the Office of Planning, Research and Evaluation, Administration for Children and Families. U.S. Department of Health and Human Services. http://www.acf.hhs.gov/sites/default/files/opre/head_start_report.pdf.

Putnam, Robert D. (1995) "Bowling Alone: America's Declining Social Capital." *Journal of Democracy* 6, no. 1: 65–78.

——. (2001) *Bowling Alone: The Collapse and Revival of American Community.* Touchstone Books.

Putnam, Robert D., Lewis Feldstein, and Donald J. Cohen. (2004) *Better Together: Restoring the American Community.* Simon and Schuster.

Quadagno, Jill. (1996) *The Color of Welfare: How Racism Undermined the War on Poverty.* Oxford University Press.

Radcliffe-Brown, Alfred R. (1922/1967) *The Andaman Islanders.* New York: Free Press.

Ragin, Charles C. (2008) *Redesigning Social Inquiry: Fuzzy Sets and Beyond.* University of Chicago Press.

Ragin, Charles C., and Lisa M. Amoroso. (2010) *Constructing Social Research: The Unity and Diversity of Method.* Sage.

Raijman, Rebecca. (2001) "Determinants of Entrepreneurial Intentions: Mexican Immigrants in Chicago." *Journal of Behavioral and Experimental Economics* 30, no. 5: 393–411.

Raudenbush, Stephen W., and Robert Sampson. (1999) "Systematic Social Observation of Public Spaces: A New Look at Disorder in Urban Neighborhoods." *American Journal of Sociology* 105, no. 3: 603–651.

Real Clear Politics. (2011) "Neal Boortz on the Moocher Class." Video. http://www.realclearpolitics.com/video/2010/10/14/neal_boortz_on_the_moocher_class.html.

Rector, Robert, and Patrick Fagan. (1996) "How Welfare Harms Kids." Backgrounder no. 1084 on Welfare and Welfare Spending. Heritage Foundation.

Rector, Robert, and Rachel Sheffield. (2011) "Air Conditioning, Cable TV, and an Xbox: What Is Poverty in the United States Today?" Backgrounder no. 2575 on Poverty and Inequality, Heritage Foundation.

Reich, Robert. (1992) *The Work of Nations: Preparing Ourselves for 21st Century Capitalism.* Vintage.

——. (2011) *Aftershock: The Next Economy and America's Future.* Vintage.

Richardson, Joseph B. (2010) "Men Do Matter: Ethnographic Insights on the Socially Supportive Role of the African American 'Uncle' in the Lives of Single-Female Headed Households and At-Risk African American Male Youth." In *Social Work with African American Males: Health, Mental Health and Social Policy* (Waldo E. Johnson, ed.): 81–100. Oxford University Press.

Rischin, Moses. (1962), *The Promised City: New York Jews 1870–1914.* Harvard University Press.

Roder, Anne, and Dorie Seavey. (2006) *Investing in Low-Wage Workers: Lessons from Family Child Care in Rhode Island.* Public/Private Ventures.

Roediger, David R. (2006) *Working toward Whiteness: How America's Immigrants Became White: The Strange Journey from Ellis Island to the Suburbs.* Basic Books.

——. (2007) *The Wages of Whiteness: Race and the Making of the American Working Class*. Verso.

Rose, Tricia. (2008) *The Hip-Hop Wars: What We Talk about When We Talk about Hip-Hop—And Why It Matters*. Basic Civitas Books.

Rothstein, Richard. (2004) *Class and Schools: Using Social, Economic, and Educational Reform to Close the Black-White Achievement Gap*. Teachers College Press.

Royster, Deidre A. (2003) *Race and the Invisible Hand: How White Networks Exclude Black Men from Blue-Collar Jobs*. University of California Press.

Rubin, Lillian B. (1994) *Families on the Fault Line*. Harper Perennial.

Saez, Emmanuel. (2013) "Striking It Richer: The Evolution of Top Incomes in the United States (Updated with 2012 Preliminary Estimates)." http://elsa .berkeley.edu/~saez/saez-UStopincomes-2012.pdf

Sampson, Robert J. (2013) *Great American City: Chicago and the Enduring Neighborhood Effect*. University of Chicago Press.

Sampson, Robert J., D. Morenoff, and F. Earls. (1999) "Beyond Social Capital: Spatial Dynamics of Collective Efficacy for Children. *American Sociological Review* 64, no. 5: 633–660.

Sampson, Robert J., D. Morenoff, and Thomas Gannon-Rowley. (2002) "Assessing 'Neighborhood Effects': Social Processes and New Directions in Research." *Annual Review of Sociology* 28: 443–478.

Sampson, Robert J., and Stephen W. Raudenbush. (1999) "Systematic Social Observation of Public Spaces: A New Look at Disorder in Urban Neighborhoods." *American Journal of Sociology* 105, no. 3: 603–651.

Sánchez-Jankowski, Martín. (1991) *Islands in the Streets: Gangs and American Urban Society*. University of California Press.

Sassen, Saskia. (1999) *Globalization and Its Discontents*. New Press.

——. (2001) *The Global City: New York, London, Tokyo*. Princeton University Press.

——. (2008) *Territory, Authority, Rights: From Medieval to Global Assemblages*. Princeton University Press.

——. (2014) *Expulsions: Brutality and Complexity in the Global Economy*. Oxford University Press.

Schiff, Jacob. (2009) "The Persistence of Misrecognition." Paper prepared for the Political Theory Workshop at the University of Chicago, January 12.

Schiraldi, Vincent, and Jason Ziedenberg. (2003) "Race and Incarceration in Maryland." Policy analysis commissioned by Maryland Legislative Black Caucus. Justice Policy Institute. Washington, DC.

Schlossman, Michael B. (2013) "Not Quite Treatment, Not Quite Punishment: A Case Study of American Juvenile Justice in the Get-Tough Era (1987–2009)." PhD diss., Princeton University.

Schuman, Howard, Charlotte Steeh, Lawrence Bobo, and Maria Krysan. (1997) *Racial Attitudes in America: Trends and Interpretations*, rev. ed. Harvard University Press.

Schumpeter, Joseph A. (1942/1975) *Capitalism, Socialism and Democracy.* Harper.

Sealander, Judith. (2003) *The Failed Century of the Child: Governing America's Young in the Twentieth Century.* Cambridge University Press.

Seavey, Ormond, ed. (1999) *Autobiography and Other Writings—Benjamin Franklin.* Oxford University Press.

Sennett, Richard. (2000) *The Corrosion of Character: The Personal Consequences of Work in the New Capitalism.* W. W. Norton.

———. (2007) *The Culture of the New Capitalism.* Yale University Press.

Sennett, Richard, and Jonathan Cobb. (1993) *The Hidden Injuries of Class.* W. W. Norton.

Sharkey, Patrick. (2013) *Stuck in Place: Urban Neighborhoods and the End of Progress toward Racial Equality.* University of Chicago Press.

Shefner, Jon, and Patricia Fernández-Kelly. (2011) *Globalization and Beyond: New Examinations of Global Power and Its Alternatives.* Penn State Press.

Shields, Mark. (2013) *PBS NewsHour,* June 21.

Shonkoff, Jack P., and Deborah Phillips. (2000) *From Neurons to Neighbourhoods: The Science of Early Child Development.* National Academies Press.

Siisiäinen, Martti. (2000) "Two Concepts of Social Capital: Bourdieu vs. Putnam." Paper presented at ISTR Fourth International Conference "The Third Sector: For What and for Whom?" Trinity College, Dublin, Ireland, July 5–8.

Skidmore, Howard. (1977) *The Story So Far, Sesquicentennial of the Baltimore and Ohio Railroad, 1827–1977.* Maryland Historical Society.

Skocpol, Theda. (1979) *States and Social Revolutions: A Comparative Analysis of France, Russia, and China.* Cambridge University Press.

———. (1995) *Protecting Soldiers and Mothers: The Political Origins of Social Policy in the United States.* Harvard University Press.

Slicker, Ellen K., and Douglas J. Palmer. (1993). "Mentoring At-Risk High School Students: Evaluation of a School-Based Program." *School Counselor* 40, no. 5: 327–334.

Small, Mario. (2004) *Villa Victoria: The Transformation of Social Capital in a Boston Barrio.* University of Chicago Press.

———. (2010) *Unanticipated Gains: Origins of Network Inequality in Everyday Life.* Oxford University Press.

Smelser, Neil, and Richard Swedberg. (2005) *The Handbook of Economic Sociology.* Princeton University Press.

Smith, C. Fraser. (1999) *William Donald Schaefer: A Political Biography.* Johns Hopkins University Press.

Solomon, Patrick. (1992) *Black Resistance in High School: Forging a Separatist Culture.* State University of New York Press.

Sowell, Thomas. (1981) *Markets and Minorities.* Basic Books.

Spencer, Herbert. (1851/2012) *Social Statics; Or, the Conditions Essential to Human Happiness Specified, and the First of Them Developed.* Ulan.

Spock, Benjamin. (1946/2012) *Baby and Child Care.* Gallery Books.

Stack, Carol. (1971/1997) *All Our Kin: Strategies for Survival in a Black Community.* Basic Books.

Steinmetz, George. (2006) "Bourdieu's Disavowal of Lacan: Psychoanalytic Theory and the Concepts of 'Habitus' and 'Symbolic Capital.'" *Constellations* 13, no. 4: 445–464.

Stepick, Alex, Carol Dutton Stepick, Emmanuel Eugene, Deborah Teed, and Yves Labissiere. (2001) "Shifting Identities and Generational Conflict: Growing Up Haitian in Miami." In *Ethnicities: Children of Immigrants in America* (Rubén Rumbaut and Alejandro Portes, eds.). Russell Sage Foundation.

Stier, Haya, and Marta Tienda. (2001) *The Color of Opportunity: Pathways to Family, Work, and Welfare.* Chicago: University of Chicago Press.

Stossell, John. (2011) "Battle for the Future." Fox Business News Video. http://www.youtube.com/watch?v=TScZwwnTN3Q.

Streensland, Brian. (2007) *The Failed Welfare Revolution: America's Struggle over Guaranteed Income Policy.* Princeton University Press.

Sullivan, Mercer L. (1989) *"Getting Paid": Youth Crime and Work in the Inner City.* Cornell University Press.

Suttles, Gerald D. (1972) *The Social Construction of Communities.* University of Chicago Press.

Swidler, Ann. (1986) "Culture in Action: Symbols and Strategies." *American Sociological Review* 51, no. 2: 273–286.

———. (2001) *Talk of Love: How Culture Matters.* University of Chicago Press.

Switzky, Bryant Ruiz. (2012) "Black Business Lending: Harder Hit, Less Rebound." *Washington Business Journal,* March 23. http://www.bizjournals.com/washington/print-edition/2012/03/23/black-business-lending-harder.html?page=all.

Taub, Richard. (1991) "Differing Conceptions of Honor and Orientations toward Work and Marriage among Low-Income African Americans and Mexican Americans." Paper presented at the University of Chicago Urban Family Life Conference, October. Published by the Center for Urban Inequality, University of Chicago.

Telles, Edward E., and Vilma Ortiz. (2008) *Generations of Exclusion: Mexican-Americans, Assimilation and Race.* Russell Sage Foundation.

Terry-Humen, Elizabeth, Jennifer Manlove, and Sarah Cottingham. (2008) "Trends and Recent Estimates: Sexual Activity among U.S. Teens." Child Trends Research Brief, Publication #2006-08. http://eric.ed.gov/?id=ED492903.

Thomas, William I., and Dorothy S. Thomas. (1928) *The Child in America: Behavior Problems and Programs.* New York: Knopf.

Thomas, William I., and Florian Znaniecki. (1918/1996) *The Polish Peasant in Europe and America.* University of Illinois Press.

Tienda, Marta, and Haya Stier. (1991) "Intergenerational Continuity of Welfare Dependence: Ethnic and Neighborhood Comparisons." Paper presented at the Chicago Urban Poverty and Family Life Conference, Irving B. Harris Graduate School of Public Policy Studies, University of Chicago.

Tienda, Marta, and William J. Wilson, eds. (2002) *Youth in Cities: A Cross-National Perspective.* Cambridge University Press.

Tilly, Charles, ed. (1975) *The Formation of National States in Western Europe.* Princeton University Press.

———. (2006) *Regimes and Repertoires.* University of Chicago Press.

Tilly, Charles, and Sidney Tarrow. (2006) *Contentious Politics.* Oxford University Press.

Tocqueville, Alexis de. (1835/2003) *Democracy in America.* Penguin Classics.

Toosi, Mitra. (2002) "A Century of Change: The U.S. Labor Force, 1950–2050." *Monthly Labor Review* (May): 15–28.

Turner, Victor. (1974) "Liminal to Liminoid in Play, Flow, and Ritual: An Essay in Comparative Symbology." *Rice University Studies* 60, no. 3: 53–92.

U.S. Bureau of Justice Statistics. (2010) "Federal Justice Statistics 2013." http://www.bjs.gov/index.cfm?ty=pbdetail&iid=4861.

———. (2013) "Prisoners in 2012—Advance Counts." http://www.bjs.gov/index.cfm?ty=pbdetail&iid=4737.

U.S. Bureau of Labor Statistics. (2011) "Union Members 2010." Press release.

———. (2012) "Civilian Labor Force Participation Rates by Age, Sex, Race, and Ethnicity." http://www.bls.gov/emp/ep_table_303.htm.

———. (2013a) "Consumer Expenditure Survey." http://www.bls.gov/cex/csxstnd.htm.

———. (2013b) "Consumer Expenditures—2012. http://www.bls.gov/news/release/cesan.nr0.htm.

———. (2013c) "Current Population Survey." http://www.bls.gov/cps/.

U.S. Census Bureau. (2007) "Survey of Business Owners." https://www.census.gov/econ/sbo/07menu.html.

———. (2011) "American Community Survey." http://www.census.gov/acs/www/about_the_survey/2011_acs_improvements/.

———. (2012a) "Employee Benefits, Government Transfer Payments, Social Assistance." https://www.census.gov/compendia/statab/cats/social_insurance_human_services.html.

———. (2012b) "State and County QuickFacts—Baltimore City, Maryland." http://quickfacts.census.gov/qfd/states/24/24510.html.

U.S. Department of Health and Human Services. (2009) "Domestic Violence and the Child Welfare System." Child Welfare Information Gateway Bulletin for Professionals. https://www.childwelfare.gov/pubs/factsheets/domesticviolence.cfm.

———. (2012) "Information on Poverty and Income Statistics: A Summary of 2012 Current Population Survey Data." ASPE Issue Brief. http://aspe.hhs.gov/hsp/12/povertyandincomeest/ib.shtml.

———. (2013) Office of Family Assistance: "Healthy Marriage and Responsible Fatherhood." http://www.acf.hhs.gov/programs/ofa/programs/healthy-marriage.

U.S. Small Business Administration. (2011) Baltimore District Office. "Local Company Moves People and Makes Profits." http://www.sba.gov/about -offices-content/2/3120.

———. (2013) "Community—Open for Business." http://www.sba.gov /community/blogs/official-sba-news-and-views/open-for-business.

Valdez, Zulema. (2011) *The New Entrepreneurs: How Race, Class, and Gender Shape American Enterprise.* Stanford University Press.

Van Maanen, John, ed. (1983) *Qualitative Methodology.* Sage.

———. (2011) *Tales of the Field: On Writing Ethnography.* University of Chicago Press.

Venkatesh, Sudhir Alladi. (2002) *American Project: The Rise and Fall of a Modern Ghetto.* Harvard University Press.

———. (2008) *Gang Leader for a Day: A Rogue Sociologist Takes to the Streets.* Penguin.

———. (2009) *Off the Books: The Underground Economy of the Urban Poor.* Harvard University Press.

Vey, Jennifer. (2012) "Building from Strength: Creating Opportunity in Greater Baltimore's Next Economy." Brookings Institution, Metropolitan Policy Program, Washington, DC.

Vigil, James Diego. (2002) *A Rainbow of Gangs: Street Cultures in the Mega-City.* University of Texas Press.

Wacquant, Loïc. (1997) "Three Pernicious Premises in the Study of the American Ghetto." *International Journal of Urban and Regional Research* 21, no. 2: 341–353.

———. (1998) "Negative Social Capital: State Breakdown and Social Destitution in America's Urban Core." *Netherlands Journal of Housing and the Built Environment* 13, no. 1: 25–40.

———. (2008) *Urban Outcasts: A Comparative Sociology of Advanced Marginality.* Cambridge: Polity.

———. (2009a) *Prisons of Poverty.* University of Minnesota Press.

———. (2009b) *Punishing the Poor: The Neoliberal Government of Social Insecurity.* Duke University Press.

Wacquant, Loïc J. D., and William Julius Wilson. (1989) "The Cost of Racial and Class Exclusion in the Inner City." *Annals of the American Association of Political and Social Science* 501 (January): 8–41.

Wagner, David, and Jennifer Barton Gilman. (2012) *Confronting Homelessness: Poverty, Politics and the Failure of Social Policy.* Lynne Rienner.

Wagner, Matthew L. (2008) "Why Some Cities Succeed More than Others at Black Entrepreneurship: An Analysis of Variables Predicted to Impact Rates of Black Business." PhD diss., University of Wisconsin, Milwaukee.

Wagner, Peter. (2012) "Incarceration Is Not an Equal Opportunity Punishment." Prison Policy Initiative. http://www.prisonpolicy.org/articles/note qual.html.

Walker, Juliet E. K. (2007) *The Dialogue of Civilizations: Capitalism, Race, and Entrepreneurship*. Palgrave Macmillan.

———. (2009) *History of Black Business in American: Capitalism, Race, Entrepreneurship*. University of North Carolina Press.

Wallis, Allan, Jarle P. Crocker, and Bill Schechter. (1998) "Social Capital and Community Building: Part One." *National Civic Review* 87, no. 3: 253–272.

Wallis, Allan. (1998) "Social Capital and Community Building: Part Two." *National Civic Review* 87, no. 4: 317–319.

Ward, Thomas W. (2012) *Gangs without Borders: An Ethnography of a Salvadoran Street Gang*. Oxford University Press.

Warner, Barbara D., and Pamela Wilcox Rountree. (1997) "Local Social Ties in a Community and Crime Model: Questioning the Systemic Nature of Informal Social Control." *Social Problems* 44, no. 4: 520–536.

Warren, Mark R., Philip Thompson, and Susan Saegert. (2001) "The Role of Social Capital in Combating Poverty." In *Social Capital and Poor Communities* (Susan Saegert, Philip Thompson, and Mark R. Warren, eds.): 1–28. Russell Sage Foundation.

Watch Tower Bible and Tract Society of Pennsylvania. (1993) *Jehovah's Witnesses—Proclaimers of God's Kingdom*. Watch Tower Bible and Tract Society.

Webb, Gary. (1999) *Dark Alliance: The CIA, the Contras, and the Crack Cocaine Explosion*. Seven Stories Press.

Weber, Max. (1912/2002) *The Protestant Ethic and the Spirit of Capitalism*. Penguin Classics.

———. (1919) *Politik als beruf* [Politics as a vocation]. Duncker and Humblodt.

Weber, Max. (2004) *The Vocation Lectures: Science as a Vocation; Politics as a Vocation*, edited by David Owen and Tracy B. Strong, translated by Rodney Livingstone. Hackett.

Western, Bruce. (2007) *Punishment and Inequality in America*. Russell Sage Foundation.

Wheeler, Etta. (1991) *The Story of Mary Ellen: Which Started the Child Saving Crusade throughout the World*. American Humane Association.

White, Harrison. (1970) *Chains of Opportunity: System Models of Mobility in Organizations*. Harvard University Press.

Wilder, Laura Ingalls. (1932) *Little House in the Big Woods*. Harper and Brothers

———. (1994) *The Complete Little House Nine-Book Set*. Harper Collins.

Wilkerson, Isabel. (2011) *The Warmth of Other Suns: The Epic Story of America's Great Migration*. Vintage.

Will, George. (1994) *The Leveling Wind: Politics, the Culture and Other News, 1990–1994*. Viking.

Willis, Paul. (1981) *Learning to Labor: How Working Class Kids Get Working Class Jobs*. Columbia University Press.

Wilson, William J. (1987) *The Truly Disadvantaged: The Inner City, the Underclass and Public Policy*. University of Chicago Press.

———. (1997) *When Work Disappears: The World of the New Urban Poor*. Alfred A. Knopf.

———. (2010) *More than Just Race: Being Black and Poor in the Inner City*. W. W. Norton.

Wimmer, Andreas. (2013) *Ethnic Boundary Making: Institutions, Power, Networks*. Oxford University Press.

Wingert, Pat, and Barbara Kantrowitz. (1993) "The Norplant Debate." *Newsweek*, February 14.

Winston, Clifford. (2006) *Government Failure versus Market Failure: Microeconomic Policy Research and Government Performance*. Brookings Institution and American Enterprise Institute for Public Policy.

Wolfe, Tom. (1987) *The Bonfire of the Vanities*. Farrar, Straus and Giroux.

Wolff, Edward N. (2010) "Recent Trends in Household Wealth in the United States: Rising Debt and the Middle-Class Squeeze." Working Paper No. 159, Levy Economics Institute of Bard College.

Wright, James M. (1921/1971) *The Free Negro in Maryland, 1634–1860*. Octagon Books.

Wuthnow, Robert. (1990) *The Restructuring of American Religion*. Princeton University Press.

———. (2007) *America and the Challenges of Religious Diversity*. Princeton University Press.

———. (2012) *The God Problem: Expressing Faith and Being Reasonable*. University of California Press.

Yokley, Raytha, Ann K. Nelsen, and Hart M. Nelsen. (1971) *The Black Church in America*. Basic Books.

Zelizer, Viviana. (1994) *Pricing the Priceless Child: The Changing Social Value of Children*. Princeton University Press.

———. (1997) *The Social Meaning of Money: Pin Money, Paychecks, Poor Relief and Other Currencies*. Princeton University Press.

———. (2007) *The Purchase of Intimacy*. Princeton University Press.

———. (2011) *Economic Lives: How Culture Shapes the Economy*. Princeton University Press.

Zhou, Min, and Bankston, Carl. (1998), *Growing Up American: How Vietnamese Immigrants Adapt to Life in the United States*. Russell Sage Foundation.

Zhou, Min, Jennifer Lee, Jody Agius Vallejo, Rosaura Tafoya-Estrada, and Yang Sao Xiong. (2008) "Success Attained, Deterred, and Denied: Divergent Pathways to Social Mobility in Los Angeles' New Second Generation." *Annals of the American Academy of Political and Social Sciences* 620: 37–61.

Zimmerman, David, and Phillip Levine. (1996) "The Intergenerational Correlation in AFDC Participation: Welfare Trap or Poverty Trap?" Institute for Research on Poverty Discussion Paper No. 1100-96. University of Wisconsin–Madison..

Zwitzky, Bryant Ruiz. (2012) "Black Business Lending: Harder Hit, Less Rebound." *Washington Business Journal.* http://www.bizjournals.com /washington/print-edition/2012/03/23/black-business-lending-harder .html?page=all.

INDEX

NOTE: Page numbers followed by *f* indicate a figure; those followed by *t* indicate a table.

Abdullah, Mohammed, 288–89
abolition movement, 47–48, 282
abortion, 236, 248
abuse. *See* child abuse
acute regulation, 118–19, 123–27, 267;
    forced sterilization as, 124–25; of
    males in welfare households, 59,
    82–83, 92–94, 124, 267, 364n1(ch.3);
    modes of resistance to, 125–27; school
    resource officers and, 3, 339–40
Adams, John Quincy, 46
adolescent motherhood, 215–16,
    230–52; as cultural capital, 241–43,
    247; cultural debates on, 238–39;
    diversified social networks and, 252;
    economic debates on, 238–40; family
    background and, 234–35; housing and,
    59; legislative responses to, 235–36;
    link with poverty of, 251–52; marriage
    promotion programs and, 237–38,
    369n5; medical and social services
    for, 59; political debates on, 235–39,
    370n8; rates of, 233–34, 235*t*, 236–37,
    369nn1–4; as symbol of adulthood, 3,
    18, 58–59, 199, 243–52; welfare depen-
    dence and, 238–40, 244–46, 370n6
adulthood. *See* transition to adulthood
Affordable Care Act of 2010, 102,
    365n1(ch.5)
agency. *See* personal agency

Aid for Dependent Children (ADC), 91
Aid for Families with Dependent Chil-
    dren (AFDC), 7, 91–92; annual costs
    of, 365n2(ch.6); monthly payments
    by, 92; pregnancy policies of, 235–36;
    regulations on males in households by,
    92–94, 124, 267
Aldridge, Stephen, 205
Alexander, Karl, 207–9
Alexander, Michelle, 127, 341
Algar, Michael H., 362n4
Alice in Wonderland (Carroll), 155–56
ambivalent benevolence, 2, 91, 171,
    350–51
American Association of Black Social
    Workers, 367n4
American Label Company, 265–66
American State: antigovernment atti-
    tudes towards, 365n1(ch.5); develop-
    ment as an industrial state of, 97–102;
    evolution of inner cities in, 103–4;
    ideological debates on poverty in,
    2–5, 171, 194, 348–55, 372nn2–3;
    immigrant mobility in, 98–103, 106–8,
    365n2(ch.5), 365n5; income inequality
    in, 345–47, 372n1; piecemeal palliative
    programs of, 119–23, 343–44; poverty
    rates in, 1, 43–45, 345, 372n1; promo-
    tion of individual and group advance-
    ment by, 3–4, 95–98, 104–5, 107,

American State (*continued*)
119–20, 343–44, 365n1(ch.5), 365n4;
systematic exclusion of Blacks from
prosperity in, 95, 103–9, 344, 347–48.
See also government social programs;
the state
anamorphosis, 116
Anderson, Elijah, 125, 362n2
Anheier, Helmut, 205
Appalachia, 102–3
The Archaeology of Knowledge (Foucault),
117
Artis, Damon, 84
Asian immigrants, 328–31, 335*t*, 336
Atkinson, Roland, 321
Atlas Storage Company, 60, 62, 133
attention deficit disorder (ADD), 121,
305–6, 319
Avalon (Levinson), 32, 50
Avoid Independent Thinking (Watch
Tower Society), 292–93

Baltimore, 38–53, 352–53, 363n7; adolescent pregnancy rates in, 233–35,
360nn1–3(ch.12); antebellum Black
population of, 46–48, 50; baseball in,
179–81; Beginning School Study in,
207–8; Black entertainment district
of, 52; Child Safe Program of, 160;
civil unrest in, 52, 298, 328, 363n8;
deindustrialization in, 5–6, 15, 39;
globalization in, 39–45, 373n4; history of, 45–47, 363nn3–4; immigrant
communities of, 46, 48, 50–51, 363n3;
incarceration rates in, 77; industrial
base of, 27–28, 38–39, 45–47, 181,
265–66, 363n5; Jewish exodus from,
32, 50, 363n6, 363n8; John Paul II's
visit to, 148; Korean population of,
182, 185; labor unions in, 47; layoffs
in, 39–40; poverty rates in, 44; SBA-
backed loans in, 334; Schaeffer's
"Renaissance" in, 48; segregated Black
neighborhoods of, 5–8, 21–24, 48–53;
twentieth-century Black population of,
48; urban revitalization programs in,
180–82; violent crime rate in, 337–38;

White flight and re-segregation of,
181–82, 298; youth sexuality rates in,
369n1(ch.12). *See also* West Baltimore
Baltimore and Ohio (B&O) Railroad, 46
Baltimore Gas and Electric Company, 28,
266, 297
Baltimore School for the Arts, 337
Baltimore Yellow Cab Company, 35
Baptist Good News Church, 287
Barclay School, 188–89
Bartlett and Hayward plant, 28–29
Bates, Timothy, 324–25
Bauer, Andre, 349
Becker, Howard S., 156
Beckford, James A., 292
Beginning School Study, 207–8
Belay, Toya, 296, 301, 304, 314
Bell, Daniel, 281
The Bell Curve (Murray), 348–49
Bench, Norma, 285–86
Bentham, Jeremy, 350
Berger, Peter, 281
Best, Wallace, 283–84
Bethlehem Steel Company, 5–6, 28, 29,
46–47, 181
Big Brothers/Big Sisters, 210–11, 368n12
Big Floyd Twigg, 17, 54–72, 108; arrests
and incarceration of, 61, 68–69, 77,
87, 93; background and education
of, 55–58, 72, 82–83; children of,
54–55, 58–64, 82–83, 85, 87, 140–43;
comparison with Donald Wilson of,
72–73; disposition of, 54–55, 62, 149;
economic context of, 64–65, 67, 72–
73; employment of, 60–62, 64, 73, 146;
goals and means of, 195*f*; intrusion of
the state and, 73; marriage to Iliad of,
70–71, 146; parenting of Little Floyd
by, 148–50, 152; perceived laziness of,
60–61, 69, 87–88, 131, 150; PISCO
and, 67–70; on reuniting the family,
62–71, 146, 149–50
biographical accounts, 10–11, 16–17,
342–43, 361n1, 362n6
birth control, 125, 236, 248, 252
Black English vernacular, 183–84, 204,
211

Black Panther Party, 337
blaming the poor, 8–11, 124, 128, 316,
    343–45, 361n2
Bloomberg, Michael, 127, 366n4
Bluestone, Barry, 39
Bobo, Lawrence, 198–99
Boissevain, Jeremy, 198, 240, 368n6
Bolton Swim and Tennis Club, 175, 190,
    206
bonding social capital, 205–6
Borjas, George J., 336
bounded solidarity, 240
Bourdieu, Pierre: on cultural capital, 242;
    on habitus, 117, 126–27; on misrecog-
    nition, 129–31, 152; on social capital,
    194, 203, 368n5; on symbolic violence,
    116–17, 127–29, 152
*Bowling Alone: The Collapse and Revival
    of American Community* (Putnam),
    202, 368n7
bridging social capital, 205–6, 209–12,
    371n1
A Brief History of Neoliberalism
    (Harvey), 12
Broh, Beckett A., 208, 209
Bronars, Stephen G., 336
Brookings Institution, 352
Brooks, Bungie, 312
Brooks-Gunn, Jeanne, 323, 371n5
Brown, Dalia, 226–27
Brown, Demetrius, 85–86
Brown, Octavia, 174–75
Brown, Ramona, 138–39
Brown, Reggie, 226–31
Brown, Reggie Shantell, 230–31
Brown, Regina, 226–27
Brown vs. Board of Education decision, 255
Buck, Carrie, 124–25
Buck vs. Bell, 366n3(ch.6)
bureaucratic interference. *See* government
    social programs; intrusion of the state
Bush, George W., 237–38, 332–33
businesses. *See* entrepreneurship
Butler, John S., 327–28

Calvert, Cecilius, Lord Baltimore, 45,
    363n3

The Calvert School, 178
Calvinism, 281
Camden Yards Park, 180
Cameron, Tyrell, 86
Campbell, Joseph, 354–55
Campbell, Marcus, 145
capital flow formations, 324
capitalism: personal responsibility and,
    123; predatory states and, 96, 103,
    365n3; state commitment to, 95
capital retrogression, 109–11, 115, 212,
    325, 338, 352
Cardigan, Alysia, 138
Carnegie, Andrew, 99
Carroll, Lewis, 155–56
Carson, Justin L., 206–7
Cavalluzo, Ken S., 336
Central American immigrants,
    365n2(ch.5)
Chan, Christian S., 211
Chapman, Lorenzo "Weedy," 186–88,
    190, 204, 214, 261–62, 269
Chapman, Reuben "Beamy" (son), 288;
    armed robbery of, 267–68; incarcera-
    tion of, 213–14, 268–69, 280
Chapman, Reuben (father), 261–62
Charm City, 363n7. *See also* Baltimore
charter schools, 200–201
Chicago school of sociology: on Black
    assimilation, 103–4; on neighborhood
    effects, 320
child abuse, 169–71; alternative policies
    on, 169–70; childhood agency and,
    153–56, 162–68; class and race fac-
    tors in, 170; definitions of, 153–56,
    159, 367n2; exaggerated reports of,
    161; legal framework of, 158–62, 170;
    origins as concept of, 156–58; printed
    material on, 160
childhood, 6–8; awareness of skin and
    hair differences in, 6, 130–31, 177;
    criminalized minor offenses of, 3, 319,
    339–40; education spending on, 2–4;
    family responsibilities of, 174, 193,
    214–15, 244, 251, 319; gang mem-
    bership and, 85–86, 136–37, 364n6;
    knowledge of liminal institutions in,

childhood (*continued*)
153, 156, 166–71, 193, 319, 368n3; neighborhood effects and, 322; social capital and, 192–212; sports, cooperation and belonging in, 175–76; summer activities in, 184–85, 194–95, 206–9, 368n10; television time in, 368n9. *See also* education; transition to adulthood; names of specific children, e.g. Twigg, Clarise

childhood agency, 151–71; awareness of social service programs and, 153, 156, 166–71, 193, 368n3; fragility of parental authority and, 153–56, 162–71, 222–26; gender identity and, 152; of immigrant children, 167–68; lying and, 160, 166–67; neighborhood power hierarchies and, 165–66, 219–20, 228; sexuality and, 166–67; sociological consideration of, 156–58, 170–71

Child Protective Services, 18, 113–14, 350–51; on children in need of assistance, 55, 137, 193; divided families and, 62; foster care under, 55, 137–40, 168, 269, 367n4; fragility of parental authority under, 154–55, 222–26; hypervigilance of, 351; immunity of workers for, 161; legal framework for, 159–62; original purpose of, 171; penalties on parents imposed by, 153, 225–26; social class of workers for, 161–62

Child Safe Program, 160

A Christmas Carol (Dickens), 124

Church of the Divine Shepherd, 286–87

Civil Rights Act of 1965, 101

civil rights movement, 20, 22, 158, 255–56, 298; Black entrepreneurship and, 328–29; legislation of, 101–2, 255; live-in maid work and, 263; religiosity and, 284; residential desegregation and, 52–53

Clarise Twigg. *See* Twigg, Clarise

class and socioeconomic status, 4; adolescent births and, 234–35; child abuse cases and, 170; educational

achievement gap and, 206–9, 368n10; immigrant mobility in, 98–103, 106–8, 365n2(ch.5), 365n5; intrusion of the state and, 73, 161–62; labor struggles and, 99–100; language differences and, 183–86, 211

Clinton, Bill, administration: economic expansion under, 76; Putnam's influence on, 202; welfare reform under, 65–66, 225, 348–49, 364n9

closure, 322

Cloward, Richard, 12

Cobb, Jonathan, 81

Coleman, James, 194; on closure, 322; on social capital, 199–203, 368n5

Collins, Frances, 269, 270

The Color of Welfare (Quadagno), 12

Coming Apart: The State of White America (Murray), 370n8

communication skills, 183–86. *See also* language and literacy skills

community mapping, 16, 362n5

community organizations, 122

Community Reinvestment Act, 123

Community School of the Holy Spirit, 140–42; academic standards at, 142; Clarise Twigg at, 179–89; homework at, 141–42, 182–83; Little Floyd Twigg at, 140–42, 152; planned closure of, 185–86; uniforms of, 179, 182, 189; White middle-class norms of, 152

community studies, 371n3

The Competitive Advantage of Nations (Porter), 121–22

"The Competitive Advantage of the Inner City" (Porter), 121–22

Conan Doyle, Arthur, 14

concentration of poverty, 238–39

conformity, 195–96

conservative principles, 3–4, 171, 195, 348–352, 372n2

contraception, 125, 236, 248, 252

Contreras, Fidel, 168

Cook, Marvin, 135

Cooper, Calvin "Blackjack," 220, 310, 312–13

Le Corbusier, 136

corporal punishment, 154–60, 167, 170
Cosby, Bill, 106–7
Coulter, Anne, 370n8
crack cocaine, 58, 109–10, 228, 279, 310–11
criminalization of poverty, 3, 319, 325, 339–40
Cuban immigrants, 327, 329, 333–34
cultural capital, 203–5, 232–33, 368n8; of adolescent motherhood, 241–52, 247; of education, 242; of religiosity, 204, 212–13. *See also* social capital
cultural explanations of poverty, 238–39
Culver, James, 61; alcohol use by, 186, 229, 269; children of, 213–15, 264–65; employment of, 269; Lydia Forrest and, 93, 133, 186, 213–15, 231, 264–67, 269–70
Culver, James, Jr., 266
Culver, James, Jr. "Mush," 215, 246, 269
Cumming, Alina, 286–87
Cummings, Marsha, 160

Davis, Kareen, 163–64
deadbeat fathers, 66–69, 93
deindustrialization, 5–6, 15, 346–47; absence of employment opportunities and, 17, 39, 56, 73, 82, 315, 363nn7–8; changing notions of masculinity and, 81; drug trade and, 19; incarceration rates and, 12–13; layoffs and restructuring of, 39–41, 43–44, 56, 108, 181, 343; race and, 5, 107–8; retraining programs and, 34–35; service-based economy of, 40, 41*f*, 48, 363n2; women in the workforce and, 73–74. *See also* globalization
Dell House, 306–7
demand distortions, 324
Democracy in America (Tocqueville), 98
demonization of the poor, 4
the deserving poor, 91, 124
developmental states, 96–102. *See also* American State
Diamond Social Club, 189–90
Dickens, Charles, 124
Dickson, Alonso, 277

dispossession of Black Americans from prosperity, 95, 103–9, 344, 347–48
distorted engagement, 2–5, 18, 95, 115–31, 212, 351–55, 372n15; absence of alternatives to, 3; as acute regulation, 3, 118–19, 123–27, 339–40; as anamorphosis, 116; liminal logic of, 116–18, 209–12; as palliation, 118–23; predatory commerce and, 338–41; qualitative differences of, 2–3; suspicion, surveillance, and control of, 2, 115, 117–18, 124–31, 316, 325, 347; symbolic violence of, 119, 127–31, 152, 339–41, 366n6
Douglass, Frederick, 47, 57
Douglass Theater, 52
Downey, Douglas B., 208, 209
downward assimilation, 365n2(ch.5)
drug trade, 19, 109–10, 115, 136, 202; age of involvement in, 246; arrest rates for, 315–16; coherent logic in engagement in, 319–20; entrepreneurship and, 318–20; mandatory sentences for, 312; of Manny Man Williams, 197, 228, 310–16, 318–20, 337; power hierarchies in, 165–66, 228; violence associated with, 58, 111, 300, 312–14, 336–39; in West Baltimore neighborhoods, 58, 111, 113, 177, 227–28. *See also* gangs
drug use, 109–12; among Whites, 111; by Clarise Twigg, 189; consumption and addiction to, 111–12; testing for, 366n4; by Towanda Forrest, 220; treatment programs for, 112
Druid Hill Avenue, 51–52, 363n6
Druid Hill Park, 49
DuBois, W. E B., 51–52, 282–83
Duneer, Mitchell, 125
Durkheim, Emile, 11, 128, 280–84

Early Childhood Longitudinal Study, 208
economic sociology, 199–203, 239–40
economics of poverty, 72–73; capital retrogression in, 109–11, 115, 212, 325, 338, 352; exclusion of Blacks from American prosperity in, 95, 103–9,

economics of poverty (*continued*)
344, 347–48; family accumulated
wealth in, 317, 330; income inequality
in, 345–47, 372n1; neoclassical version
of *Homo economicus* and, 239; palliative *vs.* investment approaches to, 118–
23, 343–44; social basis of, 199–203,
239–40; state promotion of individual
and group advancement and, 3–4,
95–98, 104–5, 107, 119–20, 343–44;
365n4; urban underdevelopment in,
108–9; of the working poor, 351–53.
See also welfare programs
Edin, Kathryn, 205
Sister Edith, 187
Edmonson Village, 51, 300, 304, 307, 315
education, 2–4, 108; adolescent motherhood and, 241–42, 247–49; of African
American women, 78–79; attention deficit disorder diagnoses and,
121, 305–6, 319; charter school and
voucher programs in, 200–201; Coleman Report on, 199–203; criminalization of minor offenses and, 3, 319,
339–40; embodied knowledge and,
207; entrepreneurial success and, 330;
legal desegregation of, 101; mentoring
programs in, 210–12, 368nn11–14;
at Morrill Land-Grant colleges, 105;
in parochial schools, 9–10, 140, 172,
178–88, 192–93, 200, 371n5; poverty
and, 44, 178, 184–85, 194, 198–99;
in private schools, 178–79; public
funding of, 95, 100, 108, 343; school
resource officers and, 3, 339–40;
self-esteem boosting projects of,
172; in sex education, 252; summer
achievement gap and, 184, 194–95,
206–9, 368n10; television and, 368n9;
transition to maturity and, 86–90; in
West Baltimore, 57, 82. *See also* social
capital
Eisenhower, Dwight D., 332
The Elementary Forms of Religious Life
(Durkheim), 280–81
embedded autonomy, 1–2, 96–98, 116,
372n15

embodied knowledge, 117–18, 126–27,
243; of business know-how, 317–18;
education and, 207
employment, 73–79, 372n1; of African
American men, 75–78, 83*t*, 364n5,
372n1; of African American women,
75, 78–79; after the Great Recession of
2008, 76–77; Baltimore manufacturing base and, 27–28, 38–39, 45–47,
181, 265–66, 363n5; Black masculinity and, 79–83, 249; as domestic help,
258, 262–63, 276; economic sociology
and, 240; Great Migration and, 79–80;
impact on parenting of, 164–65; in
the informal economy, 364n1(ch.4);
labor struggles and, 99–100; limited
opportunities for, 315; in low-wage
jobs, 351–53; symbolic skills in, 77;
of White women, 81; of the working
poor, 351–53. *See also* deindustrialization; entrepreneurship
Enfield, Lucille, 139–40
enforceable trust, 240
England, 123–24
entrepreneurship, 315–41; accumulated
wealth and, 317, 330; aspiration and,
320, 337; capital flow formations and,
324; demand distortions and, 324;
developmental government action
and, 332–36; educational factors in,
330; embodied knowledge of, 317–18;
financial resources for, 316–18, 371n1;
generational perspectives on, 317–18;
Great Recession and, 372nn12–13;
interaction hypothesis of supply and
demand and, 336; liminal government
programs and, 302–3, 316, 324–26;
of Manny Man Williams's drug trade,
197, 228, 310–16, 318–20, 341; of Marcus Williams's hauling business, 303–
5, 307–8, 315–18, 320, 341; neighborhood effects and, 316, 317, 320–26,
334, 371n5; in the penury industry,
8, 121, 325, 341, 343–44; predatory
commerce and, 316, 336–41; race and
ethnicity factors in, 326–31, 335*t*, 336,
371nn8–9, 371–72nn11–14; rates of

success in, 327–28, 331–32; social capital and, 317. *See also* drug trade; Small Business Administration

Entwisle, Doris, 207–9

Equality of Educational Opportunity (Coleman), 199–203

ethnography, 13–17, 361n1; biographical accounts in, 10–11, 16–17, 342–43, 361n1, 362n6; community mapping in, 16, 362n5; empathy and, 16–17, 362n6; identification of experiential patterns in, 14; participant observation in, 16; refinement of deep theory in, 14–15, 362n4, 362n6. *See also* research methods

Evans, Peter, 1–2, 18, 95–98, 372n15

exclusion of African Americans from prosperity, 95, 103–9, 344, 347

Fairlie, Robert W., 330

faith. *See* religiosity

Families on the Fault Line (Rubin), 81

family law, 159

Farrakhan, Louis, 67, 288

Federal Deposit Insurance Corporation (FDIC), 40

femininity, 79, 90; government patriarchal imperatives of, 91; in transition to adulthood, 244. *See also* gender relations

feminism: gender relations and, 93; working women and, 74–75, 364n1(ch.4)

fetal alcohol syndrome, 139

fictive kinship, 16

financial institutions, 324

firearm violence, 267–68, 310, 313–16, 337, 339

fire hydrants, 185

First Baptist Church, 22–23, 300

Fitzgerald, F. Scott, 118

Fitzpatrick, Davinia, 89

Fitzpatrick, Sarah, 205

Flag House, 65, 67, 145

food stamp program, 366n4

forced sterilization, 124–25, 366n3(ch.6)

Ford, Henry, 99

"Forms of Capital" (Bourdieu), 203

Forrest, Deborah, 263–66

Forrest, Felicia, 62, 137, 214–15, 264–65, 269

Forrest, Gertrude "Gertie," 254–55, 263–64, 269

Forrest, Jonah, 253–61, 265, 275

Forrest, Lydia, 18, 131, 253–74; appearance of, 262; on Big Floyd Twigg's shortcomings, 61, 69, 87–88, 150; childhood and family background of, 253–61, 275; children with James Culver of, 213–15, 264–65, 269; children with Reuben Chapman of, 261–63, 267–69; on Clarise Twigg's appearance, 177, 204; custody of Clarise Twigg of, 62, 70, 138, 172–73, 177–78, 187–93, 215, 269–70; education of, 254, 260–61; employment and cleaning work of, 222–26, 262–64, 266, 271–73, 276; goals and means of, 195f, 196; incarcerated son of, 213–14, 268–69, 280; integrity and self-respect of, 272, 276; investigation for child abuse of, 222–26; James Culver and, 61, 93, 186, 213–15, 264–67, 269–70; Little Floyd Twigg and, 138, 143; middle-class dreams of, 271; move to the George Murphy Homes of, 269–70; religiosity of, 61, 69, 179, 186–88, 190, 192, 196, 204, 268–76, 286, 289–95; role in family of, 133–34, 137, 173, 205–6, 213, 271–72; social capital and, 192–98, 204–5; on Towanda Forrest's children, 230–31; welfare assistance of, 266–67, 272, 276

Forrest, Margaret, 145, 263; childhood of, 254–55; family background of, 253–55; Melinda Twigg and, 62, 66, 137–38, 150, 166, 249, 269

Forrest, Missie, 253–65, 268, 275; Benita and, 58–59, 132–34; Little Floyd Twigg and, 138

Forrest, Towanda, 18, 189, 213–31, 264–65, 348; academic skills of, 220, 230–31, 249; appearance of, 214, 219; Clarise Twigg and, 174, 177, 198,

Forrest, Towanda (*continued*)
215–16; conflict with mother of, 218,
222–26, 269; drug use by, 220; goals
and means of, 195*f*, 244–45; leadership
of, 218–23, 226; motherhood of, 131,
230–31; on pregnancy, 213, 221, 230;
Reggie Brown and, 226–31; suspen-
sions and expulsion from school of,
226, 249; toughness of, 216–18, 220,
226, 228
the 47 percent, 349–50
Forty Acres and a Mule program, 105–7
foster care, 55, 137–40, 168, 269, 367n4
Foucault, Michel, 117, 118
"The Fox and the Grapes" (Aesop), 199
Franklin, Benjamin, 98
Frazier, E. Franklin, 283, 329
Freeman, Anton, 84
Freud, Anna, 158
Freud, Sigmund, 158
Friedman, Milton, 40–41
Fromm, Erich, 158
Furstenberg, Frank, 245

Gaddis, S. Michael, 210, 368n11
gangs, 85–86, 136–37, 309–14, 364n6.
   See also drug trade
Gangs of New York (Scorsese), 364n6
gangsta limp, 309
Gans, Herbert, 11, 347
Garfinkel, Harold, 156
Garland, David, 12–13
Garrett. Deiondre, 220–23
Geertz, Clifford, 17, 362n6
gender identity, 147–49, 152
gender relations, 17, 73–94; adolescent
   motherhood and, 248–50; in Black
   female headed households, 80, 83–
   84, 88; employment and, 73–79, 81,
   364nn4–5; gang membership and,
   85–86, 364n6; government patriarchal
   imperatives and, 91; intrusion of the
   state into, 73, 90–94, 267, 364n9; male
   resentment and, 88–90, 250, 370n11;
   masculinity and, 73, 79–83, 316;
   media portrayals of, 87–88; parenting
   roles and, 83–85; perceptions of male

laziness and, 60–61, 69, 81, 87–90;
   religiosity and, 283–85; in transition
   to adulthood, 86–90, 244–46, 250,
   370n11; welfare regulations and, 59,
   82–83, 364n1(ch.3)
George Murphy Homes, 20, 49, 206;
   Benita Wallace's unit at, 59, 133–34,
   137; Lydia Forrest's unit at, 172, 226,
   270–71, 369n2; mixed-income plan
   for, 136; social capital in, 206; violence
   at, 135–37
ghetto vernacular, 309–10
GI Bill, 101, 105, 107, 119–20, 333,
   343–44
girls in urban poverty. *See* adolescent
   motherhood; childhood; transition to
   adulthood
Glasmeier, Amy K., 122
Glass-Steagall Act of 1933, 40
Glen Oaks subdivision, 31–33
global cities, 353, 363n2
globalization, 38–45, 346–47, 363n1,
   373n4; attacks on government and, 41;
   economic deregulation of, 40; hourly
   wage declines and, 42–43; incarceration rates and, 12–13; income distribution and, 44, 45*f*, 345–47, 372n1; labor
   union membership and, 41–42; layoffs
   and restructuring of, 39–41, 43–44, 56,
   343; poverty rates and, 43–45; service
   jobs and, 40, 41*f*, 48, 363n2; the
   working poor and, 351–53. *See also*
   deindustrialization
Goffman, Erving, 116
gold teeth, 246, 312
Gordon, David M., 39–40
Gould, Stephen Jay, 124–25, 366n3(ch.6)
government social programs, 1–5, 95,
   102–7; acute regulation of, 3, 118–19,
   123–27, 154–55, 160, 267, 339–40; for
   addiction, 112; adversarial relationships with clients of, 114–15, 117–18,
   124–31, 169–70; ambivalent benevolence of, 2, 91, 171, 350–51; budgetary
   allocations of, 114; concentration in
   poor areas of, 2–3, 113–15, 245–46,
   325, 364n9; design and administration

of, 120–21; embedded autonomy of, 1–2, 96–98, 372n15; for entrepreneurship, 302–3, 316, 324–26, 332–36; liminal logic of, 116–18, 209–12; mainstream institutions of, 116–18, 201, 323, 365n1(ch.6); neoliberal policies and, 12–13; New Deal origins of, 91, 100, 124; piecemeal palliative approach of, 118–23, 343–44; profits to be made from, 8, 121, 325, 341, 343–44; research investigations of, 11–12, 120–21; self-improvement focus of, 90–94, 112, 124–25, 344, 351–52, 364n9, 372n3; symbolic violence of, 119, 127–31, 152, 339–41, 366n6; unintended consequences of, 155, 350–51; workers for, 161–62, 170. *See also* intrusion of the state; liminal institutions; names of specific programs, e.g. Child Protective Services

Grace and Saint Peter School, 178–79

Granovetter, Mark, 85, 194, 201, 240

Great Black Migration, 21–24, 48, 51, 103–4, 362n2; demographic changes of, 104; dispossession and, 106–9; employment opportunities and, 79–80, 254–56; religiosity and, 283–85

Great Depression, 100, 180

Great Recession of 2008, 40, 44, 346, 352; entrepreneurship and, 372nn12–13; jobless rates after, 76; marriage rates and, 238; wealth inequities of, 106

Grossman, Jean B., 211

Gunder Frank, Andre, 103, 108, 365n3

gun violence, 267–68, 310, 313–16, 337, 339

Guzmán, Alex, 167

Guzmán, Marisa, 167

habitus, 117–18, 126–27, 317–18. *See also* embodied knowledge

hair picks, 312

Halperin, David, 205

Haney, Lynne, 126

Hanford, Buford, 268

Hardwick, Iliad, 54, 63–71, 85, 140–50; Flag House apartment of, 65, 67, 145;

Little Floyd Twigg and, 142–43, 145–47; marriage to Big Floyd Twigg of, 70–71, 146, 149–50

Harrison, Bennett, 39, 122

Harvey, David, 12–13

Haymarket Affair, 99

Head Start, 120

health care reform, 102, 365n1(ch.5)

Henry Fite House, 363n4

heroin, 109–10

The Hero with a Thousand Faces (Campbell), 354–55

Heyns, Barbara, 194, 207, 209, 368n9

The Hidden Injuries of Class (Sennett and Cobb), 81

hip-hop, 89–90, 124–25

Hirschman, Charles, 283

Hispanic immigrants, 327–31, 333–34, 336, 365n2(ch.5)

historically specific types, 197

Holiday, Billie, 52

Holy Spirit school. *See* Community School of the Holy Spirit

Homestead Act of 1862, 104–5, 107, 365n4

Homo economicus, 239

horizontal social capital, 205

hourly wages, 42–43

housing projects. *See* public housing

Hunter, Moriah, 278

Husock, Howard, 122–23

ideological debates on poverty, 2–4, 171, 195, 348–352, 372n2

Immergluck, Daniel, 334

immigrant communities, 98–103; in Baltimore, 46, 48, 50–51, 363n3; childhood agency in, 167–68; economic and social mobility of, 95, 103–8, 365n2(ch.5), 365n5; entrepreneurship in, 328–31; impact of group membership on, 367n2; labor struggles of, 99–100; social capital in, 202–3

Immigration and Nationality Act of 1965, 101–2

incarceration, 246, 340–41, 364n2(ch.4); deindustrialization and, 12–13; drug

incarceration (*continued*)
    trade and, 19; masculinity and, 277;
    race and, 77; rates of, 340; religion
    and, 280, 288–89; as state violence, 127
income inequality, 345–47, 372n1
individual agency. *See* personal agency
industrial decline. *See* deindustrialization
Industrial Workers of the World
    "Wobblies," 100
infantalization of the poor, 4, 344
Inner Harbor, 48
innovation, 195–97, 368n2. *See also*
    entrepreneurship
interaction hypothesis, 336
intrusion of the state, 1–6, 17–19, 73,
    109, 112–31, 202; acute regulation
    in, 3, 118–19, 123–27, 154–55, 160,
    267, 339–40; child abuse and, 153–
    62; childhood agency and, 166–71;
    criminalization of poverty and, 3, 319,
    325, 339–40; ethnographic analysis of,
    13–17; gender relations and, 17, 73,
    90–94, 364n9; immunity of workers in,
    161; liminal logic of, 116–18, 209–12;
    Manny Man Williams's criminalization
    and, 318–20, 340; palliative piecemeal
    programs of, 118–23, 343–44; research
    and writing on, 11–13; restricted
    rights to privacy and, 366n4; symbolic
    violence of, 119, 127–31, 152, 339–41,
    366n6; through suspicion, surveil-
    lance and control, 2, 115, 117–18,
    124–31, 325, 347; welfare reform and,
    65–66. *See also* distorted engagement;
    government social programs; liminal
    institutions
Islam, 287–89, 294

Jacobs, Jane, 362n10
Jehovah's Witnesses, 367n5; inclusivity of,
    291–92; instruction in, 270, 292–93;
    Kingdom Hall meetings of, 177, 190,
    270, 291, 293, 367n5; Lydia Forrest and,
    61, 69, 179, 192, 268–76, 286, 289–95;
    medical practices of, 294; member-
    ship, growth, and retention rates of,
    290–92; political neutrality of, 293–94;

proselytizing by, 269–70, 367n5; restric-
    tions on independent thinking in, 292–
    93; values and beliefs of, 69, 204, 215,
    273–74, 280, 293; *Watch Tower* manual
    of, 187–88, 190, 270; Weedy Chapman
    and, 186–88, 190
Jencks, Christopher, 241, 243, 320–21
Jeter family, 36–37
John Paul II, Pope, 148
Johns Hopkins Institute for Policy
    Studies (IPS), 9–10
Johns Hopkins University, 70
Johnson, Lyndon B., 1, 346–47
Jones, Oliver Wendell, Jr., 366n3(ch.6)
juvenile detention, 227, 306–7, 319

Katz, Michael, 11
Keelty, James, 300
Kendall, Jeremy, 205
Kesey, Ken, 366n5
Key, Francis Scott, 363n4
Keynesian economic measures, 101
King, Martin Luther, Jr., 52, 255, 284,
    298, 328
kinship nomenclature, 215–16
Kintrea, Keith, 321
Kohn, Melvin, 367n2
Koppers Company, 26–36, 38, 362n9,
    363n5
Korean population, 182, 185
Kotlowitz, Alex, 250–51
Krysan, Maria, 198–99

labor force participation. *See*
    employment
labor unions, 41–42, 56, 99–100, 352
Lacan, Jacques, 130
Lafayette Square, 51–52
Lancy, Clara, 219
Land, Emory Scott, 29
Lane, Rose Wilder, 365n4
language and literacy skills, 183–86,
    211; Black English vernacular and,
    183–84, 204, 211; ghetto vernacular
    and, 309–10; library reading programs
    and, 368n9; parochial schools and,
    144, 371n5; summer achievement gap

and, 206–9; vocabulary and, 184, 186, 371n5. *See also* linguistic markers
Latin American cities, 346
Laughton, Maggie, 279–80
Lein, Laura, 205
Lemann, Nicholas, 284
Levinson, Barry, 32, 50
Lewis, Marvin, 299
Lewis, Oscar, 238
liberal principles, 2–5, 91, 171, 350–51
libertarianism, 365n4
Liberty Heights (Levinson), 50
Liberty Heights neighborhood, 5, 48–50
Liberty Ships, 29, 363n5
Liebow, Elliott, 125
Light, Ivan, 336, 371n8
liminal institutions, 116–18, 209–12, 347; criminalization of poverty by, 3, 319, 325, 339–40; embodied knowledge of, 117–18, 126–27; entrepreneurship and, 324–26; familiarity of, 153, 156, 161, 166–71, 245–46, 319, 366n4, 368n3; immunity of staff of, 161; impact on parenting of, 153–55; juvenile detention facilities as, 227, 306–7, 319; *vs.* mainstream institutions, 116–18, 201, 323, 347, 365n1(ch.6); misrecognition of inequality in, 129–31, 152; predatory capital and, 316; predatory commerce and, 338–41; subliminal resistance to, 125–26, 366n5; suspicion, surveillance and control by, 2, 115, 117–18, 124–31, 325, 347; symbolic violence of, 116, 119, 127–31, 152, 339–41, 366n6
linguistic markers: of Black English vernacular, 183–84, 204, 211; of ghetto vernacular, 309–10
Lipsky, Michael, 114, 162, 339
Little Floyd Twigg, 18, 132–53; adulthood of, 151; appearance of, 132, 133, 140, 144, 152; buffeting from home to home of, 137–40, 142–43, 146, 149, 152, 269; educational experiences of, 140–44, 148, 152, 371n5; family background of, 58, 60, 62–65, 132–38; gender identification of, 147–49,

152; goals and means of, 195*f*; sexual molestation of, 139, 145, 152, 166; survival strategies of, 140, 144; violence experienced by, 135–36, 366n1(ch.7)
Little House on the Prairie (Wilder), 365n4
Losing Ground: American Social Policy (Murray), 65, 348–49
Loury, Glen, 368n5
Lower Park Heights neighborhood, 17, 35–36, 48, 290
Luker, Kristin, 236
Lydia Forrest. *See* Forrest, Lydia
lynching, 282

mainstream institutions, 116–18, 201, 323, 347, 365n1(ch.6)
Manny Man Travis (Emmanuel Travis Williams), 19, 296–314; arrests and detentions of, 227–28, 306–7, 312, 319; childhood and education of, 304–7, 310, 319; death of, 314; drug dealing by, 197, 228, 310–16, 318–20, 337; family background of, 296–304; goals and means of, 195*f*, 196–97, 368n2; street attitude of, 307–10, 370n4; temperament of, 305–7
maquiladoras, 43
Marble Hill, 52
marriage promotion programs, 237–38, 360n5
Marsh, Tito "Gem," 267–68
Marsh, Trevor, 286
Marshall, Thurgood, 22, 52
Martin, Eva, 292–93
Martin, Lucinda, 220
Marvin, Latishia, 248–49
Marx, Karl, 99, 128
masculinity, 73, 79–83; displays of dominance in, 245–46, 250, 277, 316, 337, 370n11; employment and, 249; gang membership and, 85–86, 364n6; gangsta limp and, 309; government patriarchal imperatives of, 91; hair picks as symbols of, 312; parenting roles and, 83–85; resentment of women and, 88–90, 250, 370n11; sexual pressure on women and, 251;

masculinity (*continued*)
through fathering a child, 230, 244; in transition to adulthood, 86–90, 244. *See also* gender relations
Mason, Kiyah, 88
Massey, Douglas, 350
maturation process, 86–90. *See also* transition to adulthood
Matute-Bianchi, Maria Eugenia, 199
Mayer, Susan, 320–21
McCormick Reaper Company, 181
McCormick Spice Company, 28
McCullough, Jovan, 189–90
medicalization of poverty, 121, 319
Memorial Stadium, 179–81
Menjívar, Cecilia, 202
mentoring programs, 209–12, 368nn11–14
Merrill, Lachonda, 305
Merton, Robert K.: on children as a strategic site of research, 156; on *Homo economicus*, 239; on social capital, 87, 194–99, 361n2, 367n1(ch.10); on social time, 250–51
Mexican immigrants, 327–31, 365n2(ch.5)
middle class assumptions, 9–10; on adolescent motherhood, 244; on blaming the victims of poverty, 8–11, 124, 128, 316, 343–45, 361n2; on court appearances, 66–67; on definitions of adulthood, 243–44; of educational opportunities, 184–85; of fire hydrant play, 185; on gender roles, 91; on material incentives for children, 152, 164; on parental discipline, 148–49, 152, 161–62, 367n3; on receiving mail, 67–69; on school behavior, 152; on state promotion of individual and group advancement, 3–4, 95–98, 104–5, 107, 119–20, 343–44, 365n1(ch.5), 365n4; on transition to adulthood, 246
middle classes, 3–4; ghetto style among youth of, 125–26; mainstream government institutions of, 116–18, 201, 323, 347, 365n1(ch.6); research on poverty by, 9–10, 361n2; segregated Blacks among, 51–52, 363n6

Mill, John Stuart, 350
Miller, Angus, 296–97
Miller, Gene, 269, 270
Miller, Latricia, 163–64
Mills, C. Wright, 15, 197
minimum wage, 70
misrecognition, 129–31, 152
Mitchell, Leona, 291
Mitchell, Tammina, 314
Mondawmin Mall, 148, 221
Monroe, Pearl, 254, 257–58
Moore, Chantal, 168
Moore, Helen, 167–68
Moore, Lester, 149
More than Just Race: Being Black and Poor in the Inner City (Wilson), 5
Morgan State University, 296–97
Morrill Land-Grant Acts, 105
Mossy, Big Bolly, 312–13
motherhood. *See* adolescent motherhood
Mount Vernon neighborhood, 28
Moynihan, Daniel Patrick, 369n5
Mullen, Erin, 334
multiplexity, 240, 368n6
Muncie, Durell, 69
Murray, Charles, 65, 106, 239, 348–49, 370n8
Muslims, 287–89, 294

Nathanson, Constance, 236
National Road (U.S. Route 40), 46
Nation of Islam, 288–89
negative social capital, 202–3
The Negro Church (DuBois), 282–83
The Negro Family: The Case for National Action (Moynihan), 369n5
neighborhood effects, 316–17, 320–26, 334, 371n5; concentration of resources in, 323; ecometric study of, 322; locational deficiencies in, 325–26; mechanisms of, 322–25; predatory commerce in, 336–41; real estate ownership in, 321; research on, 321–22, 371nn3–4
neoconservatism, 171, 195, 348–355
neoliberalism, 12–13, 40, 44, 45f. *See also* globalization
Newman, Katherine, 125

New Rehoboth Baptist Church, 33
New York Society for the Prevention of
   Cruelty to Children (SPCC), 157
Nicaraguan Contra insurgency, 110
normative goals and social performance,
   195–96, 241–43, 367n1(ch.10)
Norplant patch, 125
Nortwest Ordinance of 1787, 105
not-for-profit sector, 121

Obama, Barack, 102, 333, 365n1(ch.5)
O'Conor, Herbert Romulus, 29
Ogbu, John U., 199
Old Bethel AME Church, 22
old heads, 23, 362n2
Oliver, Melvin, 104, 106
Olson, Linda, 207–9
Omar, Suhira, 288
One Flew Over the Cuckoo's Nest (Kesey),
   366n5
the Orioles, 179–81
Owens, Amanda, 278–79

Pager, Devah, 127
palliative programs, 118–23, 343–44
panopticism, 118
parents/parenting, 83–85; corporal
   punishment by, 154–60, 167, 170;
   fragility of authority of, 148–50, 152–
   55, 166–71, 222–26, 367n3; impact of
   unemployment on, 164–65; intergenerational transmission of welfare dependence and, 238–40; as involuntary
   clients of the state, 162; middle class
   assumptions on, 148–49, 152, 161–62.
   See also adolescent motherhood; child
   abuse; transition to adulthood
Park, Robert E., 104
the penury industry, 8, 121, 325, 341,
   343–44
People of Islam Security Company
   (PISCO), 67–70
Perkins, Frances, 124
personal agency, 90, 120, 125, 151–71
Peters, Stephen, 148–49
Peterson, Isabel, 365n4
Pettit, Becky, 77

philanthropic giving, 8
Piaget, Jean, 158
Pigtown neighborhood, 36
Piore, Michael, 40
Piven, Frances Fox, 12
Poe, Edgar Allan, 46
police departments, 114
Porter, Michael, 121–22
Portes, Alejandro, 194, 202, 329,
   365n2(ch.5), 365n5
Port of Baltimore, 181
poverty: as deviant, 87, 90–91; ideological debates on, 2–4, 171, 195, 348–352,
   372n2; income inequality and, 345–47,
   372n1; profits to be made from, 8, 121,
   325, 341, 343–44; rates of, 1, 43–45,
   345; in White Appalachia, 102–3. See
   also government social programs;
   intrusion of the state
predatory capital, 109, 110–12, 115, 316
predatory commerce, 315–16. See also
   drug trade
predatory states, 96, 103, 365n3
prisons, 114, 340–41. See also
   incarceration
probation and parole, 77, 127
Professional Air Traffic Controllers
   Organization (PATCO), 41–42
prostitution, 113, 262
The Protestant Ethic and the Spirit of
   Capitalism (Weber), 123–24
psychology (as field), 158
public assistance. See welfare programs
public housing, 65–66; at Flag House, 65,
   67, 145; at George Murphy Homes,
   20, 49, 59, 133, 226, 269–70, 369n2;
   at Pratt Street, 146; under Section 8,
   70–71; social capital in, 205; vertical
   architecture of, 136; violence at, 135–
   37; youth power hierarchies in, 165–66
Public School No. 58, 188–89
public service agencies. See government
   social programs
Puerto Rican immigrants, 365n2(ch.5)
Punishment and Modern Society: A Study
   in Social Theory (Garland), 12
Putnam, Robert, 201–3, 368n7

Quadagno, Jill, 12
Quakers, 282

race/racial minorities: adolescent births
and, 234, 235*f*, 360n3; adoptions and,
367n4; America's obsession with,
346; child abuse cases and, 170; civil
rights movement and, 20, 22, 52–53,
101–2, 158, 255–56; color-based
discrimination towards, 4, 98–99,
107–9; concerns about appearance
differences among, 6, 130–31, 177,
190, 198, 243; deindustrialization
and, 5; employment rates and, 75–78,
81–82; entrepreneurship and, 326–32,
335*t*, 336, 371nn8–9, 371–72nn11–14;
incarceration rates and, 12–13, 19,
77, 127, 364n2(ch.4); interaction
hypothesis of supply and demand and,
336; language differences and, 183–86,
211; poverty and, 1, 44, 345; residential segregation by, 6, 21–22, 48–53;
skin color and, 177; of social workers,
161–62; systematic exclusion from
prosperity of, 95, 103–9, 344, 347–48;
urban underdevelopment and, 108–9;
wealth inequities of, 106–7; welfare
payments and, 79, 364n3(ch.4). *See
also* immigrant communities
Rand, Ayn, 365n4
Randall, Agatha, 304
Raudenbush, Stephen W., 322
reading and writing skills, 184
Reagan, Ronald: decertification of
PATCO under, 41–42; on social legislation, 348; social program cutbacks
under, 65–66, 332–33; stagflation
under, 265–66, 303–4
real hourly wages, 42–43
redlining, 108, 352. *See also* residential
segregation
Regulating the Poor (Piven and
Cloward), 12
Reich, Robert, 77
relationship between the state and the
urban poor. *See* government social
programs; intrusion of the state

religiosity, 18, 275–95; abolition movement and, 282; in African American
history, 22–23, 227, 257, 273–74,
281–84, 314; among the poor, 278–87;
civil rights movement and, 284; of
Muslims, 287–89, 294; residential
segregation and, 276; sacred ritual
practices of, 278, 280–81, 284–87;
socially isolating practices of, 289–95;
sociological study of, 280–81; stories
of downfall and redemption in,
277, 280, 370n1(ch.14); as symbolic
capital, 204, 212–13. *See also* Jehovah's
Witnesses
repeat arrests, 127
research methods, 7–11; biographical
accounts in, 10–11, 16–17, 342–43,
361n1, 362n6; community mapping
in, 16, 362n5; ethnography in, 13–17,
361n1, 362nn4–6; interviews in, 6,
13–16; participant observation in, 16;
sample of households in, 83*t*, 357–59;
theory and analysis in, 15–17
re-segregation, 181–82, 298
residential segregation, 6, 21–22, 48,
298, 338, 352; Black English vernacular and, 211; Black entrepreneurial
activity and, 328; block-busting and,
108; concentration effects of poverty
and, 238–39; employment opportunities and, 81–82; prisons and, 340–41;
religion and, 276
respect, 249, 370n10
Richardson, Joseph B., 84
Ritalin, 306
Robb, Alicia M., 330
Robinson, Paula, 217
Roland Park neighborhood, 180
Romney, Mitt, 349–50
Roosevelt, Franklin D./New Deal, 40, 91,
100–101
Royal Theater, 52
Rubin, Lillian, 81

Sabel, Charles, 40
Saegert, Susan, 205
Sampson, Robert, 322–24

Sandtown-Winchester neighborhood, 5, 17, 48; adolescent pregnancies in, 215–16, 233–34; middle-class Black enclaves in, 51–52, 363n6; population of, 290; public service agencies in, 113–14; religiosity in, 290
Schaeffer, Donald, 48
Schmidt, John, 56
Schmoke, Kurt, 49
school resource officers, 3, 339–40
Schuman, Howard, 198–99
Schwab, Charles M., 99
Schwartz, Sarah E. O., 211
Schwitzer, Marlin, and Tzabo Attorneys at Law, 263–65
Scorsese, Martin, 364n6
Section 8 housing, 70–71
self-employment. *See* entrepreneurship
self-hatred, 130–31
Sennett, Richard, 81
Servicemen's Readjustment Act of 1944 (GI Bill), 101, 105, 119–20, 333, 343–44
sex education, 252
sexual abuse, 139, 145, 152; children's understandings of, 166–67; legal definition of, 159
sexuality, 166–67; forced sterilization and, 124–25, 366n3(ch.6); gender identity and, 147–49, 152; power conferred by, 230; rates of, 369n1(ch.12)
sexual revolution, 73–74
Shakur, Tupac, 337
Shapiro, Thomas, 104, 106
Shields, Mark, 366n4
Simpson, Moira, 165–66
Simpson, Taresha, 165–66
single mothers. *See* adolescent motherhood
situational explanations of poverty, 238–39
Skocpol, Theda, 11
slavery, 47, 87, 263, 265, 340–41; informal commerce in, 327–28; manumission/freed Blacks from, 47, 50, 104; religious narratives of, 281–82
Small Business Administration (SBA), 302–3, 332–36, 341; application process of, 333; budgetary cuts to, 332–33; color-blind criteria of, 334, 371n11; loans to minority-owned businesses by, 333–36, 372nn12–13; private lenders to, 335
Smith, Damon, 313–14
Smithson, Annette, 206
social capital, 18, 192–212, 232–33, 368n5; bonding and bridging types of, 205–6; Bourdieu's conception of, 203; *vs.* cultural capital, 203–5, 232–33, 242, 368n8; definition of, 199–200, 203; economic sociology of, 199–203; educational impact of, 184, 194–95; historically specific types of, 197; mentoring programs and, 209–12, 368nn11–14; Merton's analysis of, 87, 194–99, 361n2, 367n1(ch.10); political analysis of, 200–202; shift in perceived locus of efficacy in, 199; strong and weak ties in, 201–3, 317, 368n6; summer achievement gap and, 206–9, 368n10
social networks, 252
Social Security Act of 1935, 100–101, 124
Social Statistics (Spencer), 372n2
"Social Structure and Anomie" (Merton), 194–99, 361n2
social time, 250–51
socioeconomic status. *See* class and socioeconomic status
Southeast Crips Gang, 336–37
Sowell, Thomas, 106
spanking, 154
Sparrows Point plant, 5–6, 46–47, 363n5. *See also* Bethlehem Steel Company
Spencer, Herbert, 124, 349, 372n2
Spencer, Katrina, 279
Spencer, Mary, 287
Spock, Benjamin, 158
Spreckels, Claus, 99
Stack, Carol, 125
Starlight Limousine Company, 297
the state: definition of, 96; developmental forms of, 97–102; embedded autonomy of institutions of, 1–2, 96–98, 372n15; predatory forms of, 96, 103, 365n3. *See also* American State;

the state (*continued*)
  government social programs; intrusion of the state
Steeh, Charlotte, 198–99
Stier, Haya, 370n6
stigmatizing speech, 128–29, 366n6
stop-and-frisk policies, 127
*Street-Level Bureaucracy: Dilemmas of the
  Individual in Public Service* (Lipsky),
  114
strong ties, 201–2, 317
summer achievement gap, 184, 194–95,
  206–9, 368n10
*Summer Learning and the Effects of
  Schooling* (Heyns), 207
Supplemental Income for the Disabled
  Program, 7
Supplemental Nutrition Assistance
  Program, 7
symbolic capital, 203–5, 212–13, 232–33,
  247, 339–41, 368n8. *See also* cultural
  capital; social capital
symbolic violence, 116, 119, 127–31, 152,
  366n6; misrecognition of inequality in,
  129–31; of stigmatizing speech, 128–
  29, 366n6; of vertical charity, 127–28
systematic exclusion of African Americans from prosperity, 95, 103–9, 344,
  347–48

A Tale of Two Cities (Dickens), 124
Taub, Richard, 370n11
Taylor, Davon, 165–66
teen pregnancies. *See* adolescent
  motherhood
Temporary Assistance for Needy Fami-
  lies (TANF), 7, 93; budget of, 119–20;
  family focus of, 364n9; race and, 79,
  364n3(ch.4)
Thomas, Amelia, 88
Thomas, Dorothy S., 156
Thomas, William I., 156
Thomas Theorem, 156, 367n2
Thompson, Maurice, 139
Thompson, Philip, 205
Tienda, Marta, 370n6
Tilly, Charles, 11

Tin Men (Levinson), 50
Tocqueville, Alexis de, 98
Toleration Act of 1649, 363n3
Towanda Forrest. *See* Forrest, Towanda
transition to adulthood: accelerated
  development in, 250–52; adolescent
  motherhood and, 3, 18, 58–59, 199,
  230–52, 360nn1–4; adolescent yearnings for, 243; cultural capital of, 232–
  33, 241–43, 246–47, 312; definitions of
  adulthood and, 244–47; fathering of
  a child in, 230, 244; intergenerational
  transfer of welfare dependence in,
  238–40, 244–46, 370n6; male displays
  of toughness in, 245–46, 250, 319–20,
  370n11; middle class assumptions on,
  246; respect in, 249, 370n10
triangulation, 15, 362n4
Sister Trinita, 179, 181–82, 185–88
*The Truly Disadvantaged: The Inner
  City, the Underclass, and Public Policy*
  (Wilson), 5
Turner, Tina, 221
Twigg, Alma, 55–57, 82
Twigg, Belinda, 249
Twigg, Clarise, 18, 54–55, 60, 131, 172–
  91; appearance of, 173, 188–89, 204;
  aspirations of, 176, 186, 190–91, 193;
  brawling with other kids, 174–75, 188;
  concerns about appearance of, 131,
  177, 190, 198, 204; extracurricular
  interests of, 9, 131, 175–77, 190, 193;
  family background of, 58, 61–62,
  70–71, 172–73, 193; goals and means
  of, 195*f*, 197–98; linguistic code
  switching by, 183–84, 186, 197–98;
  Lydia Forrest's custody of, 62, 70, 138,
  172–75, 177–78, 187–88, 215, 269–70;
  motherhood of, 191; parochial school
  progress of, 9–10, 140, 172, 178–88,
  192–93, 273, 371n5; public school
  experiences of, 188–92, 198–99, 249,
  273; responsibilities of, 174, 193;
  sexual molestation of, 189–90; social
  capital and, 192–98, 204; Towanda
  Forrest and, 174, 177, 198, 215–16
Twigg, Ernie, 55–57, 82

Twigg, Floyd Mitchell, Sr. *See* Big Floyd Twigg
Twigg, Little Floyd. *See* Little Floyd Twigg
Twigg, Lucy, 57–58
Twigg, Melinda: adulthood of, 151; family background of, 54–55, 58–59, 66–67, 70–71; Margaret Forrest's custody of, 62, 66, 137–38, 150, 166, 249, 269; motherhood goals of, 244–45; return to Big Floyd Twigg's of, 146–47; sexual molestation of, 166–67; suspensions from school of, 249
Twigg, Otis, 191
Twigg, Persia, 146–47
Twigg, Rita "Boo," 55, 62–64, 138, 143–45, 150
Twigg-Hardwick, Shatirya, 54–55, 63–64, 71, 85, 142, 146
T-Zee, 151

the undeserving poor, 92, 124
The Undeserving Poor: America's Enduring Confrontation with Poverty (Katz), 11
union membership. *See* labor unions
United States. *See* American State
United Steelworkers of America, 56
Upton neighborhood, 5, 17, 48–53; adolescent pregnancies in, 215–16, 233–34; middle-class Black enclaves in, 51–52, 363n6; public service agencies in, 113–14
urban revitalization initiatives, 121–23
urban underdevelopment, 108–9
U.S. Department of Veterans Affairs, 119
U.S. Maritime Commission, 29

Van Maanen, John, 17
vertical charity, 127–28
Veterans Administration, 119
violence, 251, 366n1(ch.7); drug trade and, 58, 111, 300, 312–14, 336–39; firearms and, 267–68, 310, 313–16, 337, 339; in housing projects, 135–37; symbolic forms of, 116, 119, 127–31, 152, 339–41, 366n6; violent crime rates of, 337–38

virtual aggression. *See* symbolic violence
vocabulary skills, 184, 186, 371n5
von Hippel, Paul T., 208, 209
voucher programs, 200–201

Wacquant, Loïc, 12–13, 125, 127; on negative social capital, 202, 204; on the prison industry, 340–41
Walker, Juliet, 327–28
Wallace, Benita, 58–62, 69, 87; family background of, 263–65; Lydia Forrest's support of, 58, 206, 269, 272; as parent, 58, 62, 132–39, 193; substance use by, 58, 60, 138–39, 173, 269
War on Poverty, 1, 346–47
Warren, Mark R., 205
Washington, Dante, 244
Washington, Mary, 92–93
Watson, Darnell, 86
Waverly neighborhood, 179–82. *See also* Community School of the Holy Spirit
weak ties, 201–2, 317
wealth ratios, 106–7
Weber, Max, 11, 362n6; definition of the state of, 96–97; on inequality, 128; on principles of diligence, 123; on religious beliefs and practices, 281; on self-perpetuating government bureaucracies, 169, 339
welfare programs: annual costs of, 365n2(ch.6); average payments of, 348; intergenerational transfer of dependence on, 238–40, 244–46, 370n6; race and, 79, 364n3(ch.4); reforms of, 65–69, 93, 225, 348–49. *See also* government social programs
West Baltimore, 5–8, 10, 17, 48–53, 352–53; absence of employment opportunities in, 363nn7–8; adolescent pregnancies in, 215–16, 233–34, 237; banks in, 113; churches in, 22–24, 52, 286–87, 290; D. B. Wilson's description of, 21–24; decay of buildings in, 113; drug trade in, 58, 111, 113, 136, 177; educational opportunity in, 57, 82; Great Migration settlement of, 21–24, 48, 51, 362n2; history of poverty

West Baltimore (*continued*)
in, 50–53; household sample of, 83*t*;
housing projects in, 135–37; Islam
in, 287–89, 294; middle-class Black
enclaves in, 51–53, 363n6; Mondaw-
min Mall in, 148, 221; public service
agencies in, 113–14; social capital in,
205–6; streetfront businesses in, 36,
52, 328, 363n8; White flight and re-
segregation of, 298
Western, Bruce, 77, 127
West Side Story, 364n6
*When Work Disappears: The World of the
New Urban Poor* (Wilson), 5
White flight, 181–82
Whiteness (as category), 108
Wilder, Laura Ingalls, 365n4
Wilkins, Frank, 80–81
Wilkins, Jared, 80–81
Wilkins, Lucinda, 80–81
William Pienderhughes Elementary
School, 172
Williams, Alfonso, 89
Williams, Emmanuel Travis. *See* Manny
Man Travis
Williams, Latanya, 247–48, 251
Williams, Marcus, II, 297–301
Williams, Marcus, III, 296–305; ambition
of, 296–97, 302–3, 318, 320; education
of, 296, 299; entrepreneurial career of,
303–5, 307–8, 315–18, 320; separation
from Sharon of, 308
Williams, Minerva, 299
Williams, Nellie, 297–301, 314
Williams, Romulus, 299

Williams, Sharon Belay, 296–306, 308,
311, 314
Williams, Shennelle, 296, 300–301, 304
Williams, Tamika, 302, 304
Willis, Monsta, 311–12
Wilson, Beverly Elaine Jeter, 27, 29–32,
36–37
Wilson, Donald B., 6, 17, 20–39; background and education of, 20–22,
24–27, 72; cabdriving job of, 20–21,
35–36; on change in West Baltimore,
21–24, 36, 52; children and grandchildren of, 31; comparison with Big
Floyd Twigg of, 72–73; employment
at Koppers of, 27–35, 73, 362n9,
374n4(ch.4); normative goals of, 195*f*,
196, 367n1(ch.10); personal principles
of, 20–21, 25, 31–32, 38; temperament
and resourcefulness of, 72
Wilson, Geneva Radisson, 25–26
Wilson, Henry, 24–26
Wilson, William J., 5, 82, 350; on concentration of poverty, 238–39; on permanently marginalized populations, 321
Wolken, John D., 336
the working poor, 351–53
working women, 73–75, 364n1(ch.4)
Wulff, Mary, 183–84
Wuthnow, Robert, 281

Yiu, Jessica, 329
Young, Marquis, 86

Zelizer, Viviana, 239–40
Zhou, Min, 365n2(ch.5)